Vickery's Law and Accounts of Executo
Administrators and Trustees

MW00682814

Vickery's Law and Accounts of Executors, Administrators and Trustees

Twenty-first Edition

JOHN KIMMER, FTII
GRAHAM SCRIVEN, FCA, ATII
RUSSELL STANFIELD, Solicitor, LLB

ASSELL

Cassell Educational Limited:
Artillery House
Artillery Row
London SW1P 1RX

British Library Cataloguing in Publication Data
Vickery, B.G.
   Vickery's law and accounts of executors,
   administrators and trustees.—21st ed.
   1. Decedents' estates—England—Accounting
   I. Title II. Kimmer, John III. Scriven,
   Graham IV. Stanfield, Russ V. Vickery,
   B.G. Law and accounts of executors,
   administrators and trustees
   344.2065′6′024657   KD1530.A3

   ISBN: 0-304-31389-0

Typeset by DP Press Ltd, Sevenoaks
Printed and bound in Great Britain by Mackays of Chatham Ltd

Copyright © 1987 by Cassell Educational Ltd
All rights reserved. This book is protected by copyright. No part of it may be reproduced, stored in a retrieval system, or transmitted in any form or by any means, electronic, mechanical, photocopying or otherwise, without written permission from the publisher.

Last digit is print no: 9 8 7 6 5 4 3 2 1

Contents

List of Abbreviations

IT	Income Tax
CGT	Capital Gains Tax
CTT	Capital Transfer Tax
IHT	Inheritance Tax
CT	Corporation Tax
ED	Estate Duty
SI	Statutory Instrument
ESC	Extra Statutory Concession
IRPR	Inland Revenue Press Release
PR	Personal Representative

STATUTORY REFERENCES

TIA 1961	Trustee Investments Act 1961
ICTA 1970	Income and Corporation Tax Act 1970
TMA 1970	Taxes Management Act 1970
CGTA 1979	Capital Gains Tax Act 1979
CTTA 1984	Capital Transfer Tax Act 1984
FA 1978/1986	Finance Act 1978/1986

Preface

It is over seven years since the last edition was published in July 1979. In preparing this edition, the authors have reflected all the changes in the law which have occurred since the last edition was published. The chapters dealing with Wills reflect the fact that the Administration of Justice Act 1982 made considerable amendments to the legal formalities relating to Wills. The last six years have seen dramatic changes to the capital transfer tax regime, and the chapters dealing with this tax have been expanded and largely rewritten to reflect all the changes made by the various Finance Acts up to and including the Finance Act 1985. As a result of the passing of the Finance Act 1986, a separate chapter has been included dealing with the changes arising from the abolition of Capital Transfer Tax and the introduction of Inheritance Tax with effect from 18 March 1986. In addition, a chapter dealing with income tax in relation to estates has been included for the first time.

The aim of the authors in preparing this latest edition has been to include, in one volume, an up-to-date, comprehensive and lucid coverage of the specialized and often complicated laws and practices relevant to the administration of the estates of deceased persons. Over the years, the book has become essential reading for those studying for various professional examinations, as well as being a standard reference book for practitioners in the legal and accountancy professions. With the needs of the students in mind, many detailed and practical examples and exercises have been included to enable the text to be readily understood.

The authors would like to thank a number of colleagues for their many helpful suggestions, also our secretaries for patiently typing the final text, and our long-suffering wives for putting up with our absences whilst preparing this edition. We would also like to thank the Institute of Taxation for its much appreciated permission to reproduce past examination questions.

Any errors readers may discover remain the sole responsibility of the authors.

The law is stated as at 30 September 1986.

John Kimmer
Graham Scriven
Russell Stanfield

Table of Statutes Cited

Table of Cases Cited

1
Introduction

The law relating to executors and administrators and the administration of estates appears, at first sight, complicated, but is in fact based upon sound equitable principles arising mainly from judicial decisions made by the courts.

The responsibility of administering a deceased's estate may fall theoretically upon virtually anyone, thus necessitating a clear knowledge of the law and practice relevant to the performance of the duties of a personal representative. Usually, the administration is entrusted to a solicitor, although there are signs that the current government may attempt to lift the monopoly enjoyed by the solicitors' profession relating to the extraction of grants etc. for profit.

A number of technical expressions appear constantly in any discussion of administration and the more common terms are set out below.

TESTATES AND INTESTATES

The capacity of every deceased person will be one comprising testate (i.e. having died possessed of a will), intestate (i.e. having died not having been possessed of a will) or partially intestate (i.e. having died possessed of a will but one which either was to some extent invalid or did not cover all the deceased's assets).

A person's estate will include everything which was owned beneficially at death, e.g. cash, stocks and shares, personal effects, furniture, land, buildings. Such assets are also described as tangible assets, but intangible assets, such as rights (e.g. to be paid on an outstanding debt) would also form a part of the deceased's estate.

A testate person (testator if male or testatrix if female) leaves a will in which the testator states how his assets are to be distributed after his death. An intestate leaves no will so that his assets will devolve to those persons entitled under the prevailing rules of intestacy.

The testator's will usually appoints a person or persons to act as executor (executrix if female) whose prime responsibility is to administer the estate — i.e. collect in the assets, pay outstanding debts including any inheritance tax due — and distribute the net balance in accordance with the terms of the will.

In the estate of an intestate or, in the case of a testate appointing no executor, an interested person, usually a close relative, will apply to the court to be appointed as an administrator to administer the estate.

Executors or administrators are often referred to collectively as the 'personal representatives' of the deceased's estate.

REAL AND PERSONAL PROPERTY

Real property (or real estate) consists mainly of freehold land and buildings.

Personal property (or personal estate) consists of all moveable articles, both tangible and intangible, e.g. furniture, stock, money, interest in a partnership.

It should be noted in particular that a leasehold interest is classified as personal estate and not real estate.

GIFTS BY WILL

Gifts of property made by a will may be either legacies or devises.

Legacies are gifts of personal property and the recipient is known as a legatee. Devises are gifts of real property and the recipient is known as a devisee.

An annuity is the right to an annual sum of money usually for the duration of the life of the recipient (known as the annuitant), e.g. a testator's will might bequeath 'to my widow the sum of £400 per annum for her life'.

Both legacies and devises may be either absolute or on trust. A trust is an arrangement whereby property is transferred to persons known as the trustees who have legal ownership, for the benefit of a person or persons known as the object or the *cestui que trust*.

By way of a simple example, X leaves property by will 'to A in trust for B for life'. A is the trustee possessed of the legal ownership of the property whilst B is the object of the property. B is the life tenant entitled to enjoy and receive the net income generated by the trust property for his life. If the will makes no provision as to the vesting of the trust property after B's death, the property will revert back to the estate of X the original testator. Usually, however, a will directs that 'upon B's death, the property should go to C'. C is said to be the remainderman entitled to an interest in remainder (sometimes also referred to inaccurately as a reversionary interest). Reversions can be either vested or contingent. For example, 'to B for life and then to C' would entitle C or C's estate to the trust capital even if C pre-deceased B. In contrast 'to B for life and then to C provided he shall be living at B's death' would mean that C would only become entitled if he satisfied the contingency of surviving B. The latter is therefore known as a contingent remainderman.

A settlement is a name given to an arrangement by which property is held on trust, generally for several beneficiaries. However, whilst technically different from a trust, it is common for the two expressions to be interchangeable.

A power of appointment is an authority given to a person (known as the donee) to select the persons who shall take the property of the estate of the person creating the power. For example, a will may say 'to B for life and then to such of B's children as B may by deed or will appoint'.

In the event of the donee not exercising the power of appointment, a will usually goes on to provide for the devolution of the property in default of appointment. Where the power specifies the persons among whom the property is to be appointed, it is known as a special power of appointment. When no class of person is specified, the power is known as a general power of appointment and this could include an appointment to the donee himself of the power.

RESIDUE

Residue is what remains of a deceased's estate after the funeral expenses and debts, inheritance tax and administration costs and specific legacies and devises have been dealt with. The person stated in the will as being entitled to the residue is known as the residuary legatee (or residuary devisee if the property comprises real estate).

Exercise 1

1. Who are an executor, an intestate, an administrator?
2. Explain the following terms: legacy; devise; *annuity*; *cestui que trust*.
3. What is a power of appointment? How may such a power be exercised? What is the difference between a general and a special power?
4. What is residue? Who is entitled to it?

2
The Will: Is It Valid?

GENERALLY

The legislation enabling every person possessing testamentary capacity to deal with his estate by will is contained in the Wills Act 1837 as amended (substantially) by the Administration of Justice Act 1982.

The legislation requires precise and proper formalities relating to the execution of a will and, if such formalities are not strictly observed, the law will refuse to recognize the intentions of the testator as set out in his will and order the distribution of his estate as if he had died intestate.

Freedom of testamentary disposition

Originally, every person having testamentary capacity was free to dispose of his estate as he thought fit. However, in the interest of public and social policy, that freedom has been eroded by a succession of family provision Acts culminating in the current legislation contained in the Inheritance (Provision for Family and Dependants) Act 1975. This Act applies to testators (and intestates) dying after the 31 March 1976 and gives the court certain powers relating to financial provision to be made out of the estate of a deceased for the benefit of certain applicants. (See p.13.)

CAPACITY TO MAKE A VALID WILL

Although section 3 of the Wills Act 1837 enables every person to make a will, later parts of the legislation mean that there are limitations upon certain types of individuals, and those limitations relate either to age or to the mental state of the testator.

As to age, section 7 of the Wills Act 1837, as amended by the Family Law Reform Act 1969, provides that no will made by any person under the age of 18 shall be valid. However, privileged wills made by persons under 18 engaged on actual military service, are valid (section 11, Wills Act 1837).

As to mental incapacity, the decision in *Banks* v. *Goodfellow* (1870) established that testamentary capacity exists only if the testator had an understanding of three essential elements:

a. The nature of the act and its effects in a broad sense.
b. The extent of the property of which he is disposing, again with a broad understanding.

c. The claims to which he ought to give effect, i.e. the testator must have in mind, or be able to recall to mind, those persons whom he wishes to benefit.

Problems arise in the case of testators whose mental state varies. There is a rebuttable presumption that a person who suffers from bouts of mental illness lacks testamentary capacity. Generally, mental capacity will be analysed at the time the will is executed.

The old division of 'lunatics' into 'persons certified insane' and 'persons insane, although not certified' has been largely replaced by the terms of the Mental Health Act 1983. Section 96 of this Act empowers the Court of Protection to make a will for an adult mental patient. A mental patient is defined as someone incapable, by reason of mental disorder, of managing his own affairs. A 'statutory will' of this nature can make any provision and disposition which could have been made by the person had he the mental capacity.

MAKING A WILL

Section 9 of the Wills Act 1837, as substituted by section 17 of the Administration of Justice Act 1982, lays down the formalities now required for a valid will. These formalities now require that the will must be in writing and signed by the testator, or by some other person in his presence and by his direction and it must appear that the testator intended by his signature to give effect to the will. Further, the signature must be made or acknowledged by the testator in the presence of two witnesses present at the same time and each witness must either attest and sign the will or acknowledge the signature in the presence of the testator but not necessarily in the presence of the other witness.

The three essentials for the execution of a valid will are therefore:

a. writing,
b. signature, and
c. attestation.

Writing

No precise form of wording is necessary and the writing may be in the testator's own handwriting (in which case it is termed a holograph will), in typewritten or printed form, or any combination of these.

The only exception to the requirement of writing relates to those entitled to make privileged wills under section 11, Wills Act 1837, as amended by section 2, Wills (Soldiers and Sailors) Act 1918. This concept is designed mainly to apply to military personnel on actual military service. A privileged will can be made informally and comprise merely an oral statement substantiated by appropriate witnesses.

In the case of a soldier, privilege applies when a state of war exists. A sailor or merchant seaman may, however, claim the privilege from the time he joins his ship to the time he receives his discharge.

Whilst generally persons under the age of 18 cannot make a valid will (section 7, Wills Act 1837, as amended by the Family Law Reform Act 1969), a privileged will may be valid in the case of a soldier or sailor aged under 18 dying on actual military service.

Those wishing to pursue this subject in detail will find a large number of High Court decisions discussing the meaning of the expression 'actual military service'.

Signature

Provided the intention can be substantiated, a signature by way of the testator's mark or thumb-print or set of initials will suffice. The old requirement that the signature had to be at the foot or the end of the will was done away with by the 1982 Act so that it now suffices if the signature appears so that 'the testator intended by his signature to give effect to the will'.

It will take time to see how this requirement is construed by the courts. A signature on a separate sheet annexed to the end, or indeed the beginning, of a will will probably suffice, but it would seem that the actual signature, rather than any other descriptive words of the testator, will be an essential.

The courts have been inclined to interpret the requirements of the Wills Act 1837 fairly liberally as demonstrated in *Re Horne, Deceased; Bowden and Another* v. *Embledon* (1958) where the testatrix had signed her name on the envelope containing her will; the will itself was signed by two witnesses. Probate was granted of the two documents — the unsigned will and the signed envelope which contained the will.

Again, in *Re Chalcraft deceased* (1948), the testatrix, being in great pain, had been unable to write more than 'E Chal'. The courts held this to be an effective signature.

The amended requirements allow the signature of the testator or the signature of some other person signing at the direction of the testator. There is no restriction on whom this person might be and could be one of the witnesses. For the avoidance of doubt, however, it would appear preferable for the person signing to sign using his own signature and to state he is signing on behalf of, by his direction and in the presence of the testator.

Attestation

The amendments made by the Administration of Justice Act 1982 continue to require that the signature of the testator must be either actually made by him or acknowledged by him in the presence of at least two witnesses, who must also sign and witness the will in the presence of the testator. It is not necessary that the witnesses should know that the document is a will. They are witnessing the testator's signature rather than verifying the nature of the document. A minor, if capable of understanding what is happening, may attest a will, but for obvious reasons a blind person cannot: *Re Gibson* (1949).

Each witness must sign in the testator's presence but need not be present when the other signs.

A standard will will conclude with an attestation clause comprising a short statement above the signatures of the witnesses which declares that the will has been duly signed in the presence of the witnesses who attest the will and sign it in the presence of the testator and of each other. Whilst not essential, such a clause is advisable so as to facilitate the obtaining of probate. Further, it is customary to include the addresses of the witnesses as it might be necessary to trace them to give evidence in the case of any challenge of the validity of the will etc.

Model will

The following is a simple form of Will with a 'short form' attestation clause.

THIS IS THE LAST WILL AND TESTAMENT of me ALBERT LACY of Brettenham Manor Banbury Oxon made this . . . . . . day of . . . . . . 1986 revoking all former Wills and testamentary dispositions made by me.

1. I APPOINT JOSHUA CHECK of No. 10 The Broadway, Westminster, London Builder and my wife EILEEN LACY of Brettenham Manor aforesaid to be my Executors.
2. I REQUEST that my body be cremated.
3. I GIVE my son BRIAN LACY also of Brettenham Manor aforesaid £10,000 free of all taxes payable in connection with my death.
4. I GIVE the residue of my estate both real and personal whatsoever and wheresoever situate subject to the payment of my debts and funeral and testamentary expenses to my said wife EILEEN aforesaid absolutely but if she shall predecease me then to my said son BRIAN absolutely.

IN WITNESS whereof I have hereunto set my hand.

Signed by the said   )
ALBERT LACEY in our)
Joint presence and   )
then by us in his   )

Conditions

Condition subsequent

A *condition subsequent* is a condition on the happening of which the interest in the property concerned ceases.

Where a legacy or an annuity is subject to a condition subsequent:

a. against disputing the will;
b. against marriage with a particular person; or
c. against marriage without the consent of a certain person;

that legacy or annuity is void unless there is a gift over. The origins and extent of the rule were discussed in *Leong* v. *Lim Beng Chye* (1955). The reasoning is that, if there is no gift over, it would appear that the condition in the will was intended to be a mere threat to coerce the donee. By making a gift over to another person, it would seem that the testator wanted the latter to benefit if the condition were broken. For example, given the condition 'I leave £500 to *B* on the condition that he does not marry *X*', the legacy is void as there is no gift over. The legacy or annuity need not actually be given to a third person; it is sufficient for the testator to direct that it shall fall into residue or be revoked or forfeited and void: *Re Hanlon* (1933); the mere fact that the gift would fall into residue in any event is not sufficient: *Wheeler* v. *Bingham* (1746).

An executor is under no duty to give a legatee notice of any such condition. Consequently, where there is a gift over, a condition is good even though the legatee has no notice of it and even though the executor is the person entitled in default: In *Re Lewis* (1904).

A condition subsequent is always void in the following circumstances.

a. If it is contrary to public policy, e.g. if it is in total restraint of marriage (not including a second or subsequent marriage).
b. If it is repugnant to the nature of the gift, e.g. if it is in total restraint of alienation.
c. If it becomes impossible. Thus in *Re Parrott's Will Trusts* (1946), a condition that the beneficiary should by deed poll assume a certain name which involved his changing both his surname and his Christian name was held to be impossible, because a Christian name could not be altered by deed poll.

d. If it is uncertain. In *Re Jones* (1953) a condition for forfeiture if a beneficiary 'should have social or other relationship with X' was held void for uncertainty.

Condition precedent

A *condition precedent* is one which must be fulfilled before the property concerned can pass to the beneficiary.

Codicils

A *codicil* is a supplementary clause attached to or referring to a will with the object of adding to, cancelling or altering the provisions of the will. A codicil is, however, only valid if executed and attested in the manor required for the valid execution of a will.

Model codicil

THIS IS A FIRST CODICIL to the Will of me ALBERT LACEY dated the first day January one thousand nine hundred and eighty six.

1. I HEREBY REVOKE clause 3 of my said Will.
2. I GIVE my son BRIAN LACEY of Brettenham Manor Banbury Oxon £20,000 free of all taxes payable in connection with my death.
3. In all other respects I confirm my said Will.

In Witness whereof I have hereunto set my hand this . . . . . . day of . . . . . . 198 .

Signed by the said   )
ALBERT LACEY in our)
joint presence and   )
then by us in his   )

Gifts to witnesses

Section 15 of the Wills Act 1837 makes void any gift of property to any witness or to the spouse of any witness.

The harshness of this rule was relaxed somewhat by the Wills Act 1968 applying to testators dying after 29 May 1968. This amending Act provides that where, for example, there are three witnesses to a will, one of whom is a beneficiary, that beneficiary may still take his gift because the will would be valid (having been witnessed by two other witnesses) without his signature.

THE EXECUTION OF A WILL

Ideally, a solicitor should be present at the execution of a will to ensure that all formalities are adhered to. However, in practice, this is not always possible and wills tend to be sent through the post to clients for execution. In this case, the solicitor should ensure that a covering letter sets out explicitly the relevant procedure with particular warnings that no beneficiary or spouse of such beneficiary should be a witness together with the requirements relating to signature etc.

REVOCATION OF WILLS

All wills are said to be ambulatory until the testator's death, i.e. a will may be revoked at any time before death.

A will or codicil may be revoked at any time before death by:

a. marriage,
b. divorce, or
c. destruction.

Revocation by marriage

Section 18 of the Wills Act 1837, as substituted by section 18 of the Administration of Justice Act 1982, provides that every will shall be revoked by the subsequent marriage of the testator.

However, section 18(3) states that a will is saved from revocation if the will makes it clear that the testator was expecting to be married to a particular person and that he intended that the will should not be revoked by this marriage. Although the Act offers no explanation as to how to meet this requirement, a clause in the will explaining that the will is made in expectation of a marriage to a specific person and that the intention of the testator is that the will is not to be revoked by this marriage to this specified person will probably suffice.

Section 18(4) of the Act provides a comparable saving provision in respect of the saving of one disposition in the will.

As a relatively minor matter, section 18(2) of the Act provides that the exercise of a power of appointment contained in the will remains valid despite any subsequent marriage.

Revocation by divorce

This new concept was introduced by section 18(2) of the Administration of Justice Act 1982. It appears as section 18(A) of the Wills Act 1837. Upon the dissolution of a marriage, the will of either party to the marriage is to be construed as if (a) any appointment of the other spouse as an executor (or trustee) were omitted, with the result that letters of administration will be necessary, and (b) any devise or bequest to the former spouse becomes void. This provision only applies in respect of a dissolution of marriage obtained by court degree and does not apply to other less formal arrangements such as a separation.

Revocation by destruction

Section 20 of the Wills Act 1837 provides for the express revocation of a will or codicil by burning, tearing or otherwise destroying personally by the testator, or by some other person in the presence of the testator acting on his instructions with the intention on the part of the testator of revoking the will. Thus two things are necessary, namely a physical act of destruction, and an intention to revoke (*animus revocandi*). Symbolic destruction, e.g. the drawing of lines across the will, is insufficient, even if the words 'this Will is revoked' are written across its face (*Cheese* v. *Lovejoy* (1877)).

The execution of another will or codicil showing an intention to revoke any former will also has the effect of revoking that earlier will. It is desirable that some express declaration of revocation be included in the later will or codicil, for otherwise, where two wills of different dates exist, both will be valid and read together. However, if they purport to deal with the whole of the estate and are mutually inconsistent, the later will prevail over the earlier — *O'Leary* v. *Douglass* (1878).

A second will which expressly revokes a former one may have been invalidly executed. In those circumstances it will not be effective to revoke the earlier will. Similarly, should a disposition under a second will which does not expressly revoke a former will fail on account of the sole beneficiary being a necessary attesting witness, then the first will will not be revoked: *Re Robinson* (1930).

In *Simpson* v. *Foxon* (1907), a testator executed two wills on different dates and the later began: 'This is the last and only will and testament of . . .'. It was held that these words were not sufficient to revoke the earlier will. The testator's intention must be gathered from all the testamentary documents he leaves. Consequently, if the last will disposes of all the testator's property, then earlier wills will be presumed to be revoked. If the last will does not dispose of all the testator's property, and does not expressly revoke them, then it will be read in conjunction with the earlier ones.

As a general rule, an oral revocation without a physical act of destruction is not sufficient, so that if a testator says, 'I revoke this Will', and throws it into a waste-paper basket without tearing it up, the will is not revoked; but a mere declaration of revocation will be sufficient if made by a soldier or airman in actual service or a seaman at sea. Thus in *Wood* v. *Gossage* (1921), a soldier before leaving for the front gave his will to his fiancée for safe keeping. While in France he wrote to her instructing her to destroy the will as he had decided to revoke it. The will was not destroyed, but the court held that it had been revoked by the letter ordering its destruction.

Accidental destruction

If a will is accidentally destroyed, it is not revoked, as no *animus revocandi* accompanied the act of destruction. A copy of the will, or even a draft, may be admitted to probate, but the person seeking to establish the will must be able to prove that the destruction was purely accidental. In every case where a will cannot be found after a person's death, and that person is believed to have made a will, it is presumed that the will has been destroyed by the testator with the intention of revoking it.

In *In the Estate of Lintott* (1941), a will was deposited by the executors' solicitors in their office safe. The offices were destroyed by fire as a result of enemy action, and no trace of the will could be found. Probate was accordingly granted on a copy supported by the solicitors' affidavit deposing to its correctness. Somewhat similar circumstances arose in *Re Webb, Deceased; Smith* v. *Johnston and Others* (1964) where a completed draft will was admitted to probate. In one case where a testator's will had disappeared, the court allowed his daughter, who had been his secretary, to recite its contents from memory and probate was granted: *Sugden* v. *Lord St Leonards* (1876).

The cases show an inclination by the courts to lean against the presumption of an intestacy. They are willing to accept the accidental destruction of a will rather than the intention to revoke.

In the case of a condition precedent, there is no need for a gift over to make it effective.

Provided it is not illegal, the condition must be fulfilled, even though it is impossible, unless:

a. it becomes impossible through the act of the testator, except in the case of realty: *Re Turton* (1926); or
b. it was rendered impossible by operation of the law before the will came into operation: *Re Thomas' Will Trust* (1930); *Re Wolfe* (1953).

Partial revocation

Any alteration to an executed will must itself be subject to the necessary formalities. Where, however, a part of the will has become obliterated so that it is impossible to read, verbal evidence as to the former state of the will is inadmissible, and a blank must be left.

In *In the Estate of Nunn* (1936), two or three lines of a will had been cut out so that the will was severed into two parts. The severed parts had then been sewn together and it was held that the presumption was that the words had been cut out by the testatrix with the intention of revoking that part so the will in its existing form was admitted to probate.

In *Re Zimmer* (1924) a testatrix left her whole estate to 'my three dear children in equal shares'. One of the three children predeceased leaving issue of her own surviving, whereupon the testatrix obliterated the words 'three' from her will and substituted the word 'two' and then placed her signature in the margin. The alteration was not attested by the necessary two witnesses so that the alteration was ineffective. Accordingly, the statement should have been read as if the alteration had not been made, which would have enabled the children of the deceased child to claim a one-third share of the estate. As it was not possible, however, to read the word which had been obliterated, a blank had to be left, with the result that the estate was given to 'my *blank* dear children in equal shares'. The surviving children therefore divided the whole estate and the issue of the deceased child received nothing.

Alteration by obliteration is only accepted if the means of obliteration is such that it is impossible to ascertain from the face of the will what were the previous words of gift. Thus in *Re Itter* (1950), after executing her will, the testatrix painted over the amounts of certain legacies, and inserted slips of paper on which she wrote, without the necessary formalities, the amounts she wished to bequeath. The Court held that obliteration was ineffective and admitted to probate the will in its original terms as ascertained by infra-red photography.

Dependent relative revocation

As a will cannot be properly revoked if the testator has no intention of so doing, the destruction of a will under a misapprehension as to the effect of the destruction or of a subsequent testamentary disposition will not revoke the will destroyed. The assumption in these cases is that the operation of the revocation depended upon the result contemplated by the testator, so that if that result does not or cannot occur, the revocation will be inoperative. Thus, in *In the Estate of Southerden* (1925), a testator had made a will leaving his whole estate to his wife. Before his death, he revoked the will, believing that as he left no children his wife would get all his property if he died intestate, but as a widow does not necessarily obtain the whole of her deceased husband's property absolutely upon intestacy, and in fact in this case she would not have obtained it, the court refused to recognize the revocation and gave effect to the will under the doctrine of dependent relative revocation.

Similarly if a testator, with the intention of reviving a previous will, destroys a will by which he revoked all previous wills, the destruction will not have the effect of revoking the will, because under section 22 of the Wills Act, 1837, a revoked will can only be revived by re-execution thereof or by a codicil executed as the law requires showing an intention to revive the revoked will (see p. 12), but if the original will is 'destroyed' it is no longer capable of being revived.

A testator who makes a valid first will and then makes a second will which is invalid, e.g. by reason of its execution being defective, does not revoke the first will if he destroys it under the mistaken impression that the second will is valid. Thus, in *Re Dey* (1932), the testator had executed two testamentary documents, one in May 1925, and one in July 1930. The later will was not properly executed. The testator destroyed the earlier will in the belief that it was no longer of any use and that the document executed in July 1930 was a valid will. Consequently, the earlier will, the contents of which had been reproduced in a document before the court, was revived and probate of it was granted.

Similarly, in the case of *In the Estate of Addison, Deceased* (1964) a will was withdrawn from his solicitor by the testator, with the intention of making a new one, following the death of his wife. No will could be found at his death. The doctrine was held to apply because it was assumed that the testator had destroyed his will, intending to make a new one, but had not in fact made a new one. A carbon copy of the will withdrawn from the solicitor was admitted to probate.

Where, however, in such a case as the last, it proves impossible to arrive at a knowledge of the contents of the will intended to be revoked, an intestacy will arise.

In *In the Estate of Brown* (1942), a testator made a will completely disposing of his property, and later drew up a second will which contained a clear revocation clause but which, although duly executed, was incomplete in that he failed to state in the principal clause the names of the beneficiaries and the interests they were to take. The court held that the doctrine of dependent relative revocation ought to be applied on the ground that the testator put in the revocation clause only on the condition that a second will was a complete will disposing of his property, and that, in the circumstances, the second will ought to be admitted to probate with the first will, but that the revocation clause in the second will should be excluded from the probate.

The case of *In Re Feis Deceased (Guillaume and Ors.* v. *Ritz-Remorf and Ors.)* (1963) shows that a revocation based on a mistake of law can sometimes be valid. The testatrix made a codicil stating that her will should apply only to property in England, stating that she had 'made separate arrangements' in respect of property in Germany. These 'arrangements' were ineffective under German law, but it was held that there was a clear intention to take away the German property from the legatees under the will. The German property was thus undisposed of.

Reviving a revoked will

Section 22 of the Wills Act 1837 enacts that 'no Will or codicil, or any part thereof, which shall be in any manner revoked, shall be revived otherwise than by the re-execution thereof, or by a codicil executed in the manner herein – before required, and showing an intention to revive the same.'

In *In the Estate of Davis, Deceased* (1952), the deceased made a will in 1951 leaving all his estate to Ethel Phoebe Horsley, whom he appointed his executrix. In the following year he married her. In 1953 he wrote on the envelope containing the will the words 'The herein named Ethel Phoebe Horsley is now my lawful wedded wife', this statement, like the will, being properly attested. It was held that the document constituted a codicil, and that the circumstances showed an intention to revive the revoked will.

A codicil cannot revive a will that has been revoked by destruction; it can revive a revoked will only if it is still in existence, and the intention to revive the will must appear on the face of the codicil: *In the Goods of Steele* (1868), confirmed by *In the Estate of Taylor, Goldie* v. *Adam* (1938).

It is important to note that, conversely revocation of a codicil, which alters a previous will, does not revive the original provisions of that will. If a codicil is revoked with the intention of reviving provisions of a will this revocation is ineffective under the 'dependent relative revocation provisions'.

It is probate practice that a revoked codicil should always be produced and such a codicil will be admitted to probate if it contains an alteration to a will and to an earlier codicil.

THE INHERITANCE (PROVISION FOR FAMILY AND DEPENDANTS) ACT 1975

Under this Act, if a testator (or testatrix) dies domiciled in England and Wales (on or after 1 April 1976) and leaves a widow (or widower), a former wife (or husband) who has not remarried, a son or daughter, any person who, although not a child of the deceased, was treated as such by the deceased, and any other person who, immediately before the death of the deceased, was being maintained (either wholly or partly) by the deceased; then any one of these dependants can apply to the court under section 2 of the Inheritance (Provision for Family and Dependants) Act 1975 on the ground that under the will or intestacy the applicant has not received reasonable financial provision.

An ex-wife or ex-husband can claim 'reasonable maintenance', which means reasonable in relation to the legal obligation the testator was under before death. If the deceased was under no obligation to make financial provision, the ex-wife or husband is unlikely to succeed in their claim.

'Son' and 'daughter' respectively mean natural sons or daughters, and 'reasonable provision' would be what the court felt was required in relation to the estate and the financial responsibilities of the applicant.

'A person who, although not a child of the deceased, was treated as such' covers illegitimate children and adopted children. A grandchild, however, would not normally have a claim, unless his or her parent had died before the deceased.

'Any other person who immediately before the death of the deceased, was being maintained (wholly or partly) by the deceased' covers mistress, lover, brother, aunt, etc.

The provision which the court may make for the maintenance of such dependants is governed by section 2 of the 1975 Act, but is, of course, at the discretion of the court. It will cover periodical payments for a specified time (the life of the surviving spouse or his or her re-marriage). These payments are normally a percentage of annual income, but the court may provide for them to be made up by payments of capital, payment of a lump sum, transfer of specified property, or any marriage settlement for the benefit of the applicant.

Generally, the court will have regard to the following matters, when making the award:

a. the present resources of the applicant and his reasonable prospects (earning capacity and other inheritance);
b. the amounts the deceased donated during his life and/or under his will;
c. the size of the estate and the number of other beneficiaries;
d. whether the applicant suffers from either physical or mental disability.

It should be noted that the 1975 Act not only consolidated the law on the subject, superseding earlier Acts and judicial interpretations, but also extended the number of potential applicants, going well outside the immediate family, i.e. to widows and dependent children. It is open to the court, in certain circumstances, to award to any person, not nominated by the deceased, property being the subject of a *donatio mortis causa* (see p. 93) the subject-matter of lifetime gifts made by the deceased, provided:

a. the gift was made less then six years before death;
b. the property was a gift and not a transfer for value; and
c. there is sufficient evidence to satisfy the court that the transfer was made with the intention of defeating an application for financial provision under the terms of the 1975 Act. In order to be effective, an application under the 1975 Act must be made with *six months* immediately following the date when grant of representation is first taken out, unless the court at its discretion agrees to extend the period.

Exercise 2

1. What formalities are required by the Wills Act 1837 for the making of a valid will? Can an oral will ever be admitted to probate?
2. What pecuniary disadvantages may result to persons who attest a will or a codicil?
3. A will was signed by the testator and witnessed by two witnesses, but there was no attestation clause. It was afterwards found that one of the witnesses thought the will was a lease, and the other was a legatee. Do you consider the will was valid?
4. What persons are (a) totally and (b) partially incapable of disposing of property by will?
5. How may a will be revoked?
6. What is the effect of the accidental destruction of a will by the testator or some other person?
7. In what circumstances is a will revoked by the marriage of the testator?
8. How should alterations to a will be made? What is the effect of an improperly made alteration?
9. Explain the doctrine of dependent relative revocation.
10. In what cases may a revoked will be revived? How can this be done in those cases?
11. Explain the following terms: attestation clause; nuncupative will; holograph will; codicil; *animus testandi*; *animus revocandi*.
12. What are the main provisions of the Inheritance (Provision for Family and Dependents) Act 1975?

3
Intestacy

DISTRIBUTION OF RESIDUE

Where a person dies intestate the residue must be distributed among those entitled by law to an intestate's estate. The distribution of this residue is regulated mainly by the Administration of Estates Act 1925, as amended by the Intestates' Estates Act 1952. The various amounts due to specified relatives are varied from time to time by way of Statutory Instruments called Intestate Succession Orders.

The rules governing distribution applying at present came into force in respect of persons dying intestate on or after 1 March 1981 and are as follows.

The widow or widower

a. Where the deceased has left a spouse surviving, that spouse will receive: all personal chattels (furniture, personal effects, etc.).
b. If there is issue the surviving spouse will receive a sum of £40,000. This sum carries interest at 7 per cent per annum from the date of death to the date of payment.

If there is no issue, but a surviving parent or brother or sister (or issue thereof) of the whole blood, a sum of £85,000, again carrying interest at 7 per cent per annum.

Under the 1952 Act, the surviving spouse has the right to have the matrimonal home appropriated as part of the statutory legacy if the value permits.

The interest on the net sum of £40,000 (or £85,000) is charged against the income of the intestate's estate to the extent that the income is sufficient. If there is insufficient income to meet the payment of interest in full, the deficiency must be made good out of capital so that the surviving spouse does not suffer.

After payment of the amounts due to the surviving spouse, the entitlement to the balance of the intestate's estate varies with the nature of the intestate's surviving relatives, as follows.

If issue survive the intestate

Issue includes all lineal descendants whether legitimate, illegitimate, or legitimated. Since the enacting of the Family Law Reform Act 1969 with effect from 1 January 1970, it can be said illegitimate and legitimate children are placed on the same footing in relation to the inheritance of property.

Where issue survives the intestate, the balance of the estate, after deducting the personal chattels and statutory legacy due to the surviving spouse, must be halved. One-half will be held on trust — called the statutory trusts — for the issue of the intestate, but the income arising from it will be paid to the surviving spouse for life. The other half will be held on the statutory trusts for the issue free from any claim on the part of the surviving spouse.

For example, *A* dies intestate on 1 October 1985 and is survived by a widow and two children. After payment of all debts and administration expenses, £140,000 plus personal chattels remain to be distributed. The widow will take the personal chattels and her statutory legacy of £40,000 as her absolute property. Of the remaining £100,000, £50,000 will be held upon the statutory trusts for the children and the income will be paid to the widow for her life; the other £50,000 will be held upon these statutory trusts direct for the two children.

Should the widow die before the children attain the age of 18 or marry under that age, the sum of £50,000 will continue to be held upon the statutory trusts for the children in the same way the second sum has been held.

If the deceased leaves issue but no surviving spouse, the whole of the residue will be held on the statutory trusts for the issue.

If no issue survive the intestate

If no issue survive the intestate, nor parents or brothers or sisters of the whole blood, the whole estate goes to the surviving spouse (i.e. widow or widower). If the intestate leaves parents but no issue, the surviving spouse takes half the residue absolutely and the other half goes to the parents absolutely or will be held on trust for the relatives of the intestate in the order given below. The relatives of the intestate will take the residue (subject to the deduction of the absolute interest of the widow or widower, where appropriate) in the following order.

If *both parents* survive the intestate, the residue will be held in trust for the father and mother in equal shares absolutely. Stepfathers and stepmothers have no claim.

If *only one parent* survives the intestate, the residue will be held in trust for that parent absolutely.

If *no spouse, issue or parents* survive the intestate, the residue will be held in trust for any of the following persons who are living at the death of the intestate, in the following order and manner.

a. On the statutory trusts for the *brothers and sisters* (or issue thereof) *of the whole blood* of the intestate; but if no person takes an absolutely vested interest under such trusts, then —
b. on the statutory trusts for the *brothers and sisters* (or issue thereof) *of the half-blood* of the intestate; but if no person takes an absolutely vested interest under such trusts, then —
c. for the *grandparents* of the intestate and, if more than one survive the intestate, for them in equal shares; but if there are no members of this class, then —
d. on the statutory trusts for the *uncles and aunts* (or issue thereof) of the intestate (who are *brothers and sisters of the whole blood* of a parent of the intestate); but if no such person takes an absolutely vested interest under such trusts, then —
e. on the statutory trusts for the *uncles and aunts* (for issue thereof) of the intestate (who are *brothers and sisters of the half-blood* of a parent of the intestate).

Brothers and sisters of the half-blood, grandparents and uncles and aunts receive no benefit if the intestate leaves a widow or widower.

Steprelations should be carefully distinguished from relations of the half-blood. If A, a widower with two children, B and C, marries D, who already has two children, E and F, by a previous marriage, E and F become steprelations of B and C. If, on the other hand, A, a widower with two children, B and C, marries D and by her has two children, E and F, the latter are relations of the half-blood to B and C. Steprelations are not recognized, and cannot benefit, under intestate succession.

If no person takes an absolutely vested interest under any of the foregoing provisions, the residuary estate will belong to the Crown, or to the Duchy of Lancaster or to the Duchy of Cornwall (if the property is within either of these areas) as *bona vacantia*, or ownerless, property.

THE STATUTORY TRUSTS

These are contained in section 47, Administration of Estates Act 1925, and are as follows.

Where more than one member of the class concerned exists, the residue must be divided into as many shares as there are members of the class and must be held in trust for such persons, contingent upon their attaining the age of 18 or marrying. As soon as any member of the class attains full age or marries, he or she attains an *absolutely vested interest*, when survival will not be necessary to entitle him or her to a share of the capital. It should be noted, however, that although a vested interest is attained upon reaching the age of 18 or upon earlier marriage, the share will not, in the event of marriage before 18, be paid over until full age is reached. In this case, the whole income may be paid to the married minor until he or she is entitled to receive the capital. If any member of the class dies unmarried before attaining the age of 18, his or her interest fails and the share will be divided among the surviving members of the class, still subject, however, to the statutory trusts.

Thus, if A dies intestate leaving no widow, but three sons, all under age and unmarried, surviving him, one-third of the residue of his estate will be held upon the statutory trusts for each of the three sons. Should one of them die before he has attained an absolutely vested interest, i.e. before he has married or attained full age, then one-half of the deceased child's share will continue to be held upon the statutory trusts for each of the surviving children, who would accordingly receive ultimately one-half of the original residue. On the other hand, if the deceased child had married, upon marriage he would have attained an absolute vested interest and his share should not go absolutely to his brothers, but would pass to the deceased child's estate and be disposed of according to the terms of his will, if he left a will, or according to the rules relating to the distribution of intestate estates set out above, if he died intestate.

The case considered above is a comparatively simple one, for all A's children were living at his death. If another child had predeceased him, the position might have been different, according to the circumstances. If the deceased child left no issue of his own which survived A, no difference would result, even if the deceased child had been married and had left a widow, for the widow of the deceased child would have no claim to any portion of A's estate. If, on the other hand, issue of the deceased child had survived the intestate, the share which their parent would have received, had he been living at A's death, would be held upon the statutory trusts for the issue, who would be A's grandchildren. Thus, the estate would in such a case be divided into four portions: one for each of the three surviving children of A, and one, which in turn would be divided into equal shares, for the issue of the deceased child.

It should be noted that the issue of the deceased child take amongst them only the share to which their parent would have been entitled: that is, they share *per stirpes* or according to their stocks and not *per capita* or according to the number of such issue left.

Similar trusts apply where brothers and sisters, or aunts and uncles, form the class entitled to the residue; that is the issue of deceased brothers and sisters (nephews and nieces) and the issue of deceased uncles and aunts (cousins) will take their deceased parent's share *per stirpes*.

RIGHTS OF SURVIVING SPOUSE

In the case of intestacies arising on or after 1 January 1953, the surviving spouse is entitled to have his or her life interest (where issue survive) redeemed by payment of the capital value which is calculated in accordance with certain specified rules. After such redemption, the residuary estate may be distributed and dealt with free from the life interest of the surviving spouse. The normal time limit for this election is twelve months from the date when representation to the intestate's estate is taken out.

Furthermore, where the residue includes a dwelling-house in which the surviving husband or wife is residing at the time of the intestate's death, such spouse may require the personal representative to appropriate the said dwelling-house in or towards satisfaction of an absolute interest (where no issue survive) or the capital value of a life interest (where issue survive) of such spouse in the residuary estate. This right must also normally be exercised within twelve months of taking out representation to the estate and the personal representative may not sell the dwelling-house during this period without the written consent of the surviving spouse except in the case of a deficiency of assets to meet liabilities, inheritance tax, etc.

Example 1

Anthony Jones died intestate and a bachelor on 1 August 1985. He was the only child of the late Henry and Susan Jones, so that no widow, issue, parents, brothers or sisters survived him. In addition, all four of his grandparents were dead. Susan Jones, his mother, had at one time a sister, who had, however, been dead for some years, but this sister left two children of her own, who survived Anthony, both being minors at the time of his death. Henry Jones, Anthony's father, was the only child of his mother, Martha, but his father John had married again late in life, and two of his children by his second wife, Maud, were living at the time of Anthony's death, their names being Charles and James.

In considering any problem of intestate succession, it is usually advisable to draw up a family tree, which in this case would be as follows:

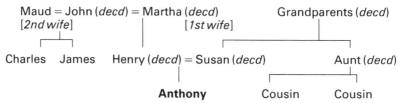

In this case, Anthony's estate would be held on the statutory trusts for the two children of his mother's deceased sister (his cousins), who is his aunt of the whole blood. If these two children die before they attain an absolutely vested interest, the residue of Anthony's estate would go to Charles and James, his uncles of the half-blood. His grandfather's wife, Maud, would get nothing, as she is in no way related by blood to Anthony. She is not his grandmother.

Example 2

Robert Hare died on 21 January 1985 leaving no will. He was survived by his widow, two unmarried sons aged 24 and 17 respectively, a married daughter who had one child, and two grandchildren, the sons of a deceased son. After payment of all debts etc. his property consisted of £125,000, including personal effects valued at £5,000.

The following statement shows how the estate will be distributed.

	£
Total estate	£125,000
Widow:	
Personal chattels	5,000
Statutory legacy	40,000
Life interest in half of balance	40,000

The balance of £40,000 will be distributed as follows:

Elder son	10,000
Younger son (on statutory trusts)	10,000
Married daughter	10,000
Two grandchildren (in equal shares on statutory trusts)	10,000
	£40,000

On the death of the widow, the sum of £40,000 in which she had a life interest, will be distributed according to circumstances as they exist at that time.

TABLE SHOWING DISTRIBUTION OF INTESTATE'S ESTATE

The following table is in accordance with the Administration of Estates Act 1925 as amended by the Intestates' Estates Act 1952, the Family Provision Act 1966, and the Family Provision (Intestate Succession) Order 1981, with regard to deaths on or after 1 March 1981.

Intestate dies leaving: –	*Distribution of estate*
Husband or wife and no issue and no parent or brother or sister (or issue thereof) of the whole blood.	Husband or wife takes the whole estate absolutely.
Husband or wife and issue.	Husband or wife takes: a. Personal chattels absolutely. b. £40,000 free of tax and costs with interest (payable out of income) at 7 per cent per annum to date of payment. c. A life interest in one-half of the balance. Subject to this life interest the residue is held on statutory trusts for the issue.
Husband or wife and no issue but a parent or brother or sister (or issue thereof) of the whole blood.	Husband or wife takes: a. Personal chattels absolutely.

b. £85,000 free of tax and costs with interest (payable out of income) at 7 per cent per annum to date of payment.

c. One-half of the residue absolutely. The other half of the residue will be taken by the parent(s) absolutely, or if no parent survives it will be held on statutory trusts for the brothers and sisters (or issue thereof) of the whole blood.

Issue but no husband or wife.

The whole estate is held on the statutory trusts for the issue.

Parent or parents but no husband or wife or issue.

Parents take the whole estate in equal shares absolutely, or if only one survives, that one takes the whole estate absolutely.

Relatives, but no husband or wife, issue or parents.

Relatives take the whole estate in the following order:

a. brothers and sisters (or issue thereof) of the whole blood on statutory trusts;

b. brothers and sisters (or issue thereof) of the half-blood on statutory trusts;

c. grandparents in equal shares absolutely;

d. uncles and aunts (or issue thereof) of the whole blood on statutory trusts;

e. uncles and aunts (or issue thereof) of the half-blood on statutory trust.

No husband or wife or relatives.

Whole estate to the Crown, Duchy of Lancaster, or Duchy of Cornwall, as ownerless property.

Exercise 3

1. *R* died intestate in 1985 leaving a widow and a father surviving him. How will *R*'s property be distributed?
2. *X* died intestate in 1985, leaving the following property:

House valued at	£50,000
Personal chattels valued at	£2,000
Cash and securities	£30,000

The following relatives survive: a widow, two sons, a granddaughter who was the child of a deceased daughter, two grandsons, who were the children of a deceased son, a father, and two brothers. How will *X*'s property be distributed?
3. Mrs *X* died intestate in 1985 leaving the following relatives: two brothers, three nieces who were daughters of a stepsister, a stepmother, and a husband. How will her property be distributed?
4. How should the estate of an intestate (who died in 1985) be distributed, assuming he leaves a widow, one son aged 30 (who has two children), two daughters aged 24 and 17 respectively, and three daughters of a deceased son (all minors).
5. Explain the following terms: personal chattels; statutory trusts; *bona vacantia*; *per stirpes*; *per capita*; half-blood.
6. An illegitimate person dies. Who has a claim to any property he may have had at death?

4
Probate

ADMINISTRATION OF THE ESTATE

Upon the death of any person, the personal representatives must administer the estate by gathering together the deceased's assets, paying all debts, taxes and expenses, and then distributing the residue among those so entitled under the testator's will, or by the laws of intestacy.

Any person who takes possession, or who in any way administers any part of the estate, must obtain probate or letters of administration as soon as possible after the death.

Acts of administration before probate

An executor derives his title and powers from the will itself, which speaks from the moment the testator dies. The obtaining of a grant of probate merely ratifies legally his title of executor. Whilst in theory, therefore, an executor can exercise all of his powers without obtaining a grant, there are in practice, restrictions on him. An executor can collect all the assets, receive payment of debts and pay any debts due, but he will not be able to sell or transfer any securities, or dispose of any real property as he himself cannot give evidence of his title, which a purchaser will require, without producing a copy of the grant of probate. An executor will not be able to withdraw money from the deceased's bank account or do any other acts that require proof of title.

THE EXECUTOR

Probate cannot be granted to more than four persons in respect of the same part of the estate of a deceased person (section 114(1), Supreme Court Act 1981). Should any dispute arise where more than four persons are appointed, such disputes are settled by a registrar in the Principal Probate Registry. At least one executor must always be appointed.

Only an executor named in the will is entitled to obtain probate. If there is an executor, he must be appointed by the will (or codicil thereto), either:

a. expressly, or
b. by implication.

An *express* appointment is made where the testator in the will either:

a. names his executor, e.g. thus: 'I appoint James Smith, of 51 London Road, Blackheath, to be my executor'; or
b. empowers some other person to nominate an executor, e.g. thus: 'I empower James Brown to appoint some trustworthy person to act as my executor.' In this latter case, the person nominated by James Brown will be the executor who is entitled to obtain probate and, in fact, James Brown can appoint himself.

An *implied* appointment is made where the testator does not expressly nominate a person as executor, but requests some person to perform acts which are normally performed by an executor, e.g. where he states in his will, 'I wish James Smith to collect my assets and pay my debts.' The person thus nominated by implication is called an executor *according to the tenor*.

Should there be any doubt as to who is really intended to be executor, owing to some ambiguity in the will, verbal evidence will be admitted to remove the doubt only in the case of a *latent* ambiguity and not in the case of a *patent* ambiguity.

A *latent ambiguity* is one which is not apparent on the face of the will, but arises from independent circumstances, e.g. if two persons, both of the name of James Smith, live at 51 London Road, Blackheath, there will, in the first example given above, be a latent ambiguity as to which is meant, and verbal evidence would, in such a case, be admitted to show which person the testator intended to appoint.

A *patent ambiguity*, is one which is apparent on the face of the will, e.g. where the will says, 'I appoint James Smith to be my sole executor, and I bequeath to Henry Brown, who is to be my sole executor, £100.' Here no verbal evidence as to which person was intended wilbe admitted, and the appointment would probably fail for uncertainty.

If no properly appointed executor exists, or the person nominated will not or cannot act, some person interested in the administration of the estate will have to apply to the court for *letters of administration, cum testamento annexo*, but probate in such a case could not be granted.

Capacity to act as executor

Any person who has attained his majority and is of sound mind may act as executor if properly nominated by the will. In the case, however, of a bankrupt or criminal, the court has a discretion to appoint some other person (section 116, Supreme Court Act 1981).

In the case of mentally disordered persons, probate will be granted to a person of age on behalf of the mentally disordered person.

If a firm is appointed as executor, probate will be granted to not more than four members of the firm individually, who were members at the date of the execution of the will. In *Re Horgan (Deceased)* (1969), where the testator appointed a firm of solicitors as his executors 'who may act through any of the partners not exceeding two in number', it was held that the appointment was valid and not void for uncertainty.

Infants

The Judicature Act 1925 provides that if a minor is appointed executor, he cannot act for any purpose or obtain a grant of probate until he has attained the age of 18.

In such a case, letters of administration *cum testamento annexo et durante minore aetate* may be granted to the minor's guardian pending the attaining of majority by the minor.

If the minor is one of several executors, then the others may prove the will and power will be reserved to the minor to obtain a grant on attaining majority.

The public trustee

The public trustee, as a trust corporation, may be appointed executor of a will and is regulated by the Public Trustee Act 1906. A testator need not obtain the consent of the public trustee to act as his executor but, although the public trustee has a discretion as to whether he will act, it may not refuse to act only by reason of the small size of the estate.

The expression 'trust corporation' includes the various banking, insurance and trust companies, and also includes the Treasury Solicitor, the Official Solicitor and any person holding any other official position prescribed by the Lord Chancellor.

Probate is granted to the trust corporation itself, but when a trust corporation other than the public trustee applies for a grant of probate or administration, the official authorized to act on behalf of the corporation must lodge in the Probate Registry a certified copy of the resolution appointing him.

Appointing a trust corporation as an executor can be both advantageous and disadvantageous. It is advantageous in that a corporation cannot die so that there is always an executor with unquestionable security, and some one is always available to deal with the administration. The disadvantages include the fact that the scale of fee which must be charged (by law) by the public trustee can be out of proportion to the size of the estate plus the fact that the public trustee has an impersonal relationship with the family of the testator which can sometimes cause inconvenience.

Limited executors

It is practicable for a testator, if he thinks fit, to appoint more than one executor, and where this is done, he may either appoint them all as general executors, in which case they act together jointly, or limit the powers of each to a certain portion of his property. Thus, *A* and *B* may be appointed as joint executors, both having power to administer the whole estate, or *A* may be appointed executor of the real estate and *B* executor of the personal estate, in which case each would enjoy powers only over his own particular portion of the estate. Or *X* may be appointed as general executor, and *Y* as a 'special' executor for example, to administer the testator's property abroad.

Where, in any case, limited powers are given to an executor, only a limited grant of probate will be issued, so that in the case quoted above, if *A* applied for probate, a grant would be made entitling him to administer that portion of the estate which was not reserved for *B* to administer — called a *grant save and except* — while if *B* also applied for probate, a grant would be made to him of the rest of the estate — called a *grant caeterorum*.

An executor may be appointed for a definite period only, e.g. for three years following the testator's death or until the testator's son comes of age. Again, his duties may be made to commence at a future time, e.g. three years after the testator's death or upon his son's marriage. If, in such cases, there happens to be no executor empowered to act during any particular period, a grant of administration will be made to some other person.

Where an executor is appointed to act until the testator's son comes of age, the latter, on attaining his majority, will be entitled to a *cessate grant* of probate, which is a supplementary grant made after a grant limited in duration has expired by the effluxion of the time for which it was granted. Another illustration of a cessate grant is where a grant of administration during the insanity of the appointed executor (*durante dementia*) has been made to some other person: the appointed executor will be entitled to a cessate grant of probate on his return to sanity.

The testator may make the appointment of an executor conditional, e.g. conditional on giving security (condition precedent) or on proving the will within a specified time (condition subsequent).

Settled land

In connection with limited grants of probate section 22 of the Administration of Estates Act 1925 provides that a testator may appoint as special executors the persons who are, at the time of his death, 'trustees of the settlement', and that probate limited to the settled land may be granted to such trustees.

Section 22 does not apply where the settlement comes to an end with the death of the testator. In that case there is no need for special executors: *Re Bridgett and Hayes Contract* (1928).

Refusal of office

In no case can the person nominated as executor be compelled to apply for a grant of probate. Renunciation of the office must be made in writing to the probate registry, but an executor who has once accepted office cannot thereafter renounce, nor may he assign it to another person.

Renunciation can also take place by the executor refusing to take the executor's oath, and once he has renounced, he cannot withdraw the renunciation without permission of the Principal Probate Registry.

Death of executor

Should the person nominated as sole executor die *before* obtaining probate, the right to probate will be lost, and his own personal representative will have no right to obtain a grant in his place. In such a case, the will and estate of the original testator must be treated as if the deceased executor had renounced or had never been nominated, and some person interested in the estate must apply for a grant of administration *cum testamento annexo*.

On the other hand, where an executor dies *after* obtaining probate but before completing the administration of the estate, the position is entirely different. If a number of executors have been appointed to deal with the whole estate, the surviving executors will carry on the administration; but if the deceased executor is sole executor, or the last survivor of a number of executors, his own executor, if any, will become executor of the original testator.

Where, however, the sole executor or last surviving executor dies intestate, or does not appoint an executor, or the executor whom he does appoint fails to obtain probate of his will, the 'chain of representation' is broken, and some person interested will have to obtain a grant of administration *de bonis non administratis* to enable him to administer the undistributed residue of the estate of the original testator.

Where, however, the chain of representation is unbroken, every person in that chain has the same rights in respect of the real and personal estate of the original testator as the original executor would have had if living, and is, to the extent to which the estate of that testator has come to his hands, answerable as if he were the original executor — section 7, Administration of Estates Act 1925.

Executor *de son tort*

Any person who interferes with the property of a deceased person by performing duties which are normally those of a personal representative, and who has not been expressly or impliedly appointed executor by the will or who has not obtained letters of administration, becomes an executor *de son tort*, or an executor by his own wrong. Such a person is not really an executor at all, and is not entitled to apply for a grant of probate, but by reason of his wrongful act may incur the following penalties.

a. He may be sued for conversion by the true executor or administrator.
b. He is liable for the due payment of inheritance tax.
c. He may be sued, as if he were a true executor, by creditors or beneficiaries of the estate.

But an executor *de son tort* is not liable for:

a. taking the amount of any debt for valuable consideration and without fraud on creditors or others due to him from the deceased at the time of his death, or
b. making any payment which might properly be made by a personal representative (section 28, Administration of Estates Act 1925).

The liability of an executor *de son tort* is generally limited to the extent of the assets that have come into his hands.

The following acts have been held sufficient to give rise to this liability, namely:

a. applying for debts due to the deceased — *Re Stevens* (1897);
b. carrying on the business of the deceased — *Hooper* v. *Summersett* (1810);

but such acts as burying the deceased (*Harrison* v. *Rowley* (1798)) or feeding his cattle (*Long* v. *Symes* (1832)) being purely acts of kindness, will not render a person liable.

Even though administration may subsequently be granted to an executor *de son tort* he is nevertheless liable as an executor *de son tort* for acts done prior to the grant which he has no right to do.

PROBATE

Probate is usually defined as the legal recognition of the validity of a will, but the term is often used to express the certificate of validity which is granted to the executor. This certificate establishes the right of the executor to administer the estate in accordance with the terms of the will and is evidence that the inheritance tax and fees incidental to obtaining a grant of probate have been paid.

Where a testator appoints more than one executor and probate is granted to some of them, power may be reserved to the others to apply later for a similar grant.

Probate jurisdiction and registries

Non-contentious probate matters are dealt with generally either in the Principal Probate Registry of the Family Division of the High Court in London or one of the district registries. It will be a matter of convenience whether an application is made to the principal registry or to a district registry but the latter have virtually the same powers as the Principal Registry so that it is only rarely that the issue of a grant has to be referred to the Principal Registry.

Probate courts

Non-contentious probate matters are dealt with by the Family Division of the High Court and contentious matters by the Chancery Division of the High Court. In contentious matters the county court has jurisdiction in respect of estates of less than £30,000. The county court has no jurisdiction in non-contentious matters and section 128, Supreme Court Act 1981, defines 'non-contentious business' as:

> 'the business of obtaining probate and administration where there is no contention as to the right thereto, including —
> (a) the passing of probates and administrations through the High Court in contentious cases where the contest has been terminated and,
> (b) all business of a non-contentious nature in matters of testacy and intestacy not being proceedings in any action, and
> (c) the business of lodging caveats against the grant of probate or of administration.'

As may be envisaged, nearly every probate case is non-contentious and is therefore dealt with entirely by the Family Division. Generally, the matter will commence as non-contentious and will only become contentious when a dispute occurs relating to documentation or an entitlement to take out a grant.

Presumption of death

Where there is no direct evidence of the testator's death an application has to be submitted for leave to swear to death; this application is made to the Registrar at the Principal or District Probate Registry.

The application for leave to swear to death has to be supported by an affidavit setting out:

a. particulars and value of the estate;
b. whether the deceased left a will;
c. what attempts have been made to trace the deceased (with copies of any advertisements exhibited);
d. whether any insurance company has admitted any claim arising from the presumed death;
e. the names of the persons entitled to share in the estate and stating who if any are *non sui juris*;
f. the facts relied on in the presumption of death;
g. that the person making the affidavit believes the 'deceased' to be dead;
h. details of any inquest held (if, for example, a body has been found and has been presumed to be, but not identified as, the deceased);
i. whether any communications have been received by any person since the deceased disappeared.

The order giving leave to swear to death must be produced with the other papers when applying for a grant.

Probate of foreign wills

Property situate in the United Kingdom — so that a grant of probate is necessary — may form part of the estate of a deceased person who has left a foreign will.

The Wills Act 1963 provides the rules governing the validity of the form of a will. By way of a brief summary, this Act provides that a will shall be treated as property executed if its execution is in accordance with the internal law in force in the place:

a. where the will was executed; or
b. where the testator was domiciled; or
c. where the testator has his habitual residence; or
d. where the testator was a national.

(a) must relate to the time and place of execution of the will, but (b), (c) and (d) expressly relate to the place either at the time of execution of the will or at the testator's death.

Section 4 of the Act provides expressly that a change in the testator's domicile after the execution of the will shall not alter the construction of that will.

It should be mentioned that domicile is a concept of international law and means the country where a person, of whatever nationality, has his permanent home and where he intends to end his days. Unlike residence, which is based mainly on fact, domicile is a concept of *animus* or intention. A husband and wife need not necessarily have the same domicile.

PROBATE IN COMMON FORM

The majority of probate matters are not contentious and do not require litigation. A grant of probate obtained from a registry without application to the court is termed probate in *common form*. Generally, it is not possible to obtain a grant until 7 days have elapsed after the death of the deceased.

The application for the grant can be made either by the personal representative personally or by a solicitor acting on his behalf. Other professions have no power to apply on behalf of clients although, as mentioned earlier, the monopoly enjoyed by solicitors in this respect may disappear during the next few years.

The procedure relates to the production of certain documents together with the payment of probate fees and capital transfer tax. The following documents are necessary.

a. *The executor's oath.* This is an ordinary affidavit sworn before a Commissioner for Oaths, declaring that the executor believes the will to be the true and last will of the deceased, who died on a specified date at a specified place, and that he will carry out all the duties of administration. It must also declare the gross value of the estate.
b. *The Inland Revenue account* (if necessary) This comprises an inventory of the deceased's estate in which it is compulsory to disclose any interest of the deceased in settled property together with chargeable gifts made by him prior to his death.

    In the case of the estate of a deceased person which is straightforward and small, generally not exceeding £40,000, the relevant account (Form No. 202) comprises one sheet only. Larger and more complicated cases require a more detailed account on Form No. 200. For completeness, it should be mentioned that where a deceased is deemed domiciled in the United Kingdom for inheritance tax purposes (but not domiciled in the United Kingdom under the general law) Form No. 201 is the correct account.

    At this state, it is relevant to refer to 'excepted estates'. No Inland Revenue account need be submitted in respect of an 'excepted estate' and, with effect from 1 April 1981, these are the estates of deceased persons who in general terms:

    i. died possessed only of assets passing under the will or intestacy or possessed of an interest as joint tenant;

    ii. the total gross amount of the property does not exceed £25,000;

    iii. not more than 10 per cent of the total value or £1,000, whichever the higher, relates to assets situated outside the United Kingdom; and

    iv. the deceased died domiciled in the United Kingdom without having made any chargeable gifts for inheritance tax purposes.

In general terms therefore no account need be submitted in the case of the deceased who died with a small estate having made no chargeable transfer for inheritance tax purposes in his lifetime.

With the introduction of inheritance tax in respect of events on or after 18 March 1986, it is assumed that new forms will be issued in due course. However, for the moment, the Inland Revenue has confirmed that the existing capital transfer tax forms can continue to be used.

c. *The actual will.*

Unlike former practice, it is not now necessary to submit the account to the Capital Taxes Office for scrutiny before the obtaining of the grant except in certain circumstances, including where a deceased is claimed to have died outside the United Kingdom, where conditional exemption from inheritance tax is claimed in respect of certain works of art etc., where it is desired to pay by instalments the inheritance tax on shares in private companies, and certain other circumstances.

The documents listed above are taken to the probate registry where the registrar considers the application and, if all is in order, a grant will in due course be issued to the executor.

If the estate is complicated with, say, a large number of quoted securities, it would be of great assistance to order several copies of the grant, and such copies can be obtained for a small fee.

In establishing the validity of a will, an attestation clause is not essential but, if no such clause exists, evidence of due execution will be required. The registrar will accept affidavits from the witnesses that the will was duly executed.

Probate of a lost will may, in exceptional circumstances, be granted in common form if there is strong evidence that a will existed at the time of the testator's death, or that a will was made and afterwards destroyed without the testator's knowledge or consent. Evidence of the contents of the will must, of course, be given, e.g. the production of a solicitor's draft copy. Normally, however, it is necessary to prove a lost will in solemn form.

PROBATE IS SOLEMN FORM

If there is any doubt as to the validity of a will, or any likelihood that its validity may be questioned, the executor should prove the will in *solemn form* in order to safeguard his own position and the interests of all parties. Thus, probate in solemn form should be obtained by the executors where there are beneficiaries who claim under a codicil which the executors do not believe to be a true codicil of the deceased, for the executors cannot protect themselves by merely citing the beneficiaries under the disputed codicil to propound and prove it (*Re Benbow* (1862)) or where the executor has reasonable grounds for doubting the testamentary capacity of the testator. To prove a will in solemn form, an action must be commenced in the High Court or the county court, as the case may require, by means of writs and citations, all persons who may be interested in the invalidity of the will being called upon to show cause, if any, why probate should not be granted.

Probate obtained in solemn form is regarded as conclusive evidence of the validity of the will, so far as all those who were cited are concerned, although even probate in solemn form can be revoked in exceptional cases. Probate in common form, on the other hand, can be questioned and, if necessary, revoked upon a petition calling upon the executor to prove in solemn form, presented within thirty years of the first grant of probate.

In the case of *In the Estate of Jolley, Deceased, Jolley* v. *Jarvis and Sands* (1964) it was emphasized that an executor who has proved in common form cannot be made to commence proceedings to prove in solemn form. It is for the person seeking to have the grant revoked to issue a writ.

REVOCATION OF PROBATE

A grant of probate will be revoked:

a. where a later will (or more usually codicil) is discovered;
b. where probate was obtained by fraud;
c. where probate has been granted to the wrong person;
d. where probate was granted whilst a caveat was in force;
e. where, as is most unlikely, the testator is found to be alive.

As regards the effect of revocation, section 27 of the Administration of Estates Act 1925 provides that any bona fide payment made under a revoked grant is not to be affected by the revocation. Further, section 37 of the same Act provides that all conveyances of any interest in real or personal estate made to a purchaser by a person to whom probate has been granted remain valid, notwithstanding any subsequent revocation of the grant.

Exercise 4

1. Which, if any, of the following can act as executor, and with what limitations?
   a. A married woman.
   b. A minor.
   c. A mentally disordered person.
   d. An undischarged bankrupt.
2. Distinguish between an ordinary executor, an executor *de son tort*, and an executor according to the tenor.
3. Mention the various steps which an executor must take in order to obtain probate of a will.
4. What are the powers of an executor before obtaining a grant of probate? What risks are involved in the exercise of these powers?
5. How can an executor be appointed? Can the appointment be in any way limited or qualified?
6. The executor of X dies without having proved the will. By his own will, however, he nominates his own executor to be executor of X. Would the office be transmitted? If not, what would happen to X's estate?
7. According to the provisions of what systems of law can wills be executed?
8. Upon what grounds may probate be revoked? How does the revocation affect the position of an executor who has made payments, or that of a third party who has paid money or delivered property to him?

5
Letters of Administration

INTRODUCTION

Where a deceased dies intestate or testate but without appointing an executor, a person or persons materially interested in the administration of the estate must apply for letters of administration, and the person appointed is called the administrator.

Grants of letters of administration are regulated by statutory provisions, but the procedures preceding a grant are very similar to those necessary in applying for a grant of probate.

Acts of administration before letters granted

Unlike an executor, an administrator has no title to the estate of the deceased until letters of administration have actually been granted, so that strictly an administrator has no right to perform any acts of administration before letters have been granted to him. Consequently, all acts so performed before the grant are strictly *ultra vires* and ineffective. Thus, if a would-be administrator contracts to sell a portion of the estate before letters have been granted to him, the contract is not binding.

But letters of administration are retrospective in their operation and relate back to the death of the deceased. Consequently if the applicant does eventually obtain letters of administration, all past acts which were for the benefit of the estate, but not those prejudicial to it, are valid and binding: *Kenrick* v. *Burgess* (1583); *Morgan* v. *Thomas* (1853).

If the applicant does not eventually obtain a grant of administration, an eventual administrator can ratify the acts of his predecessor, but if such acts are not ratified in this way they will be void.

In *Ingall* v. *Moran* (1944), it was held that an administrator as such has no cause of action vested in him before he has obtained letters of administration, and that the doctrine of relation back of his title to the date of the intestate's death upon the grant of letters of administration has no application to an action commenced by the administrator as such before the grant was made.

APPLICATION FOR LETTERS OF ADMINISTRATION

Who may apply

The Non-Contentious Probate Rules 1954 lay down the following order of priority of rights to a grant of administration where the deceased died wholly intestate. Persons having a beneficial interest in the estate are entitled to a grant of administration in the following order of priority.

a. i the surviving spouse;
   ii. the children of the deceased (including any persons entitled by virtue of any enactment (e.g. the Family Law Reform Act 1969) to be treated as if they were the children of the deceased born in lawful wedlock), or the issue of any such child who has died during the lifetime of the deceased;
   iii. the father or mother of the deceased;
   iv. brothers or sisters of the whole blood, or the issue of any deceased brother or sister of the whole blood who has died during the lifetime of the deceased.
b. If no person in any of the classes mentioned in (ii) to (iv) above has survived the deceased, then in the case of a person dying wholly intestate without leaving a surviving spouse, the persons entitled to a grant in order of priority are:
   i. brothers and sisters of the half-blood or their issue;
   ii. grandparents;
   iii. uncles and aunts of the whole blood or their issue;
   iv. uncles and aunts of the half-blood or their issue.
c. In default of any person having a beneficial interest, the Treasury Solicitor on behalf of the Crown.
d. Creditors.

Here, again, it must be borne in mind that steprelations, as distinct from relations of the half-blood, are not recognized.

Where a number of persons are entitled to share in the residuary estate, as where an intestate leaves a widow and a number of children, letters of administration will not be granted to all of them, for section 160 of the Judicature Act 1925 provides that in no case shall representation be granted to more than four persons in respect of the same estate. In such cases the court will decide which of a number of applicants are most suited for the office.

Section 160 further provides that if, under a will or an intestacy, a life interest arises or a benefit is given to a minor, representation shall be granted either:

a. to a trust corporation with or without an individual; or
b. to not fewer than two individuals.

This rule is established in order to allow more perfect protection to the persons thus benefiting, and in such cases, if a will exists and only one executor is named (not being a trust corporation), the court may, upon the application of any person interested, or of the guardian, committee or receiver of any such person, appoint one or more personal representatives in addition to the one appointed by the will.

The Non-Contentious Probate (Amendment) Rules 1967 (SI 1967, No. 748) make provision for the grant of administration to one or more assignees to whom the persons entitled have assigned their whole interests. They also provide for a grant to be made to both parents of a minor who would himself be entitled to a grant but for his minority.

Grants to outside parties

No person can be compelled to apply for letters of administration and, although there are persons entitled to the residue of the deceased's estate, it may be that no application for a grant is made. In such a case, a creditor of the deceased may apply with a view to having his debts paid.

The application

The person applying for letters of administration may lodge at the Principal or a District Registry virtually the same documents as those lodged by an executor applying for probate, except where the deceased died intestate no will can of course be submitted.

As in the case of an executor, an administrator must be sworn to an oath deposing as to the validity of the facts declared etc. The administrator also swears that he will administer the estate according to law etc.

Any opposition to a grant of letters of administration may be launched in the same manner as opposition to a grant of probate with the procedure being along similar lines.

Guarantees

The requirement enforced for many years for all administrators to enter into bonds was abolished by the Administration of Estates Act 1971. Further relaxations were contained in section 120 of the Supreme Court Act 1981 which specifies that sureties (guarantors) may be required to make good any loss suffered as a result of a breach of duty by the administrator.

The Non-Contentious Probate Rules 1954 specify that a registrar will only normally ask for a guarantee where the grant of letters of administration is made to a person obtaining a grant on behalf of a minor, a creditor, a person living outside the United Kingdom and one or two other specified circumstances. Even in these cases, the guarantee can be dispensed with if the person applying is a trust corporation or a solicitor with a practising certificate.

Grants made to the Treasury Solicitor, the Official Solicitor and other public bodies never require guarantees.

SPECIAL AND LIMITED GRANTS

As with probate, the court may at its discretion issue grants of administration confined to special purposes, assets or periods of time, so that, for example, separate administrators of real and personal estate respectively may be appointed. Examples of such special and limited grants are as follows.

Administration *cum testamento annexo*

Where a testator does not nominate an executor in his will, or where the executor nominated will not or cannot apply for probate, or where the executor nominated dies before obtaining probate, and in other cases where there is a will but no executor, a grant of administration, with the will annexed, known technically as a grant *cum testamento annexo*, will be made by the court, having regard to the rights of all persons interested in the estate concerned. In such cases letters of administration will usually be granted to the principal legatee or devisee under the will. The grantee in these cases, though an administrator and not an executor, must carry out the terms of the will in the same manner as the executor would have done.

The Non-Contentious Probate Rules 1954 lay down the following order of priority for a grant of administration with the will annexed:

a. the executor;
b. any residuary legatee or devisee holding in trust for another person;

c. any residuary legatee or devisee for life;
d. the ultimate residuary legatee or devisee or, where the residue is not wholly disposed of by the will, any person entitled to share in the residue not so disposed of (including the Treasury Solicitor when claiming *bona vacantia* on behalf of the Crown), or, subject to paragraph (3) of rule 25 of the Non-Contentious Probate Rules 1954, the personal representative of any such person:

'provided that where the residue is not in terms wholly disposed of, the Registrar may, if he is satisfied that the testator has nevertheless disposed of the whole or substantially the whole of estate as ascertained at the time of the grant, allow a grant to be made to any legatee or devisee entitled to, or to a share in, the estate so disposed of, without regard to the persons entitled to share in any residue not disposed of by the will';
e. any specific legatee or devisee or any creditor or the personal representative of any such person or, where the estate is not wholly disposed of by the will, any person who, notwithstanding that the amount of the estate is such that he has no immediate beneficial interest therein, may have a beneficial interest in the event of an accretion thereto;
f. any legatee or devisee, whether residuary or specific, entitled on the happening of any contingency, or any person having no interest under the will of the deceased who would have been entitled to a grant if the deceased had died wholly intestate.

Beneficiaries may nominate certain persons, including a trust corporation, to act for them, and the court, in its discretion, may grant letters to those nominees.

De bonis non administratis

This is a grant made 'in respect of property not administered' and it is made in two cases:

a. where a sole or last surviving *executor* dies after obtaining probate but before completing the administration and without appointing an executor of his own; and
b. where a sole or last surviving *administrator* dies after obtaining letters of administration but before completing the administration, whether or not he appoints an executor of his own. A grant *de bonis non* in this case will not necessarily be a grant *cum testamento annexo*.

In each case a grant is made giving powers of administration only over that portion of the estate which has not yet been administered.

Such a grant may be made to any person interested in the estate, as, for example, a creditor or residuary legatee, or one of the persons entitled to a share of the residue on an intestacy.

Durante minore aetate

A minor cannot obtain a grant of any description. During his minority, a grant of administration *durante minore aetate* may be made to his guardian or to such other person as the court thinks fit, giving powers of administration only until the minor attains the age of 18. Rule 31 of the Non-Contentious Probate Rules 1954 lays down the order of persons entitled to obtain a grant *durante minore aetate* as follows:

a. both parents or guardian (usually a surviving parent); or
b. if there is no guardian and the minor is over 16, the minor's next of kin; or
c. a person appointed by a registrar (there being no one else eligible).

Durante absentia

This grant is made 'during absence abroad'. If at the expiration of twelve months from the death of a person, any personal representative of the deceased to whom representation has been granted is residing out of the jurisdiction of the High Court, upon the application of any creditor or person interested in the estate of the deceased, the court may grant to such creditor or person powers of administration *durante absentia* to be exercised until the true personal representative returns within the jurisdiction.

Section 164 of the Judicature Act 1925 provides that in such a case the court may order the transfer into court of any money or securities belonging to the estate, and that if the true personal representative returns to and resides within the jurisdiction of the High Court while any legal proceeding to which a special administrator is a party is pending, such representative shall be made a party to the legal proceeding, and the costs of and incidental to the special administration and such legal proceeding shall be paid by such person and out of such fund as the court in which the proceeding is pending directs.

Durante dementia

When a sole executor becomes temporarily insane, a limited grant is made during his insanity to his committee or to the person appointed to manage his property, or, with the consent of the committee, to the residuary legatee, devisee or next of kin. Similarly, during the temporary insanity of a sole administrator, administration will usually be granted to his committee or to the manager of his property, or, failing such, to the persons next entitled.

Pendente lite

This is a grant made by the Court 'while an action is pending'. Section 163 of the Judicature Act 1925 provides that while any legal proceeding touching the validity of the will of a deceased person, or for obtaining, recalling, or revoking any representation, is pending, the court may grant administration *pendente lite* to an administrator who shall have all the rights and powers of a general administrator, other than the right of distributing the residue, but shall be subject to the immediate control of the court to act under its direction. Such an administrator may be allowed a reasonable remuneration for his services out of the estate.

Ad litem

A grant *ad litem* is made 'for the purpose of an action'. Where the person to whom probate or letters of administration have been or should be granted refuses to take part in an action in Chancery which concerns the estate, a grant of administration *ad litem* may be made to enable some person to represent the estate in the action. The appointee's powers are limited by the court, and cease with the action, but remuneration may be awarded.

Ad colligenda bona defuncti

This is a grant 'for the preservation of property', made in order to protect the assets during a delay in the application for probate or letters of administration. Any interested person may be appointed, but the powers are usually limited to those of a receiver, without power to distribute the residue.

DEATH OF ADMINISTRATOR

Upon the death of a sole administrator before the completion of the administration, some person interested in the estate must apply to the court for a grant of administration *de bonis non administratis*. No title whatever to such a grant is transmitted to the executor of the deceased administrator, as no chain of representation was created between the original deceased and the administrator.

If, on the other hand, more than one administrator is originally appointed, the survivors, upon the death of one of their number, continue to act (section 18, Trustee Act 1925).

REVOCATION OF ADMINISTRATION

A grant of letters of administration will be revoked:

a. where a will is discovered;
b. where the grant was made to the wrong person;
c. where the grant was obtained by fraud, or without citing the proper parties;
d. if the administrator becomes incapable of acting or cannot be found;
e. if the intestate is found to be alive.

As to the effect of revocation, sections 27 and 37 of the Administration of Estates Act 1925 provide the same protection as in the case of the revocation of a grant of probate.

Exercise 5

1. Compare the position of an administrator before a grant of letters with that of an executor before grant of probate.
2. Who has the right to be granted letters of administration in a case of total intestacy?
3. Mention the grounds for the issue of the following grants: *de bonis non administratis; durante minore aetate; durante absentia; cum testamento annexo; pendente lite; ad litem.*
4. In what cases may letters of administration be granted to persons who are in no way related to the deceased?
5. What happens in regard to the estate upon the death of an administrator after letters have been granted?
6. Upon what grounds may letters of administration be revoked? How does revocation affect the position of a personal representative who has made payments, or of a third party who has paid money or delivered property to him?
7. How does the office of an administrator differ from that of executor in respect of the method of appointment?

6
Executors and Administrators

PERSONAL REPRESENTATIVES

The term 'personal representative' is a collective expression to denote either an executor or an administrator. Their functions are very similar and, in the course of an administration, their primary duties comprise:

a. to get in and realize the deceased's assets and make any necessary investments;
b. to pay the deceased's debts, administration expenses and all taxes due, included inheritance tax; and
c. to distribute the residue to those entitled in accordance with the terms of the will or the intestacy rules.

A right of estate is vested in a person as soon as he becomes absolutely entitled to it, e.g. when the issue of an intestate attain majority. An interest may be vested without being vested in possession, e.g. where a person is entitled absolutely to a legacy, but payment to him is postponed.

As already discussed, the estate of a testator vests automatically in the executor immediately upon the death, except where the sole executor is a minor or otherwise incapacitated. The estate or an intestate, however, cannot vest in the administrator until letters of administration have been granted.

For practical reasons, however, a personal representative does not have the same rights over the property as he enjoys over his own and it is necessary therefore to examine carefully the duties and rights of personal representatives.

Rights and duties of personal representatives

After arranging for the deceased's burial or cremation, the personal representative must undertake the preliminaries necessary for obtaining a grant of probate or administration. This will involve:

a. opening a suspense account at the bank into which payments can be made pending the obtaining of a grant;
b. perusing the deceased's papers and documents;
c. collecting in where possible rents and debts;
d. generally compiling the information necessary to complete an Inland Revenue account necessary for the grant of probate or administration.

Having obtained the grant, the personal representative must then proceed with all speed to administer the estate.

Remuneration

As a general rule, a personal representative is expected to give 'labour of love' and is not entitled to remuneration for his services. He is entitled to be reimbursed for all reasonable expenses which he has incurred, but cannot include compensation for loss of time, and even if he is a professional man, such as a solicitor or an accountant, he can charge only for actual out-of-pocket expenses and not for profit costs, notwithstanding that he may render services which only a professional man could render. In such a case, another professional man may be employed to do the professional work, and his full costs will be allowed, but if the personal representative elects to do the work himself he can charge only his out-of-pocket expenses, as he is not bound to do any professional work which could not be done by an ordinarily executor.

The only exceptions to this rule are as follows.

a. Where the will expressly authorizes the executor to make 'the usual professional charges'. In this case the executor can charge only for actual professional work and not for work which a non-professional executor could do: *Newton* v. *Chapman* (1884). The profit costs so chargeable are in the nature of a legacy and so must abate on a deficiency of assets: *Pennell* v. *Franklin* (1898). It must be remembered, however, that the remuneration clause in a will may cover *all* work, including work of a non-professional character.

A usual form of 'remuneration clause' to be found in modern wills is as follows: 'Any executor or trustee being a person engaged in any profession or business shall be entitled to be paid all usual professional or proper charges for business transacted, time expended and acts done by him or any partner of his in connection with the trusts hereof, including acts which an executor or trustee not being in any profession or business could have done personally.'
b. Where a judicial trustee or the public trustee is appointed.
c. Where a trust corporation is appointed by the court and the court authorizes the corporation to charge for its services.
d. Where the beneficiaries, being all *sui juris* (i.e. not subject to legal disabilities), agree, particularly in the case of a trust corporation, that it shall receive remuneration.
e. Where an administrator *pendente lite* is appointed (see above, page 34).
f. Where a solicitor acting as personal representative acts as solicitor in any legal proceedings, even of a friendly nature, on behalf of himself and his co-personal representatives jointly, except to the extent of the parties: *Cradock* v. *Piper* (1850).

A personal representative who is a member of a professional firm is allowed to pay the profit costs of a partner if he has agreed that the partner shall do professional work on behalf of the estate and receive the profits of his own benefit: *Clack* v. *Carlon* (1861).

If a solicitor acting as personal representative who has no power to charge profit costs employs his firm to act for him in legal proceedings, the firm's profit costs will not be allowed out of the estate, even if he agrees with the other partners not to share them, for he would even then get an indirect benefit: *Re Gates* (1933).

In *Re Hill* (1934), a trustee without power to charge profit costs employed the firm of solicitors in which he was a partner to do certain of the trust work. Another partner had for many years attended to the trust, and, during the material time, the plaintiff received under an agreement with the firm, a fixed annuity instead of a share in the partnership profits. The court held that the profit costs should be disallowed, as, although the plaintiff's share of profits was limited to a fixed sum, this still constituted an interest in the profits made by the firm.

It should be noted that where a legacy is left to an executor as such, it is presumed to be given as compensation of his services, and will lapse if he renounces office, unless the will or the surrounding circumstances show a contrary intention: *Re Appleton* (1885).

As to the charging of professional services in general, it is fair comment to state that, nowadays, it will be unusual to find a will or trust documents not containing the 'usual professional charging clause'.

COLLECTION OF ASSETS

Section 32 of the Administration of Estates Act 1925 provides that the real and personal estate of a deceased person, to the extent of his beneficial interest therein, and the real and personal estate of which a deceased person in pursuance of any *general* power disposes by will, are assets for payment of his debts and liabilities.

Thus, it will be seen that any beneficial interest in property enjoyed by the deceased which does not terminate upon his death is an asset which must be called in by the personal representative, and, if necessary, applied towards the payment of the debts. By Section 25 of the Act, the court has power to require the personal representative to exhibit on oath in the court a true and perfect inventory and account of the real and personal estate of the deceased, and an administrator is bound by the terms of his oath to do this if required.

In any case it is advisable for a personal representative to prepare a list of the deceased's estate.

The collection of tangible assets such as clothing, jewellery, furniture and other personal chattels should not cause much difficulty, but there are other types of assets where the position of the personal representative is not so clear. The most important of these are dealt with separately and in detail below.

It should be noted that section 15 of the Trustee Act 1925 provides that, subject to the provisions of the Act as to the giving of receipts, any personal representative or trustee may, if he thinks fit:

a. accept any property before the time at which it is payable; or
b. separate or apportion any trust funds or properties which have been amalgamated; or
c. pay or allow any debt or claim on any evidence that seems to him sufficient; or
d. accept any composition or security for any debt or claim; or
e. allow time for the payment of any debt; or
f. compromise, abandon, or submit to arbitration any debt, claim or account;

without incurring personal liability for any loss which may result to the estate, provided the power is exercised in good faith.

Receipts signed by one personal representative, where there are more than one, will bind the others, except where the receipt is for the proceeds of the sale of settled land, or of land held on trust for sale, or for other capital money under a settlement, in which cases, all must sign unless the personal representative signing is a trust corporation. A sole personal representative, however, can give valid receipts for capital money.

Money

Money, whether in the house or at a bank, vests in the personal representative, and immediate notice of the death must be given to the banker of the deceased, as this notice terminates the authority of the banker to pay cheques signed by the deceased which are subsequently presented for payment. The personal representative, or all of them if more than one, should furnish the banker with specimen signatures and open an account in their own names in a representative capacity, as, for example, 'A. B., C. D. and E. F., Exors. of the Estate of Jack Jones, decd.' After probate or letters of administration have been obtained, the balance standing to the credit of the personal current account of the deceased should be transferred to this account. The deceased's deposit account should be left to earn interest, although it will now stand in the personal representatives' names. It is advisable to stipulate that cheques drawn upon the executors' account shall be signed by more than one executor, if more than one exist, but it is usual to arrange that any one executor may on behalf of himself and his co-executors indorse cheques payable to the deceased.

As various duties and taxes have to be paid to the Revenue authorities before a grant of probate or letters of administration can be obtained, a temporary loan should be obtained from the deceased's bankers on the personal security of the personal representatives, then the amount of this loan, which is to be set off against the balance on the deceased's own account, can later be merged in the banking account opened in the name of the personal representatives. In practice this loan is made on the personal undertaking of the personal representatives to pay the loan out of the first proceeds of the estate.

Contracts and torts

Any debt or other obligation due to the deceased and payable upon a contract made by him, and not statute-barred (i.e. not rendered unenforceable by statute through lapse of time), is an asset of the estate and may, if necessary, be enforced by means of action or other legal process.

The personal representative may, if he thinks fit, arrange a composition with any debtor of the estate, but if he himself owes a debt to the estate he cannot arrange a composition with himself. If, however, there is more than one personal representative, any one of them may compound a debt owing by another to the estate.

Contracts which involve the personal skill of the deceased, e.g. contracts of personal service, cannot be enforced, as they are terminated with the death.

Torts are civil wrongs, e.g. being negligent or causing a nuisance. The Law Reform (Miscellaneous Provisions) Act 1934 provides for the survival of certain rights of action, in contract and in tort, provided such actions are commenced within the period allowed by the Limitation Act 1939.

In the case of *Rose* v. *Ford* (1937), the House of Lords decided that damages could be awarded not merely for injury but also for shortened expectation of life, notwithstanding that the deceased died before the date of the action.

Apart from the 1934 Act, the Fatal Accidents Act 1846, as amended, provides that personal representatives may bring an action for damages for the death of any deceased person whose death was due to the tort of the another person. The damages awarded are based on the actual pecuniary loss to the relatives. Such an action must be brought in three years of the death. Relatives for whom the right of action under this Act exists include the usual close relatives including a grandchild and stepchild.

Whilst damages recovered under the 1934 Act form part of the deceased's estate and are subject to inheritance tax, any sum recovered under the 1846 Act does not form part of the estate and is not subject to tax.

Actions can sometimes be brought under both Acts for the same tort.

Mortgages

The rights of the deceased, both legal and equitable, in mortgaged property pass to the personal representative upon death. If the deceased was the mortgagor (the person borrowing the money), the personal representative will obtain the right of redemption (i.e. the right to recover the property on payment of principal and interest), and if the deceased was the mortgagee (the person lending the money), his personal representative will obtain, *inter alia*, the right of foreclosure (i.e. the right to obtain the full beneficial title to the property), and the right of sale.

It is advisable for the personal representative to redeem the mortgaged property as soon as practicable in order to put an end to the liability to pay interest, and to extinguish the personal covenant. In this connection section 35 of the Administration of Estates Act 1925 provides that where real or personal property is left by will subject to a charge, the person taking the property will be primarily liable for the payment of the charge, unless the will provides otherwise.

Thus mortgages and charges on property disposed of by will or passing on an intestacy are primarily payable out of the property concerned, and not out of the other parts of the estate, unless the will or some other instrument in writing signifies otherwise.

Choses in action

A right to obtain possession of money or property, if necessary by means of an action, is a chose in action. Choses in action form assets in the hands of the personal representatives and examples are stocks and shares, a share in a partnership and book debts.

Stocks and shares

These, in common with other assets, vest in the personal representative of a deceased shareholder, who is entitled upon production of his authority to deal with them as he thinks fit. Upon receiving proof of title from the personal representative, the company may, if so requested, register the shares in the name of the personal representative, according to the provisions of the articles of the company. The personal representative has to sign a form of request or form of transfer, undertaking to hold the shares subject to the conditions of issue. The personal representative is then primarily *personally* liable for calls, with a right to be indemnified out of the estate. On the other hand, the personal representative may, without having the shares registered in his name, transfer them direct to a third party. In such a case he will, of course, have to produce evidence to the company that he is the duly appointed personal representative. This will be done by production of either probate or letters of administration. Shares of a hazardous nature should be sold as soon as possible.

Bills of exchange

Although not common now, bills payable to the deceased as assets which may be enforced by the personal representative by action. He may discount, indorse or assign a promissory note or bill payable to the deceased or his order (*Rawlinson* v. *Stone* (1745)), but if he wishes to escape personal liability, he should be careful to indorse in a representative capacity, e.g.

'For and on behalf of John Jones, deceased, so far as assets only.

James Smith
Executor'

Where there are more than one executors, any one may indorse on behalf of the others, e.g. 'For self and co-executors'.

Where the deceased has received from a debtor a blank acceptance for a certain sum, his personal representative may fill up the paper as a bill payable to drawer's order, insert his own name as drawer and enforce payment against the acceptor: *Scard* v. *Jackson* (1876).

Shares in partnerships

Except in the case of a registered limited partnership, and unless the articles of partnership contain a provision to the contrary, dissolution of the whole firm automatically follows the death of one of the partners, and the personal representative then has power to compel the winding-up of the firm. This will involve the realization of the assets of the firm, the payment of its debts, and the application of any surplus according to the provision of section 44 of the Partnership Act 1890: namely, first, in payment of advances made by partners in excess of capital contributions; and secondly, in repayment of the capital interests of the various partners. Any surplus remaining after the repayment of these items is distributed among the partners according to the proportions in which profits were shared under the partnership agreement.

The right to claim the deceased partner's share of the distribution is vested in his personal representative, and may, if necessary, be enforced by application for a winding-up by the court.

Section 42 of the Partnership Act 1890 provides that where upon the death of a partner the surviving partners continue to carry on the business of the firm with its capital or assets without making any final settlement of accounts with the deceased partner's personal representative, the latter is entitled at his option to claim either 5 per cent per annum interest on the deceased partner's share of the firm's assets, or such share of the profits made after death as the court may find to be attributable to the use of his share of the assets. In practice, of course, where the personal representatives take a share of profits, they normally agree the amount of the profits with the surviving partners without recourse to court.

Continuation of the deceased's business

The goodwill, if any, of a business carried on by the deceased alone, vests in his personal representative as an asset which should, in the absence of contrary instructions in the will, be sold as soon as possible. It may be necessary for the personal representative to carry on the business until a purchaser can be found so that it may be sold as a going concern — any profits made whilst carrying on the business will be assets of the estate — as follows:

a. where, in the absence of any direction in the will that the business should be carried on, it is carried on purely for the purpose of preserving the goodwill and disposing of the business to the best advantage;
b. where the will authorizes the executor to carry on the business longer than is necessary for winding-up, if he shall think fit, and it is carried on with the consent of the deceased's creditors and in the interests of the beneficiaries;
c. where the will instructs the executor to carry on the business.

In (a) and (b) above the right of indemnity extends to *all* the assets of the deceased, whilst in (c) the right of indemnity extends only to the assets which the testator has authorized the executor to employ in the business.

If the will authorizes the executor to carry on the business, he must obtain the express authorization of the deceased's creditors if he intends to carry on the business beyond the period necessary for realization, otherwise he will become answerable to the creditors of the deceased if the business results in a loss.

The administrator of an intestate, not having his authority from the terms of a will, is entitled to carry on the business only for the purpose of realization, including the preservation of the goodwill, unless, as is likely, the administrator's statutory power to postpone sale of the assets gives him the right to carry on the business until a favourable opportunity for sale arises.

POWERS OF THE PERSONAL REPRESENTATIVE

Power of appropriation

Instead of paying a general pecuniary legacy in cash, an executor may agree with the legatee that the latter shall take some specific asset available in full or partial satisfaction of the legacy. This is what is known as the personal representative's power of appropriation. Wide provisions as to appropriation are contained in section 41 of the Administration of Estates Act 1925 which provides that the personal representative may appropriate any part of the real or personal estate in its actual condition in or towards satisfaction of any legacy or any other interest or share in the deceased's property, whether settled or not. An appropriation, however, must not affect prejudicially any specific devise or bequest. Generally speaking, certain consents are required, such as the consent of the person of full age and capacity, absolutely and beneficially entitled in possession, or, in the case of a settled share, the consent of the trustee or of the person for the time being entitled to the income, or of his guardian or committee. An appropriation will bind all persons interested whose consent is not made requisite. The section applies whether the deceased died intestate or not, and it extends to property over which a testator exercises a general power of appointment and it authorizes the setting apart of a fund to meet an annuity by means of the income of that fund or otherwise.

Any property duly appropriated under section 41 is to be treated as an authorized investment, and may be retained or dealt with accordingly.

For the purposes of the appropriation the personal representative is empowered to ascertain and fix the value of the respective parts of the real and personal estate and liabilities of the deceased as he may think fit, and he must for that purpose employ a duly qualified valuer in any case where such employment may be necessary. The value of the property appropriated will be taken as at the date of appropriation: *Re Wragg* (1919).

Trust for sale

Section 33 of the Administration of Estates Act 1925 provides that, on the death of a person dying intestate, his estate shall be held by his personal representatives, as to the real estate upon trust to sell the same and as to the personal estate, upon trust to call in, sell and convert into money such part thereof as may not consist of money.

The administrator is, however, given power to postpone the sale of the estate as he shall think fit, without liability, and it is also provided that in the absence of special circumstances personal chattels are not to be sold except for the payment of debts, or for some other special reason, nor are reversionary interests to be sold until they fall into possession.

Out of the net money arising from the sale of the estate and the ready money left by the deceased, the administrator must pay all such funeral, testamentary and administration expenses, debts and other liabilities as are properly payable thereout, and out of the residue set aside a fund sufficient to provide, in case of a partial intestacy, for any pecuniary legacies bequeathed by the will of the deceased.

An executor has similar duties, except in so far as the will makes provisions to the contrary or bequeaths or devises specific assets which will not be held on trust for sale. An executor has, however, no statutory power to postpone sale of pure personalty, i.e. personalty other than leaseholds.

Powers of management

Section 39 of the Administration of Estates Act 1925 provides that, in dealing with real and personal estate of the deceased, his personal representatives shall for the purposes of administration have:

a. full powers to deal with or dispose of the property, including the power to raise money by mortgage or charge; and
b. so far as land is concerned, all the powers, discretions and duties conferred or imposed by law on trustees holding land upon an effectual trust for sale; and
c. all the powers conferred by statute on trustees for sale.

Contractual powers

Every sole personal representative has complete power to dispose of the real and personal estate of the deceased at his discretion by sale, assignment or mortgage, and any such contract made by a personal representative is valid and binding against creditors and legatees, even if the sale appears to them unnecessary, and any conveyance of any interest in real or personal estate made to a purchaser by a person to whom probate or letters of administration have been granted is valid, even if the grant is subsequently revoked or varied (section 37, Administration of Estates Act 1925).

This provision aims at protecting persons who purchase property from personal representatives. Property which is specifically devised or bequeathed should not, however, be sold unless necessary for the payment of debts, and if it is wrongfully sold, the devisee or legatee can recover damages from the personal representative.

As the personal representative is not merely an agent of the deceased, since the estate which he is to administer is actually vested in him, he can delegate his duties to agents, and the maxim *delegatus non potest delegare* ('an agent cannot delegate his authority') will not apply. The agents must, however, be carefully chosen, and the duties delegated must not be other than those which are ordinarily delegated to businessmen. Thus, duties may be delegated to bankers, brokers, solicitors and similar agents in all cases where similar duties are normally delegated in the ordinary course of business. For example, an accountant may be employed to write up the book of the estate, and a personal representative who is an accountant is not called upon to do this work himself but may, if he desires, employ another person. In all such cases, where the agent has been properly chosen, and employed in good faith, the personal representative will not be held personally liable for loss suffered by the estate through the negligence, or even the fraud, of the agent (section 23, Trustee Act 1925).

It must be shown, however, in all cases that the personal representative himself has not been guilty of negligence, for he will be liable to the estate if, had he acted properly and with due caution, no loss would have been occasioned. Negligence in this sense means a wilful default implying either a consciousness of a breach of duty or recklessness in the performance of a duty: *Re Vickery* (1931). In that case an executor was held guilty only of an error of judgment in employing a solicitor who turned out to be dishonest.

Thus, if a personal representative employs a broker to sell investments and allows the purchase money to remain in the broker's possession for an unreasonable period, he would be liable for loss suffered by the estate through the fraudulent appropriation of the funds by the broker.

Where there are two or more executors, their interest in the estate of the deceased is a joint interest, and is subject to the incidence of 'survivorship', which characterizes joint interests. Consequently, upon the death of one of two or more personal representatives, the whole estate passes to the survivor or survivors, as the case may be (section 18, Trustee Act 1925). It is therefore provided by section 2 (2) of the Administration of Estates Act 1925 that where in respect of *real estate* there are two or more personal representatives, a conveyance of real estate shall not (except in the case of settled land, which is conveyed by the tenant for life) be made without the concurrence of *all* or an order of the court. The rule does not, however, apply where two or more executors have been named in a will and only one of them obtains a grant of probate, such executor being entitled to convey the real estate without the concurrence of the others who have not at the time obtained probate (section 8, Administration of Estates Act 1925). A sole personal representative can sell land and give a valid receipt for the purchase money, and such a sale at a considerable time after the date of death does not now put the purchaser upon enquiry as to whether it is a proper sale. In this way, the appointment of a second trustee may sometimes be obviated when a sale of land is contemplated and only one personal representative has been appointed by the will.

On the other hand, although one personal representative cannot generally convey real estate without the concurrence of the others, any contract or conveyance in respect of pure personal estate made by one, even without the concurrence of the other, will be valid and binding on all.

LIABILITIES OF THE PERSONAL REPRESENTATIVE

In his representative capacity

The estate of the deceased will, as explained earlier in this chapter, be liable generally for debts arising out of the deceased's contracts, and it will generally be liable to actions arising out of the deceased's torts.

In all these cases the personal representative is liable only in his representative capacity, and not out of his own estate, so that he may plead in defence of any such actions not only any defence which could have been pleaded by the deceased himself, but also the special defence of *plene administravit*.

By entering this plea the personal representative pleads that he has no assets belonging to the deceased with which to satisfy the debt claimed, and where this is in fact the case, such a plea should always be entered or the personal representative may find that he has to pay the claim out of his own pocket with only a right to be indemnified out of any assets of the deceased which *may* subsequently come into his hands.

Personal liability

As already stated in connection with the carrying on of a deceased person's business, the personal representative is *personally* liable upon all contracts made by him *after* the death, even if he contracts in his representative capacity, though if the contract is made in good faith and in furtherance of the administration he can claim to be indemnified in respect of such liability out of the estate. Nevertheless, in all cases the primary liability falls upon the personal representative himself, and if the assets of the estate are insufficient to meet the claim, any deficiency must be made good out of his own estate.

Similarly, there is a personal liability upon him for all torts committed by him in the course of his administration, and in such cases indemnity from the assets is allowed only where the tort was reasonably committed in proper furtherance of the administration. For example, in *Re Raybould* (1900), where the executor in continuing to work a mine let down the surface, he was held to be entitled to a right of indemnity against the assets for damages awarded against him.

Co-executors are, in general, answerable each for his own acts only, and not for the acts of the other or others of them, for each executor has, independently of his co-executors, a full and absolute control over the affairs of the deceased and is competent to give a valid discharge therefor by his own separate act. But an executor is liable for the defaults of his co-executor if the default was occasioned or facilitated by his negligence, e.g. where he has knowingly allowed estate moneys or property unnecessarily to get into or remain in the hands of his co-executor, or has not seen to the proper application of assets in the possession of the co-executor.

Liability for *devastavit*

Just as a personal representative enjoys all the powers exercisable by trustees, so is he liable as a trustee for all breaches of trust committed by him in the course of his administration. This liability may be incurred by a *devastavit*, i.e. the wasting of the estate, due to acts which are clearly wrongful, as, for example, a misappropriation of the assets to his own personal use; or even to acts which, though not absolutely tortious, result in loss to the estate.

Thus, the payment of exorbitant funeral expenses, or of unenforceable debts, the employment of improper agents, neglect to realize assets at a favourable time, the non-investment of surplus cash balances, or any other act which causes a loss to the estate which could have been avoided with proper care, may amount to a *devastavit* upon which the personal representative may be compelled to make good the loss thus incurred by the estate. Generally, however, he may pay a statute-barred debt, i.e. a debt rendered unenforceable through lapse of time, provided that the court has not declared it to be statute-barred.

In *Re Diplock's Estate* (1950), where next-of-kin claimed from certain charitable institutions sums paid out to them in error by the executors as legacies, the House of Lords upheld, *sub nom. Ministry of Health* v. *Simpson* (1950), the Court of Appeal's decision that the next-of-kin had an equitable right to recover the money paid by mistake, even though the mistake was one of law. In the first instance, the right was against the executors, and the extent of the claim against the charities was limited to the amount not recovered from the executors. Where a charitable institution had mixed with its own money money received from the executors, and had employed the mixed fund in the purchase of property, the next-of-kin were entitled to a charge on the property, but not where the money had been used in the alteration or improvement of assets already owned by the institution or in paying off an existing encumbrance on land.

The personal representative can also be compelled to account 'upon the footing of wilful default', i.e. to account not only for property which actually did come into his hands, but also for that which ought to, and would, have come into his hands but for his own negligence.

Section 29 of the Administration of Estates Act 1925 provides that on the death of a personal representative who has wasted or converted to his own use any part of the estate, his own personal representative shall, to the extent of the assets of the defaulter, be liable for the waste or conversion as the defaulter himself would have been if living.

Liability for payment of the deceased's debts

The personal representative must be careful to pay the debts of the deceased according to the proper order of priority, for certain types of debts take precedence of others, and if a debt of lower is paid before one of higher precedence, and there are not sufficient assets remaining for the payment of the debt of higher precedence, he will be *personally* liable for the deficiency.

It may be, however, that the personal representative does not discover the existence of the higher debt until after he has paid the lower. In such a case, if the personal representative advertises for claims, and notifies his intention to distribute the property in the *London Gazette* and in a newspaper circulating in the locality in which land owned by the deceased is situated, no personal liability for the debt which is claimed too late will be incurred by the personal representative. An example of the usual form of advertisement is as follows:

> FLORENCE MARY SMITH deceased. Section 27 Trust Act 1925. All persons having any claims against the estate of Florence Mary Smith late of 31 St Saviour's Road, Brixton, Spinster (who died on the 30th August 1985 and probate of whose Will was granted by the Principal Registry on the 2nd November 1985 to Walter Percy executor therein named), are required to send particulars thereof to the undersigned on or before the 11th February 1986 after which date the estate will be distributed having regard only to the claims then notified.
> Dated this 9th December 1985
>
> NORTON & CO., 111 Old Bank Street
> Solicitors for the Executor.

At lease two months from the date the advertisement appears must be allowed for the making of claims.

The personal representative must not rely entirely upon the advertisements, but must communicate with the usual creditors of the deceased and also make searches similar to those which an intending purchaser would be advised to make, for, if charges upon the estate have been registered as bills of sale or as land charges, ignorance of such at the time of the distribution of the estate would not, in spite of the advertisement, free the personal representative from liability.

Right to follow property

It must not be supposed, however, that the creditor who fails to enter a claim within the time specified by this notice will, of necessity, lose the amount of his debt, for the only effect of the notice is to protect the personal representative from personal liability for unknown claims. In other words, the debt is still owed by the estate, but if all assets are distributed before the debt is claimed, no action can be maintained against the personal representative. The creditor may, however, by virtue of section 27 of the Trustee Act 1925 and section 38 of the Administration of Estates Act 1925 follow assets which have been distributed among the beneficiaries into the hands of such beneficiaries or their representatives, or of any other person, not being a bona fide purchaser for value, who may have received them, or in whom they may be vested, and recover the amount of his debt from such beneficiaries or other persons.

Liability on leaseholds etc.

It is further provided by section 26 of the Trustee Act 1925 that where a personal representative who is liable as such on any convenant in respect of leasehold property, or in respect of liability on land granted subject to a rent charge, or for any indemnity given in respect of either, satisfies all accrued liabilities to date and, where necessary, sets apart a fund sufficient to meet any future claim in respect of any fixed and ascertained sum which the deceased has agreed to lay out on the property, then he may convey such property to a purchaser, legatee, devisee, or other person entitled to demand a conveyance, and he will thereupon be free from further liability. The assets may, however, be followed by the claimant as before.

The reason for this provision is that, apart from such protection as is given in it, a convenantor or his estate is liable on the covenant even though he assigns the lease or other contract of which the covenant was a term.

In practice, however, this section operates only in exceptional circumstances. In *Re Owers (No. 2)* (1941), it was held that if a personal representative takes possession of the premises, e.g. collects rent from a subtenant, section 26 affords him no protection, because it applies only to the liability of a personal representative *as such* and has no application where he has incurred personal liability. When, therefore, a personal representative has incurred such personal liability by reason of doing anything tantamount to taking possession of the premises, he must insist on setting aside a sufficient indemnity fund to protect him from liability for rent and in respect of repairing and other covenants, unless, instead, he is content to rely upon the covenants of indemnity given by the beneficiary or purchaser to whom the lease is assigned. It is the practice of must trust corporations to insure against leasehold liability, this being effected by arrangement at a nominal premium.

PAYMENT OF DEBTS

If the estate is solvent, the personal representatives can pay the debts in any order they think fit. However, should there be the slightest doubt about the solvency of the estate, the order set out below relating to an insolvent estate should be adhered to carefully. The estate is solvent if there are sufficient assets to pay all the debts, even though there may not be enough to meet the legacies or devises in full.

Order of priority of debts

Where the estate is insolvent, the order of payment is laid down by section 34 of the 'Administration of Estate Act 1925 and Part I of the First Schedule thereto. Certain creditors preferred by law will be entitled to priority of payment in the order specified below.

The first charge upon the deceased's estate comprises all funeral, testamentary and administration expenses, including the costs of obtaining probate together with any legal costs awarded against the estate and all similar charges. Under this heading would be included any solicitor's or accountant's charges necessarily incurred by the personal representative in connection with the obtaining of probate or letters of administration and the preservation of the assets, and all charges incurred in connection with the administration of the estate generally.

1. Secured creditors out of the proceeds of their security; these may rely on their security, or realize it and prove for any deficiency, or value the security and prove for any deficiency, or surrender the security and prove for the full amount.
2. Specially preferred debts:
   a. money or property belonging to any friendly society in the possession of the deceased as an officer of the society (Friendly Societies Act 1974);
   b. money or property belonging to any trustee savings bank in the possession of the deceased as an officer or employee of the bank (Trustee Savings Bank Act 1863);
   c. expenses properly incurred by the trustees under a deed of arrangement which may have been avoided by the subsequent bankruptcy of the deceased.
3. Preferential creditors under section 33 of the Bankruptcy Act 1914 or under other legislation:
   a. local rates having become due within twelve months before death and all assessed taxes to 5 April previous to the date of death but not exceeding one year's assessment. It must, however, represent a full year's assessment, and the 'one year' need not be the year immediately preceding the death. All sums deducted by an employer under the 'Pay As You Earn' regulations within twelve months before the date of his death;
   b. wages and salaries of workmen, clerks and servants for four months before the date of death but not exceeding £800 per individual;
   c. employers' contributions under the National Insurance Acts for twelve months before the date of death;
   d. value added tax, up to any amount due in the twelve months before the date of death.
   All these debts are payable *pari passu*.
4. Unsecured creditors of all classes *pari passu*, including debts due to the Crown not given preference in bankruptcy.
5. Debts deferred by particular statutes:
   a. loans to a person engaged or about to engage in business, if the lender is to receive a rate of interest varying with the profits, or sums due for the goodwill of a business sold in consideration of a share of the profits: Partnership Act 1890;
   b. money or other estate lent or entrusted by a husband to his wife or by a wife to her husband for the purposes of her or his trade or business: Bankruptcy Act 1914;
   c. Claims under an agreement in consideration of marriage for the future payment of money or settlement of property in respect of which the settler had no interest at the date of the marriage, under section 42 (2) and (3), Bankruptcy Act 1914.

Administration in bankruptcy

Where the estate of a deceased person is insolvent, a creditor or the personal representative himself may present a petition to have the administration carried out by the Official Receiver, which will generally render the estate subject to the laws of bankruptcy.

As such an administration falls within the sphere of bankruptcy law, it cannot be discussed at any length in a volume of this nature, but it is important to note that as soon as notice of the petition has been served on the personal representative, he should refrain from making any further payments to creditors.

It must be observed, however, that certain statutory provisions which normally apply to a bankruptcy administration, with resulting benefits to the bankruptcy assets, will not apply in a deceased insolvent administration, e.g. those applicable to reputed ownership, to avoidance of settlements and to fraudulent preferences.

Set-off

Where a creditor of the estate also owes money to the estate, the personal representative is entitled to set off one claim against the other if both debts are liquidated, i.e. of a fixed ascertained amount currently due and capable of being enforced by action. The ordinary rules of set-off between individuals will apply, so that debts owed to the estate by a company in process of liquidation, in which the deceased holds shares, cannot be set off against calls made by the liquidator in respect of the shares.

Where a person to whom a pecuniary legacy is left by the will of the deceased owes a debt to the estate, the personal representative may, even if the debt is statute-barred, retain the legacy until the debt has been paid, and though this is not strictly a set-off, the right in effect amounts to the same thing. The right can be exercised over a pecuniary legacy or a share of residue, but not in respect of a specific legacy unless it is represented by cash in the hands of the personal representative, and the debt must be owing at the time and not contingent or future. If the legatee becomes bankrupt after the testator's death, the right may still be exercised by the personal representative. If the legatee was bankrupt before the testator's death, the right of set-off cannot be exercised and the personal representative must prove in the bankrupt's estate for the debt and pay over the full amount of the legacy to the bankrupt's trustee.

PAYMENT OF LEGACIES AND DEVISES

Marshalling the assets

It should be emphasized again that an estate is insolvent only when the assets are insufficient to pay all the debts. If there are not sufficient assets available, after payment of all debts, to satisfy all the various bequests and devises in full, the estate will still be solvent. Legacies and devises may be marshalled, in the same way as debts, according to their order of precedence. If the assets remaining after the payment of all debts are not sufficient to meet all the legacies and devises, it does not therefore follow that all legacies will receive less then their full entitlement, for those legacies which are of highest rank must, as far as possible, be paid in full before legatees of a lower rank receive anything at all. In the event of a shortage of assets, therefore, it is essential that the personal representatives marshall them in their proper order.

The order of application of assets where the estate is solvent is laid down by Part II of the First Schedule to the Administration of Estates Act 1925 and is the order in which the real and personal estate of the deceased must, subject to any contrary intention in the will, be applied towards the discharge of his funeral, testamentary and administration expenses and debts. The order may be varied by the will of the deceased, either by express words or evidence of a contrary intention, and many wills do in fact instruct the executor to apply the assets in some order other than that prescribed by the Act.

The will must clearly indicate the intention of the deceased in order to vary the statutory order of application of assets (*Re Littlewood, Clark* v. *Littlewood* (1931), and it may be, of course, that the wording of the will varies the order for payment of debts but not the order for payment of expenses and legacies; or varies it for payment of debts and expenses but not for legacies, and so on.

Statutory order of application of assets

1. Property of the deceased undisposed of by will, subject to the retention thereout of a fund sufficient to meet pecuniary legacies.
2. Property of the deceased not specifically devised or bequeathed but included (either by a specific or generally description) in a residuary gift, subject to the retention out of such property of a fund sufficient to meet any pecuniary legacies, so far as not provided for as aforesaid.
3. Property of the deceased specifically appropriate or devised or bequeathed (either by a specific or general description) for the payment of debts.
4. Property of the deceased charged with, or devised or bequeathed (either by a specific or general description) subject to a charge for the payment of debts.
5. The fund, if any, retained to meet pecuniary legacies.
6. Property specifically devised or bequeathed, rateably according to value.
7. Property appointed by will under a general power, including the statutory power to dispose of entailed interests, rateably according to value.

When considering what property is 'undisposed of by will' under 1 above it should be noted that a lapsed share of residue is treated as undisposed of and is accordingly subject to the payment of debts, expenses and legacies before the effective gifts of other shares of the residue are resorted to (*Re Lamb, Vipond* v. *Lamb* (1929)), but, as pointed out above, this is subject to a specific contrary intention expressed by the deceased in his will: *Re Petty, Holliday* v. *Petty* (1929).

Undisposed-of property also includes a gift which fails for a reason other than lapse, for example because the legatee's wife was an attesting witness (*Re Tong* (1931)), and, on the authority of the same case, undisposed-of income arising after death.

If it is necessary to apportion payments between realty and personalty, they bear the payments rateably in proportion to the respective values at the date of death: *Re Harland Peck* (1941).

Under heading 2, the rule established in the *Harland Peck* case again applies. If a particular portion of the residue is subject to a secret trust, that portion is excluded from this heading: *Re Maddock* (1902).

Property included in 4 is that subject to either an express or an implied charge.

The value of the property as mentioned in 6 is the net value where the devise is of land subject to a mortgage, but where an asset is specifically given subject to legacies the value in the gross value: *Re John* (1933). An option to purchase property is not a specific gift (of the difference between the true value and the option price) and if such property, which should be the last to be resorted to, is required for payment, then the option is destroyed: *Re Eve* (1956).

Alterations to the statutory order

It is now necessary to consider what provisions in a will can be regarded as altering the statutory order of application of assets.

The fact that there is a residuary disposition does not, by itself, vary the statutory order but where, as an additional feature of the will, there is an express or implied charge of the debts and expenses on the residuary property, a variation is effected (*Re Petty* (1929), and *Re Kempthorne* (1930)), and the debts and expenses are to be paid from residue before a division into shares is made. Merely giving property upon trust or subject to a charge for payment of debts does not effect a variation of the order but where there is, in addition, an indication of exonerating other property from payment, then the order is varied and it has been shown by *Re Littlewood* (1931), *Re James* (1932) and *Re Meldrum* (1952) that such an indication is readily inferred by the courts. A residuary gift in addition to the charge is a sufficient justification for this inference: *Re James* (1947).

The avoidance of the statutory liability under section 35 by the testator's contrary intention is of primary importance when the terms of the will or other documents are being drafted, and the following cases will assist.

a. In *Re Wilson* (1908) where a will gave *A* an option to purchase at a stated price in respect of property subject to a charge, it was held that the option to purchase could be exercised at the stated price and *A* could require the property to be transferred to him free of the charge, which would have to be discharged out of the residue.
b. In *Re Holt* (1916) where the will made separate gifts of two properties to *A* it was held that a mortgage deficiency on one of the properties was not chargeable to the other property but was payable out of the residue of the estate – it would have been otherwise if there had been a single gift of the two properties (*Re Kensington* 1902)).
c. In *Re Valpy* (1906) a direction to pay debts except mortgage debts if any on Blackacre out of residue indicated an intention that the residue should discharge other mortgage debts; but in *Re Birch* (1909) where property had been directed by the terms of a will to be sold to pay off a mortgage debt on specified property, any deficiency in the proceeds of sale must still remain charged on the specified property.
d. In *Re Phuler's Will Trusts* (1964) *D*, a testator, directed that his executors and trustees should secure remuneration for their services 'free of duties'. He also gave a freehold property to *A* but made no directions as to duties on that property, which was followed by a gift of three pecuniary legacies 'free of all duties'. The residue (which included freehold properties) he directed to be sold to pay funeral, testamentary expenses, debts, legacies and 'all death duties'. It was held that any charges (for estate duty) in respect of the freehold property to *A* were not released and *A* was liable to pay them.

Variation of the statutory order is effected where the whole real and personal residuary estate is given to trustees upon trust to pay the debts and expenses therefrom and to hold the balance on trust for the beneficiaries (*Re Petty* (1929)) and where the whole real and personal estate is given to trustees 'after' or 'subject to' payment of debts and expenses thereout to hold for the beneficiaries: *Re Kempthorne* (1930) and *Re Harland Peck* (1941). In *In Re Cruse* (1930) where residue was settled on *X* for life and then on A and B absolutely, when the gift to A lapsed during A's lifetime, it was held that the primary fund to pay debts was the whole residue and not the lapsed share of the residue. As the debts had to be paid immediately and not postponed until after X's death residue could only be ascertained after all debts had been paid.

In *In Re Worthington* (1933) where the testator, after making certain pecuniary legacies, bequeathed the residue to X and Y equally, and when Y predeceased the testator it was held that on his death the lapsed share of the residue was the primary fund for payment of debts. A similar decision was also arrived at in *Re Midgley* (1955). In *Re Martin* (1955) the will gave all the real estate to a beneficiary (who predeceased the testator) and then gave the residuary personalty to the personal representative with directions to pay the debts and expenses thereout and to hold for the beneficiaries, and it was held that the residuary personalty was primarily to bear the debts and expenses and the next of kin should take the realty free. This applies only in so far as there is not a deficiency of personalty.

It is important to note that the term 'testamentary expenses' now includes capital transfer tax both on personal estate and on real estate. The law prior to 1983 treated personal and real estate differently but the Scottish decision of *Re Dougal* (1981) caused a change in the statutory rules applicable to England and Wales and effect was given to the change in the Finance Act 1983.

Donationes mortis causa, i.e. gifts of personal property made in prospect of, and conditional upon, the donor's death, are available for the payment of debts on a failure of all other assets, as would also be any fraudulent conveyances of property which could be set aside if necessary to pay debts of the estate.

It is to be noted that the residuary funds (1) and (2) mentioned in the order of application must (before being available for debts) be appropriate to the pecuniary legacy fund, which itself becomes available for debts later in group (5).

It is, therefore, necessary for the personal representative to *marshal the assets* in the order given, paying the debts primarily out of the first fund (the undisposed-of residue), and if that is insufficient, then out of the next fund, and so on, as in the following example.

Example

A dies, leaving the following assets:

		£
Freehold house	valued at	100,000
Farm	valued at	80,000
Shares in the A.B. Co. Ltd	valued at	40,000
Cash	valued at	6,000
Jewellery	valued at	1,000
Motor-cars	valued at	20,000
Furniture	valued at	1,000
		£248,000

A was also trustee of £20,000 over which he enjoyed a general power of appointment. By will A made the following bequests:

a. To X— £1,000.
b. To B— his furniture and jewellery (which are specific legacies).
c. To M— his freehold house (a specific devise).
d. His shares in the A.B. Co. Ltd were to be sold and the money applied in payment of his debts.
e. His cars were to be given to his chauffeur Z, subject to payment of his debts.
f. W was to receive one-half of the residue of the estate.

g. *Y* was appointed to the £20,000 under the general power of appointment.

The assets should therefore be marshalled in the following order:

1. Undisposed of residue.	Half of share value of farm (£40,000) and £2,500 cash (i.e. one-half × £6,000 cash after deducting legacy of £1,000).
2. Residuary estate to *W*.	Half share value of farm (£40,000) and £2,500 cash.
3. Property specifically appropriate for payment of debts.	Shares in A.B. Co. Ltd.
4. Specific legacy to *Z* subject to payment of debts.	Cars.
5. Pecuniary legacy to *X*.	£1,000.
6. Specific legacy to *B*, and devise to *M*.	Furniture and jewellery.
7. *Y*'s fund under the power of appointment.	£20,000.

If the debts of *A*'s estate exceeded £42,500, *W*'s legacy would have to be applied in payment thereof; if they exceeded £48,000 the shares would have to be sold and applied, and if that did not produce enough, then the cars would have to be sold and so on.

If the assets in any one fund used for the payment of debts are more than sufficient, the surplus remaining in the fund after payment of the debts will be divided proportionately among the beneficiaries entitled to that particular fund. Thus, if the shares were not wholly or partly required for the payment of debts the amount not required for the payment of debts would form part of the residue.

Exercise 6

1. What constitutes the assets of a deceased person?
2. What is the position of a personal representative with regard to the bank account of the deceased?
3. Can a personal representative recover damages for torts committed against the deceased during his lifetime?
4. Discuss the position of a personal representative as regard mortgages and shares which form part of the deceased's estate.
5. What is meant by a personal representative's power of appropriation? To what extent can he exercise it?
6. How can a personal representative protect himself from liability on leaseholds?
7. In what cases, if at all, is an executor personally liable for (a) on the debts of the deceased, and (b) for debts incurred by himself in winding up the deceased's estate?
8. In cases where there are two or more executors, what power has any one of them do the following:
   a. transfer shares or stock standing in the name of the testator;
   b. accept payment of a debt due to the testator, and give an effective receipt;
   c. convey freehold property.
9. What liability may be incurred by a personal representative who carries on the business of the deceased?
10. Can a personal representative delegate any of his duties without incurring personal liability for the misdeeds of the agents employed?
11. What steps should a personal representative take in order to protect himself from liability for claims of creditors? What are the rights of creditors where such steps have been taken?
12. In what order must a personal representative pay the debts of the deceased when the assets are insufficient to pay the debts in full? What liability will the personal representative incur if he pays out of the due order?
13. What debts are preferred, and what deferred, by special statutes?
14. How should a personal representative treat (a) statute-barred debts; (b) debts due from a legatee; (c) debts due to himself?
15. Explain what is meant by marshalling the deceased's assets.

7
Trusts

TRUSTS AND POWERS

A trust has been defined as 'an equitable obligation binding a person (who is called a trustee) to deal with property over which he has control (which is called the trust property) for the benefit of persons (who are called the beneficiaries) of whom he may himself be one, and any one of whom may enforce the obligation'. Trusts are generally created by deeds in lifetime or by will.

A trust must be distinguished from a power, especially from a power of appointment. A power is 'an authority to dispose of some interest in land but confers no right to enjoyment of the land'. A power is discretionary, while a trust is imperative: a trustee is bound to do as the settlor directs. As regards the distinction between a trust and a power of appointment, the objects of a power have no right of action against the appointor, in the absence of fraud, if he does not appoint, whereas if property is left on trust to divide, the court will compel its division.

Certain powers with the characteristics of trusts are known as 'powers in the nature of trusts'. Whether or not a power is a power purely and simply, or a power in the nature of a trust depends upon the settlor's true intention as gathered from the wording of the creating instrument. Thus in *Burrough* v. *Philcox* (1840), the testator gave his property to trustees on trust for his two children for their lives, remainder to their issue, and in default of issue the survivor was to have power to dispose of the property by will amongst the testator's nephews and nieces, either all to one or to as many as the surviving child thought proper. The testator's children died without issue and without an appointment having been made, and it was held that a trust in favour of the nephews and nieces had been created. Where, however, there is a gift over in default of appointment this is sufficient to negative the presumption of a trust.

CREATION OF A TRUST

The three certainties

Every trust must possess the 'three certainties':

a. *certainty of intention* — the words must be imperative, showing clearly the intention to create a trust;
b. *certainty of subject-matter* — the property which the trust is to affect must be precisely set out, otherwise the trust will fail for uncertainty;

c. *certainty of objects* — if the persons intended to benefit cannot be ascertained from the terms of the trust, the whole trust will fail.

Consideration of several decided cases will help to make clear the purpose of these requirements. The testamentary wording often gives rise to doubts whether or not a trust is intended. Thus in *Re Adams and the Kensington Vestry* (1884) the testator used the following words in giving his estate to his wife: 'in full confidence that she would do what was right as to the disposal thereof between her children either in her lifetime or by will after her decease', and in *Re Diggles* (1888) the testatrix used the words 'it is my desire that she allows . . . an annuity of £25 during her life'. The modern tendency of the courts is against construing such precatory words as a trust, and in both these cases it was held that the beneficiary took absolutely and not wholly or partly as a trustee.

In dealing with the second requirement, that of certainty of subject-matter, the essential is that the property over which the trust is to operate shall be clearly ascertainable. Thus in *Mussoorie Bank* v. *Raynor* (1882) where the testator left his estate to his widow 'feeling confident that she will act justly to our children in dividing the same when no longer required by her' it was held that, as there was no certainty as to the property the children should enjoy, there was no trust.

In *Re Ball* (1947) the term 'his dependants' was held to be too uncertain an object and no trust was created, and in *Re Wood* (1949) it was held that a gift of a fund on trust to pay £2 a week to the 'Week's Good Cause' was not effective in creating a trust as the objects were uncertain, and because the will delegated the choice of beneficiaries to the BBC, thus clashing with the doctrine that the law does not permit a testator to appoint someone else to make his will for him. The authority for this doctrine is the case of *Grimond* v. *Grimond* (1905).

The effect of the failure of a trust because the three certainties are not fulfilled is:

a. if the trust fails under (a) the person to whom the property is given subject to the precatory words takes absolutely;
b. if the failure is under (b) or (c) the gift lapses. An exception to this arises where a beneficial interest is given subject to a further interest which fails, and in this case the first interest become absolute.

Precatory trusts

Trusts may arise from the use of precatory words, in which case they are known as *precatory trusts*, e.g. where a person gives property to another and accompanies the gift with words of wish, hope, desire or entreaty that the donee will dispose of the property in some particular way. Such cases chiefly arise under wills, and it is frequently very difficult to determine whether the testator intended an absolute gift leaving it to the discretion of the donee to comply with his wishes or not, or whether he intended the donee to be a trustee of the property, and, as such, bound to dispose of it in accordance with the wish or desire expressed. Such a question can be answered only by an examination of the whole of the intrument, although the tendency in modern times is against construing precatory words as creating a trust.

Variation of the terms of trusts

For many years various schemes for altering the terms of trusts have been placed before the courts for approval, but in *Chapman* v. *Chapman* (1954) the House of Lords decided that the courts were not possessed of unlimited inherent jurisdiction to modify or vary trust intruments. The Variation of Trusts Act 1958 was subsequently passed to extend the court's jurisdiction and it authorizes the court to approve any arrangements for varying or revoking the trust or enlarging the trustees' powers of management or administration, and covers the case where some of the beneficiaries cannot give consent because of the protective trusts which would otherwise make them liable to forfeiture. There have been several cases where the court has extended the trustees' investment powers, e.g. *Re Dame Edith Coates' Will Trusts* (1959), and *Re Bing's Will Trusts* (1959), but following the Trustee Investments Act 1961 only special considerations now warrant the court giving additional powers. In *Chapman* v. *Chapman (No. 2)* (1959) it was directed that applications under the Act must be heard in open court and not in chambers.

In *Re Drewe's Settlement; Drewe and Others* v. *Westminster Bank Ltd and Another* (1966) the Court approved a scheme of rearrangement of the trust, this being primarily to save estate duty on the life tenant's death. Here the life tenant had a protected life interest in a one-quarter share of the fund and this was to pass on his death to his three children. The arrangement was that the life tenant released part of his life interest to the children while they released part of their interest to him.

In recent years, a number of applications have been made to the courts under the Variation of Trusts Act 1958 with a view to authorizing the removal of the jurisdiction of the trusts from the United Kingdom to another country, usually with a view to saving or avoiding tax. The courts have been known not to approve such a request where the avoidance of tax has been the only motive; they have been inclined to consider whether the removal of the trust would be for the overall benefit — construed in a wider sense — for the beneficiaries concerned.

Rule against perpetuities

One of the basic principles of English law is that property must be capable of free alienation and that an owner of property must not be able to tie up the disposal of property indefinitely. The rule against perpetuities was therefore devised to prevent this, and it operates to render void any future interest which will not vest within the stipulated period.

Prior to the passing of the Perpetuities and Accumulations Act 1964 the effect of the rule against perpetuities was that any future disposition or limitation of real or personal estate was totally void if there was any possibility that the gift would not vest in the lifetime of a life or lives in being at the date of the gift plus a further period of twenty-one years. For this purpose a life in being may be considered as any person mentioned in the deed or will (or the relevant portion thereof) under which the limitation is created. The life in being need not be a beneficiary but can be any specified person. It was at one time common practice to limit the disposal of property by reference to the living descendants of Queen Victoria, but a warning against his practice was given in *Re Scarborough's Will Trusts* (1958) and such a limitation might well now be held void for uncertainty.

Thus under the old rule a limitation of property to a minor *A* for life, with remainder to his eldest (and as yet unborn) child for life, with remainder to his first born grandchild who attained twenty-one years absolutely, would necessarily infringe the rule. The limitation would be effective so far as *A* is concerned, and similarly *A*'s eldest child would benefit since his interest must vest within twenty-one years of the death of the life in being, who is of course, *A* (in fact the child's interest vests immediately upon the death of *A*). There is, however, the possibility that, as *A* is the only life in being, the interest of his first-born grandchild to attain twenty-one years will not vest within twenty-one years of *A*'s death since *A*'s children may be childless at the date of *A*'s death. Under the old rule, therefore, it would be clear from the outset that no grandchild of *A* could possibly benefit.

The Perpetuities and Accumulations Act 1964 introduced two main new concepts. The first of these was the provision of a 'wait-and-see' rule, so that a limitation is not now to be judged at the time when it is made and in the light of any possibility which might affect its validity, but is to be judged in the knowledge of events which do actually happen in the applicable perpetuity period. The example quoted in the preceding paragraph illustrates how this provision can operate for the benefit of future potential beneficiaries. If, in the example, *A* at his death was survived by a grandchild who subsequently attained the age of twenty-one years, the rule against perpetuities would no longer be offended under the Act of 1964.

The second main provision of the 1964 Act was the introduction of a new perpetuity period. In any deed of disposition it is now possible to stipulate any number of years not exceeding eighty as the perpetuity period, and where a fixed period is so stipulated, it is to be accepted for all purposes of the rule against perpetuities. Where a period of years is not stipulated, the perpetuity period remains as the lifetime of a life or lives in being plus a further period of twenty-one years.

The rule against perpetuities does not apply to charities, so that, for example, the income of an estate may be bequeathed to charities in perpetuity with no residuary gift.

Rules against accumulations

A further rule prevents the accumulation of income from property. This rule is stated in sections 164–6, Law of Property Act 1925, and the effect is to permit accumulation:

a. if the sole object of accumulating the income is to produce a fund for the purchase of land during the minority of some infant(s) who would be entitled to that income if he (they) were of full age;
b. if the income is being accumulated for some other purpose than the purchase of land, either:
   i. during the minority of the person or persons entitled (as above); or
   ii. during the minority of any other person(s), living or conceived, when the testator dies; or
   iii. for twenty-one years from the testator's death.

Section 13 of the 1964 Act adds two further periods for which income may be accumulated, namely (a) a period of twenty-one years from the date the disposition is made, and (b) the duration of the minority of any person in being at that date.

If accumulation offends the rule, it is void as regards the excess period, but if the accumulation also offends the perpetuity rule, then it is completely void.

The Family Law Reform Act 1969 reduced the age of majority from 21 to 18 years with effect from 1 January 1970. Periods of accumulation permitted by reference to the duration of any minority are therefore effectively reduced accordingly. However, the Family Law Reform Act 1969 provides specifically that, in the case of dispositions executed before 1 January 1970, the age of majority will remain 21 with accumulations permitted accordingly. In the case of dispositions executed on or after 1 January 1970, accumulation is only permitted until the beneficiary in question attains 18.

TYPES OF TRUST

Life interest

One of the most common types of trusts is the life interest trust which creates a life interest with remainders of capital over. This kind of trust is not infrequently created by will or is acquired by a surviving spouse upon an intestacy.

In such cases, the deceased's personal representatives will, after dealing with all the matters relative to the administration of the deceased's estate, assume the responsibilities of trustees, unless (unusually) other persons are appointed as trustees in the will.

Upon the death of the life tenant, the interest will pass either to a succeeding life tenant or the capital will pass to a remainderman. If no such provision is made, then a resulting trust will arise in favour the deceased's relatives.

By way of examples:

a. *A* by will leaves property to *B* for life, with remainder to *X*. Upon *B*'s death the property passes to *X* or to his personal representatives if he predeceases *B*.
b. *A* by will leaves certain specific property to *M* for life, but does not state what is to happen to the property afterwards, as where he does not dispose of the residue of his estate. Upon the death of *M* there will be a *resulting trust* to *A*'s kindred, i.e. the persons who would take *A*'s property upon his intestacy.
c. If in the last case *A* had bequeathed the residue of his estate to *P*, then upon the death of *M* the property would pass to *P*.

Proof of the continued existence of the life tenant was necessary in *Re Wilson, Deceased* (1964) to enable the trustee to continue to pay the income of the estate to the life tenant's wife under a sequestration order. The onus of proof was held to be on the wife and the court could make no presumption of continuance of life in respect of the life tenant. The court has power to presume death, but not the reverse.

Life tenant and remainderman

No matter however many successive life tenants, there must eventually be a remainderman in whom the capital will invest when all the life interests have expired.

It falls to the trustees therefore to strike a balance, particularly with regard to investment policy, between maximizing income for the life tenant and having regard to capital appreciation for the remainderman.

The trustee must endeavour to preserve an equitable balance between the two unless the trust instrument shows a contrary intention and instructs the trustee to favour one or the other. Most of the rules laid down for governing the conduct of trustees are intended to preserve such a balance.

Protective trusts

A protective trust is one the subject of which is to protect not merely the capital but also the income of the trust fund.

Where any income is directed to be held on protective trusts for the benefit of any person for his life or a shorter period, section 33 of the Trustee Act 1925 provides that the said income shall, during the trust period, be held, without prejudice to any prior interest, on the following trusts:

a. upon trust for the principal beneficiary during the trust period or until he does or attempts to do or suffers any act, or until any event, other than an advance, happens, whereby, if the said income were payable absolutely, he would be deprived of the right to receive any part of it, in any of which cases, the trust shall fail;

b. on failure of the trust, the said income shall, during the residue of the trust period, be held upon trust for the application thereof for the maintenance or support or benefit of all or any one or more of the following persons, as the trustees may, in their absolute discretion, think fit:

   i. the principal beneficiary and his or her wife or husband and his or her issue;

   ii. failing wife, husband or issue, the principal beneficiary and such persons as would, if he were dead, be entitled to the trust property or its income.

Secret trusts

Once the personal representatives of a deceased person have assented to the gift, the recipient of property bequeathed or devised is normally entitled to enjoy it for his own benefit. Thus if it was the desire of the testator that the donee should hold the property upon trust for other persons, his will should say so; otherwise those persons have generally no means of compelling the donee to recognize their claims, since the Wills Act 1837 requires testamentary dispositions to be in the form required by law.

Equity does not, however, permit the donee of a gift by will to retain it beneficially – by pleading this statute – if he expressly or impliedly promised the testator that he would hold the gift for those other persons, since that would permit the donee to benefit by his own fraud.

The principle underlying the equitable doctrine of secret trusts is that equity will not allow a person to profit by his own fraud. Suppose that *A* makes his will and leaves £10,000 to *B*, the gift on the face of the will being absolute in terms. If, subsequently to the execution of the will, *A* informs *B* that he does not intend that *B* shall take the legacy beneficially, but shall hold it in trust for *C*, then either *B* must decline to carry out *A*'s wish, in which case *A* will, of course, alter his will, or *B* must assent to *A*'s wish. If *B* assents to *A*'s wish, it is clearly inequitable to allow *B* to deny the trust in *C*'s favour after *A*'s death, as *A* has left the legacy unrevoked on the faith of *B*'s promise to hold the same on trust for *C*. Similar principles would apply if *B* induced *A* to leave him £10,000 in his will, promising that he would hold the legacy in trust for *C*.

It is necessary to distinguish carefully between those cases where the person intended to act as trustee is apparently a *beneficial owner* on the face of the will, and those cases where he is expressly designated as a *trustee*.

a. *Where the trustee takes beneficially on the face of the will.* In this case, if the trusts are communicated to the trustee in the testator's lifetime, the Court will compel the trustee to carry out the trusts on the principle stated above. If, however, some document purporting to be a direction to a beneficiary is found after the testator's death, it will be ineffectual, as the conscience of the legatee is not affected by any trust.

The same principle applies where an heir induces a father not to make a will by promising that he will provide for other dependants of the father: *Sellack* v. *Harris* (1708).

In *Re Stirling* (1954), there was a gift to a bank (executor and trustee of the will) with a request that the bank should dispose of it in accordance with any memorandum signed by the testator, but such memorandum was not to form part of the will or to have testamentary character. There was no communication of the testator's wishes to the bank during his lifetime, but a memorandum indicating his wishes was found among the testator's papers after his death. It was held that the bank took beneficially. In view of the express wording, this was treated as a case where the trustee took beneficially on the face of the will.

b. *Where the trustee takes as trustee upon the face of the will.* Where property is bequeathed to a person as trustee, he can never take beneficially. But if after the will is proved, a document is found directing him to hold the property in trust for certain persons, this is ineffectual unless the document was executed as a will, as otherwise the provisions of the Wills Act would be rendered valueless. There is, therefore, a resulting trust in favour of the testator's residuary legatee or devisee, or, if none or if the trust be imposed on a residuary legatee, in favour of the persons entitled on intestacy.

The same principles apply where, although the trustee takes beneficially on the face of the will, he has accepted the capacity of a trustee in the testator's lifetime but the testator has omitted to communicate the identity of the beneficiaries prior to his death: *Re Boyes, Boyes v. Carritt* (1884).

Where the testator communicates the object of the trust to the trustee during his lifetime, a distinction is drawn between cases where the communication of objects is made at the time of the will, or before, and cases where it is made in the testator's lifetime, but after the will.

a. *Where the communication takes place at or before the making of a will.* After much uncertainty, it was laid down by the House of Lords in *Blackwell* v. *Blackwell* (1929), that in such cases the trustees hold on trust for the beneficiaries whose names have been so communicated. In this case, a testator gave £12,000 by codicil to five persons, to apply the income 'for the purposes indicated by me to them', with power to pay the capital sum of £8,000 to persons indicated to them. Detailed *parol* instructions were given to one of the trustees, and the scheme was known in outline to all the trustees and accepted by them before the codicil was executed. It was held that there was a binding trust for the objects indicated.

b. *Where the communication takes place after the will is made.* In these cases, the authorities appear to establish the proposition, although the point is not free from doubt, that the intended trust is ineffective, and the trustee holds on trust for the residuary legatee, residuary devisee, or persons entitled on intestacy, as the case may be. The case of *Re Keen* (1937) is not a clear authority in favour of the above proposition, as it turned upon a rather narrow point of construction. In principle there would appear to be no logical distinction between cases where the communication of the identity of the beneficiaries is made before, and cases where it is made after, the will.

In *Re Colin Cooper* (1939), a testator left £5,000 to trustees on secret trusts, the nature of which he had already communicated to them. By a later will he purported to increase this sum to £10,000. It was held that the secret trust was invalid as to the additional £5,000.

In *Re Gardner's Will Trusts* (1936), where a will gave property to *A* to be disposed of as already directed, it was held that a memorandum drawn up by *A* after the testatrix's death was not admissible in evidence after *A*'s death to prove the terms of the trust as it was not against *A*'s pecuniary or proprietary interest. This decision is reversed by section 1 of the Evidence Act 1938.

Secret trusts are unaffected by the Wills Act 1837 since the forms required by that Act are entirely disregarded. Persons who take beneficially under secret trusts do not take by virtue of a gift under the will but by virtue of the secret trusts imposed on a beneficiary who in fact takes under the will. A beneficiary who takes under a secret trust does not, therefore, forfeit his legacy if he has attested the will: *Re Young* (1950).

The case of *Re Tyler*; *Graves* v. *King and Others* (1967) demonstrated that the doctrine of secret trusts also applies to gifts *inter vivos*. The testatrix paid £1,500 to the donee in March 1951, and in May 1951 wrote him a letter setting out briefly the terms of the secret trust. The testatrix died in 1954, and subsequently the donee signed a memorandum stating how he was to administer the trust.

Charitable trusts

In the case of *Re Cole, Westminster Bank Limited* v. *Moore* (1958), Lord Evershed, MR, said: 'Notwithstanding the passage of three centuries during which the courts have been able to attach the charitable label to large numbers and varieties of dispositions and reject the claim to qualify in no less a number of cases, the underlying idea seems to remain as elusive as ever. The truth may be that the possible variations of expressed intention by testators and settlors are as the sands of the sea and that no catalogue of illustrations, however long, can exhaust or confine charity's scope.'

This quotation serves to illustrate how difficult it has been found by the courts to decide which gifts are charitable in their objects and which are not. The leading case on the subject is *Commissioners of Income Tax* v. *Pemsel* (1891) in which the term 'charitable purposes' was defined as covering trusts for the relief of poverty, the advancement of education and of religion, and also trusts for any other purpose which is beneficial to the community. It is this last heading which has given rise to the extensive litigation. Difficulties have often arisen because the wording of the trust instrument is wide enough to permit the application of the trust funds to non-charitable in addition to charitable purposes. Where this is so, and the trust involves a perpetuity (as it did in *Re Cole*), the whole gift is void even though the trustees may have every intention of applying the trust funds solely for purposes which come within the definition of charitable. In *Re Cole* the words used were 'general benefit and general welfare of the children . . .' and these words were held to be wide enough to allow the application of money in ways outside the technical definition; and in *Chichester Diocesan Fund* v. *Simpson* (1944) a bequest to such charitable or patriotic or benevolent object as the executors select failed as a charitable trust, as 'patriotic or benevolent' objects are not necessarily charitable; but if the objects of the bequest are in fact charitable it will not fail merely because the testator had mentioned the name or address of a particular 'institution' which no longer existed or which never did exist or had changed in name and/or address.

In *Re Robinson* (1950) a trust for good persons was held to be charitable, while a trust for the education of the descendants of certain named persons was not so regarded (*Re Compton* (1944)) as it was not for the public benefit.

There are certain characteristics of charitable trusts, as follows.

a. The doctrine of *cy-près*.
b. A charitable trust will not fail for uncertainty so long as there is a clear intention that the trustees are to select the charitable objects.
c. The rule against perpetuities does not apply provided that the trust is wholly charitable.

The case of *Re Gillingham Bus Disaster Fund* (1958) demonstrated how vitally important it is for the trust instrument to show clearly how the trust funds are to be used. In this case there was no formal trust instrument, and the purpose of the fund as advertised in a letter to the press written by the town clerk did not in the court's view show a general charitable intention, and the case arose on the question of the disposal of surplus funds. It was held that the purpose of the fund had failed and that an enquiry should be made for the subscribers of the fund so that the subscriptions could be returned.

The Charitable Trusts (Validation) Act 1954, the purpose of which was to validate certain trusts with 'imperfect trust provisions' is very limited in scope, as was illustrated in *Re Harper's Will Trusts* (1961) where the testatrix directed that her trustees divide the residue 'between such institutions and associations having for their main object the assistance and care of soldiers, etc. etc.' in such manner as they may select. It was held that the Act could not be used to validate this by confining the institutions to those exclusively devoted to charitable objects.

TRUSTEES

Distinction between personal representatives and trustees

A personal representative is under a duty to apply the property vesting in him on the death of the deceased in accordance with the terms of the will or the general law. On the other hand, a trustee is a person in whom has been vested the title of property upon trust to apply the beneficial interest for the beneficiaries. His fiduciary duty, which is to deal with the property in accordance with the terms of the trust, has always been enforceable in equity if necessary, by an action in the courts on the part of the beneficiaries.

A personal representative has to swear an oath to administer the estate according to law; a trustee does not.

In many respects, however, an executor is in the same position as the trustee. His liability is limited to the assets he receives. He can discharge himself from liability only by showing that he has duly administered them or by proving that they have been accidentally lost without it being his fault.

Executor or trustee — which capacity?

The same persons may be nominated as both executors and trustees by the will. Moreover, in the administration of the deceased's estate, an executor may act partly as executor and partly as trustee, even though he may not be specifically appointed trustee by the will. In these circumstances, it is important to determine when an act is done by an executor as executor and when by him in his capacity as trustee. No definite rule can be laid down, but in general it may be said that an executor becomes a trustee of any property when he is deemed, either by his own admissions or by law, to hold that property for the benefit of certain specified persons entitled to it. Thus, upon assenting to a legacy an executor becomes a trustee of the property concerned, until it is paid over to the legatee. Similarly, when he appropriates a specific fund to the satisfaction of a pecuniary legacy, he becomes a trustee for the amount.

There are differences, however, between executors acting as executors and executors acting as trustees as follows.

a. Only one executor need be appointed, whereas, generally speaking, there cannot be fewer than two individuals (or a trust corporation) to perform a trust.
b. Where there are more executors than one, one alone can bind the estate in all dealings with personalty. He can, therefore, sell or pledge any portion of the personalty and give good title. In the case of trustees, however, one cannot give a good title without the assent of his co-trustees. Further, a majority of trustees cannot bind a minority.
c. One of several executors can give an effective receipt except where the receipt is for the proceeds of the sale of settled land or of land held on trust for sale, or for other capital money under a settlement. In the case of trustees, however, all must sign receipts, unless specifically provided otherwise. A sole executor, however, can give a valid receipt for the proceeds of sale of land, but a sole trustee cannot do so except in the case of a trust corporation.
d. As against an executor, the right to sue for a legacy is barred after twelve years. An action against a trustee, however, is barred, normally, after six years, unless the claim is based on fraud or fraudulent breach of trust, or is to recover trust property or the proceeds thereof still retained by the trustee or previously received by him and converted to his own use, in which cases there is no period of limitation.
e. An executor can have sole authority to sign on a banking account, whereas trustees must always jointly exercise their signing powers.
f. There are certain powers available to personal representatives as such given by the Administration of Estates Act 1925 which are not open to trustees. For instance the power of raising money for administration purposes (sections 39–40), the appropriation powers of section 41, and the power to appoint trustees of minors' property (section 42).

Administrator or trustee?

The distinctions between an administrator as such and one who has become a trustee are similarly important. In *Harvell* v. *Foster* (1954), an infant daughter was appointed sole executrix and sole beneficiary of her father's will. A grant *durante minore aetate* was made to her husband who, with two solicitors as sureties, duly administered the estate. At the close of the administration the husband as administrator took possession, quite properly, of the estate funds, but he then converted them to his own use. The decision in the court of first instance was that the liability of the sureties had ended with the close of the administration and the husband then held as trustee. This was, however, reversed in the Court of Appeal, which held that the administrator did not complete his duties until he handed over the estate of the infant's majority. He could, however, have obtained a good discharge by appointing two trustees or a trust corporation under section 42, Administration of Estates Act 1925.

The question of whether executors or administrators become trustees holding for the beneficiaries as soon as they have completed the administration was clarified in *Re Cockburn's Will Trusts, Cockburn* v. *Lewis* (1957), and it is now clear that they do, although in the case of an administrator he cannot be compelled to carry on the duties as trustee indefinitely and can appoint new trustees of the will to act in his place if he so desires.

Trustees for the purposes of the Settled Land Act

Under section 30 of the Settled Land Act 1925, the following persons are to be deemed trustees of a settlement for the purposes of the Act:

a. the persons who, under the settlement, are for the time being trustees with power of sale of the settled land, or with power of consent to, or approval of, the exercise of such a power of sale; or, failing such,

b. the persons for the time being who are by the settlement declared to be trustees thereof for the purposes of the Settled Land Acts 1882–1890, or of the 1925 Act; or, failing such,

c. the persons who are for the time being, under the settlement, trustees, with power of, or upon trust for, sale of any other land comprised in the settlement and subject to the same limitations as the land to be sold or otherwise dealt with, or with power of consent to, or approval of, the exercise of such a power; or, failing such,

d. the persons who are for the time being, under the settlement, trustees with future power of sale, or under a future trust for sale of the settled land, or with power of consent to, or approval of, the exercise of such a future power; or, failing such,

e. the persons appointed by deed to be trustees of the settlement by all the persons who at the date of the deed were together able, by virtue of their beneficial interests or by the exercise of an equitable power, to dispose of the settled land in equity for the whole estate which is the subject of the settlement;

f. where a settlement is created by will or arises on an intestacy, the personal representatives of the deceased shall, if there are no trustees, and until other trustees are appointed, be the trustees of the settlement, but where there is a sole personal representative, not being a trust corporation, it shall be obligatory on him to appoint an additional trustee to act with him for the purposes of the Act.

Appointment of trustees

Trustees may be appointed

a. by the settlor on making the settlement;

b. by the beneficiaries, if they are all *sui juris* and entitled between them to the whole beneficial interest;

c. by some person having a power, under the trust instrument or under section 36 of the Trustee Act 1925, to appoint new trustees; or

d. by the court.

Where the appointment is being made by the settlor or by the beneficiaries, any competent person or corporation may be appointed, but when it is being made by a person under a power to appoint new trustees, no one should be appointed whom the court would not appoint, e.g. a person under disability or outside the court's jurisdiction, a beneficiary, beneficiary's husband, wife or solicitor. When on the application of a settlor or trustee or beneficiary, the court appoints a trustee under the Judicial Trustee Act 1896, such a trustee is called a judicial trustee and is deemed to be an officer of the court.

Beneficiaries have no power to compel a trustee to appoint a new trustee: *Re Higginbottom* (1892). They have no power to direct a trustee to retire and transfer his responsibilities to a new trustee selected by themselves: *Re Brockbank* (1948).

Where a trustee is dead, or remains out of the United Kingdom for more than twelve months, or desires to be discharged, or refuses or is unfit to act or incapable of acting in the trust, or is a minor, a new trustee may, by writing, be appointed in his place:

a. by the person or persons nominated by the trust instrument for the purpose of appointing a new trustee; or

b. if there is no such person, or no such person able and willing to act by the surviving or continuing trustee or trustees for the time being, or by the personal representatives of the last surviving or continuing trustee, the person or persons exercising the power may appoint himself or themselves to be the new trustee or trustees.

Where a trustee has been removed under a power contained in the trust instrument, a new trustee or new trustees may be appointed in his place as if he were dead, or, in the case of a corporation, as if the corporation desired to be discharged from the trust.

Where a sole trustee, other than a trust corporation, has been originally appointed, or where there are not more than three trustees (none of them being a trust corporation), an additional trustee or additional trustees may be appointed in writing by the person or persons nominated by the trust instrument for the purpose or, if there is no such person, or no such person able and willing to act, by the trustee or trustees for the time being. It shall not, however, be obligatory to appoint any additional trustee unless the trust instrument provides to the contrary, nor shall the number of trustees be increased beyond four by virtue of any such appointment. An appointor cannot appoint himself to be an additional trustee: *Re Power's Settlement Trusts* (1951). Where there is a minor beneficiary or where a life interest arises, there must be at least two trustees or a trust corporation.

All these powers of appointing new or additional trustees are conferred by section 36 of the Trustee Act 1925. Under section 41 of the Act, whenever it is expedient to appoint a new trustee or new trustees and it is found inexpedient, difficult or impracticable to appoint one in any other way, the court may make the appointment, especially where the original trustee is convicted of a felony, is mentally unsound, is a bankrupt, or is a corporation which is in liquidation or has been dissolved. Thus, in *Re May's Will Trusts, May* v. *Burch* (1940), where one of several trustees was in enemy-occupied territory, the court appointed a new trustee in her place under section 41, although there was no evidence that the trustee was 'incapable of acting' within section 36.

When a new trustee is appointed, the trust property has to be vested to him. Under section 40 of the Trustee Act, the deed appointing the trustees operates, without any conveyance or assignment, to vest the property in the trustees, provided it contains nothing to the contrary.

If a testator shows an intention to create a trust but does not appoint a trustee, the personal representative is deemed a trustee. Similarly, on the death of a sole or last surviving trustee, the legal estate subject to the trust vests in his personal representatives, who, pending the appointment of new trustees, are capable of exercising all the powers of the deceased trustee. Where there are several co-trustees, upon the death of one, the survivors continue to officiate.

A person appointed trustee is not bound to act: he may disclaim the trust at any time before he has done anything showing his intention to accept it. A disclaimer may be by word of mouth or inferred from conduct. It is usually, however, effected by deed, though a deed is not essential. The disclaimer must be of the *whole* of the trust, and it operates as a disclaimer of the property, which thereupon reverts to the settlor or his personal representatives or to the other trustees, as the case may be.

A trustee, having once accepted the trust, cannot afterwards disclaim it, and an executor-trustee, by proving the will, is deemed to have accepted its trusts: *Mucklow* v. *Fuller* (1821). A trustee may, however, obtain a release from his trusteeship by retirement. Under the Trustee Act 1925, a trustee may by deed retire from the trust, provided that after his discharge there will be either a trust corporation or at least two individuals to perform the trust, and provided that his co-trustees and the person entitled to appoint new trustees consent by deed to his retirement. These conditions must be fulfilled if a trustee is to retire without a new trustee being appointed in his place. Provided it contains nothing to the contrary, the deed operates to vest the trust property in the continuing trustees. Further, by the Public Trustee Act 1906, a trustee may retire on or after the appointment of the public trustee as an ordinary trustee, without leaving two trustees and without the consents mentioned above. Again, under the Judicial Trustee Act 1896, a judicial trustee may retire on giving notice to the court of his desire so to do.

Remuneration of trustees

As a result of the rule that a trustee cannot make a profit from his trust, trustees are generally entitled to no remuneration for their time and trouble. To this, however, there are the following exceptions.

a. The beneficiaries, being all *sui juris*, may agree that they should receive remuneration.
b. The court may sanction the payment of remuneration if the trust is exceptionally onerous.
c. A judicial trustee may be paid such remuneration as the court may assign him.
d. The public trustee is allowed to charge such fees as the Treasury fixes.
e. Where the court appoints a corporation other than the public trustee the court may authorize remuneration.
f. A solicitor-trustee may charge his profit costs when acting as solicitor in any legal proceeding on behalf of himself and his co-trustees jointly, except so far as the costs have been increased by his being one of the parties.
g. The trust instrument may expressly authorize remuneration.

Although a trustee is not entitled to remuneration he does have a right to indemnity for costs and expenses properly incurred in the course of the administration of the trust and such right may be against a beneficiary. Furthermore in appropriate cases a trustee may be empowered by the court to incur costs of litigation.

Duties of trustees

Before proceeding to study the powers and liabilities of trustees, it is necessary to summarize briefly the principal duties of trustees in general. They are as follows.

a. To inspect the terms of the trust instrument and ascertain the trust's limitations and the appointment of trustees.
b. To preserve the trust property so that no loss may be suffered by the beneficiaries.
c. To pay over the trust income to those entitled to it.
d. To keep the beneficiaries informed upon matters relating to the trust.
e. To hold the scales evenly between the beneficiaries and not to favour one at the expense of another.
f. To invest only in authorized securities (i.e. securities in which trustees are permitted to invest trust funds either by the Trustee Investments Act 1961 or by the trust instrument).
g. Not to purchase trust property for their own use. This principle does not apply where there is a pre-existing contract entered into before the creation of the trust: *Re Mulholland's Will Trusts* (1949).

To make no personal profit out of the trust, unless the will gives them authority to do so. In *Williams* v. *Barton* (1927), where a trustee received a commissioin from his employers, who had been employed to value the trust estate, it was held that he must account to the trust for such commission. In *Re Macadam* (1945), where the trustees had power to appoint directors of a company and appointed themselves, it was held that the appointment was a proper one, but that the trustees must account for their directors' fees. A trustee who procures his co-trustees to give him remunerative employment must account for the benefit obtained. So also must a trustee who has the power, by means of trust votes, to control his own appointment and, by refraining from using them, causes himself to be elected to a position of profit: *Re Gee* (1948). In *Phipps* v. *Boardman* (1965), which was confirmed by the House of Lords, a solicitor to trustees together with one beneficiary acted as agents for the trustees and acquired knowledge and the opportunity to make a profit in the shares of a private company (the trust also making a profit). It was held that the profit had all to be paid to the trust. The trustee or persons who by their conduct have made themselves agents for the trustee, thus hold the money received as constructive trustee for the persons entitled in equity to benefit. Lord Cohen's obiter dictum in the *Phipps* v. *Boardman* case suggested that had the profit been derived from dealing in shares of a public company the decision would have been different.

Not to delegate the duties of trustee. The distinction must be noted between the delegation of the whole trust as permitted under section 25 of the Trustee Act 1925, as amended by the Powers of Attorney Act 1971, and the mere delegation of certain powers or duties in the administration of the trust as permitted under section 23 dealing with the appointment of agents. Further, under section 25 the trustee remains liable for the defaults of the person appointed, whereas under section 23 the trustee is not liable for the defaults of the agent if appointed in good faith.

Exceptions to this last rule are provided by:

i.   section 23, Trustee Act 1925, which gives trustees as well as personal representatives a wide power to appoint solicitors, bankers and other agents;

ii. section 29, Law of Property Act 1925, which allows trustees for sale of land revocably to delegate their powers of leasing and management;

iii. section 8, Trustee Act 1925, which allows trustees when lending money on security to delegate the duty of valuing the security; and

iv. section 25, Trustee Act 1925, which allows a trustee who intends to remain out of the United Kingdom for more than one month to delegate his powers for the period of his absence by a power of attorney.

However, the trustee is liable for the acts of defaults of the person to whom he has delegated them, as if they were his own acts or defaults.

Although personal representatives have the power to employ agents, such as solicitors, it is clear that they are under a duty to use their judgment so as to avoid unnecessary expense to the estate. The point was discussed in *Re Grimthorpe's Will Trusts* (1958), when the court had to consider the taxing of costs incurred by trustees on an originating summons taken out to vary the investment powers contained in the trust instrument. In concluding the judge said that a person engaging his own counsel may pay whatever he likes, but in the case of a trustee he must use his judgment to try to save the estate money which need not be paid out. It was, however, held that the taxation of these items should be set aside, and the items paid by the trustees in good faith, allowed.

Discretions of trustees

A trustee must observe all the rules of equity relating to trustees and cannot depart from them unless directed to do so by all the beneficiaries who are of age and entitled between them to the whole beneficial interest.

In the case of every trust for sale of land, a power to postpone sale is implied, subject to a contrary intention, under section 25, Law of Property Act 1925. Where pure personal property is vested in trustees on trust for sale and conversion and to hold the proceeds for a class of beneficiaries, with power to postpone the sale and conversion, any member of the class absolutely entitled to a share may, generally, call for immediate payment of his share, notwithstanding the trustees' power to postpone the conversion.

In the case of land, however, the vesting in possession of the share of one of the beneficiaries does not put an end to the power of postponement or entitle him to demand sale of the land.

The court exercises a general controlling influence over all trustees, even in respect of their discretionary powers, and will see that they carry out their duties, one of which is the bona fide exercise of any discretion given to them. If they refuse to exercise their discretion, the court will interfere: *Klug* v. *Klug* (1918). If, however, they have an absolute discretion as to the mode of executing the trust, the court will not interfere with their discretion, provided they exercise it in good faith: *Gisborne* v. *Gisborne* (1877). Thus, if a testator devises realty to *A* and *B* to hold upon certain trusts, with power to sell if they think fit, and *A* and certain of the beneficiaries desire a sale, but *B*, in the bona fide exercise of his discretion, refuses to sell the court will not interfere. It should be noted that when a trust is being administered by the court, the trustees cannot exercise any of the powers without the court's sanction.

STATUTORY POWERS OF TRUSTEES

The following statutory powers are given by the Trustee Act 1925 to trustees and personal representatives.

a.   Power to sell all or any part of the property by auction or private contract, where the property is held on trust for sale or a power to sell and convert is given expressly or by implication (section 12). They may sell subject to any such conditions as they think fit, may buy it at any auction, rescind any contract for sale and re-sell, without being answerable for any loss. This section does not enable an express power to sell settled land to be exercised where the power is not vested in the tenant for life or statutory owner.

b.   Power to give valid receipts for any money, securities or other personal property payable or transferable to them under any trust (section 14). It must be added, however, that where *land* is held on trust for sale, or is settled land, a receipt for the purchase money must be signed by at least two trustees, and if there is only one trustee, another must be appointed before a valid receipt can be given. This provision does not apply where the sole trustee is a trust corporation.

c.   Power to compound, compromise, submit to arbitration or otherwise settle any debt or claim relative to the estate or trust (section 15).

d.   When authorized to apply capital money for any purpose, power to raise the required money by sale, conversion, calling in or mortgage of all or any part of the trust property in possession, notwithstanding any contrary direction in the trust instrument. This, however, does not apply to charity trustees or to Settled Land Act trustees, not being also the statutory owners (section 16).

e. Power to insure property against fire, to an amount not exceeding three-fourths of the full value of the property. The premiums are payable out of income (section 19). Property may be fully insured by arrangement with the beneficiaries.

f. Power to deposit any documents with a banker or safe-deposit company. Any sum payable in respect of the deposit is payable out of income (section 21).

g. Power to require an audit of the accounts not more than once in three years (section 22 (4)).

h. Power to employ agents (see above, pp. 43 and 44), including an accountant to write up the books and prepare the accounts of the estate.

i. Power to maintain minors (see p. 86).

j. Power to apply capital money for the advancement of a beneficiary (see p. 87).

k. Power to appoint other trustees (section 36).

The *trustees of the settlement* of settled land will not have many of the above powers; (a) and (c)–(f) will be exercisable instead by the tenant for life. Where the title has been vested in the tenant for life under the Settled Land Act 1925, the latter is regarded as the 'owner'.

Trustees are bound to sell at the best price reasonably obtainable, and they must not reject a better offer merely because negotiations for a sale have advanced so far that commercial morality prevents them from withdrawing: *Buttle* v. *Saunders* (1950). They must be careful not to sell under unnecessarily depreciatory conditions, for, though a purchaser will obtain an indefeasible title on conveyance except where he acted in collusion with the trustees, yet if the purchase price has been rendered inadequate by the unnecessarily depreciatory conditions, the beneficiaries can stop the sale before completion, and in any case they can hold the trustees personally liable for the loss.

The receipt in writing of the trustees for the money paid by the purchaser is sufficient discharge for the same and effectually exonerates him from seeing to the application of the money or being answerable for any misapplication thereof.

LIABILITY OF TRUSTEES

A trustee may be sued by any beneficiary who suffers loss through the trustee's breach of trust. A breach of trust is committed whenever one of the duties imposed upon a trustee has not been performed, as where a trustee makes a personal profit out of the trust, or makes unauthorized investments, or sells trust property in improper circumstances, or delays in investing surplus moneys of the estate.

To be liable for breach of trust, a trustee must personally have been guilty of some improper act, neglect or default. Under section 30 of the Trustee Act 1925, a trustee is answerable only for his own acts or defaults, and is chargeable only for money and securities actually received by him, notwithstanding his signing any receipt for the sake of conformity. The mere fact that a co-trustee has committed a breach of trust or that a banker has absconded with trust money will not make him liable, unless the loss is due to his own wilful default. To be guilty of 'wilful default', a trustee must know that he is committing, and intends to commit, a breach of his duty, or he must be recklessly careless, not caring whether his act or omission is a breach of duty or not.

Where two or more trustees are liable for a breach of trust, each of them may be sued for the whole amount of the loss, and if they are all sued, the judgment may be executed against any one of them. When the judgment against two co-trustees is satisfied in part by one of them, and the other trustee subsequently goes bankrupt, the judgment creditor may prove in his bankruptcy for the whole original judgment debt and not merely for the balance left unsatisfied: *Edwards* v. *Hood-Barrs* (1905). Generally, as between themselves, trustees must bear the burden equally so that, if one pays more than his share, he can claim contribution from the others, but there are four cases in which one trustee must indemnify the others:

a. where one trustee has received the trust money and misappropriated it, or is otherwise the only morally guilty party;
b. where one of the trustees, acting as solicitor to the trust, advised the commission of the breach of trust;
c. where the guilty trustee is a beneficiary, in which case the breach of trust will be made good, as far as possible, out of his beneficial interest; and
d. where an acting trustee has obtained a personal benefit in which the others have had no share.

The measure of a trustee's liability for breach of trust is the loss caused to the trust estate, except that, where the breach of trust consists in advancing too much money on an otherwise authorized security, his liability is confined to the excessive advance. The money lost must be replaced with interest, the rate of which is in the discretion of the court.

A new trustee is not liable for breaches of trust committed by his predecessors. Unless he has reason to think otherwise, he is entitled to assume that they have done their duty.

A retiring trustee, unless duly released, remains liable for breaches of trust committed by him prior to retirement. He is not liable for subsequent breaches of trust, unless the object of his retirement was to enable such to be committed.

Where a trustee or personal representative has caused a loss to the trust estate by committing a breach of trust, the court, under section 61 of the Trustee Act 1925, may relieve him either wholly or partly from personal liability, if he 'acted honestly and reasonably, and ought fairly to be excused for the breach of trust and for omitting to obtain the directions of the court in the matter in which he committed such breach'. This power to grant relief enables the court to relieve even a trustee or executor who has handed over property to the wrong person. No general rules can be laid down as to the circumstances in which the court will or will not grant such relief. Each case will be decided on its own merits.

Other ways in which a trustee may escape liability for breach of trust are as follows.

a. The claims of beneficiaries may be barred by lapse of time, i.e. six years from default, but there is no period prescribed where the claim is based on fraud or fraudulent breach of trust to which the trustee was a party, or to recover trust property or its proceeds of sale if converted to his own use.
b. A trustee who obtains his discharge in bankruptcy is freed from liability unless he has acted fraudulently.
c. A beneficiary, being *sui juris* and having knowledge of all the facts, may acquiesce or concur in the breach, or may subsequently confirm the breach or release the trustee. Any other beneficiary, however, may proceed against the trustee.
d. Under section 62 of the Trustee Act, where the breach is committed at the instigation or request, or with the written consent of a beneficiary, the court may make an order for impounding all or any part of the beneficiary's interest by way of indemnity to the trustee.

An indemnity clause is frequently inserted in wills and settlements relieving the trustees of liability for breach of trust, but a trustee cannot plead this clause where he has actively and knowingly committed a breach.

INVESTMENT

Powers and duties of trustees

Where it is necessary for a trustee to invest trust moneys in securities, he must be careful to invest only in securities which are *authorized*, for if unauthorized securities are purchased or retained and depreciation in value follows, the trustee will be personally liable to make good the consequential loss to the beneficiaries. Thus, if £10,000 is invested in an unauthorized security which upon sale realizes only £8,000, the trustee will be held personally liable to the extent of £2,000. He cannot set-off a profit he has made by one breach of trust against the loss on another. Further, not only must he make good an actual loss, but also the amount of profit which he would have made but for the breach. On the other hand, if the securities employed are authorized, the trustee is not personally liable in the event of depreciation in value.

Investment in authorized securities

Authorized securities are of two kinds:

a. Those securities in which trustees are permitted to invest trust moneys by the Trustee Investments Act 1961.
b. Any other securities which are expressly authorized by the will or settlement which created the trust. Thus, an otherwise unauthorized security may be authorized for the purpose of the particular trust. Special investment clauses, however, are strictly construed.

A power to invest in 'real securities' does not authorize the trustee to purchase land, for that is an out-and-out alienation of the trust property for which an express power is required. But, under the Law of Property Act 1925, trustees for sale of land may buy land with the proceeds (*Re Wellsted's Will Trust* (1949)). Moreover, where the will directs the trustees 'to invest investments of whatsoever nature and wheresoever, which they, in their absolute discretion, think fit, and as if they were absolute owners', it has been held that such a direction allows them to go outside the statutory list of securities so as, for instance, to purchase real property: *Re Wragg* (1919). It would seem, however, from *Re Power* (1947) that the purchase must be limited to an income-bearing investment and not for the purpose of occupation by a beneficiary.

Trustees are not liable for breach of trust by continuing to hold investments which have ceased to be authorized, but further funds must not be invested in such securities.

Under section 19 of the Limitation Act 1939, an action by a beneficiary to recover trust property or in respect of any breach of trust must, generally speaking, be brought before the expiration of six years from the date on which the right of action accrued. Actions, however, in respect of any fraud or fraudulent breach of trust to which a trustee was a party, or to recover from a trustee trust property or the proceeds thereof in his possession or previously received by him and converted to his use, are not subject to any period of limitation.

Where the trust assets have remained in their original form the beneficiary has the right to 'follow' the assets in order to obtain satisfaction, but if the assets have been converted into cash or other assets the process known as tracing can be resorted to. When tracing is necessary and several trust funds have to be segregated the rule established in *Clayton's Case* (1816) applies so that the presumption is that the first trust money paid in is the first drawn out of the account. The rule does not apply where the trustee has mixed trust moneys with his personal property and the trustee is presumed to have drawn out his own money first: *Re Hallet's Estate* (1880). There is, however, no presumption of replacement of trust moneys drawn from an account, and so if a trustee draws from a mixed account more than the total of his personal funds, and subsequently pays in further personal moneys, these do not become trust money (*Rosco* v. *Winder* (1915)), but the trustee still remains liable to account for the trust money.

Tracing can be resorted to where there is a means of segregating different funds, and applies not only to a trustee's account but to any account into which trust moneys have paid. Thus, in *Re Diplock's Estate* (1950) the next of kin were held able to trace estate funds into the hands of various charitable bodies which had wrongly received the money.

Statutory powers to invest

Statutory powers to invest are provided mainly by the Trustee Act 1925, as amended by the important provisions contained in the Trustee Investments Act 1961.

The Act is not mandatory in the sense that it does not limit or vary any express powers of investment contained in the trust instrument and in this connection, it is customary for trustees to be given an unfettered discretion in their selection of investment.

Section 2(1) of the Act provides a trustee shall not have power to make or retain any wider-range investment, unless the trust fund has been divided into two parts known as the 'narrower-range part' and the 'wider-range part'. The parts must be equal in value at the time of the division, and where such a division has been made, no subsequent division of the same fund shall be made and no property transferred from one part of the fund to the other unless:

a. the transfer is required by the Act, or
b. a compensating transfer (i.e. a transfer in the opposite direction of property of equal value) is made at the same time.

At the time of division, the two parts must be equal in value but invariably, they will become unequal both by fluctuations in market values and the operation of some of the following further provisions of section 2.

Section 2 goes on to provide that property of the narrower-range part shall only be invested in narrower-range investments, and if property invested in any other manner becomes comprised in this part, it shall be re-invested in narrower-range investments or transferred to the wider-range part of the fund with a compensating transfer.

If trustees wish to make an advance to a beneficiary under section 32, Trustee Act 1925, the trustees can withdraw property from either part of the fund; in these circumstances, no compensating transfer will be necessary.

A reversionary interest is not included in the original division of the fund so that, when the reversion falls into possession or when it is sold and proceeds are received, each part of the fund must receive an equal share.

First Schedule

The First Schedule defines the categories of investment as:

Part I: Narrower-range not requiring advice: National Savings Certificates, National Savings Bank, etc.

Part II: Narrower-range investments requiring advice: fixed interest securities, loans to local authorities, debentures with specified United Kingdom companies, special deposits with building societies, etc.

Part III: Wider-range investments: building societies shares, shares in United Kingdom quoted companies who have a total issue and paid up share capital of at least £1m and who have paid a dividend on all shares for the previous five years.

Second Schedule

The Second Schedule deals with special-range property, and covers any property represented by any extension in the will or settlement of the statutory powers.

As mentioned above, the Act does not authorize the purchase of land as an investment. The acquisition of land producing no income would not be regarded as an investment at all and would never be authorized even if a very wide investment clause was specified.

If trustees sell land, it is possible that they cease to have the power to purchase further land (*Re Wakeman* (1945)). However, given that the proceeds of sale of the land remain identifiable until suitable replacement land is found, quite possibly the power to invest in land is not lost (*Re Wellsted's Will Trust* (1949)).

To avoid these problems, most wills and settlements contain an express power authorizing trustees to purchase land other than on an investment basis, particularly authorizing the purchase of a house for a beneficiary to occupy.

Special-range property is required to be carried to a separate part of the fund. If it is converted into property other than special-range property it must be transferred to the narrower- or wider-range parts of the fund, as the case may be, but so that the separate parts of the fund are increased or decreased by an equal amount. This can be achieved either by dividing the proceeds of sale equally between the two parts or by using compensating transfers.

A trustee may invest in investments comprised in Parts I and II of the First Schedule – narrower-range investments – at any time but so far as investments contained in Part II – narrower-range investments requiring advice – and Part III – wider-range investments – are concerned he must obtain proper advice from a proper person as to diversification and suitability of the investment proposed. Such person must be reasonably believed by him to be qualified *by his ability in and practical experience of financial matters* to advise as to whether the investments are satisfactory. If such advice is not obtained in writing it must be confirmed in writing for the purposes of the Act.

The provisions regarding the changes in investments which will occur from time to time are quite logical.

a. If changes occur in the *same range* of investments in any part of the trust fund no adjustment between parts is necessary.
b. If wider-range investments become included in investments of the narrower-range part of the trust fund they must be transferred to the wider-range part of the trust fund with a compensating transfer, or sold and the proceeds reinvested in narrower-range investments as soon as possible. There is no such obligation if narrower-range investments become comprised in the wider-range part of the trust fund.
c. A *compensating transfer* simply means a transfer of investments of equal value between the two parts of the trust fund concerned. It will happen most often when investments of the wider-range class are bought out of funds of the narrower-range

class or otherwise acquired and narrower-range investments are held in the wider-range part. If no such investments are held in the wider-range part of course no such transfer can be made and the only alternative is to *sell* the wider-range investments *and re-invest the proceeds* in narrower-range investments. The following example explains how this could occur. £1,000 Government Stock held in the narrower-range part of a trust fund becomes due for redemption at 101 and as narrower-range investments to the value of £2,000 are held in the wider-range part, the trustees, *after taking proper advice*, decide to invest in stock comprised in wider-range investments. The value of such stock which they purchase is £995. As this cannot be retained in the narrower-range part, narrower-range investments to the value of £995 must be *transferred from the wider-range part to the narrower-range part in exchange for the wider-range investment that has been bought*.

d. If property accrues to a part of the trust fund *by reason of the* trustees' ownership or former ownership of property in that part then *the accrual will belong to the same part of the trust fund*. This covers a bonus issue or a beneficial rights issue by providing that the issue shall belong to the same part of the trust fund as the investments in respect of which it is made.

e. In any other cases an accrual is to go in *equal shares* to the narrower-range and wider-range parts. In order to do this it may be necessary to sell one-half of the accrual and re-invest the proceeds in the appropriate range of investments, or it may be possible to apply the whole to its appropriate part and make a compensating transfer equal to one-half of its value. This provision covers such property which would have been divided in equal parts *had it been available for division when the trust fund was divided*, such as special-range property being converted into investments of other than special-range property, or a reversionary interest which is not to be taken into account for purposes of the division of the trust fund until it falls into possession or is sold.

f. The Act contains provision for property contained in the narrower-range or wider-range parts becoming special-range property to be transferred to the special-range part of the trust fund, without any compensating transfer or adjustment. The possibility of this happening would seem very remote.

A further important provision is that *costs of a capital nature* may be paid wholly out of any part or out of each part in such proportions as the trustees decide.

The trustees' discretion as to the choice of property to be taken out of a fund under the trust instrument remains unfettered.

If a fund is to be set aside *after* division of the trust fund, provision is made for it to be constituted of narrower-range and wider-range investments of actual value or of values *proportionate to the value at that time* of the narrower-range and wider-range parts of the trust fund.

Example

David Morton died on 30 June 1986 and administration was completed by the 31 January 1987 at which date the estate comprised the following investments:

	£
5,000 Marks Brothers plc £1 ordinary shares	7,500
£8,000 London County Council 3 per cent stock	3,060
£800 Agricultural Mortgage Corporation 4½ per cent debenture stock	600
6,000 Blandbury Co Ltd 5 per cent debenture stock (registered in UK)	4,800
6,000 Blandbury £1 ordinary shares (incorporated in UK, issued and paid-up capital £1 m, all dividends paid each year)	7,200
1,000 Unit Trusts – £1 units	1,250
500 Lonum Building Society £1 shares	505
3,500 Jaspers Co Ltd 50p ordinary shares net proceeds of sale	2,585

A reversionary interest valued at £6,000 on 30 June 1986 formed part of the estate. The will authorized the trustees to retain the ordinary shares of Marks Brothers for so long as they required, but subject to this power it directed them to convert the estate into authorized securities which were to be held in trust for the benefit of the widow for life with remainder over to the children.

The trustees decided to take advantage of the Trustee Investments Act 1961 in order to avail themselves of the wider investment powers. They obtained *proper advice* in accordance with the Act, the only investment deemed not suitable being Jaspers Co Ltd ordinary shares which were sold.

On the 11 February 1987 the trust fund was valued and divided in accordance with the Act. The fund would be divided as follows:

Residuary trust fund
Special-range property   £
    5,000 Marks Brothers plc £1 ordinary shares   7,500

    (Special power contained in the will)
Narrower-range investments

	£
£8,000 London County Council 3 per cent stock	3,060
£800 Agricultural Mortgage Corporation, 4½ per cent debenture stock	600
£6,000 Blandbury Co Ltd 5 per cent debenture stock	4,800
Cash (part proceeds of sale of Jaspers Co Ltd shares)	1,540
	£10,000

Wider-range investments

	£
6,000 Blandbury Co Ltd £1 ordinary shares	7,200
1,000 unit trusts – £1 units	1,250
500 Lonum Building Society Co Ltd £1 shares	505
Cash (part proceeds of sale of Jaspers Co Ltd shares)	1,045
	£10,000

Note:
1. The available cash of £1,540 in the narrower-range part would be invested in narrower-range investments and the £1,045 cash in the wider-range part would be invested in wider-range investments.
2. If the reversionary interest fell into possession during the life-tenancy, or if it was sold, its value or the proceeds of sale would accrue to the narrower-range and wider-range parts of the trust fund in *equal shares*.

Section 1 of the House Purchase and Housing Act 1959 gives the Chief Registrar of Friendly Societies power to 'designate' a permanent building society, as a result of which a trustee may invest with such society not more than £10,000 for any one trust.

Section 4 of the Trustee Act 1925 provides that a trustee shall not be liable for any breach of trust by reason only of his continuing to hold an investment which has ceased to be authorized by the trust instrument or by the general law. This section applies to all investments authorized when they were made, and the trustees will thus avoid liability for any subsequent depreciation.

Section 4 of the Trustee Act 1925 above, is now modified in terms by section 2 of the Trustee Investments Act 1961. If the retention of an investment is contrary to the paramount requirement of an even balance between the narrower- and wider-range parts of the fund a trustee will not be safe unless he remedies the position.

A direction is sometimes given to trustees 'to invest in investments of whatsoever nature and wheresoever, which they, in their absolute discretion, think fit, and as if they were absolute owners.' It was held that such a direction allows the trustees to go outside the statutory list of securities and, for example, purchase real property: *Re Wragg* (1919).

Section 2 of the Trustee Act 1925 provides that a trustee may hold until redemption any redeemable stock or security which may have been acquired in accordance with the powers of this Act.

Section 7 of the Trustee Act provides that, unless prohibited by the trust instrument, trustees may retain or invest in securities payable to bearer, which, if not so payable, would have been authorized investments, provided that such securities must, until they are sold, be deposited by them with a bank for safe custody and collection of income. The trustees shall not be responsible for any loss incurred by reason of such deposit, and any sum payable in respect of such deposit and collection shall be paid out of the income of the trust property.

A direction that shares shall be retained in the hands of trustees does not operate as a prohibition for the purposes of section 7.

Although section 15 of the Trustee Investments Act 1961 maintains the court's power to vary investments, the cases of *Re Cooper's Settlement, Cooper* v. *Cooper* (1961) and *Re Porritt's Will Trusts* (1961) establish the court's reluctance to give trustees powers of investment wider than those contained in the Act.

Mortgage securities

A trustee may invest trust moneys in mortgages of freeholds or leaseholds of sixty years or more in the United Kingdom provided he carries out the provisions of section 8 of the Trustee Act 1925.

Under this section, if trust moneys are lent on the security of land or other property on which the trustee can properly lend, the trustee must, if he wishes to escape personal liability for a consequential loss, obtain a report upon the value of the property from some person whom he reasonably believes to be an able practical surveyor or valuer. The surveyor or valuer must be instructed and employed independently of any owner of the property, and the loan must be made under the advice of such surveyor or valuer, as expressed in the report, and not more than two-thirds of the stated value of the property should be advanced. If, however, the trustee advances more than two-thirds of the stated value and a loss occurs through depreciation, the security may be regarded as authorized for two-thirds of the stated value, and the trustee will be liable to make good only the sum advanced in excess, with interest (section 9).

Shares in limited companies

Section 10 of the Trustee Act 1925 also provides that where securities of a company are subject to a trust, the trustees may agree to any arrangement for the reconstruction or amalgamation of the company, for the sale of the undertaking to another company; or for the release or alteration of the rights or liabilities attaching to the securities, as if they were entitled to such securities beneficially; and may accept any securities of the reconstructed or purchasing company in exchange for the securities previously held, without incurring personal liability.

If upon such an amalgamation shares in the purchasing company are issued in return for shares in the company purchased, such shares will be authorized securities to the extent that the original shares were authorized.

Where preferential rights to subscribe for further shares in the company are given in respect of the trust securities, the trustees may either exercise the right out of capital, or renounce the right, or assign it for the best consideration obtainable, such consideration being capital. In any such case if they act in good faith, they will not be responsible for any loss caused by their action.

Shares in private companies

Trustees must exercise considerable care holding a controlling interest in a private company. They should ensure that they receive such information about the company's progress as directors would receive. To allow a company to be administered by minority shareholders and obtain only such information as shareholders are entitled to will render the trustees liable should the company fail: *Re Lucking's Will Trusts; Renwick* v. *Lucking and Another* (1967).

ELECTION

The equitable doctrine of election means that if *A* by will or deed gives to *B* property belonging to *C* and by the same will or deed gives to *C* other property belonging to himself (*A*), there is an intention implied that the gift to *C* shall take place only if *C* elects to permit the gift to *B* to take effect also. *C* can either take under the instrument, in which case *B* will take *C*'s property and *C* will take *A*'s, or he can take against the instrument, in which case *C* will lose the gift of *A*'s property to the extent required to compensate *B* for the latter's disappointment. Thus, if *A* by his will gives to *B* property worth £20,000, belonging to *C*, and by the same will gives *C* a legacy of £30,000, *C*, if he elects against the instrument, will keep his own property and also receive £10,000 of the legacy, the remaining £20,000 going to *B* as compensation.

The case of *Re Edwards, MacAdam* v. *Wright* (1957) very clearly illustrates the principles of election, which are:

a. that there should be an intention on the part of the testator to dispose of certain property;
b. that the property should not, in fact, be the testator's own property;
c. that a benefit should be given by the will to the true owner of the property.

The doctrine does not apply where a testator in his will makes *separate* gifts of his *own* property. If, in such a case, one gift is beneficial and the other onerous, the donee may take the former and reject the latter.

CONVERSION

The equitable doctrine of conversion is based on the maxim, 'Equity looks on that as done which ought to be done.' It means that money directed to be employed in the purchase of land is to be considered as real property, and that land directed to be sold and turned into money is to be considered as personal property. Thus conversion turns realty into personalty and personalty into realty. The doctrine operates in four cases:

a. in the case of partnership property, where partnership land is treated as personal estate because on dissolution the land will have to be sold and the proceeds divided among the partners;
b. where the court makes an order for the sale of real estate in which several persons have equal shares, in which case the share of any one of them that dies before the sale becomes part of the deceased's personal estate;
c. when trustees are directed to sell or purchase real estate, in which case the property is regarded as converted from the moment when the instrument comes into force; and
d. when there is a binding contract to sell realty, in which case the realty is treated as part of the vendor's personalty from the date of the contract.

Exercise 7

1. What is a trust? What are the 'three certainties' in relation to trusts?
2. Explain the following terms: protective trust; life tenant; remainderman; resulting trust.
3. How do personal representatives differ from trustees?
4. In what different ways may a trustee be appointed?
5. What are the duties of trustees?
6. What are the discretionary powers of trustees? Are they subject to any control?
7. What are the statutory powers of trustees? In what cases may a personal representative or a trustee receive remuneration for his care and trouble?
8. What is meant by the right of following trust property? How far is it accurate to say that the rule in *Clayton's Case* does not apply to dealings in trust funds?
9. Define a charitable trust. In what respects does it differ from a private trust?
10. Can a trustee with power to invest in 'real securities' purchase land?
11. What restrictions are there on the power of trustees to advance money on the security of property?
12. What is meant by the equitable doctrine of (a) election, (b) conversion?
13. Salmon and Fisher are seeking to invest £80,000 which has come into their hands as trustees. They are considering the following possibilities:
    a. purchase of a detached freehold house which the only beneficiary interested in income would like to occupy;
    b. loan on the security of a mortgage bearing interest at 5 per cent on a house and shop held under a lease for 99 years;
    c. purchase of New Zealand 3¼ per cent stock.
    The sum required in each is £8,000. The transactions (a) and (b) are both recommended by the surveyor to the trustees. Advise Salmon and Fisher.

8
Distribution of Assets

Having paid all the debts of the deceased, it is necessary for the personal representatives to distribute the balance of the estate among those entitled to it according to the terms of the will or the laws of intestacy. As stated earlier, gifts made by will may be either legacies of personal estate or devises of real estate.

LEGACIES

Legacies are of various types and it is important to determine the exact class to which a legacy belongs. The various classes comprise the following.

a. *General legacies*, i.e. gifts which cannot be identified specifically, e.g. a gift of £100. General pecuniary legacies are payable out of the personal estate alone: *Re Rowe, Bennetts* v. *Eddy* (1941).
b. *Specific legacies* are gifts of specific assets which can be identified precisely, e.g. 'a gift of my horse Dobbin', or 'all my shares in British Telecom'.
c. *Demonstrative legacies* are gifts of money payable out of a specific fund, e.g. '£1,000 payable out of my holding of ICI shares'.

There are other classifications of legacies, as follows.

a. *Vested legacies* are gifts of personal estate payable in any event, though the time of payment may be postponed, e.g. '£500 to *X* payable on his attaining 18'. Should *X* die before attaining 18, the legacy will be payable to his estate.
b. *Contingent legacies* are gifts of personal estate payable on the happening of a specified but uncertain event, e.g. '£500 to *X* provided that he attains 18'. If *X* should die before attaining 18, unless the bequest has a gift over to a remainderman, the legacy will revert to the estate of the testator.

 Conditions other than the attaining of a certain age can exist. For example, a condition of total restraint of marriage is void but a gift with partial restraint is valid, e.g. a condition that the legatee should not marry a person of certain religious persuasion. A gift to a surviving spouse until remarriage is valid.

 In *Re Parrott's Will Trusts* (1946), where the plaintif was left property by a testator on condition that by deed poll he altered his Christian name and surname, it was held that, since no one could alter or part with a Christian name by deed poll, the condition was void, and the plaintiff was absolutely entitled to the property.
c. *Cumulative legacies* are gifts of personal estate to the same person, additional to one previously given, e.g. a gift by codicil to *X* of a gold watch, following a gift to *X* by will of £500.

d. *Residuary legacies* are gifts of whole or part of the residue of any estate after payment of all debts, taxes and other classes of legacy.

Where there is an inconsistency between the words and figures relating to the amount of a legacy, the latter of the two inconsistent provisions prevails. Thus, in *Re Hammond, Hammond* v. *Treharne* (1938), where the testator bequeathed 'to Miss May's Mission, Great Arthur Street, London, the sum of One hundred pounds (£500)', it was held that the legacy must be regarded as one of £500.

Legacies of 'money and jewellery'

The word 'money' when used in a will is generally construed in the strict sense as cash of which payment could be claimed immediately at the testator's death, such as the balance of his account at the bank. There are cases in which a wider construction has been placed on the term, but in all of these there has been something in the context to indicate an intention on the part of the testator that this should be so. Thus, a gift of 'money remaining after payment of debts' in a will where there was no other residuary gift was held to pass the residuary personalty; and such words in such circumstances have been held to pass all property liable to the payment of debts. The meaning of 'money' is a matter of construction of the particular will. In *Re Hodgson, Nowell* v. *Flannery* (1935), it was held that where a testator possessed cash at a bank and some National Savings Certificates, the latter did not pass under a bequest of 'my money'.

In *Re Morgan, Perrin* v. *Morgan* (1943) a wider construction was placed on the term 'money'. The testatrix in this case, after making specific bequests, provided that 'all moneys' of which she should die possessed should be shared by her nephews and nieces, there being no other residuary gift. The estate consisted of investments, dividends, rents, household goods and small freehold properties. The House of Lords, reversing the decision of the Court of Appeal, held that the expression, 'all moneys', in this particular will must not be construed strictly according to the old rule but must be interpreted widely to cover all the net personalty of the estate, including the investments and household goods.

'Moneys' in the bank would cover such items as cash on both current and deposit accounts and traveller's cheques, but not share certificates, savings certificates and such other items where proof of title is involved: *Re Trundle* (1960).

'Jewellery' covers precious stones, or jeweller's work of an ornamental character designed for the adornment of the person, but does not include utilitarian articles such as plain gold watches, pencil cases or cigarette cases unless specially ornamented or jewelled: *Re Pulley, Midland Bank* v. *Carter* (1948).

Disclaimer

A legatee is not bound to accept a legacy. If he disclaims the gift, the subject-matter falls into residue. If, however, the gift is one of residue, the subject matter devolves as upon an intestacy.

ABATEMENT

For the purposes of the abatement of estates rules already discussed (see pp. 50–52), demonstrative legacies are in the same position as, and abate with, specific legacies, to the extent that they can be satisfied out of the specified fund.

It may happen that the fund available for general legacies is only utilized partially for debts so that something remains for the general legatees, although not sufficient to pay them in full. In this case, the general legacies must abate *pari passu* among themselves, i.e. they are all reduced proportionately:

$$\frac{\text{Fund available}}{\text{Total amount of general legacies}} \text{ of the legacy bequeathed.}$$

Thus, if in the above case X was left £1,500, he would receive from the personal representative:

$$\frac{5,000}{10,000} \text{ of £1,500} = \text{£750.}$$

A similar process may have to be applied among the specific devises and legacies if the fund available for the general legacies has been entirely exhausted and debts still remain unpaid, though in such a case, of course, the general legatees would get nothing, as specific legacies cannot abate until the fund out of which general legacies should be paid has been entirely exhausted.

The capital value of an annuity is treated as a general legacy for purposes of abatement, and thus annuities abate rateably with the other general legacies.

The treatment of a demonstrative legacy in respect of abatement depends on whether the fund out of which it is payable is existent or non-existent. If the fund exists, a demonstrative legacy abates after general legacies but at the same time as specific legacies. If, however, the fund is non-existent, a demonstrative legacy ranks as a general legacy and abates as such. If the fund exists but is insufficient to meet the demonstrative legacy in full, then that part of the legacy which can be met out of the fund will rank with specific legacies for the purpose of abatement, whilst the balance of the legacy will rank as a general legacy for this purpose. It follows therefore that the circumstances of each particular case will determine how a demonstrative legacy is to be treated where abatement is involved.

The forgiveness by will of a debt owing to the testator is a specific legacy and is not liable to abate with the general legacies; *Re Wedmore* (1907). But a legacy given in satisfaction of a debt is a general legacy. Where the will authorizes the personal representative to charge for his services, this is a general legacy and will be subject to abatement, unless the will otherwise directs.

ADEMPTION

If a testator by will leaves a specific article or fund to a legatee, but before his death sells or otherwise disposes of the article or fund, the legacy is said to be adeemed and the legatee will get nothing. For example, if a testator bequeaths his collection of snuff-boxes to a legatee and before his death sold his collection, the legatee would get nothing, not even the proceeds of sale.

Where stocks and shares have been bequeathed by a testator and prior to his death have changed in form, e.g. under a capital reorganization, the legacy is adeemed if new shares give the deceased an interest in an entirely different undertaking: *Kuypers* v. *Kuypers* (1925) and *Slater* v. *Slater* (1907).

Ademption is also effected by the exercise, even after the testator's death, of an option to purchase the subject-matter of a specific legacy. In *Re Carrington* (1931) a testator by his will gave certain shares to *A*. He afterwards gave *B* an option to purchase the shares within one month after his death. It was held that the legacy to *A* was adeemed by the exercise of the option by B and that the proceeds of the sale went to the residuary legatee and not to A.

The ademption rule can, however, apply only to a specific legacy, and not to a general or demonstrative legacy. Thus, if A bequeaths to C '£1,000 payable out of my holding of 3½ per cent War Loan Stock', and to Y '£1,000 (nominal) of my 2½ per cent Consolidated Stock', and sells both investments before his death, the demonstrative legacy to X will become a general legacy, ranking as such for purposes of abatement, while the legacy to Y will be construed as a specific legacy.

Section 35 of the Administration of Estates Act 1925 provides that an interest in property left by will subject to a charge for payment of money shall be primarily liable for the payment of that charge, subject to a contrary contention in the will. Thus, if A devises to B a farm subject to a mortgage of £20,000, the farm will become primarily liable for the mortgage if B accepts the gift and B cannot claim to have the debt paid by the estate in the absence of express instructions to do so.

SATISFACTION

The doctrine of satisfaction is very technical and the comments below comprise merely an outline of its application.

Satisfaction means a transfer of property which is in fact accepted by the donee and operates in law as a complete discharge of a previous legal liability of the donor. The concept is based upon the disinclination of equity to allow any person to be paid the same debt twice. The rule applies principally in the following circumstances.

a. Where a testator leaves the legacy to a person to whom he owes the debt, equity will presume that the legacy was given in satisfaction of the debt and will allow the legatee to claim both.

   The debt will not be deemed to be satisfied by the legacy where the legacy is less than the debt or where the debt was contracted after the making of the will or where the will contains, as is customary, an express direction for the payment of debts or of both debts and legacies.

b. Where two legacies of equal amount are given in the same instrument and the same motive is expressed for each or no motive for either, a presumption arises that only one legacy was intended, and there will accordingly be satisfaction of one by the other. Even if they are given in different instruments, there will still be satisfaction if the legacies are identical both in amount and in respect of motive.

c. Where a testator by will gives a portion to a child and at a later date makes an advancement to that child, the portion is presumed to have been *pro tanto* adeemed by the advancement; and where a testator binds himself to give a portion to a child and afterwards makes a gift by will to that child, the legacy will be held to have satisfied the obligation.

Satisfaction by advancement is the most important example of the concept and requires further comment.

An advancement is a grant to a beneficiary of a part of his share of capital before the time fixed for his entitlement of an absolute interest in possession. There is an equitable rule against double portions based on the assumption that a parent wishes to provide for his children equally. If A leaves a legacy of £5,000 to his son and before his death, gives the son £4,000, the son will only be able to claim £1,000 under the will as the advancement is presumed to have adeemed the legacy in part.

It must be emphasized that this is only a presumption and that if evidence can be produced to show that the testator intended the legatee to receive both sums, the rule will not be applied.

The rule only applies where the testator stands *in loco parentis* to the legatee. If therefore, a testator leaves a legacy of £500 to a friend and later makes a gift of £500 to that friend, the latter could claim the full legacy as the rule will not apply.

LAPSE

If a beneficiary predeceases the testator, the gift will usually lapse and the subject matter of the lapsed legacy will fall into residue so that the residuary beneficiary will take an additional benefit.

An important exception to the doctrine of lapse is contained in section 33, Wills Act 1837, as amended by the Administration of Justice Act 1982. The combined effect of these provisions is to specify that where a devise or bequest is made to a child or remoter descendant of the testator and that child or remoter descendant predeceases the testator leaving issue and such issue are living at the testator's death, subject to a contrary intention in the will, the devise or bequest shall take effect in favour of the issue living at the testator's death.

In the case of class gifts, e.g. a gift of a legacy to be divided 'among all the children of *A*' the issue of any child who predeceases *A* will take in substitution *per stirpes*. This is catered for by section 32(2) of the amended Wills Act 1837.

COMMORIENTES

It may happen that spouses might die in the same disaster, e.g. an aeroplane crash, and it may become necessary to determine which has survived the other. For example, a husband may leave everything to his wife by will and they may be both killed in the same accident. If the wife predeceased the husband, the residuary legacy will lapse. If on the other hand, the husband predeceased the wife, the residuary legacy would go to the beneficiaries under the wife's will or to those persons entitled under her intestacy.

Section 184 of the Law of Property Act 1925 provides that where two or more persons have died in circumstances rendering it uncertain which of them survived the other, such deaths shall be presumed to have occurred in order of seniority so that the younger will be deemed to have survived the older. In *Re Dellow's Will Trusts, Lloyds Bank Limited* v. *Institute of Cancer Research and Others* (1964), a husand and wife were found dead from gas poisoning and the court was unable to decide which survived the other so it was held that the wife, being the younger, was deemed to have survived. (As an incidental, however, it was held further in that case that the wife was guilty of manslaughter of the husband with the result that she was excluded from benefiting from his estate.)

In *Re Grosvenor, Peacey* v. *Grosvenor* (1944) two brothers sheltering in the basement of a house were killed by the same bomb. The court held that the benefit of the presumption under section 184 could be claimed successfully only if the court were satisfied that the proper inference from the facts was that the deaths were consecutive and that the circumstances rendered it uncertain which death took place first. In the case in question, the proper inference was that the brothers died simultaneously. On appeal to the House of Lords, it was held that where it could not be said for certain which of two deceased persons had died first, the older must be presumed to have died first. All that was necessary to invoke the statutory presumption was the presence in the circumstances of an element of uncertainty. In the case in question, nobody could know. The statutory presumption contained in section 184, therefore, applied.

In the case of an intestacy, there is an express exception to the operation of section 184. Section 1(4) of the Intestates' Estates Act 1952 provides that where an intestate and his wife (or her husband) die on or after the 1 January 1953, in such circumstances that it is uncertain which of the deaths occurred first, the estate will be dealt with as if the former, i.e. the intestate spouse, had left no surviving spouse.

THE TWO CERTAINTIES

Another cause of the failure of a legacy is uncertainty for all gifts must be certain as to the property transferred and certain as to the person to be benefitted.

If there is any ambiguity upon either of these points, the legacy may fail. Where either point is doubtful, the court will endeavour to discover the true intention of the testator by applying the rules laid down for the interpretation of documents. If, however, it is quite impossible to arrive at any definite conclusion, the legacy must fail for uncertainty.

However, where the will applies equally to any one of several persons, extrinsic evidence is admissible to show which one the testator meant. Thus, where a testator left one house to 'George Gord the son of George Gord', and another to 'George Gord the son of John Gord', and another to 'George Gord the son of Gord', extrinsic evidence was admitted to show who was intended to take the last house.

LEGACIES TO A CLASS

In the case of class gifts, e.g. 'to my children', it is essential to be able to determine when the legacy becomes effective. Rules known as the 'class closing rules' have therefore evolved as follows.

a. If a specific sum, e.g. £100,000, is to be divided among a class, the date when the class is established depends upon whether the gift is to take effect immediately on the testator's death, or at some future time. If the former, the class is established immediately and all those persons then living or *en ventre sa mère* will benefit. If the latter, e.g. the testator's leaves £100,000 on trust for his son for life with the capital to be divided thereafter among such of his son's children as have attained 18, the class is established when the first child attains 18. Any child born before that date can claim a share: *Re Paul* (1920).

b. If the total amount of the legacy is dependent upon the number of members of the class, e.g. where the testator leaves £500 'to each of my grandchildren', the class is established upon the death of the testator, whether the gift is immediate or postponed.

c. The decision in *Elliot* v. *Joicey* (1935) establishes that a gift 'to such of the children of X shall survive me' includes only the children alive at the death of the testator, excluding, generally, even a child *en ventre sa mère*.

CHARITABLE LEGACIES

The rules of lapse and uncertainty are not applied as strictly in the case of charitable legacies as they are to other cases. If the court is of the opinion that the will displayed an intention to be generally charitable rather than to benefit particular charities, even if the legacy cannot be carried out as specified, the court will not allow it to lapse or fail for uncertainty. The funds will be applied *cy-près* or 'as nearly as possible' in accordance with the wishes of the testator. This concept is known as the doctrine of *cy-près*.

For example, if a testator bequeaths £200,000 to endow a cottage hospital at 'Littletown' and no hospital is needed there, the court would apply the legacy *cy-près*. In *Re Knox, Fleming* v. *Carmichael* (1936), a testatrix left part of her estate to a 'nursing home' that did not exist and had never existed. It was held that, as her whole will displayed a general charitable intention, the gift should be applied *cy-près*.

From the above, it is clear that, provided the court can find a general charitable intention in the will of the testator, the charitable gift would be applied *cy-près* and not allowed to lapse.

The court may also vary the terms of a bequest in following the *cy-près* doctrine, as was demonstrated in *Re Lysaght Deceased* (1965). Here the bequest of a sum of money to found medical studentships to the Royal College of Surgeons was coupled with a proviso that no such student should be of Jewish or Roman Catholic faith. This made the gift unacceptable to the College and the bequest therefore impracticable, and the court made an order omitting the discriminating words in order to give effect to the testatrix's paramount charitable intention.

LEGACIES TO MINORS OR PERSONS ABROAD

Section 42 of the Administration of Estates Act 1925 provides that where a minor is absolutely entitled under a will to a devise or legacy, or to the residue of the deceased's estate, and such devise, legacy or residue is not devised or bequeathed to trustees for the minor, the personal representative of the deceased may appoint a trust corporation, *or* not fewer than two nor more than four individuals, to be trustees of the minor's interest. The same applies where a minor is absolutely entitled on an intestacy to a share in the deceased's residuary estate. The personal representative may appoint himself as one of the trustees. Upon delivery of the funds to such trustees, the personal representative is discharged from all further liability in respect of the minor's interest, which may be retained in its existing form or converted into money and invested in trustee securities. The section applies only where the gift or share is *absolute*, and has no application where it is *contingent*. Thus, since the interests which the issue of a deceased take on his intestacy are held upon the statutory trusts and so are *contingent* upon the attainment of the age of majority or upon marriage below that age, the section does not apply to them.

Alternatively, under section 63 of the Trustee Act 1925 the personal representative may free himself from all responsibility by paying the amount of the legacy into court. In this case, he should obtain from the commissioners of Inland Revenue directions to the Bank of England to receive the amount of the legacy and place it to the account of the Accountant-General for the credit of the minor. The cost of this procedure falls upon residue, but the cost of getting the legacy out of court falls upon the legacy when it is claimed by the beneficiary.

If the minor is a foreign national, the money may be paid out to him upon his attaining full age according to the law of his domicile, although he may still be a minor according to English law (*Re Schnapper* (1928)), but if the beneficiary is a minor by both English and foreign law, the legacy must be dealt with in accordance with English law.

Where the will appoints trustees, or leaves the legacy in trust for the minor, no difficulty will arise, as the legacy is left to the trustees named.

Where a legacy is left to a person who is absent from this country, the procedure set out in section 63 of the Trustee Act should be adopted, and the moneys paid into court by the trustees.

Maintenance from trust funds

Section 31 of the Trustee Act 1925 contains machinery allowing trustees to provide a minor with 'maintenance' out of the trust funds, subject to certain conditions.

Section 31 provides that where property is held by trustees for any person, whether such person's interest is absolute, or vested, or merely contingent, during the minority of such person, the trustees may, at their discretion, apply for his maintenance, education, or benefit, the whole or part of the income of the property. They may do so even if other funds are available for the same purpose or any person is bound by law to provide for the minor's maintenance or education. In the case of a contingent interest, however, this section applies only if the trust carries the intermediate income of the property. Under section 175 of the Law of Property Act 1925, the intermediate income is carried by a contingent or future specific devise or bequest, including a residuary devise or bequest, to trustees upon trust for persons whose interests are contingent or executory, subject to the statutory provisions relating to accumulations, except so far as such income, or any part thereof, may be otherwise expressly disposed of. A trust does not carry the intermediate income when there is a direction to accumulate: *Re Reade-Revell* (1830); *Re Stapleton* (1946).

In the case of a *contingent pecuniary legacy* which does not come under the head of a specific bequest, the rule will not, however, apply, unless the will indicates that the legacy 'carries the intermediate income', so that if a legacy is left 'to *X* on his attaining the age of 18, but until he attains the age the income is to be paid to *Y*', the trustees could not maintain *X* out of the income. If, however, the contingent legacy is left to a child of the testator or to a person to whom the testator stands *in loco parentis* and the legacy is given contingently on the legatee's attaining 18 or on some event before that age and no other fund is provided for maintenance, the legacy will be held to carry the intermediate income *up to 6 per cent per annum*. A contingent pecuniary legacy will also carry the intermediate income if the legacy is directed to be set apart from the rest of the estate: *Re Raine* (1929).

The rules relating to maintenance can be made more clear by means of some examples. In the examples below, *X* is the testator and *Y* is a minor and in no way related to the testator.

a. *X* leaves *Y* £5,000 to be paid on his attaining 18. This is a vested legacy and the income may be applied towards *Y*'s maintenance.
b. *X* leaves *Y* £5,000 contingently on his attaining 18. No provision is made as to what is to happen to the intermediate income.

 This is a contingent legacy, and no part of the income can be applied towards *Y*'s maintenance. If, however, *X* stood *in loco parentis* to *Y*, then the income on the £5,000 (up to a maximum of £300, i.e. 6 per cent per annum) can be applied towards *Y*'s maintenance.

c. *X* leaves *Y* £5,000 contingently on his attaining 18 and the will provides that the income arising from the £5,000 shall be accumulated and paid to *Y* along with the legacy.

This is a contingent legacy but as the intermediate income belongs to *Y*, it can be used for his maintenance and it makes no difference if *X* did not stand *in loco parentis* to *Y*.

Section 31 goes on to provide that any income not used for the minor's maintenance and which is not given to any other person, must be accumulated and the income resulting therefrom must be held as follows.

a. The minor's interest is vested or if on attaining 18, he becomes absolutely entitled to the property, he will become entitled to accumulations upon attaining 18.
b. In any other case, the accumulations are treated as accretions to capital on the same trusts as those on which the capital is held. But the trustees may, at any time, during the minority of such a person, apply those accumulations or any part thereof, as if they were income arising in the then current year.

ADVANCEMENT OUT OF TRUST FUNDS

Section 32 of the Trustee Act, 1925, provides that the trustees of any property *other than land* (except land held on trust for sale, which is regarded as money) may apply the *capital* moneys of the trust fund for the advancement or benefit of the beneficiary, as they think fit, even if the beneficiary's interest in the capital fund is only contingent upon his attaining a certain age, provided that:

a. not more than one-half of the person's presumptive or vested share shall be so applied; and
b. if the person advanced becomes entitled absolutely to a share of the trust property, the money advanced must be brought into account as part of the share; and
c. if any person is entitled to a prior life or other interest, whether vested or contingent, no advance shall be made to the prejudice of such a person unless he is of full age *and* gives his consent in writing.

In *Re Moxon's Will Trusts* (1958) it was decided that the word 'benefit' includes a payment direct to the beneficiary, but that nevertheless the trustees had to be satisfied that the case was a proper one for a payment to be made in that manner. In a later case, *Re Pilkington's Will Trust* (1961), it was held by the court that an advance must not only be for the benefit of the minor but such benefit must be desirable at the time. The trustees may of course still insist that the funds to be paid over shall be tied up in some manner, but it is clear that all they now have to do is to satisfy themselves that it is in the best interests of the beneficiary to have the capital paid to him and that he is able to handle the money in a proper way.

In *Re Wills' Will Trusts* (1958) it was held that trustees were entitled to make settlements of the trust property on a beneficiary. Thus, if *X* has left £5,000 in trust for *Y*, whether by way of a vested or a contingent legacy, then the trustees may in any case apply up to £2,500 to *Y* for his advancement or benefit, whether or not *Y* is a minor, but subject to the following limitations.

a. If there are persons entitled to prior interests in the £5,000, then their consent must be obtained before the advance is made. Such persons must be in existence and of full age and their consent must be obtained in writing.

b. If *Y* subsequently becomes absolutely entitled to the £5,000, he must bring into account the amount advanced to him.

The modern principle is that 'benefit' includes the discharge on behalf of the beneficiary of his moral or social obligations. Thus in *Re Clore's Settlement Trusts* (1966) the trustees sought the court's sanction to their paying a substantial sum to a charity in discharge of what the beneficiary had accepted, as a wealthy person, was his moral obligation. The beneficiary had thus benefitted by being relieved of an obligation which would otherwise have been discharged from his own pocket.

Re Pauling's Settlement Trusts (1963) is a case which is of vital importance to trust corporations. It illustrates a number of pitfalls of which corporate trustees especially should beware. A trustee department of a long-established bank had made a number of advances over the years at the request of the minor beneficiaries' father, and were challenged on the grounds of validity of these advances, but not in one instance was the honesty of the bank or the officials of its trustee department brought into question.

One paramount principle of administration appears to be that where the consent of a beneficiary in whose favour advancement had been exercised is given, but in circumstances making it a breach of trust, the court must consider all the circumstances of his consent and concurrence and if it is not fair or equitable that he should sue the trustees, he would have no action.

As mentioned above, section 32 limits the power of advancement to not more than one-half of the person's presumptive share. If the will is silent, section 32 applies by implication and will only not apply if negatived expressly in the will. It is customary for a will or settlement to widen the operation of section 32 by including a clause substituting 'the whole of the beneficiary's presumptive share' for the reference to one-half as contained in section 32.

INTEREST ON LEGACIES

A legatee to whom a *general* legacy has been left by will is entitled to claim from the estate interest at the rate of 6 per cent per annum, generally from the time the legacy becomes payable to the actual date of payment. If the will specifically mentions the date of payment, as in the case of a legacy payable at the age of 18, interest runs from that date, *but if there is no particular time specified in the will*, interest does not begin to run until one year after the testator's death, as section 44 of the Administration of Estates Act 1925 provides that a personal representative is not bound to distribute the estate before the expiration of one year from the death. A contingent legacy does not normally carry interest until the contingency has occurred.

Specific legacies, on the other hand, carry interest, or rather income, from the date of the testator's death, but only the income, if any, which is actually earned by the legacy, and out of this income are payable all the necessary expenses incurred in connection with it as from the date of the testator's death. A devise, whether residuary or otherwise, also carries net rents and profits from the date of death.

Demonstrative legacies, like general legacies, carry interest only from the time at which they become payable, but where the fund out of which the legacy is payable exists at the date of death, the demonstrative legacy will carry proportionate income from the fund from the date of death.

There are, however, certain exceptional cases in which *general legacies* carry interest from the date of testator's death, namely:

a. where a legacy is given in satisfaction of a debt upon which interest could be claimed, in which case the rate of interest is the rate agreed on in respect of the debt;
b. where a legacy is given to a minor by his parent or some person who stands *in loco parentis* to him and no other fund is designated for the minor's maintenance, in which case, under section 31 of the Trustee Act 1925, 6 per cent per annum interest is allowed if the available income is sufficient;
c. where the legatee is a minor, and the will shows an intention that the income shall be used for his maintenance, in which case the rate is the maximum earned by the legacy;
d. where a legacy is immediately segregated from the residue, e.g. where it is left 'to trustees on trust . . .', in which case the rate of interest is the rate earned by such part of the residue;
e. where the legacy is charged on land and vested, and the will makes no special provision for payment, in which case the interest is at the rate earned by the land.

ANNUITIES

An annuity is a right to an annual sum of money and ranks as a general pecuniary legacy payable by instalments. If the testator's assets are insufficient for payment of all legacies in full, an annuity will therefore abate rateably with the other general legacies.

In the absence of a contrary direction in the will, a gift of an annuity operates from the testator's death so that the first payment becomes due one year after the death.

Methods of providing for the regular payment of annuities vary depending upon the words expressed in the will. One method is a purchase of an annuity from an institution such as a life assurance company, and the capital sum required for the purchase will vary according to the annuitant's age, state of health, etc. This will be treated as a general legacy and need cause the personal representatives no further trouble. It is only open, however, to the personal representatives to adopt this course of action where the words used express clearly that the executor is to purchase an annuity or to expend so much in the purchase of an annuity.

Conversely, if the will gives no instructions as to the method of providing for the annuity, but simply bequeaths 'an annuity of £500 to *X*', the annuity is a charge upon the residuary estate.

As far as possible, the annuity should be paid out of the income generated from the residue but if this is inadequate, the capital must be drawn upon to make up any deficiency. Any capital so drawn cannot be made good out of surplus income in a succeeding year: *Re Croxon* (1915). It was held in *Re Berkeley, Inglis* v. *Berkeley* (1968) following *Re Croxon* (1915), that beneficiaries in capital were not entitled to be recouped, from surplus income of subsequent years, amounts of capital applied towards paying annuitants in prior years in which income was insufficient to meet the annuities in full.

Thus, where an annuity of £300 is left by will to *Y*, and the income derived from the residue of the estate during three consecutive years amounts to £500, £250 and £400 respectively, £50 will be taken out of capital during the second year to make up the amount of the annuity, but this £50 cannot be transferred back to capital out of surplus income in the third year.

As a matter of convenience, the personal representatives should take advantage of section 41, Administration of Estates Act 1925, which allows the appropriation of any portion of the estate towards the satisfaction of any legacy or other interest including an annuity. It will generally be necessary, however, to obtain the consent of the beneficiary in question. In exercising the power under section 41, The personal representatives must have regard to the respective rights of everybody interested in the deceased's property.

The property appropriated to meet the annuity need not be an investment authorized by law or by the will, but any property duly appropriated under section 41 thereafter becomes an authorized investment and can be retained or dealt with accordingly.

The testator may instruct the personal representatives to appropriate certain property to provide the annuity, in which case the consent of the annuitant is not required.

Particular problems arise in respect of whether the amount of an annuity is expressed in the will to be paid gross (i.e. before deduction of income tax) or net (i.e. after deduction of income tax). Annuities are subject to the deduction of income tax at the basic rate in force at the time of payment. If the will directs that the annuity is to be paid 'free of income tax' then an annuity is paid of such an amount as, after deduction of tax, will leave a specified sum. Thus, the annuitant is assured of a fixed net sum irrespective of the rate of income tax in force.

A number of judicial decisions have clarified this matter and the following rules apply.

a. Where a testator directed the payment of an annuity out of the income of his estate and there was no direction as to payment of income tax, the tax was payable by the annuitant: *Re Sharp* (1906).
b. The same rule applied where the annuity was paid out of a fund from which income tax had been deducted at source before reaching the trustees: *Re Cain's Settlement* (1919).
c. The words 'a clear annuity' were not sufficient to relieve the annuitant of liability to tax: *Re Loveless* (1918).
d. It was not a sufficient direction to give the annuity 'free of all deductions': *Re Well's Will Trusts* (1940). In *Re Hooper, Phillips* v. *Steel* (1943), it was held that under the Income Tax Act 1918 an annuity given by will was paid in part by cash given to the annuitant and in part by satisfaction of the income tax payable in respect of it, and that no 'deduction' was in law or in fact made from it.
e. A testator desiring to free an annuitant from the payment of income tax should use the words 'free of income tax': *Re Reckitt* (1932).

When an annuity is paid 'free of income tax' to an annuitant who is not liable to tax or not liable at the full rate, a claim for repayment of tax should be made, but the annuitant will be required to hand over to the trustees under the will or settlement, out of the sum recovered, an amount which bears the same proportion to the cash value of the annuitant's personal tax allowances as the gross annuity bears to the annuitant's total income: *Re Pettit, Le Fevre* v. *Pettit* (1922). For example, if the annuity is £200 gross and the total income of the annuitant is £300 (all taxed at source), two-thirds of any tax recovered must be paid over to the trustees. If the annuitant declines to make a repayment claim the trustees are entitled to require the annuitant to do so: *Re Kingcome, Hickley* v. *Kingcome* (1936). On the other hand, an annuity of 'such a sum as, after deduction of tax at the basic rate for the time being in force, will leave the clear annual sum of £x' does not come within the rule in *Le Fevre* v. *Pettit* – for the income tax comes in only for the purpose of fixing in each year the amount to be provided – and the annuitant is entitled to retain any tax recovered: *Jones* v. *Jones* (1933).

THE EXECUTOR'S ASSENT

Prior to an assent, whereby the personal representatives vest assets in a beneficiary, the beneficiary's interest in the estate amounts merely to a chose in action which comprises the right to have the deceased's estate administered in good order.

Although a legatee has a right to his legacy, subject to any creditors' claims, that right remains incomplete whilst title to all of the deceased's assets remains vested in the personal representatives. The right of the legatee is not perfected until a title has been transferred to him and this does not happen until the personal representatives have assented to the legacy. Until then, the legatee has no right to retain possession of the legacy as against the personal representatives but as soon as the assent is given, the legacy vests in the legatee.

If the executor chooses to refuse his assent to a legacy, the legacy will not fail or lapse because the right to withhold assent is given to the executor only because the legatee is or may be subject to a creditors' claim. If the legatee can prove that all creditors and others having claims have been paid in full, he can compel the executor to give his assent by application to the court.

Once given an assent cannot be retracted. Devises are also assented to by the personal representative.

The assent does not itself transfer the legal title. If title has to be transferred in a particular form, such as company shares or moneys in a Post Office Savings Bank, etc., then, once the assent has been made, the personal representatives become a trustee of the assets for the beneficiary. The completion of the particular formalities required then vests in question in the beneficiary.

The right of any person to follow the property into the hands of the person in whom it is vested is not prejudiced by the assent, and if the assets are insufficient to pay all the beneficiaries in full and the personal representative nevertheless pays in full a legacy which should have abated, the other beneficiaries can compel a refund to be made by the beneficiary who has been overpaid. But this rule does not apply when, at the time of the payment, the assets were sufficient to pay all the beneficiaries in full and the subsequent deficiency is due to accident or wilful default on the part of the personal representative. If the deficiency is due to accident, then the beneficiary prejudiced by it must suffer the loss, but if it is due to the personal representative's wilful default, then the beneficiary may compel the personal representative to make it good.

Section 38(2), Administration of Estates Act 1925, confers in effect the tracing of property etc. upon the application of a creditor, notwithstanding a previous assent by personal representatives. These rules, however, only apply to persons other than bona fide purchasers for value. If such a purchaser purchases property from the personal representatives or from the person in whom the property is vested by the executor's assent, the court has no power to take the property away from such purchaser. These provisions are contained in sections 37 and 38, Administration of Estates Act 1925.

How assent is given

As mentioned above, the assent itself does not pass the legal title. This being so, the assent of the executor may be given expressly or by implication, and may be effected by any action which shows an intention on the part of the executor to part with his interest in the legacy in favour of the legatee. Each case will depend mainly upon its particular circumstances, but such acts as handing the subject-matter to the legatee, the appropriation of assets to pay a legacy, or even an entry in the books which shows an intention to assent, may be sufficient.

In the case of land, however, the general rule is that the conveyance must be by a deed under section 52(1), Law of Property Act 1925. However, section 36 of the Administration of Estates Act 1925 confers upon the personal representatives, whether executors or administrators, the power to assent to the vesting of any estate or interest in land in any person entitled and whether by devise, bequest, devolution (i.e. under an intestacy), appropriation or otherwise. No stamp duty is payable.

Land includes a leasehold interest. A memorandum of the assent to a devise should be indorsed on the grant of probate.

If there is more than one personal representative, the assent of one only is necessary to the vesting of a legacy, but the assent of all is necessary to the vesting of land. One executor may even assent to the vesting of a legacy in himself. Whilst it is clear that an assent in respect of land must be in writing under section 36(4), Administration of Estates Act 1925, what has not been so clear is whether this formality is essential where the personal representative is to vest land in himself. The decision in *Re King's Will Trust* (1964) held that the same formalities are necessary but there has been criticism of the decision over the last twenty years. However, this appears to be the position at the moment.

EXPENSES REGARDING LEGACIES

The incidence of the costs incurred by the personal representatives in putting a legacy into the hands of the beneficiary has been the subject of several decided cases and the broad principle which has emerged is that the expenses incurred in the personal representative obtaining possession of the legacy are borne by residue while the expenses of handing over the legacy to the legatee fall on the legatee.

In the case of pecuniary legacies there will normally be little expense in making payment. In *Cockerell* v. *Barber* (1810) it was held that the costs in respect of payment such legacies are payable from the residue, so that if a personal representative has to realize securites to pay a legacy the cost of realization is borne by residue, and so is any expense of transferring the money to the legatee. If the legacy has to be paid into court, residue again bears the cost, but when the funds are paid out by the court the legacy suffers the cost: *Re Cawthorne* (1848).

A specific legacy carries with it the income it produces from the date of death to the time it is assented to the legatee and, conversely, any expenses incurred in the upkeep of the gift during this time are payable by the legatee, e.g. expenses in the upkeep of a house and its contents (*Re Rooke*, 1933), or wages paid for the upkeep of a yacht (*Re Pearce*, 1909).

LEGATEE'S RIGHT TO SUE FOR LEGACY

Under the Limitation Act 1939, a legatee or devisee, in the absence of disability, written acknowledgement or part payment as the case may be, must bring his action within twelve years from the date on which the right to receive such legacy or devise accrued. The same applies to an action claiming a share or interest in the estate of a deceased intestate. No action, however, to recover arrears of interest in respect of a legacy, or damages in respect of such arrears, can be brought after the expiration of six years from the date on which the interest became due.

Even if an executor still has the money in his possession, a legatee will be unable after a lapse of twelve years to bring an action to recover the legacy. Where, however, an executor has been constituted a trustee by the will or has made himself an express trustee of the legacy, the legatee must bring his action within six years; but where the legacy is charged on land, the period of limitation will be twelve years. In the case of an intestacy, the personal representative under section 46 of the Administration of Estates Act 1925 becomes an express trustee of the residuary estate. Here also, therefore, a beneficiary's action would in most case be barred after six years.

DONATIONES MORTIS CAUSA

A *donatio mortis causa* ('DMC') is a lifetime gift of pure personal property conditional upon death. If the death does not occur the gift is void. A DMC has some of the similarities of a legacy and some of an *inter vivos* gift.

For a valid DMC, the following must be satisfied.

a. The donor must be expecting death from a cause he cannot avoid. He need not die from the particular disorder from which he was suffering at the date of gift: *Wilkes* v. *Allington* (1931). A gift in contemplation of suicide is not a valid DMC.
b. The property given must be capable of passing so it will therefore comprise pure personal estate. Thus a DMC of freehold or leasehold property cannot be made.

   The cheque of a third party made payable to the deceased may be the subject of a valid DMC even if unindorsed and not negotiated by the donee, but a cheque drawn by the deceased donor will not be an effective *donatio* unless cash or negotiated for value by the donee before the donor's death. Such a gift is in fact a completed gift *inter vivos: Re Owen* (1949).
c. Possession of the property must be transferred to the donee at the time of the gift. In other words, there must be delivery of the subject matter of the gift to the donee or to someone on his behalf.
d. The gift must be conditional upon the donor's death. The condition need not, however, be express.

As a DMC differs from a pure gift *inter vivos* in that it is to take effect only if the donor dies, it may consequently be reclaimed by the donor at any time before his death, but it cannot be revoked by will. If the donor recovers from his illness and does not reclaim the subject-matter of the DMC, it will then be regarded as a gift *inter vivos*.

The importance of distinguishing between a pure gift and a DMC lies in the following point of difference.

a. A DMC can be claimed by the personal representative for payment of the debts of the deceased if the other assets are insufficient. Pure gifts cannot be reclaimed in this manner, unless made with an intention to defraud creditors.
b. A DMC is distinguishable from a legacy in the following respects:
   i. legacies of all classes are subject to the payment of debts before DMC;
   ii. legacies take effect from the date of the testator's death only, while the contingent possession of a DMC passes before death.
   iii. legacies require the executor's assent, while DMCs do not;
   iv. inheritance tax on legacies is payable by the executor, on DMC by the donee;
   v. a DMC may be given by an intestate, whilst a legacy implies the existence of a will.

INTERESTS OF SURVIVING SPOUSE

The Intestates' Estates Act 1952, amending section 47 of the Administration of Estates Act 1925, provides that the surviving spouse may claim to have his or her life interest reclaimed by the payment of a capital sum calculated in accordance with specified rules. The election to have the life interest capitalized must be exercised in writing within twelve months from the grant of representation and section 47(A)(2) of the Administration of Estates Act 1925 lays down a complicated formula for ascertaining the capital value. The strict rules of intestacy can be departed from if the issue entitled under the intestacy are of age and they can enter into an agreement with the surviving spouse which need not conform to the intestacy rules.

HOTCHPOT

The equitable doctrine of satisfaction operates in the case of an intestacy for any advances made by an intestate to his children, since such advances must be brought into account, or hotchpot, if those children are to share in the distribution of the residary estate.

Section 47, Administration of Estates Act 1925, provides that, where an intestate's property is held upon statutory trusts for the issue, any money or property which has been paid to or settled upon any child of the intestate, either by advancement or on the marriage of the child, must be taken into account in total or partial satisfaction of the share which such child can claim upon the death of the parent intestate, subject to the circumstances showing a contrary intention.

Further, where grandchildren obtain a share of an intestate's estate because their parent predeceases the intestate, any advance made to the deceased parent must be brought into hotchpot by the grandchildren. This does not apply, however, to any advances made to the grandchild himself.

No benefit can be derived from the hotchpot by any person who is not a descendant of the intestate, since the purpose of the rule is to equalize the shares of the children. The share of a surviving spouse therefore is deducted before bringing the advances into account.

Example 1

A dies intestate, leaving £65,000 and chattels valued at £600. No widow survives him, but three sons, *B, C* and *D*, all eighteen, are left. During his lifetime, *A* has advanced £3,000 to *B* and £5,000 to *C*. The sums payable to each son are:

	£
Value of the residue	65,600
Advance to *B*	3,000
Advance to *C*	5,000
	73,600

The residue would therefore be shared as follows:

	£	£
B's share, one-third of £73,600	24,533	
Less Advance	3,000	21,533
C's share, one-third of £73,600	24,533	
Less Advance	5,000	

	19,533
D's share, one-third of £73,600	24,534
	65,600

Example 2

As Example 1 but *A* also leaves a widow and two sons only, *X* and *Y*. An advance of £3,000 has been made to *X*.
   The residue will be distributed as follows:

	£	£
Widow — Personal chattels		600
Cash (net)		40,000
Life interest		12,500
		53,100
Value of residue, after making the above deduction		12,500
Advance to *X*		3,000
		£15,500
X's immediate share, one-half of £15,500	7,750	
Less Advance	3,000	
		4,750
Y's immediate share, one-half of £15,500		7,750
		£12,500

On the death of the widow, the amount of £12,500 in which she had a life interest will be shared equally by *X* and *Y*.

Example 3

As Example 2 but *A* leaves two sons *B* and *C*, both over eighteen, plus *E* a grandson aged 16, and the son of a deceased son *D*. Advances of £3,000, £2,000, £1,000 and £1,500 had been made to *B*, *C*, *D* and *E* respectively.
   The residue will be distributed as follows:

	£	£
Widow — Personal chattels		600
Cash (net)		40,000
Life interest		12,500
		£53,100
Value of residue, after making the above deductions		£12,500
	£	
Advance to *B*	3,000	
Advance to *C*	2,000	
Advance to *D*	1,000	
		6,000
		18,500
B's immediate share, one-third of £18,500	6,166	
Less Advance	3,000	
		3,166
C's immediate share, one-third of £18,500	6,167	
Less Advance	2,000	
		4,167
E's immediate share (on statutory trusts), one-third of £18,500	6,167	
Less Advance to deceased parent, *D*	1,000	

5,167
12,500

Note: The advance to *E* himself is ignored.

Example 4

A dies intestate leaving three sons, *X*, *Y* and *Z*. *A*'s estate consists of £14,000. During his lifetime *A* has advanced £4,000 to *X* and £12,000 to *Y*.
　The residue will be distributed as follows:

	£	£
Value of residue		14,000
Advance to *X*		4,000
		£18,000
X's share, one-half of £18,000	9,000	
Less Advance	4,000	
		5,000
Z's share, one-half of £18,000		9,000
		£14,000

Example 5

C dies intestate leaving a widow and three sons, *R*, *S* and *T*. During his lifetime *C* has advanced £9,000 to *R* and £3,000 to *T*. After providing for the personal chattels and £40,000 due to the widow, £24,000 remains for distribution.
　The residue would be distributed as follows:

	£	*R* £	*S* £	*T* £
Immediate distribution:				
Residue	24,000			
Less Widow's life interest	12,000			
	12,000			
Add Advance to *T*	3,000			
	15,000	—	7,500	7,500
Less Advance to *T*	3,000	—	—	3,000
	£12,000	—	£7,500	£4,500

Final distribution:			*R* £	*S* £	*T* £
	£	£	£	£	£
Residue		24,000			
Add Advance to *R*	9,000				
Advance to *T*	3,000				
	12,000				
		36,000	12,000	12,000	12,000
Less Advances		12,000	9,000	—	3,000
		24,000	3,000	12,000	9,000
Less Previous distributions		12,000	—	7,500	4,500
		£12,000	£3,000	£4,500	£4,500

　The doctrine of hotchpot is not only applicable to intestacy or partial intestacy, but also applies where a testator inserts a 'hotchpot clause' in his will. Such a clause is usually in the following form:

'Provided that no child or the issue of any child shall take any part of the Trust Fund hereby created without bringing into hotchpot and accounting for any advances made to the said child during my lifetime.'

DISTRIBUTION OF RESIDUE

The residue is the last part of the estate of a deceased to be distributed, and must be applied in accordance with the following rules.

Under a will

Where the residue of an estate, i.e. what remains after the payment of debts, expenses and bequests, is disposed of by the will, it must be treated by the personal representative as a legacy and will be subject to the same rules as legacies.

Under a partial intestacy

If the testator's will does not dispose of all the residue of his estate, he is said to be *partially intestate*, when the portion of the estate undisposed of will be distributed according to the rules of intestate succession. Similarly, if a share of residue should lapse, it will be distributed according to the same rules.

The provisions of the Administration of Estates Act 1925 (as amended by the Intestates' Estates Act 1952, the Family Provision Act 1966 and the Family Law Reform Act 1969), will apply, subject to the modifications contained in section 49 which apply only to a case of partial intestacy, these being:

a. that *any issue* (i.e. descendants of the deceased, including grandchildren, etc.) of the deceased who share under the partial intestacy must bring into hotchpot any beneficial interests acquired by them under the will; and
b. that the personal representative shall be a trustee of the undisposed-of estate for the persons entitled to it, unless it appears from the will that the personal representative is to take such estate for himself.

Exercise 8

1. Into what classes may legacies be divided? Why is it necessary to determine the class to which a legacy beongs?
2. How may an executor relieve himself of responsibility in respect of a legacy to a minor or to a person abroad?
3. What is the order of precedence for legacies in the application of the rule abatement?
4. Differentiate between ademption in the case of demonstrative and specific legacies.
5. Distinguish satisfaction from ademption, and explain the application of the former to debts and legacies.
6. In what cases will a legacy not lapse upon the death of a legatee before that of the testator?
7. What powers have trustees to provide for the education and maintenance of minor beneficiaries out of trust funds?
8. In what cases may a legatee claim interest upon a legacy?
9. How should annuities bequeathed by a will be dealt with by a personal representative?
10. What is meant by the executor's assent? How is assent given? Can it be withheld?
11. Is there any limitation on a legatee's right to sue for his legacy? To what extent, if at all, is the right affected by the fact that the executor continues to have the money in

his possession? Is the position of a beneficiary under an intestacy in any way different?

12. What do you understand by the terms *donatio mortis causa* and gift *inter vivos*?

13. Explain the meaning of the following terms: devise; demonstrative legacy; abatement; portion; advancement; the 'two certainties'; vested legacy; contingent legacy; hotchpot; partial intestacy.

14. *X* died intestate in 1985 leaving a widow, *A*, and three adult children, *B*, *C* and *D*, to whom advances had been made of £9,000, £2,000 and £1,000 respectively. The residue of the estate available for distribution (exclusive of personal chattels) amounted to £100,000. Show the distribution thereof.

15. *X* by his will bequeathed the following legacies:
   £1,000 to each of this three sons, *A*, *B* and *C*.
   £1,000 to *D*, who had predeceased *X*.
   £1,000 payable out of his holding of War Loan to *E*.
   £1,000 on deposit at Barclays Bank to *F*.
   £1,000 payable out of his holding of Consols to *G*.
   The War Loan had been sold and the deposit at Barclays Bank had been withdrawn by *X* before he died. The residue of the estate available for distribution, after payment of all debts, taxes and expenses, amounted to £3,400, exclusive of £1,800 Consols valued at £1,000. How much will each beneficiary receive?

16. The estate of *Z* after the discharge of all debts, expenses and death taxes, consisted of the following:

	£
Motor car and household furniture and effects	4,800
Investments	55,200
Life policies	22,500
Cash at bank	9,250

He left a legacy of £2,000 to his widow and £1,000 to his eldest son, *A*, but did not dispose of the residue of his estate. He was survived by his widow and two sons, *A* and *B*, to the letter of whom he had advanced £500 before his death. Show how the estate will be distributed, assuming that the will contained a 'hotchpot clause'.

9
Income Tax — Deceased Estates

INTRODUCTION

The deceased's personal representative will be liable to account for tax liabilities which are outstanding at the date of death, and will also be responsible for obtaining refunds where tax has been overpaid. In particular, the personal representative will be responsible for making Returns of income up to the date of death. The Returns made must be signed by the personal representative who therefore is responsible for their accuracy and completeness, and this is so even if agents such as accountants are used. Completing the tax returns, possibly for several years, may reveal that the deceased failed to disclose all of his income and, as a result, the personal representative may have to deal with a Revenue investigation. On neglect or refusal to pay the tax outstanding, the representative can be subjected to legal proceedings in the same manner as any other defaulter, but it should be noted that the liability for tax does not extend beyond the value of the deceased's assets coming into the personal representative's hands.

Where assessments have been raised prior to the death, and no appeal has been made, an appeal should be made by the personal representative within thirty days of the date of the assessment. Because of the death, this may not be possible and a late appeal, normally treated sympathetically, should be made.

The death of the taxpayer can create problems where tax has been correctly assessed before the death, but is still unpaid at the death date. There will be a delay before the tax can be paid, and an attempt should be made to settle the liability before the interest totals £30, the level below which interest is not collected. If the death occurs before the due date of payment, ESC A17 prevents interest running until thirty days after the grant of probate or letters of administration. The normal time limits within which assessments can be raised, apply. No assessments can be made later than the end of the third year of assessment following the one in which the death occurred. Where there are no irregularities, the assessments can extend back to the six years of assessment preceding the tax year in which the assessments are raised. Where there is fraud, wilful default or neglect, the assessments can cover the six years of assessment preceding the one in which the taxpayer died.

INCOME OF DECEASED AND INCOME OF THE ESTATE

It will be the personal representative's responsibility to resolve the tax affairs of the deceased, and those of the estate, Returns being required in both instances. The income of the deceased therefore has to be distinguished from estate income.

The Apportionment Act 1870 provides that receipts and payments have to be apportioned on a time basis, the part relevant to the period up to the date of death being allocated to the deceased, and the post-death part to the estate. However, it was decided in *IRC* v. *Henderson's Executors* (1931) that the Apportionment Act does not apply for income tax purposes. The Apportionment Act is therefore a matter of estate administration rather than for income tax, and is dealt with subsequently in Chapters 16 to 18.

The general rule for income tax purposes is that if the income is received prior to the death, the tax on it is assessable on the deceased; if the income is received after the day of death, the whole receipt is taxed as being income of the estate. The application of this rule can be seen in the context of annuities and life tenancies. If the deceased was in receipt of an annuity or was a life tenant, when the amount due up to the date of death is subsequently received by the estate, the personal representative is chargeable to tax on it and it should not be included in the deceased's income: *Stewarts's Executors* v. *IRC* (1952) and *Wood* v. *Owen* (1940).

The rules applying under the various Schedules and Cases, and the manner in which the income is allocated to the deceased and the estate are as follows:

a. *Schedule A* (rents from land and buildings in the UK). The amount to be assessed on the deceased will be rent (less allowable expenses) the taxpayer was entitled to receive up to the date of the death. The rents receivable after the death will form part of estate income.

b. *Schedule B* (commercial occupation of woodland). Unless an election has been made for Schedule D, Case I, the amount assessable is one-third of the annual value. The annual value for the year of assessment is apportioned on a day-to-day basis from 6 April until the day of death. One-third of the figure apportioned up to the death date is liable to tax as income of the deceased, and one-third of the balance is taxed as income of the estate.

c. *Schedule C* (income paid through paying agents). This schedule applies to United Kingdom and overseas government stocks paid through a UK paying agent. Tax is deducted at source. The income received up to and including the death date is the deceased's income, and that received after the death is part of the income of the estate.

d. *Schedule D, Cases I and II* (trades, professions and vocations). Death automatically causes a sole-trader's, or partner's, trade to cease and the cessation rules will normally apply, so that the final year of assessment will be based on the actual profits from 6 April to the cessation date. The Revenue then have the right to increase the assessments of the penultimate and prepenultimate years to actual should the actual profits for those tax years exceed the profits assessed on a preceding year basis. If a terminal loss arises it can be relieved, under section 174, ICTA 1970, against the profit of the three years of assessment preceding the year of death, and any repayment of tax will be made to the estate. Where a cessation arises on a death, by section 137(3), ICTA 1970, the rules for valuation of trading stock on a discontinuance do not apply, i.e. the stock does not have to be valued at market value but at the lower of cost or net realizable value. There are two major exceptions to the cessation rule.

Firstly, where a husband who was a sole trader dies, the widow who carries on the business after his death may continue to be assessed on the preceding year basis instead of actual, but neither unrelieved losses, nor unused capital allowances, can be carried forward to be used by the surviving spouse.

Secondly, if the deceased had been a partner, and at least one partner is engaged both before and after the change, provided that written notice is given to the Inspector of Taxes signed by all persons involved with the partnership before and after the change, then the continuation rules will apply (section 154, ICTA 1970). The election of the deceased must be signed by his personal representative. The time limit for this election is 24 months from the date of death, and, once made, the election can subsequently be revoked, provided that the revocation is also within 24 months of the death.

In making a decision, the personal representative should only consider the effect on the estate. If the election is made, even though it is not of benefit to the estate, an indemnity should be obtained from the surviving partners to the effect that they will make good to the estate any additional tax that may become payable by reason of the election. If a section 154 election is made, the assessment will remain on the preceding year basis, and the assessment for the tax year in which the death occurred will be apportioned between the partners before and after the death, in such manner as is just, normally on a time basis.

e. *Schedule D, Cases III, IV and V* (interest, overseas income). Assessed under Sehcdule D, Case III, is, *inter alia*, interest paid without deduction of tax at source, and under Schedule D, Cases IV and V, interest on overseas securities and income from overseas possessions. Death constitutes the cessation of the source and the cessation provisions will apply, the final year being assessed on an actual basis, and the Revenue may raise the penultimate year to actual. Only the income actually received up to the date of death is assessable on the deceased, no account being taken of accruals.

f. *Schedule D, Case VI* (miscellaneous income). The amount assessable is the income receivable up to the date of death, whether or not the income was actually paid to the deceased prior to death.

g. *Schedule E* (emoluments). The amount earned by the deceased will be assessable, even though all of the income may not have been paid to the deceased prior to his death. When the employer pays the remuneration outstanding at the date of death, tax should still be deducted at source under the PAYE system. Because of the spreading of personal allowances over the whole of the tax year, usually a refund of tax will have to be claimed by the personal representative. Payments made to the holder or past holder of an office, or to his personal representatives, in connection with the termination of the office or employment are potentially subject to tax, but by section 188(1), ICTA 1970, payments in connection with the termination of the office or employment by reason of death are exempted, as are payments on account of injury or disability.

h. *Schedule F* (distributions). Only dividends received before death will normally be income of the deceased. However, if the dividend is declared before the death then the dividend is due to the deceased even if paid after the death: *Potel* v. *IRC* (1971). If the dividend resolution provided that the payment date was a date subsequent to the death, then the dividend will be treated as income of the estate rather than the deceased: *IRC* v. *Henderson's Executors* (1931).

HUSBAND AND WIFE

Income aggregation

The income of the wife, whether it is earned or unearned, is aggregated with that of her husband for as long as they are living together. On the death of the husband, the wife's income until the date of the death is aggregated with that of the husband for the same period, and her income after the husband's death is assessable on her as being a separate, single person.

The death of the husband does not mean that the cessation rules will apply in respect of the wife's sources of income. The amount assessable for the year is determined in the normal way and this is then apportioned on a time basis to and from the date of death.

On the death of the wife, her income from the preceding 6 April until the date of death is aggregated with her husband's income for the whole of the year of assessment in which she died.

An exception to the principle of income aggregation and joint assessments arises under section 23, FA 1971, i.e. a claim for separate taxation of wife's earnings. Where this claim is made, the wife is treated as a separate single person in respect of her earned income only. A joint election by husband and wife is necessary before the claim can be made. The deceased's personal representative together with the surviving spouse may make or revoke such an election.

If a claim under section 23, FA 1971, is in force for the tax year of the wife's death, and the wife dies relatively early in that year, it may well be that the earnings of the wife up to her death are insufficient to enable a tax saving to be made, and indeed more tax could become payable than would be the case if the election did not apply. The situation has to be carefully reviewed and, if necessary, a revocation made by the widower and the deceased wife's personal representative.

The time limits to make or revoke a claim for separate taxation are from six months before the beginning of the tax year concerned until twelve months after the end of the year, or such later time as the Board may allow. Once the claim is made, it remains in force until it is revoked.

Liability for income tax

On death of the husband

Assessments raised prior to the death will be a liability of the estate and not of the wife. However, the outstanding assessments could be on the income of the wife that has been aggregated with the husband's. In this latter instance, where the Revenue are of the opinion that there could be a liability on the wife under section 38, ICTA 1970 (separate assessment), and the tax remains unpaid 28 days after the due payment date, an assessment can be raised on the wife (section 40, ICTA 1970).

On death of the wife

The husband remains liable for unpaid tax on the wife's income unless claims under section 23, FA 1971, or section 38, ICTA 1970, have been made. Under a section 23, FA 1971 claim for separate taxation of wife's earnings, the husband will remain liable for tax on the wife's unearned income. However, it is possible for the husband to give express notice of disclaimer. This will result in the tax on the wife's income being a liability of her estate and could therefore give rise to a small inheritance tax saving. The detailed procedure for the disclaimer is laid down by section 41, ICTA 1970:

a. the husband gives written notice to the personal representatives within two months of the grant of probate or letters of administration, with similar notice to the

Inspector or Taxes giving, in this case, names and addresses of the personal representatives;

b. the Revenue then serves a notice on the personal representatives in respect of any assessment made on or before the date of the notice served by the husband.

The tax liability is then computed as if separate assessments were in force. The two month time limit can be extended with the personal representatives' consent.

Tax repayments

Usually a tax repayment will belong to the husband. However, in *Re Cameron, Kingsley* v. *IRC* (1965), a large repayment in respect of a deceased wife's income was held to be part of the wife's assets rather than the husband's. The Revenue's view was announced on 11 August 1967 and is that, to the extent that a repayment relates to a wife's source of income, not being a source, the tax on which was paid out of the husband's pocket, the repayment will be an asset of the wife's estate rather than the husband's. To divide the repayment, where necessary, between husband and wife, the procedure on a claim for separate assessment (section 38, ICTA 1970) will normally be followed.

By section 22, FA 1978, married women will be entitled to receive directly a tax repayment arising from Schedule E income, but section 22 does not apply otherwise than under Schedule E, and even then does not apply if the husband is liable at higher rates.

Personal allowances

On death of the husband

The personal allowances for the tax year of death are available in full. There is no reduction of the married allowance even though death may occur shortly after 6 April. The full wife's earned income relief is also available against the earned income of the wife up to the death date.

The widow, as a single person from the date of her husband's death, will receive the full single allowance, and in addition, can claim the widow's bereavement allowance. The latter is equal to the difference between married and single allowances, and is available for the tax year of death and the following tax year only, and is available provided that the widow has not remarried by the end of the second tax year concerned.

As a single person not entitled to the married allowance, the widow will also be entitled to the full additional personal allowance for children, provided that there is a qualifying child resident with her for at least part of the tax year. The child must be under 16 years of age at the beginning of the tax year of claim, or, if over 16, must be receiving full time educational instruction. A child includes a stepchild, an illegitimate child where the parents have subsequently married, and an adopted child, under 18 when adopted (section 14, ICTA 1970).

On the death of the wife

Again, the husband is entitled to the full married allowance for the year, and the full wife's earned income relief. For subsequent tax years, the single person's allowance only is available. The additional personal allowance for children cannot be claimed in the tax year of the death as the husband is entitled to the full married allowance, but a claim is available for subsequent years.

There is no widower's bereavement allowance.

TAXATION LIABILITIES AFTER DEATH

The administration period

The administration period is the period during which the personal representatives of the deceased are discharging liabilities, collecting assets, and paying legacies, i.e. doing all things necessary to determine the exact amount of capital from which the income will be payable to any life tenant, or to the residuary legatees. When the period ceases is a matter of fact in each case. The period commences on the day after the death and continues until the administration is completed.

The income of the administration period is assessed on the personal representatives to basic rate tax but they are not liable to the higher rates of tax. Neither are they entitled to any personal allowances, but they are entitled to loss relief if they have to carry on the deceased's business, and to relief for interest paid.

Although no relief is given for interest paid on capital transfer tax, relief is given for interest on loans taken out to enable capital transfer tax and interest on it to be paid. Relief is allowed only for the twelve months from the date the loan was taken out. Should the allowable interest exceed the taxable income of the year in which it is paid, the excess can be carried backwards to earlier years, but cannot be carried beyond the beginning of the administration period. The excess can also be carried forward to subsequent years (Schedule 1(17), FA 1974).

Relief will also be given for mortgage interest paid by the personal representative on the sole or main residence of the deceased provided it is the sole or main residence of the surviving spouse or a dependent relative of the deceased at the time the interest is paid.

As the personal representatives are assessed to basic rate tax, any amounts paid by them to the beneficiaries on account of their entitlement will be deemed to be after deduction of tax at the basic rate, i.e. the principle of deduction of tax at source applies.

Residuary beneficiaries

It is necessary to consider two types of residuary beneficiary: a beneficiary with a limited interest in the estate, and a beneficiary with an absolute interest. A person is deemed to have a limited interest in the whole or part of the residue of an estate during any period in which he does not have an absolute interest, where the income, if it has been ascertained, would be properly payable to him, or to another in his right, for his benefit, directly or indirectly (section 432(3), ICTA 1970).

On the other hand, a person is deemed to have an absolute interest in the whole or part of the residue of an estate if and so long as the capital of the residue, if ascertained, would be properly payable to him, or to another in his right, for his benefit, directly by the personal representative, or indirectly though a trustee or any other person (section 432(2), ICTA 1970).

It therefore follows that a beneficiary who is entitled to the income of the residue, e.g. a life tenant, has a limited interest, whilst a beneficiary entitled to the capital, e.g. a residuary legatee, has an absolute interest. The distinction between the two types of residuary beneficiary is important because of special rules that apply at the end of the administration period.

On completion of the administration

As stated earlier, the principle of deduction of tax at source applies so that any sums paid to the beneficiaries during the administration period will be paid after the deduction of basic rate tax. The beneficiaries will therefore include any payments received, grossed up at the basic rate, in their tax returns for each tax year, and will be assessed to tax at the higher rates as necessary. Any payments received by the beneficiary will include payments to others on his behalf (section 432(3), ICTA 1970), assets transferred to him and debts due from the beneficiary that are set-off or released (section 432(12), ICTA 1970). No assessments at basic rate will be required unless the personal representative has authorized income to be paid direct to the beneficiary (*Williams* v. *Singer and Others* (1920) and consequently the personal representative has not been assessed on it.

On completion of the administration, in the case of a limited interest in residue, the income arising over the whole period will be deemed to have accrued evenly throughout that period on a day-to-day basis (section 426(3), ICTA 1970). This will necessitate adjustments to the income previously included in the tax returns, and these adjustments may be made before the end of the third year of assessment following the one in which the administration was completed. The spreading of the income on an even basis avoids higher rate problems where income has been paid to a beneficiary in a lump sum in one year of assessment, for example at the end of the administration period, but there is less point to the operation if there is no liability to higher rates. Even in this case there could, however, be a tax effect where the net statutory income is required for the purpose of restricting age allowance by a fraction of the excess of the income over a specified maximum or where in any year there would otherwise be unutilized allowances.

If a beneficiary with a limited interest should die before the administration is completed, sums due to him but paid subsequent to his death will be deemed provisionally to have been paid in the last year of assessment during which he was alive (section 426(2), ICTA 1970). On completion of the administration, the total income of the whole period will be divided between the deceased and his successor, if any, on a day-to-day basis.

Example 1

Mr *A* died on 23 October 1985. By his will, a life interest in the residue of the estate is bequeathed to *B* with remainder to *C* absolutely. The estate administration was completed by the executor on 10 April 1988.

During the administration, the executor paid sums of £3,550 on 1 June 1986 and £6,390 on 29 September 1987 to *B*. The final payment of £4,260 was paid to *B* on 11 April 1988.

It is assumed that the basic rate of income tax is 30% for 1985/86 and 29% for 1986/87 and 1987/88.

Initially the amounts paid to *B*, grossed up, will be treated as income of the tax year of payment.

$$1986/87 \quad £3,550 \times \frac{100}{71} = £5,000$$

$$1987/88 \quad £6,390 \times \frac{100}{71} = £9,000$$

On completion of the administration, the total income of the period will be allocated on a day-to-day basis.

$$\text{Total income if } £3,550 + £6,390 + £4,260 = £14,200$$

The length of the administration period is 900 days.

	Revised position £						Originally £	£	Adjustments required £
1985/86	$\frac{164}{900}$	×	14,200	=	2,588	× $\frac{100}{70}$ =	3,697	–	+3,697
1986/87	$\frac{365}{900}$	×	14,200	=	5,759	× $\frac{100}{71}$ =	8,111	5,000	+3,111
1987/88	$\frac{366}{900}$	×	14,200	=	5,775	× $\frac{100}{71}$ =	8,134	9,000	– 866
1988/89	$\frac{5}{900}$	×	14,200	=	79	× $\frac{100}{71}$ =	111	–	+ 111

A beneficiary with an absolute interest in the residue is entitled to his share of the residuary income that arises in any particular year of assessment (section 427(2), ICTA 1970). The residuary income for any year of assessment is defined by section 428(1), ICTA 1970) as the aggregate income of the year less:

a. annual interest, annuities or other payments forming a charge on the residue;
b. such management expenses incurred by the personal representatives as would, in the absence of an express provision in the will, be properly chargeable against income, and which are not allowable in computing the gross income of the estate;
c. any income to which any other person, e.g. a specific legatee, may be entitled out of the residue. This includes interest on legacies.

The income due to the residuary legatee cannot be accurately calculated until the administration period has ended as until then the residue cannot be ascertained, therefore sums paid to the residuary legatee during the administration period will provisionally be deemed to be residuary income of the year in which they are paid (section 427(3), ICTA 1970). Payments made must be grossed up at basic rate for inclusion in the legatee's tax returns as the principle of deduction of tax at source will apply.

When the residue is ascertained and the income of each year is known, adjustments will then be required to the residuary beneficiary's previously declared income for each tax year during which the administration continued.

Example 2

B died on 6 April 1985 having bequeathed the residue of his estate to *C*. During the administration, the executor paid *C* £1,400 on 8 March 1986, £3,550 on 10 January 1987 and the final balance of £7,100 on the completion of the administration on 5 April 1988.

The net residuary income of the estate was finally established on 5 April 1988 as £2,100 for 1985/86, £5,680 for 1986/87 and £4,260 for 1987/88.

It is assumed that the basic rate of income tax is 30% for 1985/86 and 29% for 1986/87 and 1987/88.

Initially the amounts paid to *C*, grossed up, will be treated as the income of the tax year of payment:

$$1985/86 \quad £1,400 \times \frac{100}{70} = £2,000$$

$$1986/87 \quad £3,550 \times \frac{100}{71} = £5,000$$

$$1987/88 \quad £7,100 \times \frac{100}{71} = £10,000$$

On completion of the administration, the actual income of each year will be substituted for the above amounts:

	Revised position	*Originally*	*Adjustments required*

	£	£	£	£
1985/86	2,100 × $\frac{100}{70}$ =	3,000	2,000	+ 1,000
1986/87	5,680 × $\frac{100}{71}$ =	8,000	5,000	+ 3,000
1987/88	4,260 × $\frac{100}{71}$ =	6,000	10,000	– 4,000
		£17,000	£17,000	

During the administration, the payments to the residuary beneficiary will probably have been ascertained without any distinction between the income of one year or another. To enable the payments to be related to the residuary income of each year, the payments are firstly allocated against the income of the first year, and once that income is covered, they are allocated to the second year and so on. Quite commonly the payments will exceed the income to date as a payment includes a transfer of assets. In this case the payment will be allocated to a subsequent year.

Where heavy capital liabilities arise during the administration it is possible for the amounts actually paid to the beneficiary to be less than the residuary income, so resulting in the beneficiary bearing tax on an income that he never receives. In this circumstance, by section 428(2), ICTA 1970, the residuary income of each year is reduced by a fraction equal to the proportion that the deficiency bears to the total residuary income of the period of the administration.

Where the beneficiary with the absolute interest himself dies during the administration period, the residuary income is computed for each year of assessment and each broken part of a year until the interest ceases. The adjustment at the end of the administration period is made proportionately between the successive residuary legatees (section 428(3), ICTA 1970).

The composite rate scheme

Under this scheme, a deposit-taker paying interest to UK residents deducts tax at the basic rate and pays the interest net. The payer then accounts to the Revenue for the tax deducted, but at a special rate. The system has been applied to interest paid by building societies, and, with effect from 6 April 1985, is extended to bank interest, but not to NSB ordinary and investment accounts or to National Savings income and deposit bonds. Under the composite rate scheme, where a taxpayer is entitled to a tax refund, the tax deducted under the scheme is not available for repayment. In a Statement of Practice issued in July 1980, the Inland Revenue have stated that they will not 'look through' residuary income to its source and refuse payment of tax arising from building society interest, and this practice is extended from April 1985 to bank interest etc. This practice however, only applies to absolute residuary legatees and does not extend to limited interests, i.e. life tenancies. An exception to this general rule is in the context of individuals who are not resident, or not ordinarily resident, in the UK, where the previous practice enabling them to look through to the underlying sources of the income where it is advantageous to them under double taxation agreements etc. will be continued by concession.

Absolute residuary beneficiaries — inheritance tax and income tax

Unlike life tenants, who are not entitled to income accrued before the death, an absolute residuary beneficiary will include in his tax returns income received by the personal representative after the death even though it may have accrued before the death. The accrued income will, however, be part of the capital value of the deceased's estate on which inheritance tax is chargeable, so there is an element of double taxation.

Section 430, ICTA 1970, provides some measure of relief as far as income tax at the higher rates is concerned. The net income accrued to the date of the death is computed, as is the inheritance tax chargeable on it. The inheritance tax is then grossed at the basic rate of income tax and the result reduces the absolute residuary beneficiary's residuary income chargeable to tax at the higher rates.

Example 3

D died on 1 December 1986, leaving the residue of his estate to *E* absolutely. The income of the estate for 1986/87 amounted to £6,000 before tax. Of this sum, £2,042 had accrued prior to 1 December 1986, and had been included in *D*'s estate for inheritance tax purposes. The estate attracted inheritance tax at an average rate of 14.87%.

E, who is married, had other income for 1986/87 totalling £16,000. Compute *E*'s liability to income tax for 1986/87.

E's 1986/87 tax computation:

	£	£	£
Other income			16,000
Estate income		6,000	
Less Relief under section 430, ICTA 1970:			
Accrued income	2,042		
Less Tax at 29%	592		
	£1,450		
Inheritance tax at 14.87%	216		
£216 grossed at 29%		304	5,696
			21,696
Personal allowance			3,655
			£18,041
Tax liability			
£17,200 at 29%			4,988.00
841 at 40%			336.40
			5,324.40
Add £304 at 29%:			88.16
Tax payable			£5,412.56

The £304 at 29% is added as the relief under section 430, ICTA 1970, is only available at the higher rates and is not available at basic rate.

Non-residuary legatees

Specific legatees are entitled to the income produced by the subject matter of their legacy from the date of the death. Because of problems in administering the estate, the income will quite possibly be paid late to the beneficiary, and paid in one lump sum. If the lump sum was taxed in the year that it was paid to the beneficiary, there could be a liability to higher rate tax, so to avoid this, the assessments for the years in which the income actually arose will be adjusted by allocating the income over the appropriate years.

General legatees will be entitled to receive interest from the first anniversary of the testator's death, and the interest will be paid gross, the legatee being assessed under Schedule D, Case III. By section 119, ICTA 1970, income assessable under Schedule D, Case III is taxed on the full amount of income arising. By *Dunmore* v. *McGowan* (1978), income arises when it is received or enures for the taxpayer's benefit, so it follows that if no income is actually received in any year, there is no income assessable under Schedule D, Case III. If the legatee disclaims the interest to which he is entitled, he is not assessable on it: *Dewar* v. *IRC* (1935). However, where a sum is set aside for the legatee and he refuses to withdraw that income, he is still assessable as it has enured for his benefit: *Spens* v. *IRC* (1970).

Annuities under wills

Where the will provides for the payment of an annuity, by section 52, ICTA 1970, the personal representative has to deduct income tax at the basic rate applicable to the year in which the payment is due to be paid, and the beneficiary is credited with the tax suffered by deduction. If the beneficiary is not liable to tax, a repayment of the amount deducted at source will be made by the Revenue. Where the annuity is payable in instalments, repayments can be made at regular intervals. The Revenue will normally require sight of the will, but subsequently it is sufficient to claim the repayment, supporting that claim with a certificate of the payment made and the tax deducted. The beneficiary can request the personal representative to furnish such a certificate.

Any agreement for the payment of interest, rent or other annual payment without deducting income tax is void under section 106, TMA 1970. By *Ferguson* v. *IRC* (1969), an agreement to pay a sum 'free of tax' results in the payment of such a sum as after deducting tax equals the stated amount. However, section 106 does not apply to annuities under wills or trust deeds as these are not agreements, and an annuity can be stated to be 'free of tax', so intimating that the sum to be paid is the net amount. This sum, grossed up, then becomes the taxable income of the beneficiary.

The next problem is the extent to which the beneficiary can retain any of the tax refunded to him by the Revenue that arises from the annuity. The two relevant cases are *Jones* v. *Jones* (1933) and *Re Pettit, Le Fevre* v. *Pettit* (1922).

In *Re Jones* it was held that where annuities under a will were stated to be of such amounts as after deducting income tax at the rate for the time being would amount to the yearly prescribed amounts, the annuitants were entitled to retain the refunds received from the Revenue.

By comparison, in *Re Pettit*, the will stated that an annuity was 'free of income tax'. It was held that the annuitant had to account to the trustees for a proportion of the tax refund received.

The distinction between the two situations depends on whether the annuitant is entitled to benefit to the stated extent only, *Re Pettit* then applying, or whether the annuitant is to receive the stated amount from trustees or personal representatives irrespective of his own tax position.

The rule in *Pettit* has been held to apply in the following instances:

a. 'such an amount as after deduction of tax for the time being payable in respect thereof as will leave a clear sum of £350': *Re Tatham, National Provincial Bank Ltd* v. *Mackenzie* (1944);

b. 'free of income tax at current rate for the time being deductible at source': *Midland Bank Executor Trustee Company Ltd* v. *Williams* (1945).

Re Pettit will apply to 'free of tax' clauses but not to a formula arrangement, e.g. 'such a sum as after deducting tax at the current rate shall leave a stated amount'. At first sight this appears to conflict with *Re Tatham* above, but note the important words 'clear sum' that appeared in that case. It would not be a 'clear sum' of a stated amount if the annuitant could benefit from a tax refund as well.

The question now arises as to the proportion of any tax refund the annuitant receives that has to be paid by him to the trustees under *Re Pettit*.

Example 4

An annuitant, a single person aged 67, has a *'Re Pettit'* annuity of £1,420 and no other income. The situation for 1986/87 will be:

	£		£
Gross annuity	2,000	Tax	580
Age allowance	2,850		
Taxable income	£ —	Refund	£580

The refund of £580 is due to be paid to the trustees entirely, with the result that the annuitant has benefited only to the extent of the stated sum of £1,420.

Under *Re Pettit*, the proportion of the refund that has to be paid to the trustees is the ratio of the annuity to the total income.

Example 5

The same annuitant as in Example 4, in addition to the annuity, has dividend income of £1,500 gross. The 1986/87 situation then becomes:

	£		£
Gross annuity	2,000	Tax	580
Dividends (gross)	1,500	Tax	435
	3,500		1,015
Age allowance	2,850		
	£ 650	at 29%	188
Refund due			£ 827

The part of the refund due to be paid by the annuitant to the trustee is:

$$\frac{2,000}{3,500} \times £827 = £472.57$$

The part to be retained by the annuitant is:

$$\frac{1,500}{3,500} \times £827 = £354.43$$

Apportioning the refund between the annuitant and the trustee is unsatisfactory as the amount of the refund could be dependant on whether or not the annuitant's reliefs are offset against income from which tax has not been deducted at source. To overcome this problem it is usual, in practice, not to apportion any refund between the trustee and the annuitant but to apportion the tax value of the reliefs instead.

Example 6

The facts are as in Example 5 except that instead of dividends, the income is interest paid without deduction of tax, e.g. 3½% War Loan:

	£		£
Gross annuity	2,000	Tax	580
Interest paid gross	1,500		—
	3,500		
Age allowance	2,850		
	£ 650	at 29%	188
Refund due			£392

The amount payable to the trustees is:

$$£2,850 \text{ at } 29\% = £827 \times \frac{2,000}{3,500} = £472.57$$

Working on the refund of £392 would be unsatisfactory in this case, and by apportioning the tax value of the reliefs, the same payment has to be made to the trustee as in Example 5.

It should be appreciated that the amount paid by the annuitant to the trustee then becomes income of the trust or estate. The Inland Revenue practice is to treat the grossed-up equivalent of the amount paid by the annuitant as income of the estate, the rate of tax for grossing up being the rate at the date the payment is received by the trustees. In *Re Kingcombe, Hickley* v. *Kingcombe* (1936), it was held that the annuitant must claim the refund from the Revenue, as in this respect the annuitant is effectively a trustee for the benefit of the estate.

In the absence of a contrary intention stated in the will, the annuity becomes payable as from the date of death, the first payment being due at the end of the executor's year, i.e. paid yearly in arrear. If the stated date is within twelve months after death, the annuity runs from that date, but the first payment need not be made until the end of that year. Should the estate income be insufficient to cover the annuity, then the deficiency can be made good out of capital. By *Brodies Will Trustees* v. *IRC* (1933), tax is deducted from the total payment and not just from the part met out of income. The tax on the part paid from capital is assessable on the trustees under section 53, ICTA 1970.

Section 53 applies where the payment is out of income not liable to tax. Tax is deducted from the payment and the recipient is credited with the tax deducted, a direct assessment being made on the payer. The tax rate for section 53 is the rate when the payment is made, not the rate when the payment is due, as is the case under section 52, ICTA 1970.

By section 230, ICTA 1970, where an annuity is purchased, a part of each receipt is capital, and tax is only deducted from the income portion. Section 230 does not, however, apply to annuities purchased under a direction in a will; neither does it apply to purchased annuities arising from a will or settlement out of the income of property disposed of by that will or settlement. Therefore, in the case of annuities under wills, tax is deducted from the whole of the payment. Under the *Saunders* v. *Vautier* (1841) rule a beneficiary can call for the legacy before the stated date provided that the beneficiary is *sui juris*, and no other person can take any beneficial interest in any circumstance, i.e. the beneficiary has a vested interest. The annuitant therefore can have the right to demand a capital sum rather than have an annuity purchased for him. On receipt of the capital sum, it could be used for an annuity purchase, with the result that part of the receipt will be capital and not subject to income tax.

STATEMENTS OF TRUST INCOME

Personal representatives and trustees must complete a statement of trust income annually, showing the income of the estate or trust, charges on that income, income that has been allocated to specific purposes, administration expenses incurred by the trustees, and the division of the income between the beneficiaries. Income from all sources is included together with the tax paid or payable on it. Where expenses are directly related to a particular source, they are deducted from that source, but expenses of general administration are shown separately.

Example 7

An annuity of £1,000 is payable to the deceased's widow out of the residue of the estate, and the balance of the residuary income is to be divided with one-quarter to the son and three-quarters to the daughter.
    The estate income for the year to 5 April 1987 consists of:

	£	£
Dividend income, including tax credits		1,850
Loan stock interest (gross amount)		3,150
Furnished lettings	1,200	
Allowable expenses	400	800
National Savings Bank interest		
(investment account)		200

During the year to 5 April 1987, the personal representatives incurred management expenses of £71. The interest from the National Savings Bank account for the year to 5 April 1986 had been £180.

Statement of Trust Income for the year to 5 April 1987:

	Gross	Tax at 29%
	£	£
Schedule F dividend income	1,850	536.50
Loan stock interest (tax deducted at source)	3,150	913.50
Schedule D, Case VI furnished lettings	800	232.00
Schedule D, Case III NSB interest (preceding year basis)	180	52.20
	5,980	1,734.20
Annuity to widow	1,000	290.00
Total income	£4,980	£1,444.20
Expenses incurred by trustees	£ 71	

Summary:	£	£
Total income		4,980.00
Less Income tax	1,444.20	
Expenses	71.00	1,515.20
		£3,464.80

Division of income:	Share	Paid to beneficiary
	£	£
Son (¼)	866.20	862.65
Daughter (¾)	2,598.60	2,587.95
	£3,464.80	£3,450.60

The amounts actually paid to the beneficiaries differ from their share of the income computed above because of the Schedule D, Case III income being assessed on a preceding year basis rather than on an actual basis. The difference between the income (£3,464.80) and the amounts paid (£3,450.60) is actually £200, *less* assessed £180 = £20, *less* tax at 29%, i.e. £14.20.

Beneficiaries must be issued with a form R185E by the personal representatives. This is a certificate showing, in particular, the gross income to which they are entitled and the tax deducted from it.

The R185Es to be issued to the beneficiaries in Example 7 will be as follows:

Gross amount of beneficiary's share	*Amount of tax suffered thereon by the trust*	*Amount of net payment to beneficiary*	*Amount of the payment made out capital*
(1)	(2)	(3)	(4)
For the widow			
£1,000.00	£290.00	£710.00	None
For the son			
£1,220.00	£353.80	£862.65	None
For the daughter			
£3,660.00	£1,061.40	£2,587.95	None

Note that the figures for the son and daughter in the gross column (1) are found by taking their respective net shares (£866 and £2,598.60) and grossing up by 100/71.

The general expenses of the administration of the estate are not allowable for tax purposes and are met out of the net income after tax. These expenses should therefore be grossed up in the statement to arrive at the gross income of the beneficiaries.

If this approach is adopted in the circumstances of Example 7, the result will be as follows:

	Gross £	*Tax at 29%* £
Total income as per Example 7	4,980	1,444.20
Less Expenses 71 × 100/71	100	
Distributable income (gross)	£4,880	
Division of income	*Share* £	
Son: ¼ × 4,880	1,220	
Daughter: ¾ × 4,880	3,660	
	£4,880	

The gross amounts to be shown on the R185Es will then be the same as in Example 7.

Administration expenses may be allocated against the source of income most advantageous to the taxpayer and it would be beneficial to allocate the expenses against income on which a notional tax credit is not available for repayment, e.g. building society interest, so maximizing the tax which has actually been paid.

Normally, a trustee's remuneration for services rendered is an administration expense payable out of income that has already borne tax. However, where the payment is of the nature of an annual sum, it will be allowable against estate income before tax. Where the expense is of the nature of a fee based on time spent etc. it will not be treated as an annual sum: *Baxendale* v. *Murphy* (1924).

FOREIGN ESTATES

This chapter has covered the situation where the estate is a United Kingdom estate. If the estate is a foreign estate the procedures are subject to modifications.

A foreign estate is an estate other than a UK estate. A UK estate is defined in Section 432(8), ICTA 1970, as being one the income of which comprises only income which either has borne UK income tax by deduction or direct assessment, and is not an estate any part of the income of which is exempt because the personal representatives are not resident, or not ordinarily resident, in the United Kingdom. The distinction therefore rests on whether the income is liable to UK tax, the personal representatives being UK residents, and not on the location of estate assets, or the residential status of the deceased.

Where a limited interest exists in the residue of a foreign estate, if none of the income has borne tax in the UK, any amounts paid as income during the administration to a UK beneficiary are treated as being gross amounts assessable under Schedule D, Case IV, as being income derived from foreign securities (section 426(4), ICTA 1970).

On proof of the facts on a claim, should part of the aggregate income of the estate in any year have borne tax in the UK, the tax charged on the beneficiary is reduced by the proportion of the tax charged that the income after UK tax bears to the aggregate net income of the estate (section 426(5), ICTA 1970).

Example 8

The income of a foreign estate for 1986/87 is as follows:

	Gross	Tax at 29%	Net
	£	£	£
Income subject to UK tax	4,000	1,160	2,840
Income not subject to UK tax	1,000	—	1,000
	£5,000	£1,160	£3,840

The life tenant, resident in the UK was paid £3,840.

The life tenant will, initially, be assessed on £3,840 at 29% under Schedule D, Case IV. The tax payable will be £1,113.60.

If a section 426(5) claim is made, this will be revised to:

		£
UK tax paid		1,113.60
Less $\frac{2,840}{3,840} \times 1,113.60$		823.60
		£ 290.00

The £290 is, of course, the tax at 29% on the £1,000 which had not suffered UK tax in the estate.

The beneficiary's income for inclusion in his own tax computation will then be (gross) £5,000. The tax already borne on the £5,000 is £1,160 by the estate and £290 by assessment, i.e. £1,450.

In the case of absolute interests in the residue of foreign estates, sums paid during the administration are deemed to be on account of gross residuary income (as opposed to net residuary income in UK estates), and are again assessed under Schedule D, Case IV. On completion of the administration, the beneficiary's income becomes the gross residuary income of each year and the usual adjustments to assessments are then made.

Claims under section 426(5), ICTA 1970 can then be made. When computing the claim, the calculations are made on gross income rather than the net income which is the situation where there is a limited interest.

Example 9

Taking the same facts as in Example 8, but substituting an absolute residuary beneficiary for the life tenant, the situation becomes as follows. The beneficiary is initially assessed on the £3,840 at 29% under Schedule D, Case IV. The tax payable is £1,113.60. In this example the income of the estate is now equal to the residuary income of 1986/87 so no adjustments will be made to this figure.

The claim under section 426(5), ICTA 1970, will be computed as:

	£
UK tax paid	1,113.60
Less $\frac{4,000}{5,000} \times 1,113.60$	890.88
	£ 222.72

However, for the purposes of the beneficiary's higher rate liability, the beneficiary's income remains at £3,840, no adjustment being made.

Exercise 9

1. A married man dies on 6 October of a particular year. What personal allowances will he and his wife be entitled to for that tax year?
2. What is the situation in respect of liability for income tax on the death of a husband?
3. What is the situation in respect of liability for income tax on the death of a wife?
4. Distinguish between limited interests and absolute interests in an estate.
5. State the rule in *Re Pettit* and explain when it is to be applied.
6. *A* died, aged 67, on 1 January 1987. By his will, his older sister, *B*, is given a life interest in the whole of the estate, with remainder to *C* absolutely. *C* is his deceased brother's son.

    In addition to assets which produced the income of the estate given below, *A* had two other sources of income, details of which are:

    E Plc shares: £350 cash was received as a dividend on 3 January 1987, being the final for the year to 31 August 1986. The dividend was declared to be payable on 31 December 1986. An interim of £280 cash had been received on 1 July 1986.
    F Plc shares: £497 cash was received as dividend on 11 January 1987, being the only dividend for the year to 30 November 1986. The declaration was made on 28 November 1986 and the dividend was declared payable on 10 January 1987.

Both of the above shareholdings were sold shortly after the death and no further dividends were received.

The estate administration was completed on 6 October 1988.

Details of the estate income for taxation purposes, but excluding the dividends above, together with payments made, for each year of assessment are:

	Income			Payments made	
	Gross	Tax	Net	to B	to Z on B's behalf
	£	£	£	£	£
1986/87	1,100	319	781	510	200
1987/88	6,300	1,827	4,473	4,260	—
1988/89					
(to 6/10/88)	3,000	870	2,130	—	—
1988/89 Final payment of the administration period				2,250	

You are required to state:

a. the effect that the dividends above will have on the estate income for taxation purposes, adjusting the estate income as you consider appropriate;
b. the original amounts to be included in *B*'s taxable income for 1986/87 and 1987/88;
c. the final amounts to be included in *B*'s taxable income for each year on the completion of the administration; and
d. two reasons why the total of the gross amounts for *B* may differ from the gross income of the estate for income tax purposes.

You are to assume that the basic rate of income tax remains at 29% throughout.

7. *T*, a widower, died on 6 April 1986. By his will *S*, his accountant, was appointed executor, and the whole estate was left in trust to his son *U*, for life, with remainder to *V*, his grandchild, absolutely. The will did not bar the application of the Apportionment Act 1870, but empowered *S* to continue *T*'s business so that it could be sold as a going concern. By the will, *S* is allowed a fixed annual sum of £500 for his services as executor.

   T's income-producing assets consisted of:

   — a sole trade (detail below);
   — £2,000 10% loan stock in X Plc — interest receivable 31 July and 31 January;
   — building society deposit — interest receivable 30 June and 31 December;
   — property let unfurnished (detail below).

   The sole trade was long established with accounts being made up to 5 April each year. Draft accounts were produced by an employee of *S* for the years to 5 April 1985 and, subsequently 5 April 1987, showing tax adjusted profits of £7,200 and £6,000 respectively. Stock at 5 April 1986 had been included in both sets of accounts at estimated market value of £1,940. The equivalent cost value is £1,520. The stock at 5 April 1987 was included at a cost of £1,760. All expenditure ranks for relief under section 130, ICTA 1970, and no depreciation has been charged. The unfurnished lettings produced rental income during 1986/87 of £1,130 with allowable expenses of £430. *T*, at 5 April 1986, had unutilized losses arising from this property of £100.

   T, until his death, had been the life tenant of a settled fund, the sole asset of which was an investment of £40,000 8% debenture stock in *Z* Plc. The due dates for receipt of the interest were 6 April and 6 October. The trustees normally paid the income to *T* shortly after it was received, but paid to *S* the income due until *T*'s death, on 31 July 1986.

   The interest on the 10% loan stock was received on the due dates and *S* apportioned it between capital and income as appropriate under the Apportionment Act 1870.

   Interest of £130 was received on the building society account in June and £154 in December 1986.

   The deceased had a mortgage of £10,000 on his home, provided by a relative. The interest paid by *S* for the period from 6 April 1986 until December 1986, when the property was sold, was £900. A loan was taken out by *S* to enable capital transfer tax to be paid on the estate personalty. The loan interest charged for 1986/87 was £100.

   Certain administration expenses were paid on 31 March 1987. These were allocated as £50 for capital and £90 for income. On that date *S* was paid the annual sum of £500 due to him.

   You are required:

   a. to prepare a statement of trust income for 1986/87 together with supporting notes explaining your treatment of each of the events mentioned above; and
   b. to show the entries on the R185E to be given to *U* for 1986/87.

   You are to ignore any adjustments that may arise at the end of the administration period. The basic rate of income tax is to be taken at 29%.

8. *D* died on 6 April 1986 and, for 1986/87, the estate received income subject to UK income tax of £2,000 gross, and income not liable to tax in the UK of £3,400. The estate is administered as a 'foreign estate'. *E*, the life tenant, is resident, ordinarily resident

and domiciled in the UK and is paid £3,200 as his income due from the estate for 1986/87. His income is low and will only bear tax at 29%.

You are required:

a. to state the crucial factors which determine whether an estate is a foreign or UK estate;
b. to state how *E* will be taxed in the UK on the £3,200 that he received for 1986/87;
c. to show the final amount of UK income tax payable after appropriate claims have been made; and
d. to compute the final amount to be included in *E*'s 1986/87 UK income tax computation.

10
Capital Transfer Tax I

INTRODUCTION

Capital transfer tax (CTT) was introduced in the Finance Act 1975 to replace estate duty. Unlike estate duty, which broadly was charged on a person's estate on death and gifts made up to seven years prior to death, the original conception of capital transfer tax was of a tax running 'from the cradle to the grave' with a cumulative system running throughout the lifetime of an individual, the final transfer being deemed to have been made immediately prior to the date of death, this comprising the individual's estate at his death.

The original provisions included in the Finance Act 1975 have been substantially amended by subsequent Finance Acts and the comments in this and the subsequent chapters on capital transfer tax are based on the law following the Finance Act 1985, but prior to the Finance Act 1986 which abolished capital transfer tax with effect from 18 March 1986. The new rules in respect of inheritance tax are explained in Chapter 14, but it was felt appropriate to provide completely updated chapters on capital transfer tax quite separate from the new provisions for inheritance tax.

NATURE OF THE TAX

The principle of CTT is that gifts or other gratuitous transfers of capital are taxed (subject to certain exemptions or reliefs) during the individual's lifetime and on his or her death. Two scales of rates of tax apply, the lifetime scale and the death scale. Gifts made within three years of the date of death are subject to tax at the death rate and any tax previously calculated by reference to the lifetime scale must be recalculated using the death scale in respect of gifts made within this period. Perhaps the most substantial change in the original concept of CTT is the limitation of the period of cumulation to a period of ten years; previously there was no limit so that all chargeable transfers made by an individual had to be taken into account in determining the CTT payable on his death. The old criticism of estate duty that it was an 'avoidable tax' can now be levied equally against CTT, although CTT can arise on lifetime transfers which was not possible under the old estate duty rules.

SCOPE OF THE TAX

If the transferor is domiciled in the United Kingdom, the tax applies to his property wherever situated. If he is domiciled abroad, the tax usually applies only to property situated in the United Kingdom. *Domicile* is a common law conception. It has received no settled definition in the courts. Every person has one, and only one, domicile at a particular time. A person's domicile may be stated shortly as his permanent home to which, if he is not resident there at a particular time, he has not abandoned all intention of returning. There are three kinds of domicile:

a. *Domicile of origin.* This is normally the country of a person's birth.
b. *Domicile of choice.* This can be acquired by an individual who is of age and involves:
   i.   his leaving his country of origin, and
   ii. his residence (physical presence) in the country of choice, and
   iii. his having the clear intention of making a permanent home in the country of choice, see *Commissioners of Inland Revenue* v. *Cohen* (1942).
c. *Derivative domicile.* This is acquired by a woman on marriage, normally her domicile becoming that of the husband; another example is the domicile of a child during his or her minority. The position of married women has changed if they were married after 1 January 1974. If married after that date, a woman retains her previous domicile unless she changes it by *choice* as under (b). Similarly, any boy of 14 or girl of 12 or over can exercise choice.

   For capital transfer tax purposes, however, a person who is not *domiciled* in the United Kingdom under the general law is treated as domiciled in the United Kingdom at the time of a transfer if:

a. he was domiciled in the United Kingdom on or after 10 December 1974 and within three years immediately preceding the transfer; or
b. he was resident in the United Kingdom on or after 10 December 1974 and in at least *seventeen* of the *twenty* income tax years of assessment, ending with the year in which the transfer is made. (*Residence* has the same meaning as for income tax, except that the availability of an abode for the person's use in the UK is disregarded, that is to say, he has stayed in the country for six months in the income tax year and has not come here for a *temporary* purpose only.)   (Section 267, CTTA 1984)

GENERAL PRINCIPLES

In order to appreciate how a liability to CTT arises and is calculated a number of basic principles and definitions must be understood. These are fundamental to the tax and are stated at the outset as they apply throughout the chapters on CTT which follow.

Chargeable transfer

A chargeable transfer is a transfer of value (see below) made by an individual which is not an exempt transfer.   (Section 2, CTTA 1984)

Transfer of value

A transfer of value is any disposition made by a person as a result of which the value of his estate is reduced. The amount by which the value of his estate is reduced is the value transferred. This concept of the 'loss to the donor' is the basic principle which applies in establishing the value transferred. Although the value of the asset transferred will in many cases be the same as the reduction in the value of the transferor's estate, this will not always be the case, particularly where the asset transferred is a holding of shares in a company (see 'The Basis of Valuation' p. 160). The term transfer of value is also extended to include the omission to exercise a right and is also widened to include 'associated operations' within section 268.   (Section 3, CTTA 1984)

Meaning of estate

A person's estate includes all the property to which he is beneficially entitled, but a person's estate immediately prior to his death does not include 'excluded property'. This is extended by section 49 where a person is beneficially entitled to an interest in possession in settled property to include the property in which the interest subsists. Section 157 excludes the foreign currency bank accounts of non-residents for transfers on death only. Liabilities are to be deducted in valuing a person's estate, but the CTT liability payable on any chargeable transfer, if payable by the transferor, is to be deducted from the value of his estate immediately after the transfer. This provides the authority for grossing up lifetime transfers where the donor pays the tax.
                    (Section 5, CTTA 1984)

Excluded property

Excluded property is defined as property situated outside the United Kingdom if the person beneficially entitled to it is an individual domiciled outside the United Kingdom. War savings certificates, national savings certificates (including Ulster savings certificates), premium savings bonds, deposits with the National Savings Bank or with a trustee savings bank, and certified contractual savings schemes (with section 415, ICTA 1970) are excluded property if held by a person domiciled in the Channel Islands or Isle of Man.   (Section 6, CTTA 1984)

    Additional definitions of 'excluded property' in relation to settlements are given in Chapter 13 dealing with settled property. However, it is appropriate to mention at this stage that a 'reversionary interest' is excluded property, unless:

a. it has been acquired at any time for consideration in money or money's worth; or
b. it is one to which the settlor or his spouse is or has been beneficially entitled; or
c. it is the interest expectant upon the determination of a lease treated as a settlement within section 43(3), CTTA 1984.   (Section 48(1), CTTA 1984)

Transfers on death

In order to bring a person's estate at his death within the charge to CTT, it is provided that on death tax shall be charged as if, immediately before his death, he had made a transfer of value equal to the value of his estate immediately before his death.
                    (Section 4, CTTA 1984)

RATES OF TAX

Two scales of rates of tax are laid down by Parliament, a lower lifetime scale and a higher scale applicable to transfers on or within three years of death. The rates of tax applicable subsequent to 25 March 1980 are given in Appendix III. The lifetime scale is now exactly half the death rate scale. It is provided for bands of rates of tax to be increased each year by reference to the increase in the retail prices index to the previous December, although this can be overridden by statute. (Sections 7 and 8, CTTA 1984)

EXEMPTIONS AND RELIEFS

There are a number of exemptions and reliefs and they take the form of either excluding certain dispositions, or property, or a certain part of the dispositions.

1. Non-gratuitous transfers

A disposition is not a chargeable transfer of value, if it can be shown that it was not *intended* to transfer a gratuitous benefit to any person *and* (not or) was either made as an arm's length transaction, or that it was such as might be expected to have been so made.

It must be remembered that this provision does not apply to reversionary interests and to sales of unquoted shares and debentures, unless they have been transferred at 'open market value'. The valuation of shares and debentures of unquoted companies both for the purpose of CTT and capital gains tax is a very difficult business, depending in practice to a large extent on the skill of the negotiator, since the 'open market value' will always be hypothetical. (Section 10, CTTA 1984)

2. Dispositions for family maintenance

Maintenance payments for spouse, children and dependent relatives are exempt in the following circumstances.

a. If the payment is by one party of the marriage for the benefit of the other. This includes any dispositions made on the occasion of divorce even if varied afterwards.
b. If the payment is for the maintenance, education or training of a child of either party to the marriage, or of any child who is not in the care of its parents, or of an illegitimate child of the person making the disposition, up to the end of the fiscal year in which the child reaches the age of eighteen or, if older, ceases to undergo full-time education or training.
c. If the payment represents a reasonable provision for the maintenance of a dependent relative. A dependent relative in this connection is defined, as for income tax, as a relative incapacitated by old age (65) or infirmity, or the widowed or separated mother of either spouse, irrespective of age. (Section II, CTTA 1984)

3. Dispositions in the course of trade

If the payment is regarded as an allowable expense for the purpose of income tax or corporation tax, it is exempt from CTT; this covers, of course, payments to a superannuation fund. (Section 12, CTTA 1984)

4. Dispositions to employee trusts

A payment by a close company, as defined for corporation tax purposes, to a trust for the benefit of the company's employees is exempt if the persons entitled to benefit from the trust include all or most of the employees. In order to qualify under these provisions, the trust must contain property which can be applied only for the benefit of the following:

a. employees in particular occupations or of particular firms; or

b. their relatives or dependents; or
c. charities.

Moreover, the following persons must be excluded from benefit:

a. any participator (as defined for corporation tax purposes) in the company, or in any other close company which has made a qualifying transfer to the same trust (but not a participator who is beneficially entitled to less than 5% of the issued share capital of the company or less than 5% of the assets of the company on a winding up);
b. anyone who has been a participator in such a company, either after the disposition or within the previous *ten years*;
c. any person who is treated as a *connected person* with these persons.

Transfers by an individual of shares in a company to a trust for the benefit of the employees of the company as outlined above are exempt provided the following conditions are satisfied:

a. the trustees must hold more than half the ordinary shares of the company and have the majority of votes capable of being exercised on all questions affecting the company as a whole;
b. there are no arrangements whereby the condition in (a) can be changed without the consent of the trustees.

There must be excluded from benefit under the trust any participator within the limitations outlined above.   (Sections 13 and 28, CTTA 1984)

5. Waivers of remuneration and dividends

A waiver or repayment of remuneration is not subject to CTT, provided it would have been subject to income tax if it had not been waived. It is a condition of this exemption that the remuneration waived is not allowed as a deduction in computing the employer's profits for income or corporation tax purposes. Where the right to receive a dividend is waived within the twelve months before the right has accrued, this is not treated as a transfer of value for CTT purposes.   (Sections 14 and 15, CTTA 1984)

6. Grant of tenancies of agricultural property

The grant of a tenancy of agricultural property in the United Kingdom, the Channel Islands or the Isle of Man for use for agricultural purposes is not a transfer of value provided it is made for full consideration in money or money's worth.
(Section 16, CTTA 1984)

7. Changes in distribution of deceased's estate

None of the following is a transfer of value:

a. a variation or disclaimer within section 142 (see p. 154);
b. a transfer in compliance with a testator's request within section 143;
c. an election by a surviving spouse under section 47A, Administration of Estates Act 1925;
d. the renunciation of a claim to legitim within the period allowed in section 147(6).
(Section 17, CTTA 1984)

8. Transfers between husband and wife

In general, transfers between husband and wife are completely exempt from CTT. However, where the transferor spouse is domiciled in the United Kingdom, but his spouse is not, the maximum transfer exempt is £55,000. This limit, currently £55,000, was previously equal to the nil rate band. However, recent increases in the nil rate band have not been reflected in this limit.

Example 1

Mr *A*, domiciled in the United Kingdom, married Miss *B*, who retained her French domicile after her marriage on 5 October 1980. Mr *A* transferred assets to her as follows:

9 December 1980	£15,000
5 October 1982	£35,000
11 September 1985	£25,000

The transfers made in 1980 and 1982 are completely exempt, but of the transfer made in 1985 only £5,000 (£55,000 *less* £15,000 + £35,000) is exempt leaving £20,000 as a chargeable transfer subject to the availability of any annual exemption.

For CTT purposes a husband and wife still remain 'spouses' until they are divorced or one spouse dies, although the exemption is still available in respect of property passing on death, such that transfers between spouses after separation but before divorce are exempt. Furthermore, the Inland Revenue Statement of Practice SP/E12 confirms that transfers of money or property pursuant to the order of a court on divorce or nullity of marriage will be regarded as exempt, being transactions at arm's length not intended to confer any gratuitous benefit. Where, exceptionally, it is intended to confer a benefit a transfer of value will arise. (Section 18, CTTA 1984)

9. Annual exemption

There is an annual exemption of £3,000. The year for this purpose is the same as the tax year, the year ended 5 April. If the annual exemption for a year is not used, or not wholly used, the unused amount can be carried forward for one year only and can be added to the annual exemption for that year. The annual exemption for the following year must be used in priority to the annual exemption brought forward.

Where the total values transferred in a year exceed the annual exemption available, the annual exemption is set against the values transferred in the order in which they are made during the year. If two, or more, transfers are made on the same day the exemption is attributed to the transfers on a pro rata basis. (Section 18, CTTA 1984)

Example 2

Mr *C* made the following transfers of value:

1984/85:	1 October 1984 £1,000 to his son
1985/86:	20 December 1985 £3,000 to his son
	20 December 1985 £6,000 to his daughter

The chargeable transfers of Mr *C* will be as follows:

	£	£
1984/85		
Transfer of value 1 October 1984		1,000
Less Annual exemption 1984/85		3,000
Unused annual exemption		£2,000
1985/86		
Transfers of value 20 December 1985		9,000
Less Annual exemption 1985/86	3,000	
Balance annual exemption 1984/85	2,000	5,000
Chargeable transfers		£4,000

The annual exemption available for 1985/86 is allocated between the transfers made on 20 December 1985 as follows:

	Son		Daughter
	£		£
Transfer of value	3,000		6,000
Annual exemption: ⅜ × £5,000 =	1,667	⅝ × £5,000 =	3,333
Chargeable transfers	£1,333		£2,667

10. Small gifts

Lifetime transfers of value made by a transferor in any one year (year ended 5 April) by outright gift to any one person are exempt if the values transferred by them do not exceed £250. This exemption cannot be linked with any other exemption, e.g. to exempt a gift of £3,250 using both this exemption and the annual exemption.

(Section 20, CTTA 1984)

11. Normal expenditure out of income

As the name implies, CTT is designed to tax transfers of capital not income. This exemption is available where it can be shown by the transferor:

a. that the transfer was made as part of his normal expenditure; and
b. that (taking one year with another) it was made out of his income; and
c. that after taking into account all such transfers, he was left with sufficient income to maintain his usual standard of living.

It may be difficult to establish that an item of expenditure is 'normal' when the expenditure first commences, but it will usually be considered normal after three payments if there is a continuing intention to make future payments. Moreover, if there is some form of contract or it is easily shown that there is an intention to continue payments from the outset, e.g. premiums under a life insurance policy, then it should be possible to establish the payments as normal from the first of the payments.

Premiums on life assurance on the life of the transferor will not be treated as normal expenditure if an annuity on his life was purchased at any time before, at the same time or subsequently, unless it can be shown that the purchase of the annuity and the taking out of the policy of insurance were not associated operations.

The capital element of any purchased life annuity is not included as 'income' for the purposes of this exemption.

12. Gifts in consideration of marriage

Transfers of value made in consideration of marriage are exempt to the extent that they fall within the limits set out below. It is important to note that the gifts must be 'in consideration of marriage' and hence must be made prior to the marriage taking place.

The exemptions available are as follows:

a. £5,000 in respect of an outright or settled gift by a parent of a party to the marriage;
b. £2,500 in respect of an outright or settled gift by a grandparent, or other remoter ancestor, of a party to the marriage;
c. £2,500 in respect of an outright or settled gift by one party to the marriage to the other;
d. £1,000 in any other case.

(Section 22, CTTA 1984)

13. *Gifts to charities*

Outright gifts to charities are now exempt without limit. Prior to 15 March 1983 there was an overall limit of £250,000 in respect of exempt gifts to charities made on death, or within one year of death (lower limits applied previously). Section 9, F(No.2)A 1983 removed this limitation with effect from 15 March 1983. It has been confirmed by the Inland Revenue that if the loss to the donor's estate is greater than the value actually received by the charity, e.g. as a result of a valuation taking into account related property, the whole of the transfer will be treated as exempt — see Inland Revenue Statement of Practice SP/E13.

There are a number of restrictions which may apply if the transfer is conditional, defeasible or not the whole interest of the transferor in the property transferred. These tests are applied twelve months after the date of transfer to establish if the restrictions have to be applied. (Section 23, CTTA 1984)

14. *Gifts to political parties*

Gifts to political parties are exempt in much the same way as gifts to charities, with the exception that gifts made on death, or within one year before death, are exempt to the extent of £100,000 only. Qualifying political parties are defined by reference to the results at the last general election preceding the date of transfer. To qualify, the political party:

a. must have had two members elected to the House of Commons; or
b. must have had one member elected to the House of Commons and not less than 150,000 votes cast in favour of candidates who were members of the party.
(Section 24, CTTA 1984)

15. *Gifts for national purposes*

Gifts to such national bodies as the National Gallery, the British Museum, etc., are exempt. A full list of the bodies concerned is given in Schedule 3, CTTA 1984. The restrictions which can apply in relation to gifts to charities can apply equally in respect of gifts to these bodies except that the retention of a restrictive convenant over land transferred does not prevent exemption being given. There is no limit to the exemption available. (Section 25, CTTA 1984)

16. *Gifts for public benefit*

Property given for public benefit to certain non-profit-making bodies is exempt from CTT provided the Board of Inland Revenue so direct. The property which may qualify for this exemption is limited to:

a. land which is of outstanding scenic, historic or scientific interest;
b. a building which because of its outstanding historic, architectural or aesthetic interest requires special steps to be taken for its preservation;
c. land used as grounds of a building within (b);
d. an object ordinarily kept in the building and which is given at the same time as the building;
e. property given to provide a source of income for the upkeep of the property;
f. pictures, prints, books, manuscripts, works of art or scientific collections which are of national, scientific or artistic interest.

The Board will not give the necessary direction unless it is satisfied that the property given falls within (a) to (f) above and also that the body to which the property has been given is an appropriate body to be responsible for the preservation of that property. Prior to 25 July 1985 the function now performed by the Board of Inland Revenue was performed by the Treasury.   (Section 26, CTTA 1984)

17. Maintenance funds for historic buildings

Property transferred to a fund approved by the Board of Inland Revenue under Schedule 4, CTTA 1984, is exempt from CTT. The same restrictions as described in relation to gifts to charities apply in relation to gifts to these funds, such that to qualify for the exemption the gift must be an outright unconditional gift and be indefeasible.
                                             (Section 27, CTTA 1984)

18. Loans — modifications of exemptions

If the transfer of value arises not from an outright gift, but from a loan, then certain modifications are made to the provisions regarding the exemptions described above to enable them to be applied in the situation of a loan.   (Section 29, CTTA 1984)

19. Conditional exemption

Conditional exemption is available in respect of certain classes of assets designated by the Board of Inland Revenue. This exemption is only available in respect of lifetime transfers if the transferor, or his spouse, has owned the property for at least six years prior to the date of transfer, or he acquired the property on a death which was a conditionally exempt transfer.

The classes of assets which can qualify for conditional exemption include:

a. pictures, prints, books, manuscripts, works of art, scientific collections or other things not yielding income which are of national, scientific, historic or artistic interest;
b. land of outstanding scenic, historic, or artistic interest;
c. buildings of outstanding historic or architectural interest, land with those buildings and objects historically associated with the buildings.

Undertakings have to be given to the Board that reasonable steps will be taken for the preservation of the property and for securing reasonable access to the public. In the case of works of art etc. these must be retained within the United Kingdom at all times unless prior approval has been obtained from the Board.

CTT becomes payable if conditional exemption is withdrawn on the occurrence of a chargeable event. A chargeable event can include the death of the person beneficially entitled to the property, the disposal of the property, or a material breach of the undertaking given in respect of the property. A death or disposal of the property is not a chargeable event, provided:

a. the disposal itself is conditionally exempt; or
b. the undertakings previously given are renewed by the new owner (but this does not apply if the property is sold); or
c. the property is given or sold by private treaty to one of the approved bodies within Schedule 3, CTTA 1984; or
d. the property is accepted by the Board of Inland Revenue in settlement of a liability to CTT within section 230, CTTA 1984.

CTT due in respect of a chargeable event is calculated by reference to the cumulative total of the 'relevant person', usually but not always the person who made the last conditionally exempt transfer of that property at the time of the chargeable event at the lifetime rates if the 'relevant person' is alive, or at the death rates if he is dead. Generally, the amount of the chargeable event is added to the cumulative total of the person who made the last conditionally exempt transfer, not necessarily the 'relevant person', and will, subject to the ten year cumulation period, increase the rates of CTT payable on any subsequent chargeable transfers. If he is dead, the amount of the chargeable event will be added to his estate on death thus increasing the rates of CTT payable on any subsequent chargeable event.   (Section 30–34, CTTA 1984)

20. *Government securities owned by non-residents*

Certain British Government Securities are exempt from CTT provided they are owned by persons neither domiciled nor *ordinarily resident* in the United Kingdom for tax purposes. Ordinarily resident means, broadly, habitually resident. It was announced in the House of Commons on 18 March 1977 that no further exemption would be given in respect of issues of new securities until further notice. The list of exempt securities as at September 1986 is given below. The term 'domicile' in this connection means the general law definition and not the extended definition for CTT — see p. 119. If these securities are settled property, the exemption will only apply if:

a.   a person neither domiciled nor ordinarily resident in the United Kingdom is entitled to an interest in possession, or
b.   if there is no interest in possession in the settled property, all potential beneficiaries are neither domiciled nor ordinarily resident in the United Kingdom.

List of exempt securities in issue at September 1986

Savings Certificates issued before 1st September 1922 and 7th, 8th and £1 issues

3½%	War Loan	1952 or after	12¾%	Treasury Loan	1995
8½%	Treasury Loan	1984/86	9%	Treasury Loan	1992/96
6½%	Funding Loan	1985/87	15¼%	Treasury Loan	1996
7¾%	Treasury Loan	1985/88	13¼%	Exchequer Loan	1996
13%	Treasury Stock	1990	13¼%	Treasury Loan	1997
8¼%	Treasury Loan	1987/90	8¾%	Treasury Loan	1997
5¾%	Funding Loan	1987/91	6¾%	Treasury Loan	1995/98
12¾%	Treasury Loan	1992	15½%	Treasury Loan	1998
12½%	Treasury Loan	1993	9½%	Treasury Loan	1999
6%	Funding Loan	1993	8%	Treasury Loan	2002/06
13¾%	Treasury Loan	1993	5½%	Treasury Stock	2008/12
14½%	Treasury Loan	1994	7¾%	Treasury Loan	2112/15
9%	Treasury Loan	1994			

21. *Overseas pensions*

There are special rules governing pensions paid to former employees of former colonial governments to the effect that on the death of the former employee, they are not regarded as part of the estate or treated as having been paid abroad.
                (Section 153, CTTA 1984)

22. *Cash options under approved retirement annuity schemes*

Sums of money paid to a deceased person's widow or dependants in lieu of a retirement annuity for self-employed persons and the cash option are not regarded as part of the estate.   (Section 152, CTTA 1984)

23. *Death on active service*

People in the armed forces or a number of specified auxiliary bodies (such as nurses, clergy, etc.) who die on active service are exempt, provided their representatives obtain the appropriate certificate from the Defence Council or the Secretary of State.

(Section 154, CTTA 1984)

24. *Visiting forces and staff of allied headquarters*

Emoluments and tangible moveable property of members of visiting forces (other than citizens of the United Kingdom and Colonies) and certain staff of allied headquarters are exempt.

(Section 155, CTTA 1984)

INDEPENDENCE OF EXEMPTIONS

Virtually all of the exemptions reviewed above in relation to lifetime dispositions can be applied independently of the others. As such, a single transfer of value may qualify for more than one exemption. However, as indicated above, the small gift exemption cannot be used in conjunction with any other exemption and can only be applied in relation to an outright gift of no more than £250 to any one person. In general terms it is not normally important which exemption is used, but it is usually advisable to use any other available exemptions before using the annual exemption.

The following examples demonstrate the effect of partial exemption and the independence of the various exemptions.

Example 3

Mr *D* who had made no transfers of value since 6 April 1984 made the following gifts in the year 1985/86:

a. to his wife   — £5,000
b. to his son   — a reversionary interest valued at £10,000
c. to his daughter — £3,500 on the occasion of her marriage
d. to his chauffeur — £200
e. to his secretary — £1,000
f. to his nephew   — £2,000
g. to his niece   — £2,000

The position is as follows:

a. £5,000   — Exempt (Exemption 8)
b. £10,000 — Excluded property
c. £3,500   — Exempt (Exemption 12)
d. £200   — Exempt (Exemption 10)
e. £1,000   —
f. £2,000   —   } Exempt (Exemption 9, including £2,000 brought forward from 1984/85)
g. £2,000   —

Example 4

Mr *E*, who had used his annual exemption in the year ended 5 April 1985, made the following gifts in the year 1985/86:

a. 25 December 1985 — £200 to each of his four grandchildren
b. 25 December 1985 — £500 to each of his two sons
c. 14 February 1986 — £5,000 to his sister

The position is as follows:

	£
a. Gifts to grandchildren (4 × £200)	800
Small gifts exemption 1985/86 — part	800
Chargeable to tax:	Nil
b. Gifts to sons (2 × £500)	1,000
Annual exemption 1985/86 — part	1,000
Chargeable to tax:	Nil
c. Gift to sister	5,000
Annual exemption 1985/86 — balance	2,000
Chargeable to tax:	3,000

Note: The small gifts exemption cannot be used in considering the position at (b) and (c) as the gifts exceed £250.

CALCULATING THE TAX PAYABLE — LIFETIME DISPOSITIONS

Transfers of value made, after deducting the available exemptions, are known as 'chargeable transfers'. In the case of lifetime dispositions it must be established if the tax is to be paid by the donor or the donee. If the donor pays the tax, the loss to his estate will include the tax payable, hence the chargeable transfer actually made has to be grossed up in calculating the tax payable.

In order to calculate the tax payable on any chargeable transfer it is also necessary to know the transferor's previous cumulative total of chargeable transfers. This cumulative total is now limited to chargeable transfers made within the period of ten years ending with the date of the current transfer.

The following examples illustrate the method of calculating the CTT payable on lifetime chargeable transfers in accordance with the table of rates in force after 5 April 1985. The relevant scale rates are reproduced in full in Appendix III.

Example 5

Mr *F*, who had a cumulative total of chargeable transfers of £50,000, made a chargeable transfer, i.e. after exemptions, of £35,000 in the year 1985/86. It was agreed that the donee would pay any CTT due.

The CTT due is calculated as follows:

		£
Cumulative total brought forward		50,000
Chargeable transfer 1985/86		35,000
Revised cumulative total		£85,000
CTT payable:		
On first £67,000 @ Nil	=	Nil
On next £18,000 @ 15%	=	2,700.00
Total CTT payable		£2,700.00

The above example demonstrates the position if no CTT had been paid on the earlier transfers. With the rates of CTT changing, or likely to change, each year any CTT paid on an earlier transfer will probably have been computed by reference to an earlier scale of rates. The following example illustrates the calculation of CTT payable in this situation.

Example 6

Mr *G* had made gross chargeable transfers totalling £70,000. The last transfer made was a gift of £25,000 to his son in March 1985 and this gave rise to a CTT liability of £900, i.e. £6,000 @ 15%. In 1985/86 he made further chargeable transfers of £25,000. CTT payable by donee.
The CTT due is calculated as follows:

	£
Cumulative total brought forward	70,000
Chargeable transfer 1985/86	25,000
Revised cumulative total	£95,000

CTT payable:		
On first £67,000 @ Nil	=	Nil
On next £22,000 @ 15%	=	3,300.00
On next £ 6,000 @ 17.5%	=	1,050.00
CTT due on £95,000		£4,350.00

Less CTT due on £70,000:		
On first £67,000 @ Nil	=	Nil	
On next £ 3,000 @ 15%	=	450.00	450.00
CTT payable on transfer of £25,000:			£3,900.00

Note: The amount of tax paid in respect of previous transfers is ignored. It is recalculated by reference to the current rates of tax and the amount as calculated is deducted from the total CTT due to ascertain the amount payable in respect of the current transfer. Although CTT of £900 was actually paid in respect of the earlier transfer no refund is obtainable.

Examples 5 and 6 above have demonstrated the calculation of CTT payable in respect of gross transfers, i.e. where the *donee* is to pay the tax. The following two examples illustrate the calculations where the *donor* is to pay the tax, i.e. where the grossing up procedure applies.

Example 7

Mr *H* had made chargeable transfers in the year 1984/85 totalling £55,000. These were the first chargeable transfers he had made. In the year 1985/86 he transferred cash of £25,000 to his son and he agreed to pay any CTT payable in respect of this gift.
The CTT due is calculated as follows:

	£
Cash transferred — transfer of value	25,000
Less Annual exemption 1985/86	3,000
Chargeable transfer	£22,000
Net cumulative total brought forward (since the chargeable transfer in 1984/85 was within the Nil rate band the gross and net cumulative totals will be the same)	55,000
Add Net chargeable transfer 1985/86	22,000
Revised net cumulative total	£77,000

CTT payable as follows:		
On first £67,000 @ Nil	=	Nil
On next £10,000 @ 3/17	=	1,764.70
		1,764.70
Less CTT on previous transfer		Nil
CTT payable on net transfer of £22,000		£1,764.70

Gross cumulative total carried forward:	
Revised net cumulative total	77,000
Add CTT payable	1,764.70
Gross cumulative total carried foward	£78,764.70

The position becomes a little more complicated when there has been a change in rates of CTT between two net transfers. It then becomes important to follow the detailed steps in this calculation as follows:

1. Ascertain the previous gross cumulative total of the transferor.
2. Find the tax due on this amount by reference to the current rates of tax on gross transfers.
3. Deduct 2 from 1 to find the net cumulative total.
4. Add to the amount ascertained at 3 the net amount of the new chargeable transfer to ascertain the new net cumulative total.
5. Calculate the CTT payable on the new net cumulative total.
6. Deduct the tax at 2 from the tax at 5 to give the tax payable on the net gift.

Example 8

Mr *J* made net chargeable transfers in the years 1984/85 and 1985/86 as follows:

$$1984/85 \quad £70,000$$
$$1985/86 \quad £25,000$$

He had made no previous chargeable transfers.
   The CTT due is calculated as follows:

1984/85
CTT payable on net transfer of £70,000 using rates in force to 5 April 1985:

			£
On first £64,000 @ Nil	=		Nil
On next £ 6,000 @ 3/17	=		1,058.82
CTT payable on net transfer of £70,000			£1,058.82

Gross cumulative total carried forward	
Net chargeable transfer	70,000
Add CTT payable	1,058.82
Gross cumulative total carried forward	£71,058.82

1985/86
CTT payable on net chargeable transfer of £25,000:

Gross cumulative total brought forward			71,058.82
Less CTT at rates in force from 6 April 1985:			
On first £67,000 @ Nil	=	Nil	
On next £ 4,058.82 @ 15%	=	608.82	608.82
Net cumulative total brought forward			70,450
Add new net chargeable transfer			25,000
Revised net cumulative total			£95,450

CTT payable:			
On first £67,000 @ Nil	=		Nil
On next £18,700 @ 3/17	=		3,300.00
On next £ 9,750 @ 7/33	=		2,068.18
			5,368.18
Less CTT due on previous net cumulative total			608.82
CTT payable on net chargeable transfer of £25,000			£4,759.36

Gross cumulative total carried forward:

Revised net cumulative total	95,450
Add CTT payable	5,368.18
Gross cumulative total carried forward	£100,818.18

Note: Although the CTT payable in respect of the net chargeable transfer in 1984/85 was £1,058.82 and only £608.82 has been taken into account in calculating the CTT payable in respect of the net chargeable transfer in the year 1985/86, the difference of £450 is not repayable.

Full example — lifetime transfers

In order to illustrate many of the points made in respect of lifetime transfers and the calculation of CTT payable, it is proposed to work through a detailed example.

Example 9

Mr *K*, a millionaire, married with three children and five grandchildren, has made the following transfers of value since 26 March 1974:

5 October 1974:	£12,000 to his son Peter
14 July 1976:	£100,000 worth of shares to his wife
16 May 1978:	£100,000 cash to two charities equally
25 December 1979:	£250 cash to each of his five grandchildren
15 January 1980:	£5,000 cash to his son John
15 January 1980:	£5,000 cash to his daughter Mary
16 June 1984:	£50,000 cash to his daughter to help her buy a house
16 March 1985:	a car valued at £7,500 to his son Peter
25 December 1985:	£500 to each of his five grandchildren
25 December 1985:	£10,000 to each of his three children

With the exception of the gifts in December 1985, it was agreed that the donees would pay any CTT due.

You are required to calculate to the nearest £ the CTT payable in respect of the above transfers.

1974/75	£	£	£
Gift to son Peter		12,000	
Less Annual exemption 1974/75	1,000		
Annual exemption 1973/74	1,000		
Small gift exemption	100	2,100	
Chargeable transfer		9,900	9,900
CTT payable: £9,900 @ Nil =		Nil	
1976/77			
Gift to wife		100,000	
Less Exemption — section 18, CTTA 1984		100,000	
Chargeable transfer		Nil	Nil
1978/79			
Gift to charities		100,000	
Less Exemption — section 23, CTTA 1984		100,000	
Chargeable transfer		Nil	Nil
1979/80			
Gifts to grandchildren (5 × £250)		1,250	
Gifts to son and daughter (2 × £5,000)		10,000	
		11,250	

Less Small gifts exemption (7 × £100)	700		
Annual exemption 1979/80	2,000		
Annual exemption 1978/79	2,000	4,700	
Chargeable transfer		6,550	6,550
Revised cumulative total			16,450
CTT payable: £16,450 @ Nil =		Nil	

1984/85

Gift to daughter		50,000	
Gift to son		7,500	
		57,000	
Less Annual exemption 1984/85	3,000		
Annual exemption 1983/84	3,000	6,000	
Chargeable transfer		51,500	51,500
Revised cumulative total			67,950
CTT payable:			
On first £64,000 @ Nil =		Nil	
On next £ 3,950 @ 15% =		592.50	
Total CTT payable		£ 592.50	

This will be payable by Peter since transfer to him was the last transfer made in 1984/85, and therefore as CTT is payable on less than value transferred to Peter, all CTT is payable by him.

1985/86

	£
Gifts to grandchildren (5 × £500)	2,500
Gifts to children (3 × £10,000)	30,000
	32,500
Less Annual exemption 1985/86	3,000
Chargeable transfers	29,500

Since any CTT payable in respect of these gifts is payable by Mr *K*, the grossing up procedure applies as follows:

			£
Gross cumulative total brought foward			67,950
Less CTT on this at current rates:			
On first £67,000 @ Nil =		Nil	
On next £ 950 @ 15% =		142.50	142.50
Net cumulative total brought forward			67,807.50
Add New net chargeable transfers			29,500.00
Revised net cumulative total			£97,307.50
CTT payable:			
On first £67,000 @ Nil =			Nil
On next £12,700 @ 3/7 =			3,300.00
On next £11,607.50 @ 7/33 =			2,462.20
			5,762.20
Less CTT due on previous net cumulative total			142.50
CTT payable on net chargeable transfers of £29,500			£ 5,619.70

Gross cumulative total carried forward:	
Revised net cumulative total	97,307.50
Add CTT payable	5,762.20
Gross cumulative total carried forward:	£103,069.70

Note: Prior to 5 April 1981 the small gifts exemption (£100 to 5 April 1980) could be claimed regardless of the total amount of the value transferred, hence the deductions given for this exemption in the years 1974/75 and 1979/80. The small gifts exemption of £250 is not due for the years 1984/85 and 1985/86 as the transfers of value made all exceed £250.

PAYMENT OF TAX

Due dates for payment (lifetime dispositions)

Tax on lifetime transfers is due six months after the end of the month in which the transfer is made, or in the case of transfers made after 5 April and before 1 October, on 30 April in the next year.   (Section 226, CTTA 1984)

Interest on unpaid tax (lifetime dispositions)

Interest is charged on overdue CTT from the due date, as above, to the date of payment. With effect from 1 May 1985 the rate of interest charged is at the rate of 11% per annum. Prior to 1 May 1985 the rate was 8 per cent (SI, 1985/569). Any interest paid is not allowable for any tax purposes.   (Section 233, CTTA 1984)

Interest on overpaid tax (lifetime dispositions)

Any CTT overpaid carries interest from the date of payment to the date it is repaid at the same rate as would have been charged if the CTT had been outstanding. Any interest received is not income from any tax purposes.   (Section 235, CTTA 1984)

Payment of tax by instalments (lifetime gifts)

Where the CTT is payable by the donee it is possible to elect to pay the CTT by instalments if the property transferred is within the following:

a. land and buildings wherever situated;
b. shares or securities within section 228, CTTA 1984, broadly shares or securities which give the transferor control, shares or securities of an unquoted company if the Board are satisfied that hardship would arise if all the CTT was payable immediately, and certain other unquoted shares where the value transferred amounts to at least £20,000 (£5,000 pre-15 March 1983);
c. a business or an interest in a business, as defined in section 227(7), CTTA 1984.

If the person due to pay the CTT makes a formal election, the CTT can be paid by ten equal annual instalments of which the first is payable on the normal due date. In practice the CTT account, CAP — C5, includes a question concerning the payment of the CTT by instalments.

Nothwithstanding the making of an election to pay the CTT due by instalments, the outstanding balance, together with any interest arising to the time of payment, becomes payable should the property be sold or be the subject of a futher chargeable transfer other than on death.

Interest will be charged from the normal due date to the date of payment of each instalment. In practice the interest due on the outstanding balance to the date each instalment is due will be added to the instalment and collected with the instalment. However, interest will only be charged from the date each instalment becomes due if the property transferred comprised:

a. shares or securities of a company, but excluding shares in investment, or dealing companies (dealing in land or securities) unless the company is a holding company for one or more companies carrying on qualifying activities or a jobber or discount house; or
b. a business or an interest in a business.

If property transferred falls within the above classes of assets then it is possible for the CTT due to be paid by instalments over ten years without interest provided each instalment is paid on time.   (Sections 227, 228 and 234, CTTA 1984)

Acceptance of property in satisfaction of tax

The Board may accept, upon application by the person liable to pay an amount of CTT, property in satisfaction of that CTT. Acceptable property includes land, certain buildings and their contents, works of art and other items of national, historic, scientific or artistic interest.   (Section 230, CTTA 1984)

Exercise 10

1. What is a transfer of value? How is a gift valued for capital transfer tax purposes?
2. What is a chargeable transfer?
3. What is excluded property?
4. Can the small gifts exemption be added to any other exemptions?
5. How is it possible to carry forward an annual exemption?
6. If a husband who is domiciled in the United Kingdom marries a wife who is domiciled outside the United Kingdom, is there any limit on exempt transfers from the husband to his wife?
7. Mr Jones gifts cash of £25,000 to his son Peter to help him buy his own house. Assuming Mr Jones has a previous cumulative total of £50,000 made within the ten years preceding the gift of cash on 31 August 1985, what is the capital transfer tax payable if:

   a. the tax is paid by Mr Jones; and
   b. the tax is paid by Peter.

   Mr Jones made no other transfers of value after 5 April 1984.

11
Capital Transfer Tax II

The previous chapter considered the various exemptions available. In this chapter the main reliefs will be considered as these can materially reduce an individual's liability to CTT. As indicated in the introduction to Chapter 10, this chapter will only be concerned with the provisions regarding CTT up to 17 March 1986. For an explanation of the provisions regarding inheritance tax, see Chapter 14.

DOUBLE TAXATION RELIEF

Where property abroad becomes liable to capital transfer tax by reason of a chargeable transfer of value having been effected by an individual domiciled in this country, it is possible that the transfer may also be liable to tax in the country in which the property is situated. Relief in respect of the overseas tax suffered is given in the following ways.

a. *Unilateral relief.* Credit is given against United Kingdom tax for the *full amount of tax* charged by another country on *property situated in that country*. For transfers after 6 April 1976 credit is given where both the United Kingdom and another country imposes tax on:
   i. property situated in a third country; or
   ii. property which is situated both in the United Kingdom under United Kingdom law and in the other country under that country's law.
   In these circumstances the credit is for a proportion of the tax. The proportionate credit is computed by the formula:

$$\frac{A}{A+B} \times C$$

where A is the UK capital transfer tax, B is the overseas tax and C is the lower of the two taxes A or B. (Section 159, CTTA 1984)

Example 1

A taxpayer domiciled in Ruritania and treated as domiciled in the United Kingdom makes a gift of property situated in Utopia.

	£
United Kingdom capital transfer tax	1,000 (A)
Ruritanian capital transfer tax £250 (B and C)	
Double tax relief $\dfrac{1,000}{1,000+250} \times 250 =$	200
United Kingdom tax payable	£ 800

Example 2

A taxpayer domiciled in the United Kingdom holds shares in a Ruritanian company which maintains a duplicate share register in the United Kingdom. The shares are regarded as situated in the UK under British law and in Ruritania under its laws. The calculation would be the same as under Example 1.

b. *Double taxation agreements.* Agreements made previously in respect of estate duty continue in force for CTT purposes, but only apply to CTT arising on death. New agreements concluded in respect of CTT apply in respect of lifetime transfers as well as transfers on death. If relief is due under both an agreement and under (a) above, the relief given is calculated under whichever provision provides the greater amount of relief. (Section 158, CTTA 1984)

BUSINESS PROPERTY RELIEF

This relief was originally introduced by the Finance Act 1976. It was substantially revised for transfers which took place after 26 October 1977 and has been subject to various changes subsequent to that time.

Nature of the relief

The relief takes the form of a percentage reduction in the value transferred provided all the qualifying conditions are satisfied. The percentage reduction in value depends upon the nature of the property transferred. Since the relief takes the form of a reduction in the value transferred it is given *before* any other available exemptions are deducted in calculating the chargeable transfer.

Conditions for claiming business property relief

In order to qualify for business property relief the assets transferred:

a. must be 'relevant business property', and
b. must have been owned for a minimum period of time.

Each of these will now be considered in more detail.

Relevant business property

This is defined in section 105, CTTA 1984 and includes the following:

a. a business or an interest in a business;
b. shares or securities of a company which, either alone or with other shares or securities held by the transferor, give control of the company. Related property — (see Chapter 12) — is taken into account for this purpose, with certain exceptions;
c. shares in a company not within (b) and which are not quoted on a recognized stock exchange — shares quoted on the Unlisted Securities Market are not quoted for this purpose;
d. land, buildings, plant or machinery which, immediately before the transfer, was used wholly or mainly for the purposes of a business carried on by a company of which the transferor then had control or by a partnership of which he was a partner; and
e. land, buildings, plant or machinery which, immediately before the transfer, was

used wholly or mainly for the purposes of a business carried on by the transferor which was settled property in which he was then beneficially entitled to an interest in possession (see Chapter 13 dealing with settled property for a definition of this term).

Modifications to definition of relevant business property

The general definition of relevant business property above is modified to exclude certain classes of business or the whole of the business in certain circumstances as follows.

a. A business, or interest in a business, or shares or securities of a company are not relevant business property if the business consists wholly or mainly of dealing in stocks and shares or land and buildings or making or holding investments. Exceptions to this rule include jobbers and discount houses and the shares of a holding company if the shares of at least one subsidiary would qualify as relevant business property.

b. Shares or securities of a company are not relevant business property if at the time of the transfer the company has made a resolution for a voluntary winding up, a winding up order has been made or the company is otherwise in the course of liquidation. This does not apply if the business of the company is to continue, the purpose of the winding up or liquidation being to effect a reconstruction or amalgamation and this takes place within one year of the transfer.

c. Land, buildings, etc., within (d) and (e) of the previous section are not relevant business property unless the business or shares are relevant business property.

d. Property subject to a binding contract for sale at the date of transfer is not relevant business property unless the contract is to incorporate a business or reconstruct a company. Buy and sell agreements will also prevent property qualifying as relevant business property (see Inland Revenue Statement of Practice SP 12/80).

Minimum period of ownership

To qualify as relevant business property the transferor must have owned the property for a minimum period of two years. This general rule is modified in the following circumstances:

a. If the property transferred replaced other property, which had it been transferred immediately before it was replaced would have qualified as relevant business property, and the period during which the property transferred and the replaced property was owned amounts to at least two years out of the last five years, the property transferred qualifies as relevant business property, but the value on which relief is calculated cannot exceed that of the replaced property.
    (Section 107, CTTA 1984)

b. Where the transferor became entitled to any property on the death of another person he is deemed to have owned it from the date of death. Furthermore, if the property passes on death from one spouse to the other, the period of ownership of the deceased spouse is aggregated with that of the surviving spouse.
    (Section 108, CTTA 1984)

c. Property transferred within two years of acquisition can still qualify as relevant business property and be deemed to have satisfied the two year ownership test provided either the acquisition of the property or the subsequent transfer takes place on a death. The property, or property which it replaced, must have been eligible for business property relief at the time of the earlier transfer.

(Section 109, CTTA 1984)

Value for the purpose of business property relief

It is important to be able to determine the value of the property transferred in respect of which relief will be due. The following points are relevant.

a. The value of a business is the net value of the business, i.e. the value of all the assets used in the business, including the value of any goodwill, less any liabilities incurred for the purposes of the business. (See *Finch and Others* v. *IRC* (1983), later renamed *Fetherstonaugh and Others* v. *IRC* (1984) when heard in the Court of Appeal. This case was concerned with the inclusion within the terms 'relevant business assets' and 'assets used in the business' where one of the assets used, land, was settled property in which the deceased had been the life tenant. It was held that the land was relevant business property and hence its value had to be taken into account in ascertaining the net value of the business.) (See also Chapter 13.)

(Section 110, CTTA 1984)

b. Where it is necessary to value the shares of a company which is the member of a group of companies, and one or more of the companies is excluded from the definition of 'relevant business property', the shares are valued as if the non-qualifying companies are not members of the group.

(Section 111, CTTA 1984)

c. Where the business, including a business run by a company, owns assets which are not used wholly or mainly for the purposes of the business and have not been so used throughout the two years prior to the transfer, and are not required at the time of the transfer for future use for the purposes of the business, the value of those assets is excluded in determining the value of the business, or the shares if the business is run by a company. An asset owned by one member of a group, but used for the purposes of the business of another group member is not excluded under this rule. Assets excluded under this rule are known as 'excepted assets'. Where part, but not the whole, of land or buildings is used exclusively for the purposes of a business and as a result of the above rule the whole would be treated as an excepted asset, it is possible to treat the land or building as two separate assets and the value of the part used exclusively for business purposes can be included in the value qualifying for business property relief. This value is arrived at by apportioning the value of the whole in a manner which may be just, although no guidance is given as to how this apportionment should be made.

(Section 112, CTTA 1984)

Rate of relief

There are now only two rates of relief available. These are as follows:

a. 50% in respect of property falling within (a) and (b) of the definitions of relevant business property above, and
b. 30% in respect of other relevant business property.

For transfers prior to 15 March 1983 the rate of relief available in respect of property within (c) of the definitions of relevant business property above was 20%.

(Section 104, CTTA 1984)

It is specifically provided that property which received agricultural property relief (see below) is not eligible for business property relief.

(Section 114, CTTA 1984)

AGRICULTURAL PROPERTY RELIEF

Introduction

Although agricultural property relief was included within the provisions for CTT when CTT was introduced in the Finance Act 1975, the whole concept of the relief was changed for transfers made after 9 March 1981. The new scheme of relief was introduced by section 96 and Schedule 14, FA 1981, now sections 115 to 124, CTTA 1984. The description of the relief which follows is concerned with the new scheme of relief only.

Agricultural property

This is defined as agricultural land or pasture situated in the United Kingdom, the Channel Islands or the Isle of Man and includes woodlands and buildings used in connection with the intensive rearing of livestock etc. provided the occupation of the woodland or buildings is ancillary to that of the agricultural land and buildings. It also includes farm houses, farm cottages and farm buildings which are of a character appropriate to the agricultural land. The term 'agricultural' for this purpose includes the rearing and grazing of horses on a stud farm and the growing of mushrooms and tomatoes as well as sporting rights. However, the value eligible for relief is limited to the agricultural value of the land, i.e. excluding, for example, any development value of the land.

(Section 115, CTTA 1984)

Qualifying transferors

Relief is available to individual transferors and also trustees of settled property in which no interest in possession subsists.

(Section 115, CTTA 1984)

The relief available

As with business property relief (see p. 137) there are two rates of relief available as follows:

a. 50 per cent if the interest of the transferor gave the right to vacant possession or the right to obtain it within twelve months, or

the transferor had owned his interest prior to 10 March 1981 and had he disposed of the land on 9 March 1981 he would have been entitled to relief at the rate of 50 per cent under the old rules.

If there would have been a restriction of the relief under the old rules by reason of the overriding limits which then applied of £250,000 or 1,000 acres, the new relief will be similarly restricted, although any balance will automatically qualify for relief at the 30 per cent rate in (b) below.

b. 30 per cent in all other cases (20 per cent for transfers made prior to 15 March 1983). This covers broadly tenanted land to which the relief at (a) above does not apply.

Where the interests of all joint tenants or tenants in common, or the equivalent interests in Scotland, give vacant possession then each joint tenant or tenant in common is deemed to have vacant possession.

(Section 116, CTTA 1984)

Minimum period of ownership or occupation

Agricultural property relief is not available unless the agricultural property:

1. has been occupied by the transferor for the purposes of agricultural throughout the period of two years ending with the date of the transfer, or
2. has been owned by the transferor throughout the period of seven years ending with the date of the transfer and has been occupied for the purposes of agriculture, although not necessarily by the transferor.

(Section 117, CTTA 1984)

The above basic conditions are modified in the following circumstances:

a. Relief is allowed on replacement property where the property transferred, together with the property which it replaced, had been occupied for at least two years of the five years immediately preceding the transfer. In the case of tenanted property, the property transferred together with the property it replaced, must have been owned for at least seven years of the ten years immediately preceding the date of the transfer. Relief is limited to the amount which would have been available had the replacement not taken place, i.e. it is not possible to increase the relief by replacing one property by a more valuable property within the relevant period. Changes arising from the formation, alteration or dissolution of a partnership are ignored for this purpose.

(Section 118, CTTA 1984)
b. Occupation of agricultural property by a company which is controlled by the transferor is treated as occupation by the transferor. Occupation by a Scottish partnership is treated as occupation by the partners, notwithstanding the fact that a partnership is a separate legal entity in Scotland.

(Section 119, CTTA 1984)
c. Where a transferor became entitled to the agricultural property on the death of another person he is deemed to have owned it from the date of death. He is also treated as having occupied it from the date of death if he subsequently occupies it. Furthermore, if the other person was his spouse he is treated as having occupied or owned the agricultural property throughout any period for which his spouse occupied or owned it. This is so even for the purposes of the 50 per cent transitional relief available provided the transferor would have qualified for the old 50 per cent relief if he owned his interest prior to 10 March 1981 (see section (a) of the reliefs available above).

(Section 120, CTTA 1984)
d. The two year occupation test or seven year ownership test is treated as satisfied, if not otherwise satisfied, where all the following conditions are satisfied:
   i.   there are two transfers of value, known as 'the earlier transfer' and 'the later transfer' of which at least one arose on a death, and
   ii. the earlier transfer must have qualified for agricultural property relief, and
   iii. the whole, or part, of the agricultural property which was transferred by the earlier transfer became the property of the person, or his spouse, who made the

later transfer and at the time of the later transfer was occupied either by the person making the later transfer or the personal representatives of the person who made the earlier transfer, and

iv. the property, or any replacement property, would qualify for agricultural property relief apart from the minimum period of occupation or ownership.

(Section 121, CTTA 1984)

Agricultural property of companies

Where the asset transferred comprises shares or securities of a company, and the assets of the company include the agricultural value of agricultural property then agricultural property relief will be due provided:

a. the shares or securities gave the transferor control of the company, and
b. part of the value of the shares or securities can be attributed to the agricultural value of the agricultural property owned by the company, and
c. the agricultural property was occupied for the purposes of agriculture for the period of two years immediately preceding the date of the transfer, or the company owned the agricultural property throughout the period of seven years immediately preceding the date of the transfer and the property was occupied for the purposes of agriculture throughout that seven year period by the company or another person,
d. the shares or securities must have been owned by the transferor throughout the periods of two years or seven years within (c) above.

The rules regarding replacement property (see section (a) of the paragraph on the minimum period of ownership or occupation above) are available, in a slightly modified form, to enable relief to be given in respect of replacement property which, together with the property it replaced, was held for two years out of the previous five years for owner occupied property or seven out of the previous ten years for tenanted property.

Relief is in any event limited to the appropriate percentage of the value of the shares or securities which is attributable to the agricultural value of the agricultural property owned by the company.

(Sections 122 and 123, CTTA 1984)

Binding contracts for sale

Agricultural property relief is not available if at the time of the transfer the transferor has signed a contract for the sale of the land. This also applies in respect of a transfer of shares within the previous section if the transferor has signed a contract for the sale of the shares. However, there are two exceptions to this general rule as follows:

a. where the agricultural land is being sold to a company and the consideration is wholly or mainly shares or securities of the company and these will give the transferor control of the company, or
b. where, in relation to the shares or securities of a company within the previous section, the sale is being made for the purposes of a reconstruction or amalgamation.   (Section 124, CTTA 1984)

WOODLANDS

Where a person's estate on death includes the value of land which is not agricultural property within the definition given on p. 140, and there are trees growing on the land, it is possible to exclude the value of the growing timber and underwood when determining the CTT payable on death. If the timber is disposed of before the next death, whether by gift, sale or otherwise, CTT is charged on the sale proceeds or value of the timber at the time of the disposal.

It is not always advantageous to claim this relief. For example, if the timber is immature at the date of death the value of the relief may be insignificant, but if claimed a substantial liability to CTT may arise based upon the sale proceeds of the mature timber. However, if there is no disposal of the timber between the death on which the claim arises and the next death on which the timber is transferred, the relief claimed on the first death becomes permanent. Clearly each case must be examined carefully before a claim is made.

Relief is available provided all the following conditions are satisfied.

a. The land must be included in a person's estate on death and the land must not be 'agricultural property' within the definition for Agricultural Property Relief.
b. The person must have been beneficially entitled to the land throughout the period of five years ending with the date of death, or have become beneficially entitled to it within that period otherwise than for a consideration in money or money's worth. This includes a person entitled to an interest in possession in settled property.
c. A formal election in writing must be made to the Board within two years from the date of death, or such longer period as the Board may allow, by the person liable to pay the CTT.

(Section 125, CTTA 1984)

If the above conditions are satisfied, the value of the growing timber is left out of account in determining the value of the person's estate on his death.

(Section 125, (2)(a), CTTA 1984)

Where the whole or part of the timber is disposed of, other than by way of a transfer on death, a charge to CTT arises in respect of the net proceeds of sale if sold, or the net value of the trees or underwood disposed of if not disposed of for a consideration in money or money's worth. (Section 126, CTTA 1984)

In calculating the net proceeds of sale or the net value of the timber or underwood, the following expenses may be deducted:

a. the expenses incurred in disposing of the trees or underwood, and
b. the expenses incurred in replanting within three years of the disposal, or such longer time as the Board may allow, to replace the trees etc. disposed of, and
c. the expenses of replanting to replace trees or underwood previously disposed of, so far as not allowed in respect of the previous disposal,

so far as these expenses have not been allowed for income tax purposes.

(Section 130, CTTA 1984)

The charge to CTT is calculated as if the net proceeds of sale, or net value, as determined above, were included as part of the value transferred on the earlier death and as if the value formed the highest part of the estate. If the disposal giving rise to the charge to CTT is itself a chargeable transfer, for example an *inter vivos* gift, the value transferred by that chargeable transfer is reduced by the CTT payable under these provisions.

(Sections 128 and 129, CTTA 1984)

Example 3

A died in June 1985 leaving an estate of £150,000, including land and growing timber valued at £30,000. The value of the land was agreed at £8,000. The whole estate was left to *A*'s son and an election for woodlands relief was made. *A* had made no previous chargeable transfers. *A*'s son sold the timber for £55,000 in December 1985, incurring expenses of £4,500 for felling the trees, commission on sale of £500, and £2,500 for replanting. The CTT position is as follows:

		£
A's death		
Gross value of estate		150,000
Less value of timber (£30,000 − £8,000)		22,000
CTT due on		£128,000
CTT payable:		
On first £67,000 @ Nil	=	Nil
On next £22,000 @ 30%	=	6,600.00
On next £33,000 @ 35%	=	11,550.00
On next £ 6,000 @ 40%	=	2,400.00
Total CTT payable		£20,550.00

	£	£
Sale of timber		
Gross proceeds of sale		55,000
Less: Felling costs	4,500	
Sale commission	500	
Replanting costs	2,500	7,500
Net proceeds of sale		£47,500

The CTT chargeable is calculated as follows:

		£
Value of estate on death		128,000
Add Net proceeds of sale		47,500
Total		£175,500
CTT payable:		
On first £67,000 @ Nil	=	Nil
On next £22,000 @ 30%	=	6,600.00
On next £33,000 @ 35%	=	11,550.00
On next £33,000 @ 40%	=	13,200.00
On next £20,500 @ 45%	=	9,225.00
		40,575.00
Deduct CTT charged on death		20,550.00
Further CTT payable		£20,025.00

If *A*'s son had gifted the timber instead of having sold it, and the net value had been £47,500, the value transferred would have been £27,475, i.e. £47,500 less additional CTT payable of £20,025.

Exercise 11

1. Describe briefly the two forms of double taxation relief available.
2. Describe what you understand by the term 'relevant business property'.
3. Certain classes of asset, or business, are excluded from the term 'relevant business property'. What assets are excluded?
4. What rates of relief are available in respect of the classes of 'relevant business property'?
5. What do you understand by the term 'agricultural property relief'?
6. What conditions have to be satisfied before agricultural property relief is available at the rate of 50%?
7. What value is eligible for agricultural relief?
8. Describe briefly the scheme of relief available in respect of woodlands.

12
Capital Transfer Tax III

INTRODUCTION

As has been mentioned earlier, there are two scales of rates of CTT: a lifetime scale and a scale applicable to transfers made on or within three years prior to death. The appropriate scales of rates are reproduced in Appendix III. Before examining the position in relation to CTT on death it is appropriate to consider the recalculation of the CTT payable in respect of transfers made within three years of death. This chapter only deals with the position under the CTT legislation which applies to 17 March 1986. The position from 18 March 1986 under the new provisions for inheritance tax is examined in Chapter 14.

CTT payable on transfers made within three years of death

On the occasion of the transfer CTT will have been calculated by reference to the lifetime rates in force at the date of the transfer. If death occurs within three years of the date of the transfer, death on the third anniversary of the gift is not within three years, the CTT must be recalculated using the death rates in force at the date of death. Any additional CTT due is payable by the donee, regardless of the person who paid the CTT on transfer.

Example 1

Mr A made a gift of cash of £85,000, his first ever transfer, to his daughter in March 1985. The CTT due was payable by his daughter. He died in January 1986. The CTT payable is as follows:

	£	£
a. *Lifetime transfer:*		
Gross transfer		85,000
Less Annual exemption:		
1984/85	3,000	
1983/84	3,000	6,000
Chargeable transfer		£79,000
CTT payable:		
On first £64,000 @ Nil =		Nil
On next £15,000 @ 15% =		2,250.00
CTT payable		£2,250.00
b. *Recalculation of CTT on death:*		£
Chargeable transfer — as before		£79,000

CTT payable:		
On first £67,000 @ Nil	=	Nil
On next £12,000 @ 30%	=	3,600.00
Total		3,600.00
Less CTT paid previously		2,250.00
Additional CTT payable		£1,350.00

It may be that as a result of changes in the rates of CTT in force between the date of gift and the date of death that the CTT due at the new death rates is less than the CTT actually paid at the old lifetime rates. If this occurs, then no additional CTT liability arises, but none of the previously paid CTT is repayable.

The above example demonstrates the calculation required if the donee paid the CTT on the earlier transfer. The calculation is a little more complicated if the donor paid the CTT on the earlier transfer. The following example illustrates the calculation if this applies.

Example 2

Mr *B*, who had a previous cumulative total of £40,000, made a chargeable transfer, i.e. after exemptions, of £45,000 in June 1984. It was agreed he would pay any CTT due. He died in March 1986. The CTT payable is as follows:

a. *Lifetime transfer:*		£
Cumulative total brought forward		40,000
Add Chargeable transfer — net		45,000
Net cumulative total		£85,000
CTT payable:		
On first £64,000 @ Nil	=	Nil
On next £17,850 @ 3/7	=	3,150.00
On next £ 3,150 @ 7/33	=	668.18
Total CTT due		£3,818.18
Net chargeable transfer		45,000
Add CTT payable (ignoring pence)		3,818
Gross lifetime gift		£48,818
b. *Recalculation of CTT payable on death:*		£
Gross cumulative total		£88,818
CTT payable at death rates:		
On first £67,000 @ Nil	=	Nil
On next £21,818 @ 30%	=	6,545.40
		6,545.40
Less CTT on previous cumulative total prior to the gift, £40,000		Nil
Revised CTT on lifetime transfer		6,545.40
Less CTT paid by Mr *B*		3,818.18
Additional CTT payable by donee		£2,727.22

The above examples have shown the recalculation of the CTT payable as a result of the donor dying within three years of making the transfer using the same value as that taken into account in the calculation of the CTT payable on the earlier lifetime transfer. This will be the position in the majority of cases, but if the value of the asset at the date of death of the transferor is less than the value at the date of transfer, or the asset was sold prior to the date of the transferor's death by the transferee, or his spouse, by way of a bargain at arm's length and the proceeds received were less than the value at the date of the transfer, the recalculation of the CTT payable at the death rates is based on the reduced value, or proceeds of sale, provided a claim is made by the transferee. If any additional recalculation using the lower value produces a lower amount of CTT than was actually due on the lifetime transfer no repayment of CTT can be obtained. If this relief is claimed it does not affect the transferor's cumulative total. Relief cannot be claimed where the asset transferred has been given away, or sold in a bargain not at arm's length, between the date of the transfer and the date of death of the transferor.   (Section 132, CTTA 1984)

The above rules apply to assets generally, but wasting assets, i.e. assets with a predictable useful life of less than fifty years, are excluded (section 132, CTTA 1984). Also special provisions apply in respect of the following:

a.   capital receipts from shares (section 133, CTTA 1984);
b.   payments for calls on shares (section 134, CTTA 1984);
c.   reorganizations of share capital (section 135, CTTA 1984);
d.   transactions of close companies (section 136, CTTA 1984);
e.   interests in land (section 137, CTTA 1984);
f.   leases having a duration of less than fifty years at the date of the transfer (section 138, CTTA 1984);
g.   other property where there has been a change in the nature of the asset (section 139, CTTA 1984).

CAPITAL TRANSFER TAX ON DEATH

Capital transfer tax is chargeable on the net values of the estates of persons who have died on or after 13 March 1975. This date should be contrasted with the date on which the tax became operative with respect to lifetime dispositions (namely 27 March 1974). There were transitional provisions affecting deaths during the period 27 March 1974 to 12 March 1975. It should therefore be emphasized that what follows applies only to deaths on or after 13 March 1975.

The personal representatives of a deceased person have a duty to report the assets and liabilities of the estate to the revenue authorities, and they are accountable for the capital transfer tax payable on the net value of the deceased's free estate. The net value of the estate represents the gross value of the property liable to capital transfer tax, and for all valuation purposes on death there is no grossing up of the type undertaken in the valuation of lifetime gifts. The capital transfer tax due on death must be paid before the Grant of Representation can be issued to the personal representatives.

As already mentioned (see p. 120) CTT is to be charged on death as if immediately before his death the deceased had made a transfer of value equal to the value of his estate immediately prior to his death. This general rule is extended to bring into account changes which occur by reason of death. This ensures that, for example, the proceeds from a life insurance policy are brought into the estate for CTT purposes, but property passing by survivorship is excluded from this rule.   (Section 171, CTTA 1984)

In ascertaining the assets and liabilities of the deceased at the date of death, it is specifically provided that the following liabilities may be deducted:

a.   reasonable funeral expenses (section 172, CTTA 1984);
b.   costs of adminstering or realizing property situated outside the United Kingdom, up to a maximum of 5% of the value of the property (section 173, CTTA 1984);

c. income tax and capital gains tax due up to the date of death, income tax arising on certain specified items which arise as a result of the death, and CTT due on lifetime transfers so far as actually paid out of the estate (section 174, CTTA 1984);
d. certain future payments due from the estate (section 175, CTTA 1984);
e. certain value attributable to Scottish agricultural leases (section 177, CTTA 1984).

Interest on the capital transfer tax liability arising on death is payable if the tax remains unpaid at the end of the period of six months from the last day of the month in which the deceased died. Interest accrues from that time until the payment of the liability at the rate of 9 per cent (which should be contrasted with the rate of 11 per cent attributable to unpaid capital transfer tax on lifetime dispositions). If any repayment of capital transfer tax paid by the personal representatives becomes due, the overpaid tax must be refunded by the Inland Revenue with interest at the same rate and from the same date as the tax, if outstanding, would have carried interest for the benefit of the Inland Revenue.

The above rates of interest apply with effect from 1 May 1985, the rates prior to that date being as follows:

1 December 1982 to 30 April 1985	6% and 8% respectively
1 December 1980 to 30 November 1982	9% and 12% respectively
Prior to 1 December 1980	6% and 9% respectively

The starting point on the table of rates for the assessment of capital transfer tax on death is the cumulative total value of the deceased's lifetime dispositions (i.e. his cumulative total). The cumulative nature of capital transfer tax is, therefore, clearly demonstrated on the death of an individual when the net value of the free estate represents the final accumulation of the deceased's chargeable transfers. In calculating the previous cumulative total only chargeable transfers made within the ten years prior to the date of death have to be included.

The following example illustrates the cumulative nature of CTT in these circumstances in a very straightforward estate.

Example 3

Mr *C* died in September 1985 leaving a net chargeable estate of £100,000 which all passed to his children. He had made previous chargeable transfers, i.e. after exemptions, as follows:

June 1975	£25,000
December 1980	£50,000

The CTT due on his death, assuming no exemptions or reliefs are due, is as follows:

		£
Cumulative total brought forward		50,000
Add Net value of estate on death		100,000
CTT chargeable on		£150,000
CTT payable:		
On first £67,000 @ Nil	=	Nil
On next £22,000 @ 30%	=	6,600.00
On next £33,000 @ 35%	=	11,550.00
On next £28,000 @ 40%	=	11,200.00
		29.350.00
Less CTT on previous cumulative total of £50,000		Nil
CTT payable on death		£29,350.00

AGGREGATION

The principles of aggregation of the value of all property passing on the death of an individual which formerly applied to the assessment of estate duty are largely retained for the purpose of assessing the capital transfer tax due on death. The process of aggregation involves the simple addition of the values of all property which passes on the death in order to determine the total value of all assets liable to capital transfer tax and the rates of tax applicable thereto. The capital transfer tax liability thus calculated is then apportioned between the separate accountable parties.

The major categories of property which passes on a death, and the accountable parties affected by the charge to tax, may be summarized as follows:

Property passing	*Accountable Party*
a. Deceased's free estate	Personal representatives
b. Trust funds in which deceased enjoyed an interst in income.	Trustees of trust fund
c. Property held under beneficial joint tenancy	Surviving joint tenant

(Section 200, CTTA 1984)

At this point it is hoped that the following example will be sufficient to demonstrate the general principle of aggregation.

Example 4

Mr *D* died in October 1985, having made one chargeable transfer during his lifetime in July 1982, when he gave his son £35,000, after exemptions. At his death the net value of his free estate was £85,000; he had a life interest in a trust set up by his late mother and the value of the settled property was £50,000. He also had a half-share interest in a property held as joint tenants with his daughter. The half-share interest in the property was valued at £60,000. The whole of his free estate passed to his son and daughter in equal shares and the capital of his mother's trust passed to his son.

Assuming no reliefs or exemptions are available, the CTT payable will be calculated as follows:

Property passing on death:	£
Free estate	85,000
Settled property	50,000
Joint property	60,000
Total value	195,000
Add Cumulative total brought forward	35,000
CTT payable on	£230,000

CTT payable:		
On first £67,000 @ Nil	=	Nil
On next £22,000 @ 30%	=	6,600.00
On next £33,000 @ 35%	=	11,550.00
On next £33,000 @ 40%	=	13,200.00
On next £39,000 @ 45%	=	17,550.00
On next £36,000 @ 50%	=	18,000.00
		66,900.00
Less CTT on £35,000		Nil
CTT payable on death		£66,900.00

This total CTT liability must be apportioned between the person liable to pay the CTT, in accordance with the principles stated above, as follows:

Personal representatives:	$\dfrac{85,000}{195,000}$	×	£66,900	=	£29,161.54
Trustees of mother's trust:	$\dfrac{50,000}{195,000}$	×	£66,900	=	£17,153.85
Surviving joint tenant:	$\dfrac{60,000}{195,000}$	×	£66,900	=	£20,584.61
					£66,900.00

EXEMPTIONS ON DEATH

The main exemptions and reliefs have already been reviewed in Chapters 10 and 11. These will now be mentioned briefly together with other exemptions or reliefs not previously mentioned, indicating any particular aspects which have to be considered in relation to the use of these exemptions on death.

Property passing to deceased's spouse

Provided the recipient spouse is domiciled in the United Kingdom and the deceased spouse was similarly domiciled, property passing on death is completely exempt from CTT, regardless of the value passing. However, if the deceased spouse was domiciled in the United Kingdom and the surviving spouse is not, the exemption available is limited to £55,000 and any value in excess of that figure, after taking into account lifetime transfers to the spouse within the previous ten years, is chargeable to CTT in the normal way. The exemption is available in respect of property passed absolutely to the surviving spouse and also property in which the spouse becomes entitled to an interest in possession with effect from the date of death. It also applies if the property passes by will or under the intestacy rules.

If the entire estate passes to a surviving spouse then, subject to the domicile limitation mentioned, the whole of the estate will be exempt from CTT. The position becomes a little more complicated where the spouse only becomes entitled to a part of the estate on death. This is likely to arise in two main ways; firstly, where the spouse becomes entitled to a share of residue only, and secondly where the spouse is left a legacy. The first of the these situations is simply illustrated as follows.

Example 5

Mr *E* died in June 1985 having made no previous chargeable transfers. The net value of his estate is £300,000 and this is left to his wife, son and daughter in equal shares.

The CTT payable by the personal representatives is calculated as follows:

	£
Net value of estate	300,000
Less Exempt portion (to spouse)	100,000
Chargeable estate	£200,000

CTT payable:	
On first £67,000 @ Nil	Nil
On next £22,000 @ 30%	6,600.00
On next £33,000 @ 35%	11,550.00
On next £33,000 @ 40%	13,200.00
On next £39,000 @ 45%	17,550.00
On next £ 6,000 @ 50%	3,000.00
Total CTT payable	£51,900.00

In this case the CTT of £51,900 would be payable out of the non-exempt share of residue of £200,000, leaving £148,100 to be divided equally between the son and daughter.

The position is also fairly straightforward if the spouse is left a legacy and the balance of the estate passes in a non-exempt form.

Example 6

Mr *F* died in June 1985 having made previous chargeable transfers of £40,000 in 1982. The net value of his estate was £100,000. By his will he left a pecuniary legacy of £50,000 to his wife, with the residue to their son.

The CTT payable by the personal representatives is calculated as follows:

	£
Net value of estate	100,000
Less Exempt legacy to widow	50,000
Net chargeable estate	50,000
Add Cumulative total brought forward	40,000
CTT chargeable on	£90,000

CTT payable:		
On first £67,000 @ Nil	=	Nil
On next £22,000 @ 30%	=	6,600.00
On next £ 1,000 @ 35%	=	350.00
		£6,950.00

If in Example 6 the son had been left a pecuniary legacy of £50,000 with the residue passing to the widow, the CTT payable would be quite different from the above calculation, unless the will provided for the legacy to bear its own tax. The calculation of the CTT payable where there are both exempt and non-exempt shares of the estate are examined later in this chapter when further reference to this situation will be made.

Surviving spouse exemption

This exemption is one of the transitional exemptions made necessary by the change of incidence of CTT from the old estate duty rules. Under estate duty, duty was charged on the first death with relief available on the second death. This position is, of course, completely reversed under the CTT rules.

To remove the possibility of a double charge to duty it is provided that if estate duty was charged on the estate of one spouse, or former spouse, who died before 13 November 1974, and on the death of the second spouse the value of any property would have been excluded from charge under the old estate duty rules (section 5(2), FA 1894), then the property is to be left out of account in determining the CTT payable on the surviving spouse's death. The old estate duty exemption applied where the surviving spouse was entitled to an interest in possession in settled property. The exemption is not available where the surviving spouse was able to dispose of the property by his/her will, or where the widow/widower could compel the trustees to appoint capital to him/her. (Paragraph 2, Schedule 6, CTTA 1984)

Gifts to charities

There is now no limit on the exemption for gifts to charities made on death or during lifetime. The calculation of the CTT payable on an estate involving both exempt and non-exempt portions is considered later in this chapter. (Section 23, CTTA 1984)

Gifts to political parties

The exemption is limited to £100,000 in respect of gifts made on or within one year of death. The specific rules dealing with the allocation of the exemption limit where the total gifts exceed £100,000 and the calculation of the CTT payable are dealt with later in this chapter.   (Section 24, CTTA 1984)

Property devolving upon 'heritage bodies'

The value of all property bequeathed for national purposes to such heritage bodies as the National Gallery and the British Museum is exempt from charge to capital transfer tax on death. The relief operates in the same manner as the relief given to property passing to a spouse.   (Section 25, CTTA 1984)

Gifts for public benefit under wills

Certain property which is bequeathed for public benefit is exempt from capital transfer tax on death. The types of property which qualify for this relief, and the conditions attaching to the relief are identical to those described earlier in relation to lifetime gifts. Once again the exemption is assessed and allocated on the basis demonstrated in respect of property devolving upon a surviving spouse.   (Section 26, CTTA 1984)

Foreign property where the deceased is domiciled abroad

On death of a person domiciled outside the United Kingdom no account is taken of any property located abroad for the purpose of arriving at the net value of the estate. Domicile is to be construed in connection with this relief in accordance with section 267, CTTA 1984.   (Section 6, CTTA 1984)

Certain government securities where the deceased is domiciled abroad

This relief is identical to that afforded to 'exempt gilts' which form the subject-matter of gifts effected by persons who are neither domiciled nor ordinarily resident for tax purposes in the United Kingdom. Where such securities are in the beneficial ownership of the deceased, and he is not at the time of death domiciled here, their value is exempt from capital transfer tax. For the purpose of this relief, and by contrast to the exemption referred to in the previous paragraph, domicile is to be determined without reference to section 267, CTTA 1984.   (Section 6, CTTA 1984)

Reversionary interests

In assessing the value of the deceased's estate for tax purposes no account is to be taken of reversionary interests unless any such interests were acquired either by the deceased or by any person previously entitled to it for consideration in money or money's worth (i.e. unless the reversionary interests were purchased).   (Section 48, CTTA 1984)

Certain savings of persons domiciled in the Channel Islands or Isle of Man

The exclusion from charge applicable to *inter vivos* gifts of National Savings certificates, premium bonds, etc., in the beneficial ownership of persons domiciled in the Channel Islands or Isle of Man is also relevant on death. The value of such savings is not part of the estate for tax purposes. The question as to whether or not the deceased was domiciled in the Channel Islands or the Isle of Man is to be determined with respect to this exemption without reference to the provisions of section 267, CTTA 1984.
                                      (Section 6(3), CTTA 1984)

Death on active service

See p. 128.

Cash options under approved annuity schemes

See p. 127.

Overseas pensions and gratuities

See p. 127.

Emoluments and effects of visiting forces and staff

See p. 128.

Commorientes provisions

The devolution of the estates of persons who die in circumstances rendering it uncertain which of them died first has been considered on p. 83. Notwithstanding the fact that as a result of these commorientes provisions one estate may fall into another, it is provided under section 4(2), CTTA 1984, that for tax purposes the persons concerned shall be considered to have died at the same instant. The effect of this is that capital transfer tax is charged in each estate on the assets of the estate before taking into account any further assets which might fall into the estate under the commorientes rules regarding devolution.

Example 7

Tom, who was aged 26 years, and his brother Fred, aged 23, died in a car accident on 29 July 1985 in circumstances such that it was impossible to determine which of them survived the other. Neither brother has effected any *inter vivos* transfers of value, and they have no other relatives. They both died intestate, and each of their estates was valued at £50,000.

 Under the Law of Property Act 1925, section 184, Fred is deemed to have survived Tom. Tom's estate therefore falls into Fred's estate, the value of which as a result is increased to £100,000. Capital transfer tax is, however, not charged on either estate, since neither estate exceeds £67,000 in value when the value of property falling in under section 184 is disregarded.

Works of art etc.

The exemptions for gifts for national purposes (section 25, CTTA 1984) and gifts for public benefit (section 26, CTTA 1984) apply equally to transfers made on death. Conditional exemption is also available in respect of transfers made on death (sections 30–34, CTTA 1984). A full description of these exemptions is given in Chapter 10, pp. 125–126.

Woodlands

A full description of the relief available in respect of growing timber and the calculation of the additional CTT payable as a result of a subsequent sale or other disposal is given in Chapter 11, p. 142.

FURTHER RELIEFS ON DEATH

Thus far consideration has been given to the various exemptions which are available on death, but there are a number of further reliefs which have the effect either of reducing the capital transfer tax on death or of alleviating its burden in other ways. The reliefs available are considered separately below.

1. Quick succession relief

As the name implies, this relief is designed to reduce the overall incidence of CTT where the same property becomes chargeable to CTT on two separate occasions in quick succession.

The rules described below, which apply to transfers after 9 March 1981, relate to transfers of a person's free estate. The rules which apply to settled property are described in Chapter 13.

Relief is available where CTT becomes payable on death and the estate of the deceased person includes property transferred to him on an earlier transfer within the five years preceding his death. The CTT payable on death in respect of the property transferred by the earlier transfer is reduced by the following percentages of the tax charged on the earlier transfer:

Period between transfers	Percentage of tax charged on first transfer
One year or less	100%
Between 1 and 2 years	80%
Between 2 and 3 years	60%
Between 3 and 4 years	40%
Between 4 and 5 years	20%

Example 8

Mr *G* died in September 1985. Included in his estate was property valued at £20,000 which had been given to him in October 1983 by his brother. The value at October 1983 was also £20,000. The CTT paid by his brother in respect of this transfer amounted to £2,000. The total value of *G*'s estate was £120,000 all of which passed to his son. He had made no previous chargeable transfers.

CTT payable on G's death:

	£	
Chargeable estate		£120,000
CTT payable:		
On first £67,000 @ Nil =	Nil	
On next £22,000 @ 30% =	6,600.00	
On next £31,000 @ 35% =	10,850.00	
	17,450.00	

Less Quick succession relief:
Maximum relief:
$$\frac{20,000}{120,000} \times £17,450 = £2,908$$
CTT paid on value reflected in *G*'s estate:
$$\frac{20,000}{22,000} \times £2,000 = £1,818$$

Relief due 80% × £1,818 =	1,454.00	
CTT payable on G's death	£15,996.00	

(Section 141, CTTA 1984)

2. Alteration of dispositions taking effect on death

The earlier provisions regarding the variations of dispositions taking effect on death were revised with effect from 11 April 1978 by section 68, FA 1978. The comments below refer to the new rules, which represent a relaxation of the old provisions.

The disposition by a deceased person of his estate, by will or under the law of intestacy, may be varied, or disclaimed, by an instrument in writing made within two years of the date of death, by the persons, or any of the persons, who would benefit.

Variations or disclaimers, made in this way are treated as if they had been made by the deceased provided an election is made to the Board within six months of the date of the instrument, or such longer period as the Board may allow. This election must be signed by:

a. the person, or persons, making the election, and
b. the personal representatives where additional CTT is payable as a result of the variation, although the personal representatives may decline to join in the election if they hold no assets, or insufficient assets, to discharge the additional CTT payable.

It is not sufficient merely to submit the instrument of variation to the Capital Taxes Office. A formal election must be submitted within the time limit allowed, although the Capital Taxes Office have confirmed that they will accept an election incorporated within the instrument itself.

A variation can be made even after the estate has been fully, or partially, distributed, but a disclaimer cannot be made once the person wishing to make the disclaimer has received some benefit under the terms of the will or intestacy.

A variation as outlined above is not effective for CTT purposes if it is made for consideration. However, the exchange of interests, for example, in a person's estate, is not treated as consideration for these purposes.

If a variation to which these provisions apply results in property being held in trust for a person for a period which ends not more than two years after the date of death, the disposition which takes effect at the end of that period is treated as if it had taken effect from the beginning of that period. However, this does not apply in respect of any distribution or application of the property within the period, i.e. this will be chargeable to CTT in the normal way.

Although a variation of the terms of the deceased's will may be advantageous, it may not always be beneficial to elect for the variation to apply as from the date of death. For example, it may be possible to utilize the nil rate band of the original beneficiary when transferring the property to the ultimate beneficiary.

Similar provisions are available for variations for capital gains tax purposes (see Chapter 14), but no similar provisions apply for income tax purposes, with the result that the original will, or the law of intestacy, determines the destination of income arising in the period from the date of death to the date on which the instrument of variation is made.   (Section 142, CTTA 1984)

3. Agricultural property relief and business property relief

These reliefs are available in respect of transfers made on death, provided all the conditions for these reliefs are satisfied by the deceased as at the date of death (see pp. 137–142).

4. Credit for overseas tax

Where the deceased leaves property located abroad which by reason of its location is liable to overseas tax on death and by reason of the deceased's domicile is also liable to capital transfer tax, the overseas tax paid may be offset as a credit against the capital transfer tax payable provided that the overseas tax is of a nature similar to capital transfer tax (i.e. the overseas tax is chargeable on death by reference to the value of the property concerned). This relief corresponds with the similar relief provided for overseas tax incurred as a result of lifetime dispositions.

(Sections 158 and 159, CTTA 1984)

5. Payment of tax by instalments

The capital transfer tax payable on death which is attributable to certain property (referred to below as instalment property) may, if an election is made for the purpose, be paid by ten equal yearly instalments, the first of which is due for payment six months after the last day of the month in which the death occurred. Instalment property is represented by the following assets:

a. land (whether leasehold or freehold and regardless of location);
b. shares or securities of a company which gave the deceased control of the company immediately before his death;
c. other unquoted shares or securities provided either that:
    i.   not less than 20 per cent of the capital transfer tax payable on the death by the accountable party is chargeable upon the value of the unquoted shares or securities or upon other instalment property, or
    ii. the Inland Revenue is satisfied that the capital transfer tax attributable to the value of the unquoted securities or shares cannot be paid in one sum without undue hardship;
d. other unquoted shares provided that their value exceeds £20,000 and their nominal value represents at least 10 per cent of the issued shares of the company or, if they are ordinary shares, 10 per cent of the total nominal value of all ordinary shares in issue;
e. the net value of the deceased's business, or of the deceased's interest in a partnership.

Despite the fact that an election for the payment of tax by instalments may have been made, the accountable party may at any time discharge all outstanding instalments of capital transfer tax, and, in the event of a sale of the instalment property, he must do so. Where a part of the instalment property is sold, the appropriate part of the unpaid capital transfer tax falls due for payment immediately. Furthermore, notwithstanding the provisions as to interest on unpaid capital transfer tax on instalment property which are outlined below, in the event of a sale of any instalment property interest on the unpaid tax runs from the date of sale.

Generally speaking, an election for payment of capital transfer tax by instalments is appropriate on death, but tax can also be paid by instalments on qualifying instalment property where the donee of a lifetime transfer bears the tax, and where the charge to tax arises in certain specific situations on property held in trust which remains in trust following the occasion of charge. Additionally the capital transfer tax attributable to an *inter vivos* transfer of growing timber may be paid by instalments provided that the transfer serves to create a futher charge to capital transfer tax on the value of the growing timber by reference to an earlier death. The capital transfer tax arising by reference to an earlier death which is charged on growing timber may not be paid by instalments; it is only the *inter vivos* tax liability which carries this option.

Interest on capital transfer tax attributable to the following:

a. land;
b. the shares or securities of a company whose business consists wholly or mainly of dealing in land or investments (excluding jobbers and discount houses);

runs with effect from six months after the last day of the month in which the death occurred on the full amount of unpaid tax.

Interest on the capital transfer tax due on death in relation to all other types of instalment property accrues from the due date of the instalment only.

(Sections 227, 228, 229 and 234, CTTA 1984)

6. Losses on qualifying investments

Under section 45, FA 1973, it was provided for estate duty purposes that a deduction from the value of the estate may be claimed for losses incurred on the sale of qualifying investments within the period of twelve months following the death. This relief in identical form has been preserved for the purposes of capital transfer tax on death.

Qualifying investments are all quoted investments and all holdings in authorized unit trusts. It follows, therefore, that this relief is not available with respect to private company holdings. The relief may be claimed only by the accountable party to the extent that he realizes investments whilst acting in his representative capacity. Thus personal representatives may claim the relief to the extent that they sell investments in order to meet administration expenses or to the extent that they sell investments under the trust for sale applicable to the distribution of the residuary estate either under a will or upon intestacy. Such sales will be effected by the personal representatives acting as such in the general undivided estate with a view to a subsequent distribution of the cash remaining after expenses are discharged in appropriate proportions to the residuary legatees. Where, however, personal representatives appropriate investments to a residuary legatee, and thus become bare trustees rather than personal representatives, subsequent sales of qualifying investments at a loss have no effect on the capital transfer tax liability on death since such losses cannot be claimed as a deduction from the value of the estate. Similarly if the residuary estate is to be held on continuing trusts, sales by the trustees of the residuary trust fund do not qualify for relief although losses incurred on investments sold in the undivided estate before the residuary trust fund is established qualify for relief in the hands of the personal representatives.

It is, therefore, necessary for personal representatives to review all sales of qualifying investments either on the anniversary of the death or on the earlier completion of the sales of all qualifying investments. In practice, of course, reviews of this type should be carried out throughout the administration of an estate so that full advantage of the relief may, in appropriate circumstances, be taken. If the result of such a review one year after the death is that there is an overall gain on the sale of all qualifying investments by comparison with their original probate values, no relief for capital transfer tax purposes may be claimed notwithstanding the fact that individual qualifying investments may have been sold at a loss.

If, however, an overall loss arises on the sale of qualifying investments during the twelve month period, the overall loss may be claimed as a deduction from the value of the estate. In assessing the overall loss arising the personal representatives cannot claim allowance for brokerage, contract stamp and the like incurred on sales of investments. The loss, which is allowable for capital transfer tax purposes, is the loss calculated by comparing the gross proceeds of sales with probate values.

Example 9

Mr *H* dies on 14 May 1985 leaving a net estate of £100,000. The following qualifying investments are, during the administration of the estate, sold by his personal representatives:

	Probate value £	Date of sale	Gross proceeds £
XYZ Co. Plc	10,000	28 August 1985	11,000
ABC Co. Plc	28,000	28 August 1985	20,000
DEF Co. Plc	2,000	13 May 1986	2,500
KLM Co. Plc	30,000	15 May 1986	11,000

Relief may be claimed as follows:

	£	£
Value on which capital transfer tax was originally paid		100,000
Deduct: Total probate value of investments sold within one year	40,000	
Less: Total proceeds of investment sold within one year	33,500	6,500
Value on which capital transfer tax is finally paid		£93,500

NB: Since the holding in KLM Co. Plc was sold more than one year after the death, no relief is available.

The following provisions may serve to reduce the relief which might otherwise be claimed:

a. Where capital moneys are received in respect of a qualifying investment otherwise than on sale (e.g. proceeds of sale of rights in nil paid form) the capital moneys received should be added to the proceeds of sale of the holding for the purpose of establishing the loss arising on its sale.
b. Where an additional amount of a qualifying investment is acquired by the accountable party, the subsequent sale of the holding is treated as being a proportionate sale of the original holding, and the holding acquired.
c. Where a call is paid in respect of a qualifying investment on taking up new shares, the amount paid is added to the probate value of the holding in calculating the loss arising on the subsequent sale of the total holding. Where the holding is subsequently partially sold the principles outlined in (b) above are applied.
d. Where the accountable party acting in that capacity purchases additional qualifying investments during the relevant period or within two months of the end of the relevant period, the loss arising on the sale of other qualifying investments is restricted. For this purpose the relevant period is the period from the date of death to the completion of the sales of qualifying investments, or, if it is shorter, the period of one year from the date of death. It is possible, therefore, that the purchase of qualifying investments up to fourteen months from the death might affect the capital transfer tax liability. The loss arising on sales of qualifying investments in these circumstances is reduced by the proportion of the total proceeds of sale which is expended in the purchase of other qualifying investments. For example the purchase of qualifying investments at a cost of £10,000 would reduce by one-half any loss arising on the sale of qualifying investments for £20,000. In normal circumstances it is hardly likely that personal representatives would purchase investments since their duty is to distribute the estate, but this restriction is of more significance to trustees of trust funds who are also eligible for this relief for capital transfer tax purposes on the death of a life tenant.

(Sections 178–189, CTTA 1984)

7. Land sold within three years of death

Where an interest in land is comprised in a person's estate at his death and this is sold within three years of his death for a price less than the probate value at death by the person liable for the CTT on that interest, e.g. the personal representative, and a claim is made by that person, the sale value can be substituted for the probate value for the purposes of calculating the CTT liability arising on death. However, the sale of all land sold within three years of death must be substituted for the respective probate values; it is not possible to pick and choose which land to claim relief on — it is all or nothing.

A claim is not competent in any event if:

a. the sale value differs from the value at death by less than the lower of:
   i.   £1,000, and
   ii. 5 per cent of its value at the date of death.
b. the sale is by the personal representative or trustee to:
   i.   a person who, at any time between the date of death and the date of sale, has been beneficially entitled to, or to an interest in possession in, the interest in the land sold, or
   ii. the spouse, or a child or a remoter descendant of a person within (i) above, or
   iii. the trustees of a settlement under which a person within (i) or (ii) above has an interest in possession in property comprising the interest in the land sold, or
c. the vendor or any person within (b) above obtains a right to acquire the interest sold or any other interest in the same land.

As with sales of qualifying investments in 6 above, adjustments have to be made in respect of transactions in land within the period of three years from the date of death. These include the following.

a. If further land is purchased in the period which commences with the date of death and ends four months after the last sale, the relief otherwise due may be reduced. If the aggregate of all purchase prices equals or exceeds the aggregate of the sale prices, all the relief is lost. Otherwise, an addition is made to the sale price of each interest calculated as follows:

$$\left(\begin{array}{c} \text{Value on death} \\ \textit{less} \\ \text{sale price} \end{array} \right) \times \frac{\text{Aggregate of purchase prices}}{\text{Aggregate of sale prices}}$$

(Section 192, CTTA 1984)

b. If there is a change in the interest between the date of death and the date of sale, the sale price is adjusted to ensure that relief is only given for a real reduction in value, not a reduction caused by the change in interest.   (Section 193, CTTA 1984)
c. Where the interest sold is a lease of less than 50 years, as at the date of death, the sale price is adjusted to reflect the wasting away of the lease over the period from the date of death to the date of sale. This is calculated using the table in Schedule 3, CGTA 1979.   (Section 194, CTTA 1984)
d. The sale price is adjusted where the interest in land sold represents only part of the interest in land valued at the date of death.   (Section 195, CTTA 1984)
e. An adjustment may also be necessary where the interest in the land is sold to a beneficiary on exchanges of land.   (Section 196, CTTA 1984)
f. If an authority possessing compulsory purchase powers has served a notice to treat before the date of death or within three years after the date of death and the land

is actually acquired from the appropriate person after the end of the three year period, a claim to relief can be made as if the sale took place within the three year period. This provision is ignored if the sale price exceeds the value at the date of death. Furthermore, this provision does not permit any 'backdating' of a sale by way of compulsory purchase for the purposes of establishing the period within (a) above.   (Section 197, CTTA 1984)

g. The date of sale or purchase for the purposes of these provisions is defined as:
    i.   the date of the contract, where the sale or purchase is pursuant to a contract;
    ii. the date of the *grant* of the option, where the sale or purchase arises as the result of the exercise of an option where the option was granted not more than six months earlier;
    iii. where the land is acquired, otherwise than by way of a contract by an authority possessing compulsory purchase powers, the date of sale is the earlier of:
        1. the date on which the compensation is agreed or otherwise determined (variations on appeal are disregarded for this purpose), or
        2. the date when the authority enters on the land in pursuance of its powers.

Special rules apply if the land is acquired by a general vesting order under the Town and Country Planning Acts.   (Section 198, CTTA 1984)

(Sections 190–198, CTTA 1984)

8. Sales of related property within three years of death

Where the property has been valued under the related property rules and it is then sold within three years of the death for a sale price less than the valuation at the date of death, then it is possible to claim to have the value at the date of death calculated without reference to the related property. To qualify for a claim the sale must satisfy a number of conditions as follows:

a. the vendors must be the persons in whom the property vested immediately following the death, or the personal representatives, and
b. the sale is at arm's length for a price freely negotiated at the time of the sale, and is not made in conjunction with the sale of any of the related property, and
c. the vendor, or any person having an interest in the sale proceeds, is not the same as, or connected with, the purchaser or any person having an interest in the purchase, and
d. neither the vendors nor any other person having an interest in the sale proceeds obtain in connection with the sale a right to acquire the property sold or any interest in or created out of it.

Further conditions have to be satisfied if the property in question is shares or securities of a close company.

The purpose of these conditions is to prevent artificial sales being used to reduce the value of the estate for CTT purposes. Genuine arm's length sales to totally unconnected parties will qualify for relief.   (Section 176, CTTA 1984)

9. The basis of valuation

Generally speaking the value which is liable to capital transfer tax as a result of any transaction is measured by the loss suffered by the donor or trust fund as a result of the transaction. It is for this reason that on a normal lifetime disposition and on certain distributions from trust funds, the actual value of the property affected by the disposition is grossed up by reference to the effective rate of capital transfer tax payable in order to arrive at its taxable value. Clearly if an individual gives a cash sum of £20,000 to another person, the loss suffered directly as a result of the gift by the donor is both:

a. £20,000 and
b. the capital transfer tax paid.

If, however, the sum of £20,000 is given subject to the condition that the donee must meet the donor's capital transfer tax liability, the total loss to the donor is £20,000, and this is therefore the taxable value of the gift. By the same token, of course, the gift is of lesser value in the hands of the donee since he has an outstanding liability to capital transfer tax.

The accountable parties on any transaction include both donors and donees. In normal circumstances the donor is primarily accountable for the capital transfer tax payable on any transaction but there is nothing to stop him from arranging for the donee to render the relative tax account to the Inland Revenue and meeting the capital transfer tax liability. Whilst the Inland Revenue has wide powers of recovery of outstanding tax from donees, these are not normally exercised until the tax is overdue. Nevertheless the Inland Revenue is quite prepared to accept tax paid before the due date by the donee. Similarly, on the creation of a settlement the settlor may include in the settlement deed a provision to the effect that the trustees are to meet the capital transfer tax liability, in which case the actual funds settled will determine the value liable to tax without grossing up.

Section 160, CTTA 1984, provides that 'the value at any time of any property shall for the purposes of this Act be the price which the property might reasonably be expected to fetch if sold on the open market at that time.' In essence section 160 is restating the principles of valuation which have already been in force for the purposes of estate duty and capital gains tax. The underlying property affected by any chargeable event is to be valued at its full market value. Frequently, as in the case of quoted shares, the market value is readily available; in other cases, however, the full market value becomes a matter of negotiation with the Inland Revenue which has wide powers of determining any value conclusively for tax purposes. In the case of properties the accountable party normally negotiates an agreed value with the district valuer of the valuation office whilst unquoted shares of any significant value are assessed by a process of negotiation with the Inland Revenue Share Valuation Division.

The basic principle stated by section 160 is also relevant to the value of property on the death of an individual. The value liable to capital transfer tax on the death of an individual is represented by the value of his estate on the assumption that all his assets were to be sold on that date in the open market. No allowance is made for the fact that the market would be depressed if all the property was sold on the one date, for in practice care would be taken to avoid overloading the market with its consequent disadvantage to the estate. On the other hand, if the value has suffered depreciation through the death (e.g. goodwill in the case of the business of a sole trader) that fact may be taken into account. In many cases it will be necessary to employ an expert valuer. Thus furniture, chattels of all sorts, shops, land, and the goodwill of any business carried on by the deceased should be valued by some properly qualified person whose opinion will be acceptable to the Inland Revenue. The valuations provided by such competent valuers should be attached to the official account.

The provisions of section 161, CTTA 1984, must not be overlooked in relation to valuations of assets. This section requires that in valuing property comprised in a person's estate, whether in lifetime or on death, where there is related property, the value of the property must be the appropriate proportion of the aggregate value of that property and the related property. Related property is defined to include property:

a. comprised in the estate of his spouse, or
b. if it is or has been in the preceding five years:
    i.   the property of a charity, or held on trust for charitable purposes only, or
    ii. the property of a political party, a body within Schedule 3, CTTA 1984, or a body not established or conducted for profit (see section 26, CTTA 1984).

The effect of these provisions can be simply illustrated as follows: If Mr X held 40 per cent of the issued shares of an unquoted company and his wife held 20 per cent of the shares, the value of Mr X's shares is to be calculated as two-thirds of the value of a 60 per cent holding. The value calculated on this basis is likely to be considerably more than the value of a 40 per cent holding. In applying the loss to donor rule, assuming Mr X has made a transfer of half of his shares, the transfer of value would be calculated as follows:

Value before transfer (40% + 20% = 60% holding)	£A
Value after transfer (20% + 20% = 40% holding)	£B
Loss to estate of Mr X	£C

In this example £C will be far in excess of the value of a 20 per cent holding, the holding actually transferred, because the effect of including the related property is to pass from a control holding basis of valuation to a minority holding basis of valuation.

If property the value of which is not immediately ascertainable (e.g. land and buildings) is sold within a short time of the death, the gross sum realized will be used as the relevant value on death, unless the Revenue authorities consider that the sale was not 'bona fide'.

Certain features which are peculiar to the valuation on death of various types of assets will now be considered.

Bank balances

Bank balances should be confirmed by the usual certificates from the deceased's bankers, stating the interest payable or receivable, as the case may be, and any bank charges accrued, to the date of death. Income tax is allowed as a deduction from the interest which has accrued to the date of death.

National savings certificates

Unless a letter from the Director of Savings of the Post Office is attached to the official account stating the value of the certificates at the date of death, details must be given showing the number of certificates, and the price paid for, and the date of purchase of, each certificate.

Premium savings bonds

A letter of confirmation from the Bonds and Stocks Office stating the holding of the deceased should be included. This should in any event be obtained as there is no indication on a bond of the holder's name nor any registered holder's number. Bonds are eligible for inclusion in prize draws during the twelve months following death. The question as to whether any prize received after the date of death is due to income or capital is not easily resolved and it would appear that a court ruling on the point will be required.

Stocks and shares

The valuation of stocks and shares will not usually require any expert assistance in view of the fact that if a Stock Exchange quotation is given for such stocks and shares the quoted value is accepted by the Revenue authorities. Frequently, two prices are quoted — the jobber's nominal buying price (lower), and the jobber's nominal selling price (higher) — and in such cases the value for the purposes of the tax liability on death is taken as one-fourth of the difference between the two prices, added to the lower price. Thus, if the price quoted is 90–92, the value for tax purposes will be 90½, i.e. 90 + ¼(92 − 90). The quotation should be taken from the Stock Exchange Official List for the day on which the death took place. Where bargains are recorded, the valuation may be based thereon, instead of being computed according to the 'one quarter up' rule; the price at which business was done will be taken if there was only one price, otherwise the price taken will be the mean (middle price) of the different prices. If the death takes place on a day when no business is transacted upon the Stock Exchange, so that no quotation for that day is given, the price quoted on either the preceding or the following business day will be accepted. Where shares are quoted on a provincial exchange only, a copy of the official list of such exchange should be attached to the account.

Stock Exchange quotations are either *cum div.* or *ex div.*[1] If the investment is quoted *cum div.* at the date of death, the dividend accrued up to that date is included in the quoted price and there is consequently nothing further to be brought in for tax purposes. On the other hand, an *ex div.* quotation does not include accretions of dividend to date, and for tax purposes it is necessary to add a full quarter's, half year's or year's dividend, as the case may be, to the *ex div.* quotation in order to ascertain the value at the date of death. Thus, if a 3 per cent stock upon which interest is paid quarterly is quoted at 40 *cum div.* on the day of the death, the value in the account of £100 nominal value of stock will be £40, but if the quotation is 40 *ex div.* the value will be £40, *plus* one quarter's interest at 3 per cent per annum (*less tax*) on £100 (see Chapter 16).[2] This addition to the amount of interest is necessary by virtue of the fact that as the deceased held the shares on the day the quotation changed to *ex div.*, he became entitled to that interest and it is therefore part of his estate, while the reason for the inclusion of the *full* impending interest is that, by the practice of the Stock Exchange, the *cum div.* quotation was reduced by that amount in arriving at the *ex div.* quotation.

If the deceased held certain shares when the quotation changed to *ex div.*, and between that date and the date of death he sold the shares, the dividend or interest presently payable must be included in the account; the shares, of course, will not appear, but if the proceeds of sale had not been received by the deceased before his death, the amount due from his stockbrokers will appear as a debt due to the deceased.

Treasury bonds are quoted on the Stock Exchange at their capital value only, and *the actual amount of interest accrued to the date of death* must be included in the official account.

If shares held by the deceased are not quoted on any Stock Exchange, they must be fairly valued. Such a valuation should take into account the profit-earning capacity of the business, the return for the purchaser's investment, the general solvency of the

---

1. The expression *cum int.* and *ex int.* are sometimes used in connection with fixed interest bearing securities.
2. It is the practice of the Capital Taxes Office to allow income tax to be deducted from the *ex div.* interest in the case of 3½ per cent War Loan, although such interest is normally paid gross where the holding is in the form of registered or inscribed stock. A similar concession is made in the case of other stocks where income tax is not deductible at source.

company, the extent of the security in the shape of assets, the nature of the management, the objects of the company, its methods of business and the capital value of the assets of the company: *Smyth* v. *Inland Revenue Commissioners* (1931). Much of this information will be derived from the company's accounts — the number of years' accounts required by the Capital Taxes Office will depend upon the circumstances, e.g. the size of the holding, but those for three years are commonly regarded as a minimum.

If the articles of a private company contain restrictions on the transfer of shares (e.g. by providing that a holder wishing to transfer his shares must first offer them for sale to existing members at a price prescribed by the articles), the shares should be valued at the price which they would fetch if sold in the open market on the terms that a purchaser would be entitled to stand in the shoes of the deceased and to hold the shares subject to the restrictions imposed by the company's articles (*Inland Revenue Commissioners* v. *Crossman; Same* v. *Mann*, 1936).

Allowance should be made, in valuing shares, for any loss which can reasonably be expected to accrue from the cessation of the deceased's services and the loss of his personal prestige. That is to say, the valuation must proceed on the footing that the deceased is already dead: *Re Magan* (1908).

Where the holding is only a small minority holding carrying little influence over the company's policy, valuation normally proceeds on the basis of the potentialities of the shares as an income producing investment. That is to say, regard is had to the dividends an investor might expect to receive having in mind the company's profit record and prospects, together with its apparent policy as respects distributions. Frequently, the yield of the investment to be valued is compared with the yield current at the death on comparable quoted shares. An interesting case on this point, which demonstrates the degree to which even experts can disagree, is *Re Holt, Holt* v. *Inland Revenue Commissioners* (1953).

The valuation of unquoted investments requires great skill and is best regarded as a task for the expert, except in cases where the sum involved is insufficient to justify his services.

If shares are of no value and there is a liability for uncalled capital, the liability, estimated at what it would be necessary to pay a transferee to induce him to take the shares, may be deducted in computing the value of the estate.

Foreign currencies

The conversion of foreign currency values, e.g. bank deposits held abroad, is effected by taking the extreme of the quotations giving the lowest value in sterling. Thus, assuming the American rate of exchange at the date of death was 1.30 to 1.35 dollars to the £, any holdings in American currency will be converted into sterling at 1.35 dollars to the £, thereby showing the lowest value in sterling. Similarly, if the Indian rate of exchange at the date of death was 14.8 to 15 rupees to the £ any holdings in Indian currency will be converted into sterling at the rate of 15 rupees to the £.

Foreign securities

The value of securities in the USA and Canada is the sterling equivalent of the quoted price abroad converted at the appropriate rate of exchange (as set out above). Thus $100 nominal of a United States stock quoted at 105, when the rate of exchange was 1.30–1.35 would be valued at:

$$100 \times \frac{105}{100} \times \frac{1}{1.35} = £77.77$$

Formerly, 75 per cent of any premium in force was added to the quoted price, but since the abolition of exchange control regulations in 1979, the investment dollar premium no longer exists. Other foreign securities are generally valued on the 'one-quarter up' basis where two prices are given in currency and converted into sterling in accordance with the rules set out above.

Assurance policies

Policies of assurance on the deceased's own life should be valued at the amount receivable from the assurance company, including bonuses.

Share in a partnership

The deceased's share in a partnership must be ascertained by reference to the partnership agreement. The sum so ascertained is inserted as one item in the official account and is regarded as *personalty* and must be certified by all the surviving partners. A copy of the last balance sheet and a copy of all relevant clauses of the partnership agreement affecting the determination of the share of a deceased partner, duly certified by the surviving partners, must be attached to the account.

Private business

Accounts must be prepared at the date of death and each type of business asset or liability must be shown under its proper heading in the official account. Goodwill must be taken into account and valued in accordance with the custom of the trade (e.g. a given number of years' purchase of the gross fees in the case of a professional accountant's practice), or computed on the basis of so many years' purchase of the net profits.

Freehold and leasehold properties

The value of the property must be agreed with the district valuer, who is an official of the Inland Revenue. It may be desirable to employ an expert valuer to act on behalf of the personal representatives, otherwise they or their solicitors may agree the value with the district valuer.

Where the property is to be sold within a short time of the death, it is usually permissible to use an estimated value initially, and to adjust the proceeds of sale in a corrective account.

In the case of a landed estate it was held in *Duke of Buccleugh* v. *Inland Revenue Commissioners* (1967) that such an estate must be valued as if it were comprised of various smaller easily saleable units and it must further be assumed for the purpose of estate duty that all the necessary lotting, dividing, preparing and drawing up of sale particulars had been completed at the date of death so that at that date the various individual units may be sold at the best possible price. Contrast this decision with that in *Willett* v. *IRC* (1982) where the Lands Tribunal valued a tenanted farm on a discounted basis by reference to the tenant's likely period of occupation, although the farm was sold in lots shortly afterwards.

10. Statutory apportionments

An examination of the official forms reveals the fact that certain apportionments of rents and income are aggregable with the rest of the estate for tax purposes. In other words, not only is money or property which is actually in the hands of the deceased at the time of his death subject to capital transfer tax, but also all money which has been earned by him or by his investments up to the date of his death, even if such earnings are not paid or payable until after the death.

Suppose, for example, that A owned a house which he let to B for a period of three years at a rent of £1,000 per annum, payable quarterly in arrear on the usual quarter days, viz. Ladyday (25 March), Midsummer (24 June), Michaelmas (29 September), and Christmas (25 December). A died on the 30 November. The value of the house is clearly aggregable for tax purposes, but in addition the rent actually accrued up to and including 30 November must be aggregated, as, although this rent is not payable until 25 December, the next usual quarter-day, yet it had accrued before the death. The aggregable portion of the rent is arrived at by taking the number of days in the quarter concerned and apportioning the rent, thus:

Number of days in quarter:		
30 September to 25 December		87 days
Number of days up to date of death:		
30 September to 30 November		62 days
Quarterly rent payable		£250
Proportion due up to and including day of death	$\frac{62}{87}$ of £250 =	£178.16

This sum must be aggregated with the rest of the estate although it will not actually be received until the 25 December.

It will be observed that, in making the apportionment, three facts must be considered:

a. the amount apportionable;
b. the period of accrual;
c. the date of death.

It should be noted that certain authorities contend that the apportionment of rent should be calculated on the basis of the full year (in the above case, $\frac{62}{365}$ of £1,000 = £169.86), but the method indicated above is usually adopted.

A similar apportionment of interest due upon loans must be made. Thus, if A loaned B £1,000 at 15 per cent per annum interest, payable half-yearly on 30 June and 31 December, and A died on 31 March, one-half of the half-year's interest due on 30 June would be aggregable, i.e. £75.00 (gross), or £52.50 (net) if income tax is deducted at 30 per cent.[1] Strictly the apportionment should be made in days, and this should be done when dealing with examination questions, unless the question specifies otherwise, or unless the dates in the question lend themselves to apportionment in months.

In calculating the number of days accrued up to the date of death the calculation is made inclusive of the day of death, i.e. the day of death is regarded as capital.

The following are not apportionable:

a. the profits of a private partnership, or the profits of the voyage of a single ship company: *Jones* v. *Ogle* (1872);
b. any sums properly payable in advance, e.g. rent payable in advance: *Ellis* v. *Rowbotham* (1900);
c. premiums payable on any policy of assurance.

In general it may be stated that apportionments are necessary for two distinct purposes:

---

1. Income tax has been calculated at the rate of 30% where appropriate despite the recent reduction in the basic rate to 29%.

a. for the ascertainment of the net principal value of an estate in order to assess capital transfer tax, and
b. for the allocation of income, expenditure and losses between life tenant and remainderman, or between a series of life tenants.

At this stage only those involved in the ascertainment of the net principal value of the estate will be considered.

No provision in the will can prevent this apportionment for tax purposes, although it can alter it as far as the beneficiaries are concerned (e.g. the will may provide that all income received after death shall be paid to the life tenant, irrespective of the period covered by such income).

It will be recalled that special rules are adopted for the valuation of quoted stocks and shares, accrued dividends or interest being taken into account in the price. No apportionment is therefore necessary for tax purposes, though it will be seen later that adjustment may be necessary as between life tenant and remainderman. Building society deposits and local authority mortgages are not 'quoted' investments, and it is, or course, necessary to take income accrued thereon into account in computing the net principal value of the estate.

11. Deductions from the estate for CTT purposes

From the aggregate or gross value of that portion of the estate which is subject to tax, certain debts and encumbrances may be deducted, the resulting figure being the net principal value upon which the rate of tax is assessed and paid.

The charges etc., which may be thus deducted are as follows:

Funeral expenses of a reasonable nature

These will include the normal expenses of burial, having regard to the social status of the deceased, but not additional expenses such as the cost of embalming the body or bringing the body from abroad or erecting a monument to the deceased. By concession, however, where the deceased was head of the household, a reasonable sum may be allowed in respect of mourning for the family and servants.

The death grant payable under the Social Security Act 1975 is not liable to CTT, and is not deductible from the amount of the funeral expenses, nor need any reference be made to it in the Inland Revenue account.   (Section 172, CTTA 1984)

Debts due to persons resident within Great Britain

The debts in question must, however, have been incurred bona fide and for full consideration in money or money's worth, and must be *legally enforceable against the estate*.

Thus, if the deceased had by deed promised to pay a sum of money to X, such promise being purely voluntary and without consideration, this debt could not be deducted. On the other hand, if the deceased owed his grocer the price of goods supplied up to the date of death, this would be a debt which could be deducted.

A personal representative is not compelled to plead the Limitation Act, and if he pays a debt which, apart from that Act, would be enforceable, that debt can be deducted.

Liabilities due at some future date (e.g. bills of exchange) should be discounted for purposes of deduction.

Gaming debts cannot be deducted.

Moreover, if the deceased was entitled to claim reimbursement of the debt from some other person, such a debt cannot be deducted unless such reimbursement cannot be obtained. Thus, if the deceased has guaranteed a debt owed by *A* to *X*, this debt cannot be deducted unless *A* is so insolvent that it is impossible to hope for reimbursement from him.

No deduction is allowed in respect of testamentary expenses in respect of the deceased's own estate, since these liabilities do not arise until the death has actually taken place. But if the deceased had inherited real property on a previous death, and all or part of the capital transfer tax thereon remained outstanding at the time of his death, the amount thereof would be deductible in computing the value of the property.

On the death of a married woman no deduction for debts is allowed if the husband is primarily liable for such debts, but funeral expenses of the deceased married woman may be deducted.

Debts due to persons resident out of Great Britain, if the same are either payable in Great Britain or are charged on property situated in Great Britain

Debts, other than the above, which are due to persons resident out of Great Britain are deducted primarily from personal property left by the deceased situated out of Great Britain, but if it is shown to the satisfaction of the Commissioners of Inland Revenue that such debts exceed the value of the personal property abroad a repayment of capital transfer tax can be claimed. Where, however, the deceased had no property abroad, the foreign debts may, by concession, be deducted from the property in this country, to avoid a subsequent repayment.

Income tax accrued to date of death

Where a person dies during a year of income tax assessment, the actual income for the fiscal year in which the death takes place must be ascertained in order to arrive at the correct assessment.

The actual tax payable up to the date of death, if not previously paid e.g. by direct assessment or by deduction from remuneration, may be deducted from the gross value of the estate. Similarly, any arrears of tax still outstanding in respect of previous years may be deducted in arriving at the net estate.

Interest on arrears of income tax apportioned to the date of death may also be deducted in arriving at the net value of the estate.

Any tax recoverable by a repayment claim to the date of death (e.g. where the greater part of the deceased's income was taxed at the source) and any refund under the Pay-As-You-Earn provisions would require to be brought in as an asset.

In the case of the death of a married woman who was at the time of her death living with her husband, unpaid income tax can be deducted from her estate if they had claimed separate assessment or if the husband had exercised his statutory right to disclaim liability for tax in respect of her income.   (Section 174, CTTA 1984)

Income tax on investments

Income tax on the income derived from investments is usually deducted before the income is paid over to the recipient, and where any portion of this income which has accrued due up to the date of death is subject to capital transfer tax it must be aggregated less income tax.

Thus, if *A* died on 7 June 19.. leaving £1,000 of 2½ per cent Consols valued at 25 *ex div.* on the date of the death, the aggregable figure will be arrived at as follows:

	£	£
£1,000 of 2½ per cent Consols at 25 *ex div.*		250.00
Interest for one quarter	6.25	
Less Income tax at 30 per cent	1.87	4.38
Value of Consols and interest at date of death		£254.38

On the other hand, if investments are quoted *cum div.* on the day of the death, no deduction of income tax can be made as the net accrued dividend is already included in the *cum div.* valuation.

Mortgages and other terminable charges

If any portion of the deceased's estate is subject to a mortgage or bill of sale the amount of the debt for which such security has been given may be deducted from the gross value of the estate.

In addition, any interest which has accrued due up to the date of death may also be deducted.

Thus, if *A* died on 31 October 19.. leaving freehold property valued at £20,000 which is subject to a mortgage of £11,000 at 10 per cent per annum interest, payable each 30 June and 31 December, the figure upon which tax is payable would be arrived at as follows:

	£	£
Freehold property valued at		20,000
Less Mortgage debt		11,000
		9,000
Less Interest accrued to date of death:	£	
4 months at 10 per cent per annum	300	
Less Income tax thereon — at 30 per cent	90	210
Value subject to capital transfer tax		£8,790

Where the mortgage debt is payable out of the general estate the debt and accrued interest should be deducted from the personalty, but where mortgaged realty devolves subject to the charge thereon under section 35 of the Administration of Estates Act 1925, the debt and accrued interest must be deducted from the value of the property concerned.

Rent under a tenancy agreement

All rent due under a tenancy agreement up to the termination of the tenancy will be allowed as a deduction, together with any amount payable under the agreement for dilapidations, but such liability must, of course, be reduced by any rents received from permitted sub-letting until the tenancy expires.

Capital gains tax

All capital gains tax outstanding for the year of death or earlier years serves to reduce the value of the estate.

Capital transfer tax on inter vivos transfers

Capital transfer tax outstanding on transfers of value effected by the deceased in his lifetime is an allowable deduction provided that the deceased was liable for the tax.

(Section 174, CTTA 1984)

Expenses of administration and collection of foreign assets

Where the estate includes assets located abroad it is permissible to claim a deduction for the additional expenses of administration, collection and realization of the foreign assets incurred directly as a result of their location, although in no circumstances may the deduction exceed 5 per cent of the value of the foreign assets in question.

(Section 173, CTTA 1984)

12. Joint property

The general term 'joint property' covers two distinct forms of co-ownership. Under a tenancy in common each of the co-owners possesses a defined share of the joint property which he is free to sell and dispose of during his life or under his will. For capital transfer tax purposes property owned by a tenant in common is treated in the same way as any other property owned by the individual in question.

Under a joint tenancy the property is jointly owned in the sense that on the death of one of the joint tenants the property passes wholly to the survivor or survivors. Whilst during his life a joint tenant has the right to sever the joint tenancy (i.e. to convert it into a tenancy in common) no such right exists on death with the result that property held under a joint tenancy cannot pass under a will or intestacy. On the death of a joint tenant the property in question passes by survivorship into the absolute ownership of the surviving joint tenant.

Certain peculiarities arise in relation to property held under a joint tenancy. Unless the joint tenancy arose under a will or deed executed by a third party, the creation of the joint tenancy after 26 March 1974 normally amounts to a transfer of value. Thus if an individual purchases property in the names of himself and another person as joint tenants, he has in effect made a transfer of value equivalent to one-half of the value of the property and he is taxed accordingly. Obviously, however, if the joint tenants are husband and wife the creation of the joint tenancy amounts to an exempt transfer and no capital transfer tax is payable.

Where a joint tenancy has been created after 26 March 1974, the subsequent death of one of the joint tenants may give rise to a claim for capital transfer tax unless the joint tenants are husband and wife when there can never be a liability to capital transfer tax on the death of the first joint tenant. Whether or not a claim for capital transfer tax arises on the death of a joint tenant depends upon whether or not the deceased placed the property in joint names in the first instance. If he did not do so (i.e. if he benefited from the original transfer of value on the creation of the joint tenancy), there is no liability to capital transfer tax on his death. The reason for this is that the property is effectively held in a settlement and is exempt since it has reverted to the settlor (i.e. the original transferor).

If, however, the first death is that of the original transferor, there is a liability to capital transfer tax on the one-half share of the joint property which now passes absolutely to the surviving joint tenant. Furthermore if the death occurs within three years of the creation of the joint tenancy, there may be a further liability to capital transfer tax by virtue of the fact that the transfer of value on the creation of the settlement is re-assessed at the higher rates of tax due on death. In both cases the surviving joint tenant is accountable for the capital transfer tax which is payable.

Where the joint tenancy was created before 27 March 1974, the element of gift on its creation could not have been liable to capital transfer tax which did not then exist. As a consequence the element of gift is treated for capital transfer tax purposes in accordance with the normal rules for gifts *inter vivos* made before 27 March 1974. This is the principle which underlies the method of assessing capital transfer tax on the death on or after 13 March 1975 of either joint tenant. If the joint tenant who dies first benefited from the creation of the joint tenancy, a one-half share of the value of the joint property is liable to capital transfer tax on his death and the liability falls on the surviving joint tenant. If, however, the original transferor dies first, not only is the value of his severable one-half share liable to capital transfer tax but also there is a potential claim for tax on the one-half share which he effectively gave to the surviving joint tenant on the creation of the joint tenancy. Clearly if the joint tenancy was created within seven years of his death such a claim arises (subject to the normal 'taper' relief). If the joint tenancy was created more than seven years before the death a similar claim might arise (without the benefit of taper relief) if the original transferor had retained an interest in the property given. It will be recalled that for estate duty purposes a gift was not completed unless the donor completely excluded himself from benefit in respect of the property given.

Where a joint tenancy between husband and wife was created before 27 March 1974, there is no liability to capital transfer tax on the death of either party since the property devolving upon the surviving spouse is specifically exempt from charge.

References to a one-half share of joint property which are made above are not necessarily intended to mean an exact half share of the full market value of the property. In some cases (for example on the death of a joint tenant) it might reasonably be argued that the half-share in question should be valued at a discount to the full 50 per cent of the market value on the ground that the property was not freely disposable. In other cases, and in particular on the creation of a joint tenancy, the Inland Revenue might equally reasonably argue that the loss to the transferor's estate is more than a simple one-half share of the market value of the property since the value of the transferor's interest under the joint tenancy after the transfer is less than the value of one-half of the total property before the transfer.

13. Incidence of CTT on death

The parties accountable for the capital transfer tax liability arising on a death are not always the persons who bear the burden of the tax ultimately. As a simple example it is clear that on the death of a life tenant the trustees of a settlement are accountable for the capital transfer tax payable but the burden of the tax falls upon the succeeding beneficiaries of the settlement. It is in this sense that the burden of the capital transfer tax payable on death, more properly referred to as the incidence of the tax, must be considered.

The incidence of the capital transfer tax payable on death on property which does not form part of the deceased's free estate is tabulated below:

Nature of property	*Incidence of tax*
a.　Settled property	Succeeding beneficiaries
(i.e. deceased's interest in trust funds)	(i.e. chargeable against trust fund).
b.　Property held under joint tenancy	Surviving joint tenant
c.　Gifts made before 27 March 1974 but	
within seven years of death	Donees of gifts
d.　Gifts made after 26 March 1974 but	
within three years of death	Donees of gifts
(tax payable representing the	
difference between tax at the higher	

rates and tax at the lower rates)
e. Nominated property   Nominees

For reasons which are now becoming rather anachronistic the position is not quite so straightforward in the deceased's free estate (by which is meant all the property which falls to be distributed under his will or intestacy). Again the basic position is tabulated below:

Nature of property	*Incidence of tax*
a. Real property (as defined on p. 2)	Residuary estate
b. Personal property in this country	Residuary estate
c. Personal property located abroad	Beneficiaries entitled to such property
d. Property passing under general power of appointment	Appointees

It is of course open to a testator to make specific provisions as to the incidence of any tax liability which will overrule the above principles, but to the extent that a testator does not provide otherwise, the above rules must be followed. From these rules therefore it is possible to derive a number of subsidiary rules which are stated below:

a. capital transfer tax attributable to pecuniary legacies falls on residue (but see (f) below);
b. capital transfer tax attributable to specific bequests of personalty falls on residue;
c. residue bears all capital transfer tax borne by the estate apart from tax under (d) to (g) below;
d. capital transfer tax attributable to specific bequests of real property is borne by the residue unless the will provides otherwise;
e. capital transfer tax attributable to specific bequests of property located abroad is borne by the specific legatees unless the will provides otherwise;
f.   where pecuniary legacies are charged upon realty or a mixed fund of personalty and realty, the legatees must bear the appropriate proportion of the capital transfer tax attributable to the real property concerned; *Re Spencer-Cooper* (1908). Similar principles apply to property located abroad if pecuniary legacies are wholly or partially charged on such property;
g. If a beneficiary is given an option under the will to take realty as part of his share of the residuary estate, he must bear the capital transfer tax thereon: *O'Grady* v. *Wilmot* (1916).

14. Corrective accounts and certificates of discharge

Directly as a result of the requirement that an account of any transfer of value or other chargeable event must be delivered to the Inland Revenue within a specified period if the tax is to be paid by the due date (and thus interest is to be avoided) it will sometimes be necessary to submit estimated figures in the first instance. This is particularly true on the death of a person since it is obviously necessary to prepare quickly an account of the assets and liabilities of the estate in order to obtain probate or letters of administration. It follows therefore that there are amendments to the figures initially reported whenever values are altered (perhaps as a result of negotiation with the Inland Revenue) or whenever additional assets or liabilities are discovered in the case of a death. Provision is therefore made in these circumstances for the submission of a corrective account for assessment. Any further capital transfer tax due or any repayment of capital transfer tax which arises as a result of a corrective account is then calculated. In some cases more than one corrective account may be necessary. The adjustment of the tax position which is effected on the assessment of a corrective account involves the payment of interest either to or by the Inland Revenue provided that the due date for payment of the liability has passed.

On the assessment of the final corrective account, or following the assessment of the original account if no amendments arise, application may be made to the Inland Revenue for a certificate of discharge from all further claims to capital transfer tax. Such a certificate is issued when the Revenue authorities are satisfied that all tax due has been paid, and offers full protection against further claims for capital transfer tax attributable to property which has been disclosed to the Inland Revenue. A certificate of discharge does not, however, discharge any accountable party from tax in the case of fraud or of failure to disclose material facts. Furthermore, such a certificate does not affect any further tax which might be payable if it transpires that further property forms part of the estate of a deceased person. Nevertheless, it is submitted that for their own protection personal representatives and trustees should not complete the distribution of an estate or of a trust fund on the death of a life tenant until a certificate of discharge has been obtained.

FULL EXAMPLES OF THE CALCULATION OF CTT ON DEATH

Earlier examples in this chapter (Examples 5 and 6) illustrated the calculation of the CTT liability arising on a death in the more straightforward situations. The examples which follow will look at some of the more complicated calculations which may be required, although the examples given are not designed to illustrate every conceivable form of calculation which may be required.

Example 10

Mr *J* died in June 1985 having made previous chargeable transfers of £40,000 in 1982. The net value of his estate was £100,000. By his will he left a pecuniary legacy of £50,000 to his son, free of CTT, with the residue to his wife.

The facts of this example are similar to those in Example 6, but in this case the pecuniary legacy of £50,000 is payable free of CTT to his son. (Contrast the CTT payable in this example with that payable in Example 6.)

The CTT payable on *J*'s estate is calculated as follows:

	£
Gross cumulative total before death	40,000
Less CTT at death rates at date of death	Nil
Net cumulative total	40,000
Add 'Tax-free' legacy	50,000
Net cumulative total	£90,000
CTT payable on net cumulative total:	
On first £67,000 @ Nil =	Nil
On next £15,400 @ 3/7 =	6,600.00
On next £ 7,600 @ 7/13 =	4,092.30
	10,692.30
Less CTT on previous net cumulative total	Nil
CTT payable on 'tax-free' legacy	£10,692.30
Grossed up value of 'tax-free' legacy (ignoring pence)	£60,692
Exempt residue becomes £100,000 *less* £60,692	£39,308

The distribution of *J*'s estate is as follows:

'Tax-free' legacy to son	50,000
CTT to Inland Revenue	10,692
Exempt residue to widow	39,308
Total	£100,000

The example above demonstrates the grossing up procedure necessary where a 'tax-free' legacy is payable out of a share in the estate which is itself exempt from CTT. Although the exempt share of the estate in the above example arose because the residue passed to *J*'s widow, the same calculation would apply if the residue was left wholly to charity, for example, or was otherwise wholly exempt from CTT.

Where there are both 'tax-free' legacies and non-exempt shares in the estate, a double grossing-up calculation is necessary to calculate the CTT liability in respect of the estate.

The stages in the double grossing-up calculation are as follows:

Stage 1: Calculate the grossed-up value of the tax-free legacies ignoring the remainder of the non-exempt estate.

Stage 2: Using the grossed-up value of the tax-free legacies obtained in Stage 1, make a provisional calculation of the total CTT due on the estate and hence the average rate of CTT.

Stage 3: Gross up the tax-free legacies using the average rate of CTT ascertained in Stage 3.

Stage 4: Calculate the CTT on the whole estate using the revised grossed-up value of the tax-free legacies established in Stage 3.

Example 11

Mr *K* died in September 1985. The net value of his estate has been agreed as £250,000. By his will he left legacies of £15,000 each, tax-free, to his two cousins, and a legacy of £20,000 to his niece which is to bear its own tax. The residue of his estate was left equally between his widow and his daughter. In 1980 he made chargeable transfers of £90,000 gross, the donees paying the tax, and these were the only previous transfers of value made.

The CTT payable in respect of *K*'s estate is calculated as follows:

	£	£
Stage 1		
Gross cumulative total before death		90,000
Less CTT at death rates in force at date of death:		
On first £67,000 @ Nil =	Nil	
On next £22,000 @ 30% =	6,600.00	
On next £ 1,000 @ 35% =	350.00	6,950
Adjusted net cumulative total		83,050
Add tax-free legacies (2 × £15,000)		30,000
Net cumulative total		£113,050
CTT on net cumulative total:		
On first £67,000 @ Nil =	Nil	
On next £15,400 @ 3/7 =	6,600.00	
On next £21,450 @ 7/13 =	11,150.00	
On next £ 9,200 @ 2/3 =	6,133.33	
	23,883.33	
Less CTT on previous net cumulative total	6,950.00	
CTT payable on tax-free legacies	16,933.33	
Tax-free legacies	30,000.00	
Grossed-up value of tax-free legacies (ignoring pence)	£46,933	

Stage 2

Grossed-up value of tax-free legacies	46,933
Other non-exempt legacies	20,000
	66,933
Non-exempt share of residue:	
½ × (£250,000 − £66,933)	91,533
	158,466
Add Gross cumulative total before death	90,000
CTT chargeable on	£248,466

CTT payable:

On first £67,000 @ Nil	=	Nil
On next £22,000 @ 30%	=	6,600.00
On next £33,000 @ 35%	=	11,550.00
On next £33,000 @ 40%	=	13,200.00
On next £39,000 @ 45%	=	17,550.00
On next £49,000 @ 50%	=	24,500.00
On next £ 5,466 @ 55%	=	3,006.30
		76,406.30
Less CTT on previous cumulative total		6,950.00
Assumed CTT payable on death		£69,456.30

The average or assumed rate becomes: $\dfrac{69,456}{158,466}$

Stage 3

Revised grossed-up value of tax-free legacies becomes:

£30,000 × $\dfrac{158,466}{158,466 - 69,456}$ =   £53,410

Stage 4

Grossed-up value of tax-free legacies	53,410
Other non-exempt legacies	20,000
	73,410
Non-exempt share of residue:	
½ × (£250,000 − £73,410) =	88,295
	161,705
Add gross cumulative total before death	90,000
CTT chargeable on	£251,705

CTT payable:

On first £67,000 @ Nil	=	Nil
On next £22,000 @ 30%	=	6,600.00
On next £33,000 @ 35%	=	11,550.00
On next £33,000 @ 40%	=	13,200.00
On next £39,000 @ 45%	=	17,550.00
On next £49,000 @ 50%	=	24,500.00
On next £ 8,705 @ 55%	=	4,787.75
		78,187.75
Less CTT on previous cumulative total		6,950.00
CTT payable on death		£71,237.75

Distribution of Mr K's estate

Re-grossed tax-free legacies	53,410
Chargeable estate	161,705
CTT payable (ignoring pence)	71,237
Division of estate as follows:	
Tax-free legacies	30,000
CTT thereon $\left(\dfrac{53,410}{161,705} \times £71,237\right)$ =	23,529
	53,529

176 Executorship Law and Accounts

Other legacies		20,000	
CTT thereon $\left(\dfrac{20,000}{161,705} \times £71,237\right)$	=	8,810	8,810
Net legacies		£11,190	11,190
Residue of estate (£250,000 − £73,529)		£176,471	
CTT on residue:			
£71,237 − (£23,529 + £8,810)		38,898	38,898
Exempt residue to widow:			
½ × £176,471	=		88,235
Balance of residue		88,236	
Less CTT thereon		38,898	49,338
Total estate			£250,000

Exercise 12

1. Mr Green died in September 1985. He had made a chargeable transfer of £20,000 on 1 March 1984. His cumulative total of chargeable transfers at 1 March 1984, all made in the previous five years was £60,000. The donee paid the tax due in respect of the earlier transfer. Calculate the amount of any additional tax due in respect of the chargeable transfer made in March 1984.
2. What types of expenses and liabilities can be deducted in arriving at the value of a person's estate at death?
3. What do you understand by the term 'related property'? What effect can this have on the value of a gift for capital transfer tax purposes.
4. Mr Smith died in August 1985 leaving a net estate of £200,000. The whole of his estate passed to his wife and son absolutely. What is the CTT payable:
   a. assuming no previous chargeable transfers, and
   b. assuming previous chargeable transfers within the last ten years of £50,000.
   In each case show the distribution of the estate.
5. What relief can be claimed if the personal representatives sell quoted shares and securities shortly after death at a price less than the probate value?
6. Mr Brown died in September 1985 leaving an estate of £150,000. He had made chargeable transfers in the last ten years of £55,000. His estate passes as follows:
   a. legacy of £75,000 to his daughter, free of CTT;
   b. residue to his widow.
   Calculate the capital transfer tax payable as a result of the death of Mr Brown and show the distribution of the estate.
7. Describe the provisions concerning the rearrangement of a person's estate for capital transfer tax purposes. Are there similar provisions for income tax and capital gains tax purposes.
8. Mr Smith died in July 1985 leaving an estate with an agreed net value of £200,000. He had made previous chargeable transfers of £50,000 within the last ten years prior to his death. By his will he left tax-free legacies of £15,000 each to his two nieces and a legacy of £25,000 to his nephew to bear its own tax. The residue of the estate he left equally between his widow and his son. Calculate the capital transfer tax payable on Mr Smith's estate and show the distribution of the estate.

13
Capital Transfer Tax IV

The previous chapters were concerned with the effect of capital transfer tax on lifetime dispositions and on death. This chapter concentrates on the rather complex rules affecting the imposition of capital transfer tax in settlements and trust funds. The rules described are those that applied under the capital transfer tax legislation in force prior to the passing of the Finance Act 1986. This act introduced the new provisions for inheritance tax that applies from 18 March 1986. Chapter 14 deals with the changes introduced by the Finance Act 1986.

CREATION OF A TRUST FUND OR SETTLEMENT

Generally speaking, on the creation on or after 27 March 1974 of a trust fund or settlement, a charge to capital transfer tax at lifetime rates arises and the settlor is accountable for the tax payable which is assessed by reference to his accumulator. In other words the creation of a settlement amounts for all tax purposes to a gift *inter vivos*. For this reason it is necessary to gross up the net value of the property placed in trust in the manner outlined previously in order to arrive at the taxable value of the disposition. Frequently, however, if it is a provision of the settlement that the capital transfer tax liability shall fall on the trustees of the settlement, and provided that the tax is paid from the assets of the settlement, there is no grossing up, and the gift is valued simply by reference to the value of the assets settled at the date of the settlement.

Many of the exemptions which may be claimed in relation to other lifetime dispositions are available to the settlor on the creation of a settlement. For convenience the exemptions concerned are listed below.

Settlements on spouses
Where the settlor's spouse takes a life interest (or other limited interest in possession) in the settled property the creation of the settlement amounts to an exempt transfer.

Transfers of £3,000 per year
Partial or total exemption may be available if the settlor can claim under this heading. Whether or not he can make such a claim depends, of course, on other transfers effected by him within the relevant tax years.

Settlements made in consideration of marriage
Essentially marriage settlements qualify for exemption on their creation on the same

basis as outright gifts in consideration of marriage qualify. For this purpose, however, a settlement shall not be treated as made in consideration of marriage if the persons who are entitled or who may at any time become entitled to any benefit under the settlement do not fall strictly within the following categories:

a.   the parties to the marriage, issue of the marriage, or spouses of such issue;
b.   subsequent spouses of the parties to the marriage, or any issue or the spouses of any issue of a subsequent marriage of either party to the marriage;
c.   persons becoming entitled on the failure of trusts for any issue of the marriage under which trust property would (subject only to powers of appointment which may exist in favour of persons mentioned within (a) or (b) above) vest indefeasibly on the attainment of a specific age or either on the attainment of such an age or some earlier event, or persons becoming entitled (subject as above) on the failure of any limitation in tail;
d.   persons becoming entitled on the coming into operation of the protective trusts under the Trustee Act 1925, section 33, provided that the principal beneficiary is a person falling within (a) or (b) above;
e.   the trustees of the settlement provided that they benefit to the extent of a reasonable amount of remuneration only.

The limits of £5,000, £2,500 or £1,000, as the case may be, are of course imposed on gifts by way of marriage settlement (see p. 124).

Settlements on charities

For transfers made after 14 March 1983 there is no limit on the amount of the exemption available in respect of transfers to charities. This exemption covers both outright gifts to charities and also the creation of settlements for charitable purposes only. The settlement must be perpetual, not for a limited period only.   (Section 23, CTTA 1984)

Settlement of foreign assets where the settlor is domiciled abroad

As a general rule, settlements of foreign assets made by the settlor at a time when he is domiciled outside the United Kingdom are excluded property. However, for settlements created after 9 December 1974, the extended definition of domicile (section 267, CTTA 1984) must be taken into account in determining if the settlor is domiciled outside the United Kingdom.

Property is treated as being comprised in a settlement when it is introduced into the settlement (see Inland Revenue Statement of Practice SP/E9). The status of excluded property is determined immediately before the property vests: *Von Ernst & Cie SA and Others* v. *CIR* (1980).

There are no provisions within the CTT legislation for determining whether property is or is not situated abroad. Hence, the common law situs rules apply. Broadly, these are as follows:

a.   *registered shares and securities* are situated where they are registered;
b.   *bearer shares and securities* are situated in the country in which the certificate of title is retained;
c.   *land and chattels* are situated where the land or chattels are physically situated;
d.   *debts* are generally situated where the debtor resides, but if the debt is due from a bank it is situated at the branch of the bank from which it is primarily recoverable.

(Section 34, CTTA 1984)

Exempt gilts

To the extent that a settlor who is domiciled abroad includes the particular government securities qualifying for exemption in a settlement, the creation of the settlement is exempt from capital transfer tax.   (Section 48, CTTA 1984)

Certain savings of persons domiciled in the Channel Islands or the Isle of Man

National Savings certificates and the like if settled by a settlor domiciled in the Channel Islands or the Isle of Man are excluded property at the time of creation of the settlement.   (Section 6, CTTA 1984)

Reversionary interests

Unless acquired at any time by way of purchase reversionary interests are excluded from the operation of capital transfer tax.   (Section 48, CTTA 1984)

Settlements for the maintenance of the family

Section 11, CTTA 1984 applies on the creation of settlements for the particular purpose specified in the section and outlined fully in relation to lifetime gifts.

None of the other exemptions which may be claimed in relation to outright gifts is available on the creation of a settlement. Thus, the small gifts relief has no relevance on the creation of a settlement, however small the settlement may be. Settlements on political parties do not qualify for exemption, but it is possible that whilst there is no specific exemption for settlements on heritage bodies or other bodies not conducted for profit, the creation of such a settlement may escape tax if the body concerned is charitable and the settlement is made in perpetuity under the exemption provided for settlements on charities. Agricultural relief, business property relief and a credit for overseas tax paid on the same occasion may also be claimed on the creation of a settlement.

One other exemption is of some importance on the execution of a settlement. If the settlor settles property on himself for life or some other limited period, the creation of the settlement is not a chargeable event. Strictly of course this is not an exemption since there has been no transfer of value and the beneficial ownership of the property settled has not changed.

SETTLED PROPERTY — GENERAL DEFINITIONS

Before reviewing the detailed provisions regarding CTT applicable to settled property, it is appropriate to define certain of the terms used in the legislation, as without a clear understanding of these terms it will be difficult to appreciate the comments which follow.

The main definitions are as follows.

Settlement

A 'settlement' is defined as any disposition, or dispositions, of property whether effected by instrument, by parol or by operation of the law, or partly in one way and partly in another, whereby the property is for the time being:

a. held in trust for persons in succession or for any person subject to a contingency, or

b. held by trustees on trust to accumulate the whole or part of any income of the property or with power to make payments out of that income at the discretion of the trustees or some other person, with or without power to accumulate surplus income, or

c. charged or burdened (otherwise than for full consideration in money or money's worth) with the payment of any annuity or other periodical payment for a life or any other limited or terminable period.

A foreign settlement is also included within this definition if it is governed by the law of any part of the United Kingdom, or foreign law if it is governed by provisions broadly equivalent to United Kingdom law.   (Section 43(2), CTTA 1984)

A lease of property for life, or lives, or for a period only ascertainable by reference to death, unless for full consideration in money or money's worth is treated as a settlement.   (Section 43(3), CTTA 1984)

The definition is extended in Scotland to include:

a. an entail;
b. any deed by virtue of which an annuity is charged on, or on the rents of, any property;
c. any deed creating or reserving a proper life rent of any property, whether heritable or moveable.

The term 'deed' in this context includes any disposition, arrangement, contract, resolution, instrument or writing.   (Section 43(4), CTTA 1984)

The definition is also amended in its application in Northern Ireland to include references to property standing limited to persons, but to exclude a lease in perpetuity within the meaning of section 1, Renewable Leasehold Conversion Act 1894, or a lease to which section 37 of that act applies.   (Section 43(5), CTTA 1984)

Settlor

A settlor is defined as any person by whom the settlement was made directly or indirectly, and includes any person who has provided funds directly or indirectly for the purposes of the settlement or has made with any other person a reciprocal arrangement for that other person to make the settlement.

Where more than one person is a settlor in relation to a settlement and the circumstances so require, the legislation is to be applied as if the settled property were comprised in separate settlements. If there is an identifiable capital fund provided by each settlor there will be more than one settlor in relation to the settlement: *Thomas v. IRC* (1981).   (Section 44, CTTA 1984)

Trustee

The trustees of a settlement are regarded as a single continuing body of persons separate from the individuals, who are, at any given time, the trustees. The term 'trustees' is defined to include any person in whom the settled property or its management is for the time being vested. This covers the situation where no formal trustees have been appointed, for example, a lease for life.

Reversionary interest

A 'reversionary interest' means a future interest under a settlement whether it is vested or contingent. In relation to Scotland this also includes an interest in the fee of property subject to a proper life rent.   (Section 47, CTTA 1984)

Excluded property

As previously indicated, a reversionary interest under a settlement is excluded property unless it has been acquired at any time for a consideration in money or money's worth, the settlor, or his spouse, is or has been beneficially entitled to it, or the interest is expectant upon the determination of a lease for life (see 'settlement' above).

Excluded property also includes a settlement of foreign assets made by a settlor domiciled abroad (see discussion on p. 000), and a settlement of exempt government securities where the person entitled to a qualifying interest in possession is neither domiciled abroad (see discussion on p. 178), and a settlement of exempt government qualifying interest in possession all the persons for whose benefit the settled property or income from it has been or might be applied, or who are or might become beneficially entitled to an interest in possession in it, are persons neither domiciled nor ordinarily resident in the United Kingdom.

SETTLEMENTS WITH AN INTEREST IN POSSESSION

A trust or settlement, once created, assumes a legal status independent of the settlor or testator. For CTT purposes a clear distinction must be drawn between settlements with an interest in possession and settlements with no interest in possession. The term 'interest in possession' is not defined within the CTT legislation. The leading case at present on this subject is the case of *Pearson and Others* v. *IRC* (1980). This case established three guidelines in determining if a beneficiary has an interest in possession, as follows:

a. the beneficiary must have a present right to present enjoyment of the income arising;
b. where the beneficiary's right of enjoyment depends upon the trustees not exercising a power of accumulation, he does not have an interest in possession;
c. administrative powers, e.g. the trustees being allowed to charge for their services or those of professional agents, insure trust assets, pay taxes which fall due, etc. do not preclude there being an interest in possession.

It was also apparently agreed by the parties to this case that an overriding power of appointment by trustees does not prevent a beneficiary having an interest in possession provided that power cannot be used to appoint the income away from the beneficiary after it has arisen.

The Revenue's view of the term 'interest in possession' was set out in the Press Release of 12 February 1976. The views expressed in that Press Release do not appear to be inconsistent with the judgement of the House of Lords in the *Pearson* case.

The effect of section 31, Trustee Act 1925, must also be considered, where this applies in relation to the settlement. The effect in the case of minor beneficiaries appears to be to defer the entitlement to income of an infant beneficiary until he attains the age of 18, thus the infant will not have an interest in possession. Unless the settlement is within the definition of an accumulation or maintenance settlement, the settled property will fall to be dealt with under the provisions for settlements without an interest in possession. As far as adult beneficiaries are concerned, the effect appears to be to accelerate his right to receive the income such that he has an interest in possession.

The paragraphs which follow deal only with trusts with an interest in possession, and, for the sake of simplicity, reference is, in general, made to the normal situation where property is held on trust for a life tenant. The general principle of capital transfer taxation allied to such trusts is that a life interest amounts to ownership of the trust property although responsibility for payment of the tax rests with the trustees (section 49, CTTA 1984). This general principle can clearly be seen in operation on the various potential occasions of charge to capital transfer tax which are summarized below. Whether or not the trust fund was created under a will or by a lifetime settlement, and whether or not the trust commenced after 26 March 1974, the potential occasions of charge to capital transfer tax are the following.

On the death of a life tenant (or other income beneficiary)

With effect from 13 March 1975, on the death of a life tenant, the value of the trust property in which the life interest subsisted is, subject to the exemptions and reliefs mentioned below, aggregated with the value of the life tenant's free estate and other property passing on the death in order to determine the effective rate of capital transfer tax. The process of aggregation has been considered elsewhere and corresponds to the former estate duty practice, but it is apparent that the amount of capital transfer tax payable in the trust fund depends not only on the value of the trust property and other property passing on the death, but also on the deceased's life tenant's accumulator at the time of his death. The capital transfer tax payable on the death of a life tenant is assessed without reference to the level of taxation incurred on the creation of the trust fund, or on the death of an earlier life tenant.

Example 1

Mr *A* died in August 1985. He had made chargeable transfers of £50,000 within the last ten years, but all more than three years prior to his death. He left a free estate of £50,000, net, and was the life tenant of settled property having a value of £100,000 as at the date of his death.
    The CTT liability of the trustees will be as follows:

		£
Value of free estate		50,000
Value of settled property		100,000
		150,000
Add Cumulative total brought forward		50,000
CTT chargeable on		£200,000
CTT payable:		
On first £67,000 @ Nil	=	Nil
On next £22,000 @ 30%	=	6,600.00
On next £33,000 @ 35%	=	11,550.00
On next £33,000 @ 40%	=	13,200.00
On next £39,000 @ 45%	=	17,550.00
On next £ 6,000 @ 50%	=	3,000.00
		51,900.00
Less CTT on previous cumulative total		Nil
CTT chargeable on death		£51,900.00
Liability of trustees: $\dfrac{£100,000}{£150,000} \times £51,900$ =		£34,600.00

The capital transfer tax liability arising in a trust fund on the death of a life tenant is assessed at the higher rates of tax applicable on death and is due for payment by the trustees six months after the last day of the month in which the death occurred and carries interest at 9 per cent with effect from that date.

The example given above assumes that there are no exemptions or other reliefs which might be claimed on the death. The following exemptions are, however, relevant on the death of a life tenant.

Property devolving on the life tenant's spouse

To the extent that trust property devolves upon the spouse of the life tenant whether absolutely or by way of a life interest, the property concerned is exempt from capital transfer tax on the death. The exemption is identical to the exemption available in the free estate of the deceased. (Section 18, CTTA 1984)

Surviving spouse exemption

Where the life tenant was the surviving spouse of a person on whose death before 13 November 1974 estate duty became payable on the trust assets, there is no charge to capital transfer tax on the death of the life tenant, regardless of the beneficial interests which then arise. This is, in fact, a continuation of the former exemption allowed for estate duty purposes, and the exemption is available whether or not estate duty was paid on the death of the former spouse provided that the trust's assets were liable (perhaps at a nil rate) on that death. The exemption is, however, withdrawn if the deceased life tenant was fully competent to dispose of the trust property (for example, if he had a general power of appointment over the trust fund).
(Paragraph 2, Schedule 6, CTTA 1984)

Example 2

Mr *B,* who died on 5 April 1964, left the residue of his estate to his wife for life with remainder to his children in equal shares. Mrs *B* dies on 10 May 1985 and the trust fund then valued at £400,000 is distributed to the children.

Since on the death of Mr *B* estate duty was paid on his entire estate, there is no charge to capital transfer tax on 10 May 1985 when his widow dies.

It will be apparent from the above example that this exemption provides relief in cases where no relief was given on an earlier death for property which passed to the deceased's spouse.

Reverter to settlor

Where on the death of a life tenant property comprised in a settlement passes to the settlor, the property concerned is exempt from capital transfer tax provided that the settlor survives the life tenant and the settlor has not acquired the reversionary interest by purchase. (Section 54(1), CTTA 1984)

Reverter to settlor's spouse

Where on the death of a life tenant property comprised in a settlement passes to the settlor's spouse, the property concerned is exempt from capital transfer tax provided that the settlor's spouse survives the life tenant and is both domiciled and resident for income tax purposes in the United Kingdom in the year of assessment in which the death occurs, and provided that neither the settlor nor the settlor's spouse has at any time acquired a reversionary interest in the settlement by way of purchase.
(Section 54(2), CTTA 1984)

Property devolving upon charities

Property passing to charities is now exempt without limit and this exemption is available in respect of the transfer arising on the termination of a life interest on the death of a life tenant.   (Section 23, CTTA 1984)

Property devolving upon political parties

The exemption available in respect of transfers to political parties is available in respect of terminations of life interests.   (Section 24, CTTA 1984)

Property devolving upon 'heritage bodies'

Property passing to such bodies as the National Gallery and the British Museum is completely exempt from capital transfer tax on the death of a life tenant.

(Section 25, CTTA 1984)

Property bequeathed for public benefit

Property passing on the death of a life tenant to bodies established for public benefit may qualify for total exemption from capital transfer tax provided that the property concerned meets the conditions set out in detail in relation to life-time dispositions.

(Section 26, CTTA 1984)

Foreign trusts

Regardless of the domicile of the deceased life tenant, assets located abroad which are held in trusts of foreign domicile are excluded from charge to capital transfer tax on the death of the life tenant. A trust is regarded as being of foreign domicile if at the time of its creation the settlor or the deceased was himself domiciled abroad. For this purpose section 267, CTTA 1984, is to be applied in determining the domicile of the settlor or deceased at the time of creation of the trust. Assets located in this country which are held in such trusts are subject to capital transfer tax on the death of the life tenant in the normal way.   (Section 53(1), CTTA 1984)

'Exempt gilts'

Where the deceased life tenant is at the time of death neither domiciled nor ordinarily resident in this country, the specific government securities which are listed in connection with lifetime dispositions are exempt from capital transfer tax if they are held in the trust fund. For this purpose section 267, CTTA 1984, is not applied.

(Section 48(4), CTTA 1984)

Reversionary interests

If a reversionary interest remains an asset of a trust fund on the death of the life tenant, no charge to capital transfer tax arises on its value unless the reversionary interest has at some earlier date been purchased by any person. This is the case even if, for example, the reversionary interest became subject to the trust on a death in 1973 and estate duty was postponed with respect to the reversion on that date. It follows that personal representatives who in earlier years took the decision to postpone estate duty on a reversionary interest until it fell into possession have derived some benefit from the decision whilst personal representatives who paid estate duty on the value of the reversionary interest at the time of the original death have paid a levy which as a result of the abolition of estate duty and the introduction of capital transfer tax they might have avoided.   (Section 53(1), CTTA 1984)

Persons domiciled in the Channel Islands or Isle of Man

Where National Savings Certificates, Trustee Savings Bank deposits and similar assets (i.e. those mentioned in relation to lifetime dispositions) are held in a trust fund and the life tenant is domiciled in the Channel Islands or the Isle of Man, the value of these assets is left out of account on the death of the life tenant.

Death on active service

Where the life tenant of a trust fund dies on active service (as defined in relation to capital transfer tax on death) the trust fund is completely exempt from capital transfer tax.   (Section 154, CTTA 1984)

Works of art

Exemption is provided in a trust fund on the death of a life tenant for works of art provided that the necessary conditions are fulfilled. The conditions and the required undertakings are those relevant to any death of a deceased person.
                                                                       (Sections 26 and 30, CTTA 1984)

Historic land and buildings

The death of a life tenant may give rise to a claim for exemption on the value of historic land and buildings comprised within the trust fund. Again exemption is provided on exactly the same basis as the exemption for works of art. In both cases the exemption can be lost on a subsequent sale of the assets in question or on a breach of undertakings. Where the exemption is lost, the capital transfer tax payable is assessed in the manner explained in relation to capital transfer tax in the free estate of the former owner of the assets.   (Sections 26 and 30, CTTA 1984)

Timber

Subject to the conditions specified in relation to the death of the owner of growing timber, the value of growing timber owned by a trust fund may be exempt from capital transfer tax on the death of the life tenant if exemption is claimed within the relevant period. The beneficial ownership of the timber by the former life tenant is a sufficient degree of ownership for the purpose of the exemption provided that the life tenant fulfils the necessary conditions. On the subsequent sale or disposal of the timber capital transfer tax is assessed by reference to the value of the property passing on the death of the life tenant in accordance with the rules detailed in the previous chapter.
                                                                                 (Section 125, CTTA 1984)

The following further reliefs may be claimed on the death of a life tenant.

Quick succession relief

For transfers after 9 March 1981, the relief available in respect of transfers of value in quick succession of settled property is identical to that in relation to the free estate of individual transferors. The relief for individual transferors is described on p. 154 to which further reference should now be made. For transfers prior to 10 March 1981 the relief available in respect of successive transfers of settled property was different to that relative to the free estate.

Business property relief

Business property relief is available in respect of settled property, provided the other relevant conditions are satisfied, as follows:

a. where the business itself is settled property and the beneficiary has an interest in possession in that settled property, relief should be available at the rate of 50 per cent;

b. where the business belongs to the life tenant and the assets transferred are settled property which has been used for the purposes of the business, relief is available at the rate of 30 per cent under section 105(1)(e), CTTA 1984.

The above appears to be the position following the Court of Appeal judgment in the case of *Fetherstonaugh and Others* v. *CIR* (1984) (previously *Finch and Others* v. *CIR*), although the position is not wholly free from doubt and is the subject of discussion at present.   (Sections 103–114, CTTA 1984)

Agricultural relief

Where the deceased life tenant was by virtue of his life interest in a trust fund the beneficial owner of agricultural property which is subject to the trust, agricultural relief may be claimed by the trustees on the life tenant's death provided that the life tenant fulfilled the conditions required of any transferor of agricultural property who seeks relief.   (Sections 115–124, CTTA 1984)

Credit for overseas tax

As usual where the death of a life tenant gives rise both to a capital transfer tax liability and a liability to an overseas tax of a similar nature on assets located abroad, the overseas tax paid may be credited against the capital transfer tax due.
                                                                  (Sections 158 and 159, CTTA 1984)

Payment of tax by instalments

On the death of a life tenant capital transfer tax may be paid by instalments in the appropriate circumstances referred to in detail in connection with any other death. Again by virtue of his beneficial ownership of instalment property held in the trust fund the life tenant is technically regarded as the owner of such property and may therefore be considered for this purpose to have control of a company. Similarly the total personal holdings of the life tenant and the holdings which he beneficially owns by virtue of his life interest may be considered together for the purpose of deciding whether or not he had control of a company, or whether or not 10 per cent of the issued shares passed on the death.   (Section 227, CTTA 1984)

Losses on qualifying investments

The relief available applies on the death of a life tenant in the same way as it applies to any other death with the general result that the overall loss incurred by the trustees on the sale of investments held at the date of death of the life tenant during the twelve months following the death may be claimed as a deduction from the value of the trust fund at the date of death. Where the trust fund becomes absolutely distributable following the life tenant's death, the trustees become bare trustees subject only to their lien for tax and administration expenses. Nevertheless in these circumstances the relief may be claimed even if they are purely selling investments under the general trust for sale with a view to providing a cash distribution for the legatees.

Where the trust fund remains held on further trusts following the death of a life tenant, all investment transactions are carried out by the trustees acting in the same capacity. It is more likely in these circumstances that a purchase of qualifying investments might be effected during the fourteen months following the life tenant's death and as a result the overall loss arising on the sale of qualifying investments held at the date of death will be affected. Clearly before they effect such purchases the trustees of a continuing trust fund must attempt to reach delicately balanced decisions, bearing in mind both normal investment criteria and the tax implications involved.

(Sections 178–189, CTTA 1984)

Disclaimers

The disclaimer of an interest in settled property, provided the disclaimer is not made for a consideration in money or money's worth, is not a chargeable transfer. The CTT legislation is applied as if the person making the disclaimer had not become entitled to the interest. For a disclaimer to be effective, however, the person making the disclaimer must not have received any benefit from the interest he is seeking to disclaim.

(Section 93, CTTA 1984)

On the termination of a life interest (or other interest in possession)

It is provided that the termination of a life interest or other interest in possession in trust property is an occasion of charge to capital transfer tax subject to the various exemptions which are referred to below. The general rule is that, whenever a right to receive income from a trust fund ceases either wholly or partially, there is an occasion of charge to capital transfer tax. This is designed to bring within the scope of capital transfer tax what may be described as trust-breakings generally which might otherwise escape the normal liability to capital transfer tax arising on the death of an income beneficiary.

Under this heading therefore capital transfer tax is charged on *inter vivos* terminations of interests in possession in trust funds. Such terminations are regarded as equivalent to lifetime dispositions, and accordingly they attract capital transfer tax at the lower lifetime rates and the tax is assessed by reference to the income beneficiary's cumulative total. It follows therefore that the termination of an income beneficiary's interest in a trust fund serves to increase the level of his cumulative total with the result that subsequent chargeable transfers of value effected by him are taxed at higher rates than would have been chargeable if his interest had not been terminated. Frequently the termination of an interest in possession is involuntary in the sense that the event which causes the termination (e.g. the expiry of a fixed term if a life tenant's interest is under the trust instrument limited to end after a specified number of years). In such cases the trustees of the settlement are not involved in the planning or execution of the termination. There are other occasions, however, where an interest in possession is wholly or partially terminated as a result of a voluntary act on the part of the income beneficiary (e.g. if a life tenant agrees to the advance of trust funds to a beneficiary under section 32, Trustee Act, 1925). It is suggested that on these occasions prudent trustees should make it clear to the income beneficiary that the action contemplated, which is of no direct benefit to him, will on its implementation serve to increase his cumulative total and thus to increase the tax payable on future transfers effected by him.

Despite this relationship between the income beneficiary's cumulative total and the charging of capital transfer tax on the trust fund, the trustees of the trust fund are primarily responsible for payment of the capital transfer tax liability arising on an *inter vivos* termination of an interest in possession in the income of a trust fund.

At this point it might be useful to summarize the various occasions upon which an interest in possession is regarded as being terminated. It should be emphasized that the following list is not exhaustive since on any occasion on which an interest in possession in trust income ceases during the life of the beneficiary there is an *inter vivos* termination for capital transfer tax purposes.

The following are perhaps the more obvious examples:

a. the release or surrender of an interest in income;
b. the sale of an interest in income;
c. the assignment of an interest in income;
d. an advance under section 32 Trustee Act 1925, from a trust fund subject to an interest in possession;
e. the advance of capital under a power in the trust instrument from a trust fund subject to an interest in possession;
f. the expiry of a fixed term if an interest in possession is limited to end after a specified number of years;
g. the happening of a specified event if an interest in possession is limited to end on the occurrence of the event (e.g. remarriage);
h. the fulfilment of a contingency if the contingent legacy does not carry the intermediate income which is therefore payable to residuary legatees;
i. the partition of the trust fund between income beneficiaries and remaindermen.

Although each of the above transactions is an occasion of charge to capital transfer tax, rather complex rules are used in determining the value which attracts tax on each occasion. Two basic principles are involved in assessing the value which is liable to tax.

a. the concept of ownership implicit in the capital transfer tax legislation equates the beneficial ownership of an income beneficiary with absolute ownership, and as a result no charge to capital transfer tax arises on assets received absolutely by an income beneficiary from a trust fund and on consideration received by an income beneficiary on the disposal of his interest;
b. to the extent that a specific cash sum or specific assets are released from a trust fund, the grossing-up principle applies in valuing the release since the loss to the trust fund is measured by the value of the assets released plus the tax attributable to the release; but where the occasion of charge to tax is such that the capital transfer tax liability arising is borne by the property released or otherwise affected by the transaction, there is no grossing up and the capital transfer tax liability is assessed simply on the value of the trust property involved in the transaction.

With these principles in mind, let us now return to each of the potential occasions of charge on the termination of an interest in possession with a view to assessing the extent of the charge to capital transfer tax, subject of course to the exemptions and reliefs which are considered later.

a. On the release or surrender of an interest in income (e.g. a life interest) the life tenant takes no further interest in the trust property released which is either distributed to the remaindermen or held upon succeeding trusts. In either case the trustees as the parties accountable for tax discharge the tax liability prior to distribution or out of the continuing trust fund. The value of the trust fund released as at the date of the release is therefore the relevant value for capital transfer tax purposes without grossing up.   (Section 52(1), CTTA 1984)
b. On the sale of a life interest, the position is basically the same as in (a) above except that the trustees hold the income of the trust fund on trust for the purchaser and the life tenant receives consideration for the sale. The value liable to capital transfer tax is therefore the value of the trust fund on the date of the sale less the consideration received by the life tenant. There is no grossing up.
                (Section 52(2), CTTA 1984)

c.　The assignment of a life interest without consideration has the same tax implications as the release of a life interest. Following the assignment the trustees hold the income of the trust fund on trust for the assignee and are responsible for capital transfer tax on the value of the trust fund on the date of the assignment without grossing up.　　　　　　　　　　　　　　　(Sections 51 and 52(1), CTTA 1984)

d.　An advance under the Trustee Act, 1925, Section 32 can normally be expected to take the form of the release of a specified cash sum for a particular purpose to a remainderman. Under no circumstances can the life tenant benefit from the advance, and the trust fund is depleted both by the amount of the advance and the capital transfer tax attributable to the advance. The amount advanced should therefore be grossed up in order to determine the value upon which the trustees are liable to pay capital transfer tax. Exceptionally there may be occasions when trustees agree to make an advance to a remainderman on the condition that the amount of the advance is to be reduced by the tax attributable to it, and in such circumstances there would be no grossing up.

e.　An advance under a power in the trust instrument creates a capital transfer tax liability which the trustees are required to meet and which may or may not according to the circumstances require to be grossed up for valuation purposes. If the advance takes the form of a specified cash sum placed in the hands of the beneficiary, the grossing-up principle applies. Alternatively, the trustees may agree to advance a percentage of the trust fund (perhaps one half), in which case it would be normal for the share of the fund released to bear its own capital transfer tax liability and there would be no grossing up. Again, the trustees may advance funds under a power of advancement subject to a condition that the amount advanced is to be regarded as a gross sum, and the funds actually paid to the advancee shall be the gross sum less the capital transfer tax thereon. This method of advancement would also avoid grossing up.　　　　　　　　　　　　　　　　(Section 52(3), CTTA 1984)

f.　On the expiry of a fixed term where income is bequeathed to a beneficiary until the term expires (e.g. income to *X* for five years from the date of my death) the beneficiary normally will take no further interest in the trust fund which will be held on the succeeding trusts subject to the capital transfer tax liability. Accordingly the value liable to capital transfer tax will simply be the value of the trust fund on the date the fixed term expires. If, however, the income beneficiary whose interest has expired immediately becomes entitled to share in the distribution of the trust fund or to share in the income arising after the expiry of the fixed term, the value of the property due to him or from which he is entitled to receive income is to be deducted from the value of the trust fund liable to capital transfer tax.
　　　　　　　　　　　　　　　　　　　　(Section 52(1), CTTA 1984)

g.　The capital transfer tax position on the termination of an interest in possession on the happening of a specified event is identical to the position in (f).

h.　Where a legacy is bequeathed to an individual contingently upon his attaining a specified age or fulfilling some other condition, the legacy does not carry the intermediate income in normal circumstances (see pp. 88 and 89) unless the trust instrument provides otherwise, and accordingly in these circumstances the income provided by the property representing the legacy is payable pending the fulfilment of the contingency to the residuary legatees. It follows that on the fulfilment of the contingency the interest in possession in income enjoyed by the residuary legatees is terminated. The contingent legatee is normally entitled to the full amount of the legacy free of tax, and accordingly the amount of the legacy should be grossed up for capital transfer tax purposes. Clearly prudent trustees should prior to the distribution of an estate reserve funds in excess of the amount of any outstanding contingent legacy in order to ensure that sufficient funds are available to them to meet the legacy itself and the capital transfer tax attributable to it. Where insufficient funds have been retained by trustees to meet both the full amount of the legacy and the capital transfer tax liability, it would appear that both the legatee and the Inland Revenue can enforce their claims against them and the trustees may find themselves in the invidious position of attempting to recover the amount of capital transfer tax paid from the residuary legatees.

If a contingent legacy carries the intermediate income which is payable to the contingent legatee, there is of course no charge to capital transfer tax on the fulfilment of the contingency since the contingent legatee is regarded for capital transfer tax purposes as 'owning' the amount of the legacy both before and after the fulfilment of the contingency.

If, however, the income provided by a contingent legacy falls to be accumulated pending fulfilment of the contingency, there is no interest in possession in the contingent legacy fund which is as a result treated in accordance with the rules applied to trusts with no interest in possession which are explained later in this chapter.

i. On the partition of trust fund between life tenant and remaindermen, the value of the property allocated to the life tenant is deducted from the total value of the trust fund for capital transfer tax purposes as at the date of the partition. The value remaining (i.e. the value of the remaindermen's share) is liable to capital transfer tax, and, since the trustees as accountable parties will deduct the capital transfer tax payable from the remaindermen's share prior to distribution, there is no grossing up.   (Section 53(2), CTTA 1984)

One further aspect of the process of valuation of a trust fund on a termination of an interest in possession should be emphasized. If the event which causes the charge to capital transfer tax also at the same time gives rise to a capital gains tax liability, the capital gains tax attributable to the value of the property which is also liable to capital transfer tax may be claimed as a deduction from the value liable to capital transfer tax. The circumstances in which a capital gains tax liability might arise on the termination of an interest in possession are considered in Chapter 15 but at this point it should be made clear that the capital gains tax liability may only be treated as a deduction from the value of the trust fund for capital transfer tax purposes if both tax liabilities arise directly as a result of the same event, and the capital gains tax liability is borne by a person who becomes absolutely entitled to the settled property concerned.

(Section 165(2), CTTA 1984)

A number of examples of the imposition of capital transfer tax on terminations of interests in possession are given below for the purpose of illustration.

Example 3

On 22 September 1985, Mrs *C* who is life tenant of a trust fund valued at £80,000 releases her interest in the trust fund in favour of her children who are the remaindermen. Mrs *C* has made chargeable transfers within the preceding ten years of £25,000. A capital gain tax liability of £5,000 is incurred on the notional disposal of the trust assets at 22 September 1985. No hold over relief election is made.

The value of the settled property liable to CTT as at 22 September 1985, is as follows:

	£
Value of trust fund	80,000
Less Capital gains tax	5,000
Value now chargeable	£75,000

The CTT payable by the trustees is as follows:

Value now chargeable	75,000
Add Cumulative total of life tenant	25,000
	£100,000

CTT payable:

On first £67,000 @ Nil	=	Nil
On next £22,000 @ 15%	=	3,300.00
On next £11,000 @ 17.5%	=	1,925.00
		5,225.00
Less CTT on previous cumulative total		Nil
CTT payable		£5,225.00

Note: The CTT liability of £5,225 is payable out of the trust fund by the trustees, but the former life tenant's cumulative total is increased to £100,000.

Example 4

Mr *D*, the life tenant of a trust fund valued at £100,000, sells his life interest to his brother on 15 August 1985 for a consideration of £20,000. Mr *D* had made chargeable transfers of £50,000 within the preceding ten years.

	£
Value of trust fund	100,000
Less consideration received	20,000
Value chargeable	£80,000

The CTT payable by the trustees is as follows:

Value chargeable	80,000
Add Cumulative total of life tenant	50,000
	£130,000

CTT payable:

On first £67,000 @ Nil	=	Nil
On next £22,000 @ 15%	=	3,300.00
On next £33,000 @ 17.5%	=	5,775.00
On next £ 8,000 @ 20%	=	1,600.00
		£10,675.00
Less CTT on previous cumulative total		Nil
CTT payable by trustees		£10,675.00

Mr *D* now has a cumulative total of £130,000.

Example 5

Under the will of Mr *E* deceased a legacy of £20,000 is left to Mr *Z* contingently upon his attaining the age of 30 years. Mr *E* died on 10 May 1981 and since that time the trustees have paid the income from the contingent legacy fund to the two residuary legatees in equal shares. On 25 June 1985 Mr *Z* attains the age of 30. At that date the cumulative totals of chargeable transfers of the two residuary legatees are £45,000 and £70,000 respectively.

The CTT liability of the trustees will be calculated as follows:

	£
First residuary legatee:	
Share of legacy	10,000
Add Cumulative total or residuary legatee	45,000
	£55,000
CTT payable:	
£55,000 @ Nil	Nil

	£
Second residuary legatee:	
Gross cumulative total brought forward	70,000
Less CTT at current lifetime rates:	
On first £67,000 @ Nil	Nil
On next £ 3,000 @ 15%	450
Net cumulative total	69,550
Add Share of legacy	10,000
Revised net cumulative total	£75,550
CTT payable:	
On first £67,000 @ Nil	Nil
On next £ 8,550 @ 3/17	1,508.82
	1,508.82
Less CTT on previous net cumulative total	450.00
CTT payable by the trustees	£1,058.82

The revised cumulative totals of the residuary legatees become as follows:

First residuary legatee:	£55,000
Second residuary legatee:	
£75,550 + £1,508.82	£77,059

Example 6

Mr *F*, the life tenant of a trust fund valued at £200,000, agrees to the advancement under section 32, Trustee Act 1925, of a cash sum of £20,000 to his son who is one of the residuary legatees and who requires this amount to complete the purchase of a property. The cumulative total of Mr *F* is £175,000, all chargeable transfers made within the last ten years. In June 1985 the trustees sell investments for £23,000 and incur a capital gains tax liability of £3,000. On receipt of the proceeds of sale of the investments the trustees pay the cash sum of £20,000 to Mr *F*'s son.

The CTT payable by the trustees is calculated as follows:

		£	£
Life tenants gross cumulative total brought forward			175,000
Less CTT at lifetime rates:			
On first £67,000 @ Nil	=	Nil	
On next £22,000 @ 15%	=	3,300.00	
On next £33,000 @ 17.5%	=	5,775.00	
On next £33,000 @ 20%	=	6,600.00	
On next £20,000 @ 22.5%	=	4,500.00	20,175
Adjusted net cumulative total			154,825
Add Net cash advancement			20,000
Revised net cumulative total			£174,825
CTT payable:			
On first £169,550	=		24,450.00
On next £ 5,275 @ ⅓	=		1,758.33
			26,208.33
Less CTT on previous net cumulative total			20,175.00
CTT payable by trustees			£ 6,133.33

The cumulative total of Mr *F* becomes £174,825 + £26,208 = £201,033.

Note: The capital gains tax liability incurred by the trustees is not allowable in computing the CTT liability since it does not arise directly as a result of and at the same time as the chargeable event, nor is it borne by the person becoming absolutely entitled to the settled property.

Example 7

In the exercise of a power of advancement granted to them under the trust instrument, the trustees of a trust fund agree on 1 June 1985 to advance a one-third share of the trust fund to a remainderman. The trust fund is then valued at £120,000 in total, and a capital gains tax liability of £5,000 is incurred on the notional disposal on the date of the advancement. The life tenant of the whole of the trust fund is Mrs *G* whose consent is not required and who has made a total of £50,000 of chargeable transfers within the last ten years.

The value liable to CTT is calculated as follows:

	£
One-third share of trust fund	40,000
Less Capital gains tax	5,000
Chargeable to CTT	£35,000
CTT payable:	
Chargeable value	35,000
Add Life tenant's cumulative total	50,000
	£85,000
CTT payable:	
On first £67,000 @ Nil =	Nil
On next £18,000 @ 15% =	2,700.00
	2,700.00
Less CTT on previous cumulative total	Nil
CTT payable by trustees	£2,700.00

The distribution of the trust fund may be summarized as follows:

	Total value	Two-thirds remaining in trust	One-third advanced
	£	£	£
Value of trust before advance	120,000	80,000	40,000
Less:			
Capital gains tax	5,000		5,000
Capital transfer tax	2,700		2,700
Value after advance	£112,300	£80,000	£32,300

Example 8

Mrs *H* is the life tenant of a trust fund valued at £200,000. She agrees with the remainderman, her son, that the trust fund should be distributed as one half to her absolutely and one half to her son absolutely. On 10 August 1985 a deed of partition to this effect is executed by all the interested parties. At that time, Mrs *H* had made previous chargeable transfers within the preceding ten years of £40,000. As a result of the notional disposal a capital gains tax liability of £10,000 is incurred.

The value liable to CTT is calculated as follows:

	£
Value of trust fund	200,000
Less Capital gains tax liability	10,000
Net value of trust fund	190,000
Less One half share due to Mrs *H*	95,000
Value chargeable to CTT	£ 95,000

CTT payable:

Chargeable value of trust fund	95,000
Add Life tenant's cumulative total	40,000
CTT payable:	£135,000

On first £67,000 @ Nil	=	Nil
On next £22,000 @ 15%	=	3,300.00
On next £33,000 @ 17.5%	=	5,775.00
On next £ 2,000 @ 20%	=	400.00
		9,475.00
Less CTT on previous cumulative total		Nil
CTT payable by trustees		£9,475.00

The distribution of the trust fund may be summarized as follows:

	Total £	Mrs H £	Remainderman £
Total value of trust fund	200,000		
Less Capital gains tax	10,000		
	190,000	95,000	95,000
Less Capital transfer tax	9,475		9,475
Final distribution	£180,525	£95,000	£85,525

Exemptions

Although terminations of interests in possession in settled property are in many ways similar to lifetime dispositions, the small gifts exemption, exemption for normal expenditure out of income and exemption for gifts back to the donor are not available. With effect from 6 April 1981 it has been possible for the life tenant to allow the trustees to utilize his annual exemption and exemption for gifts in consideration of marriage. Prior to 6 April 1981 these exemptions could not be used. The life tenant must give notice to the trustees within six months of the chargeable event informing them of the availability of the exemption.   (Section 57, CTTA 1984)

All the examples above have assumed that no exemptions or reliefs are available. Had any exemption (e.g. for property passing to the life tenant's spouse on the release of a life interest) been available the capital transfer tax computed in each example might have been considerably reduced or eliminated. Furthermore, although capital gains tax has been shown as payable in two of the examples, it may be that on a beneficiary becoming absolutely entitled to assets from the trustees that a claim will be made to hold over the gain against the acquisition value for CGT purposes of the beneficiary (section 79, FA 1980 and section 82, FA 1982). This is considered further in Chapter 15 dealing with capital gains tax.

For full information regarding exemptions and reliefs quoted below further reference should, if necessary, be made to the position on the death of a life tenant as outlined earlier in this chapter. The exemptions and reliefs which can, in appropriate circumstances, be claimed on the termination of an interest in possession are the following:

a. property devolving upon life tenant's spouse;
b. surviving spouse exemption;
c. reverter to settlor;
d. reverter to settlor's spouse;
e. property devolving upon charities;

f.   property devolving upon political parties (see Notes below);
g.   property devolving upon 'heritage bodies';
h.   property passing to bodies established for public benefit;
i.   foreign trusts;
j.   'exempt gilts';
k.   reversionary interests (see Notes below);
l.   persons domiciled in the Channel Islands or the Isle of Man;
m.   works of art (see Notes below);
n.   historic land and buildings (see Notes below);
o.   quick succession relief;
p.   agricultural relief;
q.   credit for overseas tax;
r.   payment of tax by instalments (see Notes below).

Notes:
a.   The limit of £100,000 applicable to gifts to political parties within one year of death is relevant, and property passing as a result of a termination may incur a capital transfer tax liability if the limit is exceeded having regard to all such property passing on the death and if the life tenant dies within one year of the termination.
b.   Since reversionary interests are excluded property provided that they have not been purchased at any time, the assignment of the remainder to a life tenant who as a result can call for the distribution of the trust fund is not an occasion of charge.
c.   Where works of art or historic land and buildings are affected by a termination, there are two potential charges to tax, namely tax on the termination itself and the outstanding capital transfer tax due by reference to the last death on which they passed. The exemption previously described in relation to conditionally exempt transfers applies equally to terminations of interest in possession.
d.   Payment of tax by instalments on qualifying instalment property is only possible on a termination if the instalment property remains in trust. If the instalment property is distributed as a result of the termination the instalment option is not available.

   Attention should also be drawn to the fact that two major reliefs which can be used on the death of a life tenant are not available on a termination. There is no exemption for growing timber, and no relief for losses sustained on the sale of investments following the termination. On the other hand, the following exemptions, not available on the death of a life tenant, are relevant on the termination of an interest in possession.

a.   Section 11, CTTA 1984 dispositions for the maintenance of the family can be claimed as exempt subject to the requirements mentioned in relation to lifetime dispositions. This exemption is of particular relevance to advancements under section 32, Trustee Act 1925, for educational purposes where the remainderman advanced is the minor child of the life tenant.
b.   If a life interest held on protective trusts under section 33, Trustee Act 1925, is forfeited by an attempted alienation or bankruptcy, the forfeiture is not regarded as a termination and no charge to capital transfer tax arises. From the date of the forfeiture the trust becomes a discretionary trust and therefore subject to the taxation rules applied to trusts with no interest in possession and to protective trusts in particular. The above only applies in respect of events that occurred on or before 11 April 1978. For events occurring after 11 April 1978, the property is deemed to be held on interest in possession trust in favour of the principal beneficiary.

(Sections 73 and 88, CTTA 1984)

Since the capital transfer tax payable on the termination of an interest in possession is assessed at the lower lifetime rates of tax, the death of the former life tenant or other income beneficiary within three years of the termination causes the property affected by the termination to be reassessed at the higher rates of tax applicable on death, and the resultant capital transfer tax liability is represented by the difference between the tax payable at the higher rates and the tax already paid in accordance with the lower scale of rates. The assessment of the additional tax liability is identical to the assessment of the additional liability on the death of a transferor within three years of a lifetime gift.

The trustees of any trust fund affected by a termination are jointly liable with the beneficiaries of the trust fund for the additional tax due as a result of the death within three years of the former income beneficiary. Effectively they are accountable therefore for the capital transfer tax payable on the subsequent death of the former income beneficiary when the fund remains in trust following the termination. Where, however, the trust fund becomes available for distribution as a result of a termination, the trustees are only liable for any further tax payable on the subsequent death of the former income beneficiary to the extent that trust funds remain in their hands. If the fund has been wholly distributed, the trustees have no liability and the beneficiaries to whom the trust property was distributed are responsible for the tax payable. Trustees have no duty to withhold trust funds from beneficiaries who are absolutely entitled as a result of a termination purely for the purpose of reserving funds to meet the potential additional tax liability which might arise on the subsequent death of the former income beneficiary.   (Section 204, CTTA 1984)

SETTLEMENTS WITH NO INTEREST IN POSSESSION

Before considering in detail the provisions regarding this type of settlement it is appropriate to note that the whole regime of CTT in respect of settlements without an interest in possession was changed by the Finance Act 1982 with effect from 9 March 1982. The paragraphs which follow describe the provisions which apply from 9 March 1982. A full description of the provisions which applied prior to that date is given in the 20th Edition. The legislation is now to be found in sections 58 to 85, CTTA 1984.

A definition of the term 'interest in possession' is given at the beginning of this chapter, to which further reference should be made if necessary. The settlements with which we are now concerned are those in which no interest in possession subsists. For the sake of convenience these will be referred to as 'discretionary settlements' in succeeding paragraphs, but these will include the following types of settlement:

a. settlements where the income is to be distributed or accumulated at the discretion of the trustees;
b. settlements where the income is to be accumulated for a period which does not infringe the rule against accumulations;
c. settlements where the income is to be accumulated and capitalized pending the fulfilment of a contingency regardless of any powers of distribution for maintenance which may be available to the trustees.

Discretionary settlements are included within these special rules regardless of the fact that all the income may be distributed each year to appropriate beneficiaries. If the trustees have a discretion as to which beneficiaries income is to be distributed or the amount of income to be paid to each, or both, then the settlement is within these special provisions.

Certain privileged settlements, e.g. accumulation and maintenance settlements, are outside the scope of these provisions and these will be considered later in this chapter.

1. Overall view of provisions

In order to make it easier to understand the detailed rules which apply in relation to discretionary settlements it may be helpful to summarize briefly the overall effect of the new provisions.

A charge to CTT will arise on the following occasions:

a. when property is introduced to the settlement. This will include both the original creation of the settlement or the addition of further property to the settlement subsequently. These transfers can arise either by way of lifetime dispositions by the settlor, or on death if the settlement is created under the terms of the will of the deceased;
b. on each ten-year anniversary of the creation of the settlement a charge to CTT arises at 30 per cent of the normal rates applicable; and
c. when property leaves the discretionary settlement, for example when property is appointed to a specific beneficiary or is transferred to one of the privileged types of settlement. This charge, often referred to as the 'exit charge', covers the period from the last ten-year charge.

2. Definitions

A number of definitions have already been considered in relation to settled property generally. These included:

a. settlement;
b. settlor;
c. trustee;
d. reversionary interest;
e. excluded property;
f. interest in possession.

The following further definitions apply in relation to settlements in which no interest in possession subsists.

Relevant property

This is defined as settled property in which no qualifying interest in possession subsists, other than:

a. property held for charitable purposes only;
b. accumulation and maintenance settlements;
c. protective trusts where the failure or determination occurred before 12 April 1978;
d. settlements for disabled persons set up before 10 March 1981;
e. settlements for the benefit of employees;
f. maintenance funds for historic buildings;
g. superannuation schemes;
h. property comprised in a trade or professional compensation fund;
i. excluded property; and
j. newspaper trusts.   (Section 58, CTTA 1984)

Qualifying interest in possession

A qualifying interest in possession is an interest in possession to which an individual is beneficially entitled. It also includes an interest in possession held by a company, where the business of the company consists wholly or mainly of the acquisition of interests in settled property, provided the company has acquired the interest for full consideration in money or money's worth from an individual who was beneficially entitled to it.   (Section 60, CTTA 1984)

Commencement of settlement

The commencement of a settlement is the time when property first became comprised in the settlement.   (Section 60, CTTA 1984)

Ten-year anniversary

This is defined as the tenth anniversary of the date on which the settlement commenced, with subsequent anniversaries at ten-yearly intervals, subject to the following exceptions.

a. No date falling before 1 April 1983 is a ten year anniversary. Therefore, if a settlement commenced on 25 March 1973, the first ten-year anniversary will be 25 March 1993.
b. The date in (a) is extended to 1 April 1984 if the first ten-year anniversary would have fallen in the year ended 31 March 1984 and a payment was made out of the settlement in that year which could not have been made without the result of court proceedings. However, this rule does not affect the determination of subsequent ten-year anniversaries.   (Section 61, CTTA 1984)

Related settlements

Settlements are related if they are made by the same settlor on the same day. A settlement, the whole of the property of which is held for charitable purposes, is not related with any other settlement.   (Section 62, CTTA 1984)

Payment

This includes a transfer of assets other than money.   (Section 63, CTTA 1984)

Quarter

This means a period of three months.

3. The occasions of charge

The creation of the settlement

As indicated at 1(a) above, a transfer to a settlement will be treated as a transfer of value whether the transfer is made during lifetime or on death. The circumstances of the settlor at the time of the transfer will determine the extent of his chargeable transfer, if made during his lifetime, and the amount of CTT payable. Unless the settlement deed includes a clause requiring the CTT payable on the transfer to the trustees to be met out of the settled property, the grossing-up procedure will apply. The normal rules on death will apply to determine the amount of CTT payable on death and hence the amount of property which becomes settled.

The ten-year anniversary

CTT is charged on the ten-year anniversary on the value of all relevant property comprised in the settlement at that time at the specified rate of tax. The specified rate of tax depends upon the date on which the settlement commenced with separate rules applying in respect of settlements which commenced after 26 March 1974 and those which commenced before 27 March 1974.   (Section 64, CTTA 1984)

SETTLEMENTS WHICH COMMENCED AFTER 26 MARCH 1974

a. As indicated above the value on which CTT is to be charged is the value of the relevant property comprised in the settlement at the anniversary date. The rate at which this value is to be charged is 30 per cent of the 'effective rate'.
b. The 'effective rate' is determined by reference to an assumed, or hypothetical, transfer made by an assumed transferor with a hypothetical cumulative total.
c. The hypothetical transfer is the aggregate of the following:
    i.   the value of the relevant property at the anniversary date;
    ii. the value of any other property comprised in the settlement which is not relevant property, and has never been relevant property; at the value at which it first became comprised in the settlement, and
    iii. the value of any property comprised in a 'related settlement'.
d. The hypothetical cumulative total is determined by aggregating the following:
    i.   the value of chargeable transfers made by the settlor in the ten years preceding the day on which the settlement commenced, disregarding transfers made on that day and transfers made prior to 27 March 1974;
    ii. the amounts on which exit charges have been made in the preceding ten years, including 'distribution payments' under the legislation applying before 9 March 1982 which were made in the ten years preceding the anniversary date.
e. The CTT is to be calculated as if the hypothetical transfer as at (c) above were a chargeable transfer made by the hypothetical transferor with a cumulative total as at (d) above, the CTT being calculated at the lifetime rates.

The above situation is best illustrated by an example.

Example 9

Mr *J* settled property on two settlements on 15 June 1981 of £25,000 each. He had already used all available exemptions, but the chargeable transfers made totalling £50,000 used up his nil rate band. Settlement 1 is a discretionary settlement whereas Settlement 2 is a life interest settlement. On 15 June 1991 each settlement is worth £65,000. On the basis that there are no further changes in the rates of CTT and no prior exit charge arises, the CTT payable on the first ten-year anniversary charge will be calculated as follows:

	£
Hypothetical chargeable transfer:	
Value of relevant property at 15 June 1991	65,000
Value of property in the related settlement as at 15 June 1981	25,000
	£90,000
Hypothetical cumulative total	Nil
CTT chargeable at lifetime rates on	£90,000
CTT due:	
On first £67,000 @ Nil =	Nil
On next £22,000 @ 15% =	3,300.00
On next £ 1,000 @ 17.5% =	175.00
	£3,475.00

Effective rate $\left(\dfrac{3,475}{90,000} \times 100\right)$ = 3.861%

Rate of ten year anniversary charge becomes:
30% × 3.861%   1.158%

Ten year anniversary charge (£65,000 × 1.158%)   £   752.70

f.   A number of important conclusions can be drawn from the above example.
   i.   If the life interest settlement had been made after the discretionary settlement instead of on the same day, the two settlements would not have been 'related settlements' such that the value on commencement of the life interest settlement would not have been brought into the calculation of the hypothetical chargeable transfer. The assumed cumulative total would remain at nil, such that nil CTT would have arisen in respect of the hypothetical chargeable transfer. It follows that the charge on the ten-year anniversary would also have been nil.
         Since related settlements can easily be avoided if made during lifetime, they should be avoided. This is not possible if the settlements are created under the terms of a will since all settlements so created commence with effect from the date of death.
         It also follows that an unrelated settlement comprising property with an initial value of less than the nil rate band when the settlor has made no previous chargeable transfers should not give rise to a ten-year anniversary charge unless the property has increased in value substantially by the time of the ten-year anniversary.
   ii.   If the life interest settlement had been made before the discretionary settlement, e.g. one day before to avoid the related settlement provisions, although the initial value in that settlement would then be excluded from the hypothetical chargeable transfer calculated above, the hypothetical cumulative total would become £25,000 with the result that the charge on the ten year anniversary would become as follows:

	£
Hypothetical chargeable transfer	65,000
Hypothetical cumulative total	25,000
CTT chargeable at lifetime rates on	£90,000

CTT due:
On first £67,000 @ Nil	Nil
On next £22,000 @ 15%	3,300.00
On next £ 1,000 @ 17.5%	175.00
	£ 3,475.00

Effective rate $\left(\dfrac{3,475}{65,000} \times 100\right)$ 5.346%

Rate of ten-year anniversary charge becomes:
30% × 5.346%   1.603%

Ten-year anniversary charge (£65,000 × 1.603%)   £ 1,041.95

It follows that the order in which settlements are created can have a material effect on the rate of the ten-year anniversary charge.

SETTLEMENTS WHICH COMMENCED BEFORE 27 MARCH 1974
a.   For settlements which commenced before 27 March 1974 the charge at the ten-year

anniversary is still calculated at 30 per cent of the effective rate, but the hypothetical transfer and the hypothetical cumulative total on which this effective rate is based exclude certain of the elements which had to be included in respect of settlements which commenced after 26 March 1974.

b. The hypothetical transfer is limited to the value of the relevant property at the anniversary date, i.e. (c) (ii) and (iii) above are not included.

c. The hypothetical cumulative total includes only the amounts on which exit charges have been imposed in the ten years preceding the anniversary date, including 'distribution payments' under the legislation applying before 9 March 1982 which fall within that ten-year period.

d. Otherwise the calculation of the ten year anniversary charge proceeds as for settlements which commenced after 26 March 1974.

This situation can be illustrated by the following example.

Example 10

Mr K created a discretionary settlement on 15 September 1966, transferring property to the value of £100,000 to the trustees. The trustees made a distribution payment of £30,000 to a beneficiary in 1980 and in 1985 an exit charge arose on £25,000. On 15 September 1986, the value of the remaining property is £75,000. On the basis that the rates of CTT remain unchanged, the CTT payable on the first ten-year anniversary charge will be calculated as follows.

		£
Hypothetical chargeable transfer:		
Value of relevant property at 15 September 1986		£75,000
Hypothetical cumulative total:		
Distribution payment within last ten years		30,000
Exit charge within last ten years		25,000
		£55,000
Hypothetical transfer		75,000
Hypothetical cumulative total		55,000
Chargeable at lifetime rates on		£130,000
CTT due:		
On first £67,000 @ Nil	=	Nil
On next £22,000 @ 15%	=	3,300.00
On next £33,000 @ 17.5%	=	5,775.00
On next £ 8,000 @ 20%	=	1,600.00
		£10,675.00
Effective rate $\left(\dfrac{10,675}{75,000} \times 100\right)$	=	14.233%
Rate of ten-year anniversary charge becomes:		
30% × 14.233%	=	4.269%
Ten year anniversary charge (£75,000 × 4.269%)		£ 3,201.75

CHARGE ON SUBSEQUENT TEN-YEAR ANNIVERSARIES

a. *Settlements created after 26 March 1974:* The rules for calculating the ten-year anniversary charge on second and subsequent ten-year anniversaries are the same as those described above in relation to the first ten-year anniversary charge. However, it must be remembered that only exit charges which have arisen in the preceding ten years fall to be taken into account (see (d) (ii) on p. 199).

b. *Settlements created before 27 March 1974:* The calculation of the second and subsequent ten-year anniversary charge becomes even more straightforward than the first ten-year charge. The hypothetical transfer is limited to the value of the relevant property at the anniversary date and the hypothetical cumulative total is equivalent to the amounts subject to exit charges in the ten years preceding the ten-year anniversary date.

REDUCED RATE WHERE PROPERTY HAS NOT BEEN RELEVANT PROPERTY THROUGHOUT THE TEN-YEAR PERIOD

The paragraphs and examples above have assumed that the relevant property has been comprised within the settlement throughout the whole of the ten-year period. However, if the relevant property has not been comprised within the settlement throughout the whole ten-year period the rate applicable to that part of the property not held within the settlement for the whole ten years is reduced by one-fortieth for each complete quarter which had expired before the property became, or last became, relevant property.

This position is illustrated by the following example.

Example 11

Mr *L* created a discretionary settlement on 1 June 1980 and transferred a freehold property valued at £100,000 to the trustees. He had used all available exemptions but had made no other chargeable transfers. On 15 June 1984 he transferred stocks and shares to the trustees having a value of £30,000. On 1 June 1990, the value of the settled property is:

Freehold property	150,000
Stock and shares	40,000
	£190,000

Assuming the rates of CTT remain unchanged, the CTT payable on the first ten-year anniversary will be as follows:

	£
Hypothetical chargeable transfer:	
Value of relevant property at 1 June 1990	
Freehold property	150,000
Stocks and shares	40,000
	£190,000
Hypothetical cumulative total	Nil
CTT chargeable at lifetime rates on	£190,000

CTT due:

On first £67,000 @ Nil	=		Nil
On next £22,000 @ 15%	=		3,300.00
On next £33,000 @ 17.5%	=		5,775.00
On next £33,000 @ 20%	=		6,600.00
On next £35,000 @ 22.5%	=		7,875.00
			£23,550.00

Effective rate $\left(\dfrac{23,550}{190,000} \times 100\right)$ =   12.394%

Rate of ten-year anniversary charge becomes:
30% × 12.394%   =   3.718%

Tax payable:

Original fund (£150,000 × 3.718%)	£	5,577.00
Additional fund $\left(£40,000 \times 3.718\% \times \dfrac{24}{40}\right)$		892.32
Total CTT payable		£6,469.32

Note: There are 16 complete quarters which have expired before the stocks and shares became relevant property. Hence the rate of charge is reduced by 16/40 leaving 24/40 as the proportion of the rate chargeable.

The above example does not reflect the practical difficulties of valuing the added property separately from the original property. Clearly in many instances the settled property held at the date of the ten-year anniversary charge represent the whole of the property settled during the previous ten years and it will not be possible to readily identify the value attributable to each separate transfer to the settlement during that period. The Act gives no indication as to how this apportionment of value should be calculated.

PROPERTY ADDED TO SETTLEMENT AFTER 8 MARCH 1982

a. *Settlements made after 26 March 1974:* Where property is added to a discretionary settlement by the settlor after 8 March 1982, and before the ten-year anniversary charge, it is necessary to reconsider the hypothetical cumulative total for the purposes of calculating the ten-year anniversary charge. It is only necessary to consider these rules if two conditions are satisfied:
 i. the transfer made by the settlor is a 'chargeable transfer', and
 ii. as a result of the transfer the value of the property in the settlement is increased.

   It is clear, therefore, that if the transfer made by the settlor is an exempt transfer, the condition at (i) will not be satisfied as no chargeable transfer will have taken place.

   Also, if the amount of the settled property is not increased although the value of that property is increased by reason of a transfer by the settlor, the transfer is disregarded if it can be shown that the transfer:
 i. was not primarily intended to increase the value, and
 ii. resulted in an increase in value of not more than 5 per cent of the value immediately before the transfer.

   Apart from the exclusion above, the hypothetical cumulative total for the purposes of the ten-year anniversary charge is calculated as the higher of:
 i. the settlor's cumulative total of chargeable transfers made in the ten years prior to the commencement of the settlement, i.e. the normal amount as described at (d) (i) on p. 199, and
 ii. the settlor's total of chargeable transfers made in the ten years prior to the day on which the addition to the settlement was made disregarding:
   1. transfers made on that day;
   2. transfers made before 27 March 1974;
   3. the value of any property which is included within the hypothetical transfer at (c) on p. 199 or value attributable to property which has been the subject of an exit charge within the last ten years.

Example 12

Mr *M* created a discretionary settlement on 10 September 1980 by transferring property to the trustees valued at £50,000. The chargeable transfer as far as Mr *M* was concerned was £75,000. His cumulative total of chargeable transfers prior to the commencement of the settlement was £50,000. On 1 October 1986 Mr *M* transferred further property to the settlement valued at £30,000. His cumulative total prior to this transfer, including the earlier transfer to the trustees, was £120,000.

   The hypothetical cumulative total for the purposes of the ten-year anniversary charge on 10 September 1990 will be the higher of:

a. The settlor's cumulative total
   at 10 September 1980

£

£50,000

OR

b. The settlor's cumulative total
   at 1 October 1986

£120,000

Less Value of property which is included
within the hypothetical transfer

50,000

£70,000

Therefore, the hypothetical cumulative total will be taken as £70,000 for the purposes of the ten-year anniversary charge.

If there is more than one addition, the above calculation must be made in respect of each addition, and the addition giving the highest cumulative total is the one used for the purposes of the ten-year anniversary charge.

b. *Settlements made before 27 March 1974:* The same basic conditions as were described in relation to settlements made after 26 March 1974 (see (a) above) must be satisfied before the special rules apply. Also, the exclusion mentioned is available in respect of settlements made before 27 March 1974.

Apart from the above exclusions, the hypothetical cumulative total is calculated by adding to the hypothetical cumulative total calculated under the normal rules (see (c) on p. 201), the aggregate of chargeable transfers made by the settlor in the period of ten years ending with the date of the addition to the settlement but excluding:

i.   transfers made on the date of the addition to the settlement,

ii. transfers made before 27 March 1984, and

iii. the value of any property which is included within the hypothetical transfer within (b) on p. 201, or the value which is attributable to property which has been the subject of an exit charge within the last ten years.

Example 13

Mr *N* made a discretionary settlement on 10 May 1970. On 25 June 1980 the trustees made a distribution payment of £100,000. In 1986, Mr *N* made a chargeable transfer of £75,000. In 1989 Mr *N* transferred property valued at £25,000 to the trustees.

The hypothetical cumulative total for the purposes of the ten-year anniversary charge will be calculated as follows:

	£
Distribution payments within last ten years	100,000
Add Chargeable transfers by settlor	75,000
Revised hypothetical cumulative total	£175,000

The property valued at £25,000 transferred to the trustees in 1989 is excluded from the above calculations.

PROPERTY LEAVING AND RE-ENTERING DISCRETIONARY SETTLEMENT

If property held within a discretionary settlement ceases to be relevant property and then again becomes relevant property within the ten years between anniversaries (for example, the creation of an interest in possession in part of the capital which then falls in and the property again becomes relevant property), the hypothetical cumulative total is reduced to take account of the fact that the property, without special provisions, would be included in both the hypothetical cumulative total and the hypothetical transfer. The hypothetical cumulative total is reduced by the smaller of:

a. the amount on which the exit charge was based to the extent that this is attributable to the property becoming relevant property again, and
b. the value of the property on the anniversary date.

Effectively, therefore, the higher of the two values is left in the calculation of the ten-year anniversary charge.

If property has left the discretionary settlement and re-entered more than once during the period of ten years between anniversaries, the above reduction in the hypothetical cumulative total is made in respect of each exit and re-entry separately.

The exit charge

The exit charge, often referred to as the proportionate charge, arises when:

a. property comprised in the settlement ceases to be relevant property, or
b. in a case where (a) does not apply, the trustees make a disposition which results in the value of the property comprised in the settlement being less than it would be but for the disposition.

The occasion of charge at (b) covers depreciatory transactions which would include, for example, the grant of a lease for less than full consideration. The term 'disposition' in this connection is defined to include the failure to exercise a right unless it can be shown that the failure was not deliberate. If a disposition arises from the failure to exercise a right, the disposition is treated as made at the latest time at which the trustees could have exercised the right.

The loss-to-donor principle applies in relation to exit charges such that if the CTT is to be paid out of the settled property the grossing-up procedure applies.

EXEMPTIONS AVAILABLE

No exit charge will arise if any of the following exemptions are available to the trustees.

a. If there is a disposition within (b) above and the trustees can show that there was no intention to confer a gratuitous benefit and either the transaction is at arm's length between unconnected persons or is such as might be expected in a transaction between parties at arm's length. (Section 65(6), CTTA 1984)

   Note: This exemption is identical to that available to individual transferors under section 10, CTTA 1984. It is difficult to see how the trustees can claim this exemption if the disposition involves one of the beneficiaries.

b. If there is a disposition within (b) above and this involves the grant of a tenancy of agricultural property within the United Kingdom, Channel Islands or Isle of Man, for full consideration. (Section 65(6), CTTA 1984)
c. The payment of costs or expenses which are fairly attributable to the relevant property is not treated as property ceasing to be relevant property. (Section 65(5), CTTA 1984)
d. Where the payment is the income of any person for income tax purposes, or would be if he were resident in the United Kingdom, this is not treated as property ceasing to be relevant property. (Section 65(5), CTTA 1984)

   Note: The exemptions at (c) and (d) include the liability to make any such payment.

e. If the event occurs within the first quarter since the settlement commenced or within the first quarter following a ten-year anniversary. (Section 65(4), CTTA 1984)
f. If the property ceases to be situated in the United Kingdom and thereby becomes excluded property as defined. (Section 65(7), CTTA 1984)

g. If the settlor of the settlement was not domiciled in the United Kingdom when the settlement was made and the property comprised in the settlement is invested in exempt government securities and thereby becomes excluded property, as defined.

(Section 65(8), CTTA 1984)

h. If the property transferred is qualifying shares of a company which are transferred to a qualifying employee trust.   (Section 75, CTTA 1984)

i. If the property becomes held for charitable purposes only, or becomes the property of a qualifying political party, or the property of a qualifying body within Schedule 3, CTTA 1984, or is the subject of a gift for public benefit.   (Section 76, CTTA 1984)

THE AMOUNT ON WHICH THE EXIT CHARGE ARISES

As indicated above, the amount on which CTT is charged is calculated on the basis of the loss-to-donor rule. Hence, it is the amount by which the value of the relevant property is reduced as a result of the property ceasing to be relevant property, or the disposition by the trustees. If the CTT is payable out of the settled property, then the grossing-up procedure applies.   (Section 65(2), CTTA 1984)

THE RATE AT WHICH TAX IS CHARGEABLE

The rate at which CTT is charged depends upon whether the charge arises before or after the first ten-year anniversary charge, and also if the settlement commenced before 27 March 1974 or on and after that date. Each of these situations will now be considered in turn.

a. *Rate before first ten-year anniversary charge:*
   i. *Post 26 March 1974 settlements.* The rate of tax applicable to an exit charge is the appropriate fraction of the effective rate. This is determined as follows.

   The effective rate is 30 per cent of the rate calculated as if a transferor with a hypothetical cumulative total equivalent to the chargeable transfers made by the settlor in the ten years to the day on which the settlement commenced, disregarding transfers made on that day and before 27 March 1974, had made a chargeable transfer of an amount comprising:

   1. the value of the settled property comprised in the settlement at the date of commencement;
   2. the value of any property comprised in a related settlement at the date of commencement; and
   3. the value immediately after it became comprised in the settlement of any property added to the settlement before the date of the charge, even if it no longer remains in the settlement.

   The appropriate fraction is the number of fortieths as there are complete quarters from the date of commencement of the settlement to the day before the occasion of charge.

   The above is best illustrated by an example.

Example 14

Mr *O* settled property valued at £100,000 on a discretionary settlement on 1 December 1980. At that time he had made previous chargeable transfers of £30,000. On 15 December 1985 the trustees appoint capital of £25,000 to Mr *P* who agreed to pay any CTT due. No further property was added to the settlement and there were no related settlements. The proportionate charge is calculated as follows:

		£
The hypothetical cumulative total is		£30,000
The hypothetical transfer is:		
Value of property at commencement of settlement		£100,000
CTT due on hypothetical transfer:		
Hypothetical transfer		100,000
Hypothetical cumulative total		30,000
		£130,000

CTT due on:

On first £67,000 @ Nil	=	Nil
On next £22,000 @ 15%	=	3,300.00
On next £33,000 @ 17.5%	=	5,775.00
On next £ 8,000 @ 20%	=	1,600.00
		£10,675.00

$$\text{Effective rate}\left(\frac{10,675}{130,000} \times 100\right) \quad = \quad 8.21\%$$

30% × 8.21%	=	2.46%

Appropriate fraction		20/40ths
CTT payable by Mr *P* is as follows:		
£25,000 × 2.46% × 20/40	=	£307.50

Note: In the calculation above the CTT payable on the transfer into the settlement on 1 December 1980 has been ignored in order to keep the figures as simple as possible. Clearly, if Mr *O* had paid the CTT, the property received by the trustees would have been £100,000 but if the trustees had paid the CTT it would have reduced the value comprised in the settlement on commencement.

As with the ten-year anniversary charge, if any part of the property which is the subject of the charge has not been relevant property, or was not comprised in the settlement throughout that period, the appropriate fraction in respect of the property not comprised in the settlement throughout the period to the occasion of charge is reduced by excluding from the numerator the number of complete quarters from the commencement of the settlement to the date on which the property first became comprised in the settlement.

ii. *Pre 27 March 1974 settlements.* The rate of tax applicable to an exit charge is 30 per cent of the effective rate. This is determined as follows:

The effective rate is calculated as if a transferor with a hypothetical cumulative total equivalent to the amounts of any 'distribution payments' made between 27 March 1974 and 9 March 1982 and within the ten years before the chargeable event *plus* the amounts of any exit charges within the last ten years made a chargeable transfer of an amount equal to the reduction in value of the settled property as a result of the event or disposition giving rise to the exit charge.

This can be illustrated as follows:

Example 15

Mr *Q* created a discretionary settlement in 1968. On 15 May 1985 the trustees appoint capital of £100,000 to a beneficiary absolutely. The trustees had made a distribution payment of £20,000 in 1980. The beneficiary had agreed to pay any CTT due.

The CTT due on the exit charge is calculated as follows:

	£
Hypothetical transfer	100,000
Hypothetical cumulative total	20,000
CTT chargeable on	£120,000

On first £67,000 @ Nil	=		Nil
On next £22,000 @ 15%	=		3,300.00
On next £31,000 @ 17.5%	=		5,425.00
			£8,725.00

Effective rate $\left(\dfrac{8,725}{120,000} \times 100\right)$ = 7.27%

Rate of exit charge (30% × 7.27%) = 2.18%

CTT payable (£100,000 × 2.18%) = £2,180.00

If the tax was payable by the trustees, this would be calculated by reference to the grossed-up amount.

It should be noted in relation to pre 27 March 1974 settlements that other property in the same settlement or related settlements is ignored and there is no reduction by fortieths for property which has not been relevant property throughout the period prior to the exit charge.

Two forms of transitional relief were available in respect of exit charges which arose in the period from 9 March 1982 to 1 April 1983, or 1 April 1984 if the event giving rise to the exit charge could not have occurred otherwise than as a result of court proceedings. The relevant legislation governing these reliefs was contained in Paragraphs 4 and 6–9, Schedule 15, Finance Act 1982.

b. *Rate after first ten-year anniversary charge:*
   i. *Post 26 March 1974 settlements.* Stated simply, the rate of exit charge on events occurring subsequent to the first ten-year anniversary charge is the rate applicable to the last anniversary charge multiplied by the fraction:

$$\frac{\text{Number of complete quarters from last anniversary date to}}{\text{the day before the event giving rise to the exit charge}}$$
$$\frac{}{40}$$

However, this simple statement can be complicated by three possible situations, as follows:

1. a change in the lifetime rates between the date of the last anniversary charge and the date of the exit charge;
   Note: This is quite likely in view of the provisions of section 8, CTTA 1984, requiring indexation of rate bands subject to the increases being overridden by statute.
2. the addition of property to the settlement between the last ten-year anniversary charge and the date of the exit charge; and
3. property which was comprised in the settlement at the last ten-year anniversary, but which was not relevant property at that time becoming relevant property before the date of the exit charge.

The situation within (1) above is dealt with quite simply by recalculating the rate of charge at the previous ten-year anniversary as if the rates of tax in force at the date of the exit charge had applied at that time.

Additions of relevant property within (2) and (3) also result in the recalculation of the rate of charge at the previous ten-year anniversary. Property which has been added to the settlement for the first time is brought into the recalculation at its value on introduction to the settlement. Property previously comprised in the settlement but not relevant property, is introduced into the calculation at its value when it became relevant property. The additional property must be brought into the recalculation of the anniversary charge even if the exit charge relates wholly to property which was relevant property at the date of the last anniversary charge. However, if property becoming relevant property after the last anniversary charge is the subject of the exit charge the 'appropriate fraction' is reduced by omitting any quarter expiring before the day on which the property became relevant property.

The following example is intended to illustrate several, but not all, of the preceding points.

Example 16

Mr *R* created a discretionary settlement on 15 September 1974 by making a transfer to the trustees of £100,000 cash. He paid the CTT on this transfer. He had made no previous chargeable transfers. On 1 May 1985 he transferred further cash of £20,000 to the trustees. On 1 December 1985 the trustees appoint cash of £80,000 to a beneficiary absolutely. The beneficiary agrees to pay any CTT due. The value of the relevant property, the whole of the settled property, at 15 September 1984 is £180,000.

The ten year anniversary charge and the exit charge will be calculated as follows:

	£
Ten-year anniversary charge 15 September 1984	
Hypothetical cumulative total:	
Chargeable transfers by settlor	Nil
Amounts of previous exit charges	Nil
	Nil
Hypothetical transfer:	
Value of relevant property at anniversary date	£180,000
Hypothetical transfer	180,000
Hypothetical cumulative total	Nil
	£180,000
CTT at lifetime rates at 15 September 1984:	
On first £64,000 @ Nil =	Nil
On next £21,000 @ 15% =	3,150.00
On next £31,000 @ 17.5% =	5,425.00
On next £32,000 @ 20% =	6,400.00
On next £32,000 @ 22.5% =	7,200.00
	£22,175.00
Effective rate $\left(\dfrac{22,175}{180,000} \times 100\right)$ =	12.32%
Rate of ten-year charge (30% × 12.32%) =	3.69%
CTT payable (£180,000 × 3.69%) =	£664.20
Exit charge 1 December 1985	
Re-calculation of ten-year anniversary charge	
Hypothetical cumulative total, as before	Nil
Hypothetical transfer:	[£]
Value of relevant property at anniversary date	180,000
Value of added property at date of entry	20,000
	£200,000

CTT on £200,000 at lifetime rates at 1 December 1985:

On first £67,000 @ Nil	=	Nil
On next £22,000 @ 15%	=	3,300.00
On next £33,000 @ 17.5%	=	5,775.00
On next £33,000 @ 20%	=	6,600.00
On next £39,000 @ 22.5%	=	8,775.00
On next £ 6,000 @ 25%	=	1,500.00
		£25,950.00

$$\text{Effective rate}\left(\frac{25,950}{200,000} \times 100\right) \quad = \quad 12.97\%$$

Notional rate of ten-year charge (30% × 12.97%)   =   3.89%

If the whole of £180,000 appointed to the beneficiary comes from the original fund the appropriate fraction will be:

$$4/40 \times 3.89\% \quad = \quad 0.389\%$$

The CTT payable will be:

$$£80,000 \times 0.389\% \quad = \quad £311.20$$

If, however, £20,000 of the £80,000 relates to the £20,000 transferred to the trustees on 1 May 1985, the appropriate fraction in respect of this amount will be

$$\frac{4-2}{40} \times 3.89\% \quad = \quad 0.194\%$$

The CTT payable will be:

£60,000 × 0.389%	233.40
£20,000 × 0.194%	38.80
	£272.20

ii. *Pre 27 March 1974 settlements.* The rate of tax on exit charges in respect of pre 27 March 1974 settlements after the first ten-year anniversary charge is calculated in exactly the same way as for post 26 March 1974 settlements, i.e. by reference to the rate at the previous ten-year anniversary charge adjusted for changes in rates of CTT or additions of relevant property, as described in (i) above.

Discretionary settlements — miscellaneous points

a. Where a settlor or his spouse (spouse for this purpose includes widow or widower) is beneficially entitled to an interest in possession in property immediately it becomes comprised in a settlement, the property is not treated as having become comprised in the settlement for the purposes of the rules applicable to discretionary settlements until neither is beneficially entitled to an interest in possession. The settlement is then treated as having been made by the last of them to be beneficially entitled to the interest in possession. This is important in relation to the determination of the rate of tax on ten-year anniversary and exit charges as these reflect the cumulative total of the settlor immediately prior to the commencement of the settlement.   (Section 80, CTTA 1984)

b. If (a) above applies in relation to a settlement, the property comprised in the settlement will only be excluded property if the person deemed to be the settlor is domiciled outside the United Kingdom at the time the interest terminated.
                              (Section 82, CTTA 1984)

c. Property ceasing to be comprised in one settlement and which becomes comprised in a second settlement is treated as remaining in the first settlement for the purposes of the discretionary settlement provisions, and also those relative to maintenance funds and conditionally exempt transfers, unless someone has become beneficially entitled to the property in the meantime. Property subject to this rule is not excluded property unless the settlor of the second settlement is domiciled outside the United Kingdom at the time the second settlement is made, and the settlor of the first settlement is also domiciled outside the United Kingdom at the time the property moved to the second settlement as well as being domiciled outside the United Kingdom at the time of making the first settlement.

d. It will be useful to summarize briefly the main exemptions or reliefs which are available against an exit charge on property ceasing to be relevant property:
   i.   exemption for gifts to charities;
   ii.   exemption for gifts to political parties;
   iii. exemption for gifts for national purposes;
   iv.   exemption for gifts for public benefit;
   v.   conditional exemption for national heritage property as applied to the discretionary settlement provisions by sections 78 and 79, CTTA 1984;
   vi.   exemption in respect of orders made under section 2, Inheritance (Provision for Family and Dependants) Act 1975;
   vii. agricultural property relief — see Chapter 12;
   viii. business property relief — see Chapter 12;
   ix.   excluded property is outside the scope of the CTT provisions relative to discretionary settlements.

PRIVILEGED SETTLEMENTS

Certain classes of privileged settlements receive special treatment under the provisions dealing with discretionary settlements. These include the following.

a. *Accumulation and maintenance settlements.* See detailed comments in respect of this type of settlement later.
b. *Charitable settlements.* Broadly speaking property held is not relevant property so is not liable to an exit charge or ten-year anniversary charge. Special rules apply if property leaves a temporary charitable trust, i.e. where the property is held for charitable purposes for a limited period only.   (Section 70, CTTA 1984)
c. *Trusts for the benefit of employees or newspaper trusts.* Payments out of these trusts do not attract an exit charge, provided the payment is not to one of the excluded beneficiaries. Property leaving a discretionary trust on transfer to an employee trust is also exempt from the exit charge and the ten-year anniversary charge does not arise.   (Sections 72, 75, 86 and 87, CTTA 1984)
d. *Protective trusts.* Under the terms of section 33, Trustee Act 1925, property is held in trust for the life of the principal beneficiary. If the principal beneficiary attempts to deprive himself of the benefit of the income of the trust, this creates a discretionary trust in his favour under section 33. This is ignored for CTT purposes such that payments to the beneficiary are outside the scope of the rules relating to discretionary settlements.
e. *Superannuation schemes.* Broadly, although superannuation schemes are effectively trusts, they are taken outside the provisions dealing with both life interest and non-life interest settlements. Also, where an interest under a scheme

comes to an end on the death of the annuitant, then the value of the interest is left out of account when valuing the deceased's estate on death. If the interest under a scheme does not terminate on death a charge to CTT arises on the disposal of the interest.   (Section 151, CTTA 1984)

f. *Trusts for disabled persons*. Provided the person for whom the settlement is made is disabled at the time the settlement is made, as defined, no interest in possession subsists in the settled property and not less than half of the settled property is to be applied for the benefit of the disabled person during his life, then the person is deemed to be entitled to an interest in possession in the settled property. This takes the trust outside the discretionary settlement provisions such that capital advances to the beneficiary are not chargeable to CTT.   (Section 89, CTTA 1984)

g. *Maintenance funds for historic buildings*. Privileged treatment is given to funds set up for the maintenance of historic buildings. This includes:

   i.   exemption for transfers into the fund by individuals;
   ii. settled property transferred to a fund from a discretionary settlement does not suffer an exit charge;
   iii. property within the fund is not 'relevant property' so is not liable to the ten-year anniversary or exit charges; and
   iv. certain payments out of the fund are excluded from a charge to CTT whereas others are liable to an exit charge at a special reduced rate.

                                      (Section 77 and Schedule 4, CTTA 1984)

Although only a brief description has been given in respect of the majority of the forms of privileged trusts, it is appropriate to consider in greater detail the provisions relating to accumulation and maintenance settlements.

ACCUMULATION AND MAINTENANCE SETTLEMENTS

A qualifying accumulation and maintenance settlement, broadly, is not liable to the ten-year anniversary charge and in the majority of situations no exit charge arises when property leaves the settlement. To qualify for this special treatment the following conditions must be satisfied:

a. one or more beneficiaries *will*, on attaining a specified age not exceeding twenty-five, become beneficially entitled to the property or an interest in possession in the property, and

b. no interest in possession subsists in the settled property and the income is to be accumulated so far as not applied for the maintenance, education or benefit of a beneficiary.

The word 'will' in condition (a) above was considered by the court in the case of *Lord Inglewood* v. *IRC* (1983) which was concerned with a clause in the trust deed giving the trustees power of revocation and reappointment. As the trustees had power to appoint the capital of the fund away from the permitted class of beneficiaries, then the certainty of the word 'will' was not present. Hence, in that case, the settlement did not come within the special provisions for accumulation and maintenance settlements. It should be noted, however, that a power to appoint in favour of other members of the permitted class of beneficiaries will not prevent the settlement from qualifying for the special rules.

One further condition has to be satisfied before the settlement will qualify. This can be either of the following:

c. not more than twenty-five years have elapsed since the commencement of the settlement or, if later, the time at which the conditions at (a) and (b) above were satisfied, or
d. all the persons who are or have been beneficiaries are or were grandchildren of a common grandparent or children, widows or widowers of such grandchildren who were themselves beneficiaries but died before the time when, had they survived, they would have become entitled as indicated in (a) above.

For the purposes of these conditions 'persons' includes unborn persons (but the condition at (a) cannot be satisfied unless there is or has been a living beneficiary), and children includes illegitimate children, stepchildren and adopted children.

No charge to CTT arises in the following circumstances:

i.   when a beneficiary becomes beneficially entitled to the property or to an interest in possession in the property on or before attaining the specified age;
ii. on the death of a beneficiary before attaining the specified age;
iii. on the payment of costs or expenses fairly attributable to the property;
iv. where any payment will be income for tax purposes of any person, or would be if he were resident in the United Kingdom;
v.   in respect of any liability to make a payment at (iii) or (iv).

Otherwise a charge to CTT will arise when:

a. the settled property ceases to satisfy the conditions outlined and (a), (b) and (c) or (d) above, or
b. the trustees make a disposition which reduces the value of the settled property.

The exemptions described above in relation to discretionary settlements may be available to reduce or eliminate the charge to CTT, e.g. where the property becomes held for charitable purposes, or in relation to dispositions where the trustees can establish that they did not intend to confer any gratuitous benefit — see earlier comments on dispositions by trustees in relation to discretionary settlements generally.

The charge to tax is calculated on the loss-to-donor principle and the grossing-up procedure applies if the trustees pay the CTT. The rate of tax chargeable is calculated on a rising scale depending upon the number of quarters in the 'relevant period' which commences on the day on which the property became, or last became, held on accumulation and maintenance trusts, or 13 March 1975 if later, and ends on the day before the event giving rise to the charge. The scale is as follows:

> 0.25% for each of the first 40 quarters,
> 0.20% for each of the next 40 quarters,
> 0.15% for each of the next 40 quarters,
> 0.10% for each of the next 40 quarters,
> 0.05% for each of the next 40 quarters,

This gives a maximum rate of 30 per cent after 50 years.

The fact that property becomes held on a qualifying accumulation and maintenance settlement does not prevent a charge to CTT arising when the property is transferred to the trustees. Therefore, if an individual makes a transfer to trustees the CTT payable will be calculated in the normal way and if the capital is appointed out of a discretionary settlement to an accumulation and maintenance settlement this will be subject to an exit charge. (Section 71, CTTA 1984)

PAYMENT OF TAX

Payment of tax by instalments

Instalment property has been defined elsewhere. Where discretionary trusts are concerned the instalment option is not available on the occasion of an actual release of capital. Provided that the property remains in trust following the chargeable event capital transfer tax may be paid by instalments on instalment property on the following occasions:

a. when a person beneficially entitled to an interest in possession in any property contained in a settlement disposes of his interest;
b. on the attainment of a vested interest in the income of the trust property by a beneficiary;
c. on the occasion of the periodic charge;
d. on the attainment by a discretionary trust of the exempt status of an 'accumulation and maintenance trust'.

Where the instalment option is available, the tax may be paid by ten equal yearly instalments subject to the overriding provision that the unpaid tax attributable to instalment property which is subsequently released from the trust fund becomes payable immediately upon the release.

Although it is not strictly an exemption it is worth noting that since there is no interest in possession in discretionary trusts, there can be no question of an additional capital transfer tax liability arising on the death of any person within three years of a capital distribution or other event.

Due date for payment of tax and interest thereon

Capital transfer tax due in relation to trust funds is payable on the following dates:

a. if the liability arose on a death, the tax is due and payable six months after the end of the month in which the death occurred. Interest accrues on unpaid tax at the rate of 9 per cent from the due date;
b. if the liability arose as a result of any other event, the due date for payment depends upon the date of the event as follows:
   i. if the chargeable event occurred during the period 6 April to 30 September (inclusive), the due date is the following 30 April;
   ii. if the chargeable event occurred during the period 1 October to 5 April (inclusive), the due date is the last day of the sixth month after the chargeable event.

Interest accrues on unpaid tax at the rate of 11 per cent from the due date.

Exercise 13

1. Define the following terms:

   a. a settlement;
   b. a settlor;
   c. reversionary interest;
   d. excluded property, in the context of settled property;
   e. an interest in possession.

2. On what basis is the capital transfer tax calculated on the death of a life tenant?
3. Who is liable to pay the capital transfer tax calculated on the death of a life tenant?
4. Mr Graves died in August 1985. He made chargeable transfers within the preceding ten years in the amount of £35,000. He left a free estate valued at £65,000 net and was the life tenant of settled property having a value of £85,000 at the date of his death. The whole of his free estate passed to his son. Calculate the amount of capital transfer tax payable on the death of Mr Graves and the amount payable by the trustees.
5. In what circumstances can an annual exemption, or part thereof, be taken into account in calculating the capital transfer tax payable on the termination of an interest in possession?
6. Define the following terms:

   a. relevant property;
   b. ten year anniversary;
   c. related settlements.

7. Mr Peters settled property on the trustees of a discretionary settlement on 15 September 1982. The value of the property at that time was £50,000. Prior to 15 September 1982 he had made chargeable transfers totalling £25,000. No exemptions were available in respect of the transfer to the trustees. The value of the settled property at 15 September 1992 is £100,000. On the basis that there are no further changes in the rates of CTT after those in force from 6 April 1985 and no prior exit charges, calculate the capital transfer tax payable on the first ten-year anniversary charge.
8. Mr Davies settled property valued at £70,000 on the trustees of a discretionary settlement on 10 June 1980. He made chargeable transfers prior to 10 June 1980 of £40,000, and paid the capital transfer tax due on the transfer to the trustees. On 11 September 1985 the trustees appoint capital of £30,000 to a beneficiary who agreed to pay any capital transfer tax due. No property had been added to the settlement since it commenced on 10 June 1980 and there were no related settlements. Calculate the exit charge arising on the appointment of capital to the beneficiary on 11 September 1985.
9. What conditions have to be satisfied before a settlement qualifies as an 'accumulation and maintenance settlement' and how is this treated differently from other discretionary settlements for capital transfer tax?

14
Inheritance Tax

INTRODUCTION

As was mentioned in the introductions to Chapters 10 to 13, the Finance Act 1986 abolished Capital Transfer Tax (CTT) and introduced Inheritance Tax (IHT) with effect from 18 March 1986. To a very large extent the provisions for CTT have been retained, but in a modified form, and new provisions have been introduced to deal with matters, such as gifts with a reservation of benefit, reminiscent of the old Estate Duty rules, which were superseded when Capital Transfer Tax was introduced back in 1974.

This chapter will examine the changes introduced by the Finance Act 1986 and the provisions now in force in respect of transfers made on and after 18 March 1986. The statutory references quoted will relate to the Finance Act 1986.

Before examining the provisions in detail, it may be appropriate to summarize the changes in broad terms in order to provide an overview of the new rules that now apply. The following major changes that arise are as follows:

1. Gifts between individuals and gifts to certain favoured trusts are now completely exempt from IHT, provided the donor survives for a period of seven years from the date on which the gift was made. During this period of seven years, the gifts are known as 'potentially exempt transfers' (PETs), since, until the seven years have passed, the gifts will not become exempt gifts.
2. The cumulation period is reduced from ten years to seven years in respect of all chargeable transfers.
3. All chargeable transfers made within seven years of death are taxed at the death rates, but there is a form of tapering relief available in respect of transfers made more than three years prior to death.
4. Special rules now apply in respect of gifts made where the donor has reserved a benefit.
5. Certain debts due on the death of an individual may not be deductible in computing the value of his estate if the creditor has received gifts from the deceased.
6. Certain gifts made during lifetime will still be 'chargeable transfers', and although the Finance Act 1986 only prescribes one table of rates of IHT, these will be chargeable at half the rates prescribed in the table. (The table of rates is reproduced in Appendix III.)

RATES OF INHERITANCE TAX

1. *The Cumulation Period*

For all chargeable transfers made, during lifetime or on death, on or after 18 March

1986, only chargeable transfers made within the previous seven years are brought into account to determine the rate of tax chargeable on the later transfer.

(Para. 2, Sch. 19, FA 1986)

Although this reduces the cumulation period to seven years, from the period of ten years which applied under the CTT rules, this can produce some difficult situations, as will be seen later in this chapter, when chargeable transfers are made after potentially exempt transfers which subsequently become chargeable transfers. However, in straightforward situations, this reduction in the period of cumulation should reduce the overall impact of IHT on an individual's estate.

2. *Tax Rates*

There is now only one table of rates for the purposes of IHT, which came into operation with effect from 18 March 1986. These rates, as contained in The Capital Transfer Tax (Indexation) Order 1986 (SI 1986 No. 528), would normally have come into operation with effect from 6 April 1986. Although there is only a single table of rates, chargeable transfers made during lifetime are taxed at only 50% of the scale rates.

(Para. 2(2), Sch. 19, FA 1986)

For transfers made within seven years of death, but more than three years prior to death, the rate (or rates) of tax chargeable is calculated at the following percentages of the full rates:

Transfer made more than:

three years but not more than four years before death	80%
four years but not more than five years before death	60%
five years but not more than six years before death	40%
six years but not more than seven years before death	20%

(Para. 2(4), Sch. 19, FA 1986)

It will be noticed that transfers made more than three years but not more than five years prior to death will be chargeable at a higher rate than under the CTT rules that applied immediately prior to 18 March 1986, when 50% of the death rates applied in respect of transfers made more than three years prior to death. It is specifically provided, therefore, that the rate of tax applicable to transfers made before 18 March 1986 must not be more than the rate applicable prior to 18 March 1986.

(Para, 40(1), Sch. 19, FA 1986)

3. *Lifetime transfers that are not 'Potentially Exempt Transfers'*

Any lifetime transfer that is not a PET, for example a gift into settlement other than a favoured settlement, is chargeable to IHT at 50% of the rates of tax specified in the table. The chargeable transfer will immediately be included in the transferor's cumulative total of chargeable transfers and will remain within that cumulative total for the next seven years.

(Para. 2, Sch. 19, FA 1986)

If the transferor dies within the next seven years, the following will occur:

a. The IHT will be recalculated at the full rates applying at the date of death, subject to the taper relief mentioned above, but by reference to the value of the chargeable transfer at the date it was made, not the value at the date of death.

(Para. 2, Sch. 19, FA 1986)

b. The tax liability as calculated at (a) above is compared with the tax originally charged on the lifetime gift. If further tax is payable this will normally be payable by the transferee, although this can be recovered from the transferor's estate if it remains unpaid more than 12 months after the end of the month in which the transferor died.

(Section 101(3) and Para. 26, Sch. 19, FA 1986)

c. If the calculation of the tax liability at (a) produces a liability which is less than the liability paid on the lifetime gift at the time it was made, for example, as a result of taper relief, lower scale of rates at the date of death etc., no repayment is made.

(Para. 2(3), Sch. 19, FA 1986)

4. *Potentially exempt transfers that become chargeable transfers*

If a transferor dies within seven years of making a PET, the PET becomes a chargeable transfer. The effect of this is as follows:

a. The PET becomes a chargeable transfer which, for the purposes of calculating the transferor's cumulative total, is treated as having been made by the transferor at the time the PET was originally made. It is important to note that this will then affect the transferor's cumulative total from that time onwards and hence will affect the rates of tax applicable to subsequent chargeable transfers, PETs which become chargeable transfers and the estate of the transferor at his death.
b. It is the value of the PET at the time it was made which becomes taxable, not the value at the date of death, but it is taxable at the full rates prevailing at the date of death, subject to taper relief, not the rates in force at the time the PET was originally made.

(Para. 37, Sch. 19, FA 1986)

c. Any tax payable will normally be due from the transferee, although the Inland Revenue can recover this tax from the transferor's personal representatives if it has not been paid at the end of a period of 12 months from the end of the month in which the transferor died.

(Section 101(3) and Para. 26, Sch. 19, FA 1986)

5. *Chargeable estate at death*

IHT is chargeable on the total value of an individual's estate at his death, to the extent that the deemed transfer is not an exempt transfer, for example to a surviving spouse or to charity, at the full rates in force at the date of death and taking into account all chargeable transfers made in the seven years prior to the date of the individual's death. The earlier chargeable transfers will include previous PETs which became chargeable as a result of the death.

6. *Annual and other exemptions*

In the foregoing paragraphs, reference has been made to chargeable transfers and potentially exempt transfers. Potentially exempt transfers are considered in detail below and this will include a reference to the annual and other exemptions that still remain available. The term 'chargeable transfer' in this context means, as it did for CTT, a transfer of value that is not an exempt transfer. The exemptions described in Chapter 13 in relation to CTT apply also for IHT. The business and agricultural property reliefs have also been retained, but in a modified form. The changes in these reliefs are dealt with separately later in this chapter.

POTENTIALLY EXEMPT TRANSFERS

1. *Introduction*

Since this represents a fairly radical change from the provisions for CTT, it may be appropriate to first define what is meant by the term 'potentially exempt transfer' (PET). A PET is a transfer of value:

a. which is made by an individual on or after 18 March 1986, and
b. which would normally be treated as a chargeable transfer, and
c. which is either a gift to:

    i.   another individual
    ii. an accumulation and maintenance trust, or
    iii. a disabled trust.

(Para. 1, Sch. 19, FA 1986)

The definition above includes the term 'chargeable transfer', which retains its meaning as for CTT. Therefore, if the value transferred is wholly covered by exemptions available, there will be no transfer that would previously have been treated as a chargeable transfer and, hence, no PET.

    It follows from the above definition that a transfer of value can only be a PET if the gifted property becomes comprised in the estate of another individual, an accumulation and maintenance settlement, or a trust for the disabled. Property deemed to be held as part of a person's estate, i.e. property supporting a life interest under an interest in possession trust, is not included for this purpose.

    All PETs are assumed to be exempt transfers when they are made. Provided the transferor survives seven years from the date on which the PET is made, this exemption will be confirmed. If the transferor dies within this period of seven years, the PET becomes a chargeable transfer. The calculation of the IHT payable when a PET becomes a chargeable transfer will be demonstrated in the example at the end of this section.

    On the basis of the foregoing definition of a PET, it may be helpful if a few examples of transfers that can never be PETs are given. The following are examples of transfers that will continue to be chargeable transfers, which will give rise to a liability to IHT at the time the transfer is made, or at least count towards the cumulative total of chargeable transfers made by the transferor if only chargeable at the nil rate:

a. Gifts into settlements with an interest in possession (see definition of such a settlement in Chapter 13).
b. Terminations of interests in possession in settled property. (Although IHT is charged as if the person who was previously entitled to the interest in possession had

made a transfer of value equivalent to the value of the property supporting the interest that has been terminated, it is specifically stated that the termination is not a 'transfer of value' — Section 51 (1)(a), CTTA 1984. See also Para. 14, Sch. 19, FA 1986.

c. Gifts into discretionary settlements, strictly settlements without an interest in possession (other than the types of trusts mentioned at 1(c)(ii) and (iii) above) and payments out of such discretionary trusts.

d. Transfers of value by close companies apportioned to the participators.

It must also be noted that a transfer of value is not a PET until the transferee has assumed bona fide possession and enjoyment of the property to the entire exclusion, or virtually to the entire exclusion, of the transferor and of any benefit to him by contract or otherwise. A more detailed discussion of these provisions appears later in this chapter under the heading 'Gifts with reservation of benefit' (Section 102, FA 1986).

It has already been noted that many of the exemptions available under the previous CTT legislation have been retained for IHT purposes. Specific provisions have been introduced to deal with the allocation of the annual exemption, including any balance from the previous year, where both chargeable transfers and PETs are made in the same year. Initially, PETs are ignored when allocating the annual exemption available for any particular year. If a PET subsequently becomes a chargeable transfer it is treated, for the purposes of allocating the annual exemption, as if it were made after any chargeable transfers made during that year. It follows, therefore, that the annual exemption available for any year is allocated against chargeable transfers made during that year in the order in which they were made. It appears that this method of allocation could cause problems in relation to annual exemption carried forward by one year (see Chapter 10) in circumstances where unused exemption from one year is carried forward to the next year and set off against a chargeable transfer made in the subsequent year. If a PET made in the previous year becomes a chargeable transfer, the annual exemption carried forward may then not be available for carry forward, thus increasing the charge to IHT on the chargeable transfer made in the subsequent year.

One other amendment to an exemption previously reviewed in relation to CTT must be mentioned. This concerns the conditional exemption for works of art etc., which requires adjustment to take account of the rules for PETs. Clearly, if the transferor survives seven years from the making of the PET, the transfer will be exempt in any event and there will be no need to claim conditional exemption. If the transferor dies within seven years of making the PET such that this would then become a chargeable transfer, conditional exemption can then be claimed, but by reference to the property as at the date of the transferor's death.

(Paras. 6–12, Sch. 19, FA 1986)

One other possible disadvantage in respect of this change to PETs should be noted. It is possible for the same property to be charged to IHT more than once in respect of the same transferor. For example, if Mr A gives property to Mr B, Mr B gives the property back to Mr A two years later, and Mr A then dies six months later, the property will be chargeable as a gift made within seven years prior to Mr A's death, and the same property would seem to be chargeable as part of his estate on death. The mutual transfers relief (Sections 148 and 149, CTTA 1984) was repealed with effect from 18 March 1986, but regulations are to be introduced by Statutory Instrument to prevent double charges to IHT arising in the manner suggested in the above example.

The application of the new rules will now be demonstrated in an example, where it has been assumed that there will be no change of rates throughout the period covered by the example and that in the case of each transfer made, the transferee agrees to pay any CTT/IHT payable.

Example 1

An individual makes the following gifts and dies on 15 May 1993 leaving an estate with a net value of £200,000.

15 February 1984	Gift to son	£55,000
1 June 1986	Gift to trustees of an interest in possession settlement	£75,000
1 July 1988	Gift to daughter	£55,000
1 March 1991	Gift to trustees of a discretionary settlement	£60,000
15 May 1993	Chargeable transfer on death	£200,000

Ignoring annual exemptions, the CTT or IHT payable will be as follows:

Lifetime tax liabilities

1. 15 February 1984: gift to son of £55,000

No CTT payable, as the chargeable transfer is within the nil rate band of £60,000 then in force.

2. 1 June 1986: gift into interest-in-possession settlement of £75,000

	£	Tax
Cumulative total of chargeable transfers within last seven years	55,000	Nil
Present chargeable transfer	75,000	
Revised cumulative total	£130,000	

On first £129,000 @ Nil to 35%	=	19,100.00	
On next £1,000 @ 40%	=	400.00	
		£19,500.00	
Tax due @ 50% of full rates			9,750.00
IHT payable		=	£9,750.00

3. 1 July 1988: gift to daughter of £55,000

No liability to IHT at this time since this will be considered to be a potentially exempt transfer.

4. 1 March 1991: gift into discretionary settlement of £60,000

	£	Tax
Cumulative total of chargeable transfers within last seven years, i.e. excludes transfer made 15 February 1984	75,000	
Present chargeable transfer	60,000	
Revised cumulative total	£135,000	

On first £129,000 @ Nil to 35%	=	19,100.00
On next £6,000 @ 40%	=	2,400.00
		£21,500.00

Tax due at 50% of full rates		=	10,750.00
Less IHT on previous cumulative total			
On first £71,000 @ Nil	=	Nil	
On next £4,000 @ 30%	=	1,200.00	
		£1,200.00	

Tax due at 50% of full rates	=	600.00
IHT payable		£10,150.00

Recalculation of tax liabilities following the death of the transferor on 15 May 1993.

	Chargeable Transfer	Full Tax	% Charge	Tax Due	Tax Paid	Additional Tax
	£	£		£	£	£
1. 15 February 1984: Gift to son	55,000	Nil		Nil	Nil	Nil
2. 1 June 1986: Gift into interest in possession settlement	75,000	19,500.00	20%	3,900.00	9,750.00	Nil
	130,000	19,500.00				
3. 1 July 1988: Gift to daughter	55,000	23,050.00	60%	13,830.00	Nil	13,830.00
	185,000	42,550.00 (a)				
15 February 1991: Seven-year write- off of gift to son	(55,000)	(23,050.00)				
	130,000	19,500.00				
4. 1 March 1991: Gift into discretionary settlement	60,000	25,300.00	100%	25,300.00	10,150.00	£15,150.00
Cumulative total	£190,000	£44,800.00 (b)				

Notes

a. Calculation of IHT of £42,550 is as follows:

On first £164,000 @ Nil to 40%	=	33,100.00
On next £21,000 @ 45%	=	9,450.00
		£42,550.00

b. Calculation of IHT of £44,800 is as follows:

On first £164,000 @ Nil to 40%	=	33,100.00
On next £26,000 @ 45%	=	11,700.00
		£44,880.00

The IHT payable on the chargeable estate on death is as follows:

	£	Tax
Cumulative total of chargeable transfers within the seven years prior to death	190,000	44,800.00
Chargeable estate on death	200,000	
Final cumulative total	£390,000	

IHT payable at full rates:

On first £71,000 @ Nil =	Nil	
On next £24,000 @ 30% =	7,200.00	
On next £34,000 @ 35% =	11,900.00	
On next £35,000 @ 40% =	14,000.00	
On next £42,000 @ 45% =	18,900.00	
On next £51,000 @ 50% =	25,500.00	
On next £60,000 @ 55% =	33,000.00	
On next £73,000 @ 60% =	43,800.00	
£390,000	£154,300.00	£154,300.00
IHT payable from estate		£109,500.00

It will be noted from the above example that a substantial additional liability to IHT falls on the trustees of the discretionary settlement as a result of the transfer to the daughter on 1 July 1988 becoming a chargeable transfer following the death of the transferor. This was previously treated as a PET. The additional liability is also greater than the £10,150 that they might have expected to have to pay.

GIFTS WITH RESERVATION OF BENEFIT

Introduction

Section 102 and Schedule 20, FA 1986 introduce the provisions that deal with gifts with a reservation of a benefit. These provisions are very reminiscent of the provisions that were introduced as long ago as 1881. It is perhaps unfortunate that the draftsmen of the 1986 legislation have retained the terminology of the old legislation, using the words 'gift', 'donor' and 'donee', instead of the terms now familiar from the CTT legislation: 'transfer of value', 'transferor' and 'transferee'. This change of terminology and minor differences in the wording used in the legislation make it a little uncertain as to whether or not old estate duty cases will be conclusive in interpreting the new provisions. In view of the use of the term 'gift' instead of 'transfer of value', it may be thought that a sale at an undervalue, most certainly a transfer of value under the CTT legislation, might not be a 'gift' under these new provisions. However, it was established in the case of *Attorney-General* v. *Worrall* (1895) 1 QB 99 that this is treated as a gift with a benefit reserved.

The new provisions would not seem to apply where the donor is excluded from all benefit from the gifted property, but a benefit is reserved for the donor's spouse or widow/widower. However, a gift with reservation is treated in the same way as any gift at the time it is made. For example, if an individual makes a gift to the trustees of a discretionary settlement and the individual is one of the discretionary beneficiaries, the gift will give rise to an immediate charge to IHT at 50% of the full rates. As will be seen, the same property could also become chargeable to IHT again on the death of the individual.

From a practical point of view, it may be easiest to see the effect of these provisions by looking at the situation which arises on the death of the donor of gifts with reservation of benefits. At the date of the donor's death, each gift made, where a benefit has been reserved to the donor, must be reviewed, as far as IHT is concerned, with the following consequences:

a. If the benefit previously reserved was released more than seven years prior to the donor's death, no charge to IHT will arise.
b. If the benefit previously reserved was released within seven years before the donor's death, the gift will be liable to IHT as at the date the benefit was released and by reference to the value of the gift at that time.
c. If the benefit previously reserved had not been released as at the date of the donor's death, the gift will be liable to IHT as part of the donor's estate at the date of his death.

It will be appreciated from the above summary that it is possible for two charges to IHT to arise in respect of the same property, for example, on a gift into a settlement or to an individual within seven years of the donor's death, and also on the release of any benefit reserved, if the release occurs on or within seven years of the donor's death. Regulations are to be introduced to give relief from any double charge to IHT.

The detailed rules

The legislation defines a gift with reservation of benefit as any gift made by an individual on or after 18 March 1986 where either:

a. possession and enjoyment of the property is not bona fide assumed by the donee at or before the beginning of the relevant period; or
b. at any time in the relevant period the property is not enjoyed to the entire exclusion, or virtually the entire exclusion, of the donor and of any benefit to him by contract or otherwise.

This definition has included the term 'the relevant period', which is simply defined as the period ending on the date of the donor's death and commencing seven years before that date, or, if it is later, on the date of the gift.

(Section 102(1), FA 1986)

It must be noted that this definition is also extended to take account of the associated operations rules, such that any benefit obtained by the donor by virtue of any associated operations of which the disposal by way of gift is one shall be treated as a benefit to him by contract or otherwise.

(Para. 6(1)(c), Sch. 20, FA 1986)

Whilst the circumstances stated above continue to apply, the property gifted, in relation to the gift and the donor, is treated as property subject to reservation. (Section 102(2), FA 1986). In a press release dated 18 March 1986, the Inland Revenue gave the following examples of 'gifts with reservation':

a. where a house is given, but the donor continues to reside in it;
b. where a settlor of a discretionary settlement is also a beneficiary;
c. certain insurance schemes where the tax-payer retains a right to benefits during his

lifetime, for example, PETA [Pure Endowment Term Assurance] plans, discounted gift schemes and inheritance trusts.

As indicated in the introduction, if immediately before the death of the donor there is any property that is subject to a reservation in relation to him, that property is to be treated as property to which he was beneficially entitled immediately before his death. Hence, such property will be chargeable to IHT as if it formed part of his estate on his death. If within the seven years before his death the donor releases the reservation in his favour, such that the property is no longer considered to be a gift with reservation, the donor is treated as having made a PET at the time the reservation is released. The value of the gift is the value of the gifted property at the time the PET is made.

(Sections 102(3) and (4), FA 1986)

To the extent that the following transfers are exempt, the gifts-with-reservation rules do not apply:

a. transfers between spouses (Section 18, CTTA 1984)
b. small gifts, i.e. up to £250 per annum per donee (Section 20, CTTA 1984)
c. gifts in consideration of marriage (Section 22, CTTA 1984)
d. gifts to charities (Section 23, CTTA 1984)
e. gifts to political parties (Section 24, CTTA 1984)
f. gifts for national purposes etc (Section 25, CTTA 1984)
g. gifts for public benefit (Section 26, CTTA 1984)
h. maintenance funds for historic buildings (Section 27, CTTA 1984)
i. employee trusts (Section 23, CTTA 1984)

(Section 102(5), FA 1986)

Although the definition of a gift with reservation includes the phrase 'or virtually to the entire exclusion' of the donor, which may be very difficult to interpret in practice, the legislation does set out a number of situations in which there will be no benefit reserved. These include the following:

a. if the gifted property is an interest in land or a chattel, the donor's continued occupation, enjoyment or possession of the land or chattel is to be disregarded if it is for full consideration in money or money's worth.

(Para. 6(1)(a), Sch. 20, FA 1986)

b. if the gifted property is an interest in land and the donee is a relative of the donor, occupation of the land will not be treated as a benefit reserved if it arises in the following circumstances:

i.   it results from a change in the circumstances of the donor since the time of the gift which was unforeseen at the time of the gift;
ii. it occurs at a time when the donor has become unable to maintain himself through old age or infirmity; and
iii. it represents a reasonable provision by the donee for the care and maintenance of the donor.

(Para. 6(1)(b), Sch. 20, FA 1986)

The condition at (i) above is extended by the phrase 'and was not brought about by the donor to receive the benefit of this provision'. Clearly, any arrangement that reduces the assets of the donor to such an extent that he has to rely upon the donee to provide accommodation in the previously gifted property and maintenance will be caught by these anti-avoidance provisions. It seems that what is contemplated by this provision is a totally unexpected deterioration of the donor's financial circumstances.

There are also special rules to deal with the situation where the donee disposes of the property gifted to him, subject to a reservation of benefit in favour of the donor before the material date, i.e. the date of death of the donor or the date on which the reservation is released, if earlier. The rules provide for a tracing procedure, where the donee exchanges the gifted property for some other property, such that the property received in exchange is treated, for the purposes of the 'gifts with reservation of benefit' rules, as if it had been comprised in the original gift. If the donee voluntarily gives the property away other than for full consideration in money or money's worth, then, unless the property has been gifted back to the donor, the donee is treated, for the purpose of these rules, as if he still owned the property.

(Para. 2, Sch. 20, FA 1986)

If the original gift with reservation is cash, then the tracing procedure does not apply. Therefore, if the donee spends the cash, the property purchased will not be treated as substituted property. Similarly, if the property gifted is sold by the donee for cash, this breaks the tracing procedure and any property purchased by the donee for the cash received from the sale of the first property will not be treated as substituted property.

(Para. 2, Sch. 20, FA 1986)

Separate rules apply in relation to settled property. These apply if the gift by the donor becomes settled property by virtue of the gift and also where the property is settled by the donee before the material date. Broadly, the property comprised in the settlement is treated as the property comprised in the gift at the material date. If it can be shown that part of the settled property was not derived from the original gift, then this can be excluded, as can any accumulations of income which have been accumulated under the terms of the settlement deed.

(Para. 5, Sch. 20, FA 1986)

Although these rules deem property gifted subject to a reservation of benefit, which is still subject to the reservation at the date of his death, to be property to which the donor was beneficially entitled at the date of his death, such property cannot be the subject of a disclaimer or variation within section 142, CTTA 1984.

Practical aspects of the new rules

As indicated the 'gifts with reservation' rules will only apply if:

a. the donee does not assume possession and enjoyment of the gifted property, or
b. the gifted property is not enjoyed to the entire, or virtually entire, exclusion of the donor and of any benefit to him by contract or otherwise.

In the circumstances it will be essential to establish the exact nature of each gift. The basic principle is that what a donor keeps back is not a gift. If, therefore, an individual is retaining and excluding some beneficial interest from the gift instead of making a gift subject to a reservation, then these new rules will not apply. By way of illustration, suppose an individual makes a gift of a large estate to his son and reserves the right to live in a small cottage on the estate. In this situation it is likely that he will be treated as having reserved a benefit in the whole estate, such that the whole of the estate will be chargeable to IHT on his death. If, on the other hand, he had made a gift of the estate excluding the cottage to his son, then IHT would only be chargeable on his death, provided he survived the gift by more than seven years, on the value of the cottage.

Reference has already been made to the Inland Revenue press release of 18 March 1986, which gave some examples of 'gifts with reservation'. It is interesting to note that for estate duty purposes no duty was payable where:

a. the donor made a gift of a house to a donee and survived the gift by seven years; and
b. the donee took possession of the house and became the head of the household; and
c. the donor resided in the house as the donee's guest without any arrangement between them as to the provisions of lodging.

(A.G. v. Seccombe (1911) 2 KB 688)

In the light of the Inland Revenue press release of 18 March this would now be treated as a 'gift with reservation'. However, if for example, elderly parents make unconditional gifts of undivided shares in their house to their children, and the parents and children occupy the property as their family home, each owner bearing his or her share of the running costs, this will not be treated as a 'gift with reservation'. In these circumstances, the parents' occupation or enjoyment of the part of the house they have given away is in return for similar enjoyment by the children of the other part of the property. Thus, the donor's occupation is for full consideration. (Hansard Standing Committee G 10 June 1986). The practical problem with this type of arrangement is that the children may have their own home(s), such that only the donors may wish to live in the gifted house. It is also worth noting again that if the donor continues to occupy, enjoy or possess gifted land, the reservation will only be ignored if it is for *full consideration* in money or money's worth. This is an all-or-nothing test; there is no partial relief for partial consideration.

It is likely that a benefit will also be treated as having been reserved in the following situations:

a. Where the donor is a trustee of a settlement of which he is settlor if he is entitled to receive remuneration for his services as a trustee. If the settled property includes shares in a private company and the settlor continues to hold shares in the company in his own right, it may be unwise for him to be the first named trustee, as he would then be able to exercise the voting rights on the settled shares, in addition to the voting rights on his own personal shares. Although he would be exercising the voting rights in two different capacities, this could be construed as a 'reservation of benefit', particularly if the combined voting rights gave him control, and should be avoided if possible.
b. where the donor retains an option to repurchase the gifted property, particularly if the option is exercisable at an under-value.

Partnership transactions

A specific reference to partnership transactions may be helpful, as gifts between members of a family partnership, e.g. father and son, are not uncommon. The comments that follow are considered to represent the best view currently available, but cannot be considered to be totally free from doubt. Where these are based on old estate-duty cases, the appropriate reference has been given. It remains to be seen how far the old estate-duty cases will be binding as far as the new rules are concerned, although it is understood that the Capital Taxes Office intend to follow these earlier decisions, at least those that favour the Inland Revenue.

The following are examples of situations that are likely to arise in practice, although they do not cover every conceivable situation.

a. There should be no reservation of benefit where, for example, father retires from a partnership and gives the whole of his partnership interest to another partner, e.g. his son. However, there could be a reservation of benefit if father became an employee of the partnership at a level of remuneration which is excessive for the duties actually performed.
b. There could be a reservation of benefit where the donor partner withdrew cash, or other assets, from the partnership, gifted this to the donee partner who then reintroduced the cash or assets as additional capital of the partnership. The donor partner would effectively continue to have use of the cash or assets in his capacity as a partner.
c. There is probably no reservation of benefit where a partner, who does not wholly retire from the partnership, gifts part of his interest to another partner, e.g. his son, reducing his interest in capital and profits from, say, 50% to 25%. It is considered that, in these circumstances, the donor partner has made an outright gift of part of his interest in the partnership business, which is completely separate from the specific assets of the partnership, which continue to be used for the purposes of the partnership business by all of the partners, including the donor partner.
d. There is probably no reservation of benefit where a partner, e.g. father, owns property which is occupied rent free by a partnership of which he is a member together with other members of his family, and he gives the property to, say, his children, even though the partners, including the donor partner, continue to enjoy the rent-free use of the property. This is because the property gifted to the children is gifted subject to the existing rights of use by the partnership, and the donor's continuing benefit is obtained by reason of the partnership interest and is not referable to the gift.

(Munro v. Stamp Duty Commissioners (1934) AC 61)

e. It is considered that there will be a reservation of benefit where there is an absolute gift of land from, say, father to son, and the son is then brought into partnership with his father, introducing the land into the partnership.

(Chick v. Stamp Duty Commissioners (1958) AC 435)

It remains to be seen exactly how the Capital Taxes Office apply these new rules. Until such time as experience of the attitude of the Inland Revenue has been gained, each transaction will have to be very carefully considered in order to establish whether a reservation has been retained, or an interest retained with a reduced interest only being gifted.

NON-DEDUCTIBLE DEBTS

Under the CTT legislation, the treatment of debts incurred by an individual was quite straightforward and was explained in Chapter 12. New rules are introduced for IHT, which are concerned with the deductibility of debts on death — lifetime transfers are not affected — but the new rules only apply in respect of debts or incumbrances created on or after 18 March 1986.

The new rules are widespread with the aim of preventing any deduction for fictitious debts. However, they also ensure that properly deductible debts reduce the value of a person's estate so that IHT is not levied twice. To take a simple example, if an individual creates a debt, but receives full consideration for it, then his estate is not diminished. If the debt were disallowed, his estate would be artificially increased by the value of the debt and a double charge would arise.

Debts and incumbrances will be deductible in full if:

a. they are incurred or created bona fide,
b. for full consideration in money or money's worth
c. wholly for the person's own use and benefit, and
d. take effect out of his interest.

Debts are to be abated where any consideration for the debt has been derived from the deceased. The rules, which are based on the old estate-duty provisions, are best illustrated by an example.

Example 2

In June 1986 the deceased borrowed £30,000 from his son, John. The deceased had made previous transfers as follows:

a. £10,000 that he settled on his daughter, Alice, on her marriage in 1960.
b. A house that he gave to John in 1965 and that John sold in May 1986, the proceeds of £18,000 forming part of the loan.
c. £6,000 that he gave to John in 1985, of which John invested £4,000. The balance of £2,000 forms part of the loan. It cannot be proved that the loan was not in contemplation at the time of the gift.

The whole of the property derived from the deceased is, therefore, £34,000. Of the £30,000 consideration for the debt, £20,000, i.e. £18,000 under (b) and £2,000 under (c), *consisted* of such property and is therefore not allowable as a debt (Section 103(1)(a), FA 1986).
    The balance of £10,000 falls under the second arm of the new rules (Section 103(1)(b), FA 1986) and must be abated. The calculation of this abatement is as follows:

Total amount which could have been rendered available, i.e. (a) + (b) + (c)	=	£34,000

The amounts to be excluded are:
i. so much as is included in the consideration, i.e. the £20,000
ii. so much as was the subject matter of a disposition not made with reference to the loan. Prima facie, this covers the balance of £10,000.

The calculation is as follows:

	£	£
Amount falling under Section 103(1)(b), FA 1986		10,000
Less Amount which could have been available	34,000	
Less Amounts to be excluded	(20,000)	
	(10,000)	(4,000)
'Excess' in respect of which no abatement made		£6,000

In effect, the allowance for the debt would be abated by £4,000, leaving £6,000 of the £10,000 allowable. None of the £20,000 is allowable, as this consisted of property derived from the deceased. The total allowable is, therefore, £6,000.
    It will be noted from the above example that although only debts and incumbrances

created on or after 18 March 1986 have to be taken into account, property derived from the deceased can include dispositions made at any time before the date on which the debt or incumbrance was created and can be taken into account in determining the amount of the debt that can be deducted.

There are circumstances in which the application of the new rules within Section 103, FA 1986 could give rise to a double charge to IHT. Example 3 below illustrates this situation. The Inland Revenue has authority to make regulations to avoid such double charges (Section 104(1)(c), FA 1986).

Example 3

a. In June 1986 an individual gives his house, valued at £100,000, to his son. (This is a PET so no immediate charge to IHT will arise.)
b. In December 1986 the son sells the property back to his father for £100,000, but the purchase price is left outstanding. (Again, no immediate charge to IHT arises.)
c. In June 1988 he makes a further gift of £200,000 to his son.
d. In August 1990 the individual dies.

On death, the £100,000 debt created at (b) will be chargeable to IHT, because the debt is non-deductible (section 103, FA 1986) and the £200,000 will also be charged, because the PET is now chargeable. Alternatively, if the £200,000 were given in satisfaction of the debt, only the £200,000 will be chargeable to IHT, because £100,000 would have discharged the debt, and under section 103(5), FA 1986 this is treated as a PET made at that time, and the balance of £100,000 would be a PET in its own right.

BUSINESS AND AGRICULTURAL PROPERTY RELIEFS

1. *Partially exempt estates*

Under the old CTT rules it was possible to achieve substantial savings of CTT where the estate of a deceased person included agricultural or business property and part of the estate was left by way of a pecuniary legacy which was exempt. The following example demonstrates how the CTT rules were applied in these circumstances.

Example 4

An individual died on 15 December 1985 with an estate comprising:

	£
Farm	400,000
Business assets	200,000
Stocks and shares, etc.	150,000
Total estate	£750,000

In his will, he left the business assets to his two sons, subject to CTT, a pecuniary legacy of £300,000 to his widow, and the residue to his daughter.

The calculation of the CTT liability would have been as follows:

	£
Farm (£400,000 less 50% agricultural property relief	200,000
Business assets (£200,000 less 50% business property relief	100,000
Stocks and shares, etc.	150,000
	450,000
Less exempt legacy to widow	300,000
Chargeable estate	£150,000
CTT payable	£29,350

These rules have been changed by section 105, FA 1986, so that specific gifts of agricultural or business property are reduced by the relief attributable to the property, and in the case of other specific gifts, reliefs are spread between exempt and non-exempt parts of the estate.

The value of any specific gifts that do not attract either business or agricultural property relief are taken into account at the 'appropriate fraction of their value'. The 'appropriate fraction' is defined as follows:

a. The numerator is the difference between the value transferred and the value, as reduced by the appropriate relief, of any specific gifts of business or agricultural property.
b. The denominator is the difference between the unreduced value transferred and the unreduced value of any specific gifts of business or agricultural property.

(Section 105, FA 1986)

This is probably most easily demonstrated by applying these new rules to the facts in Example 4 above.

Example 5

Facts as in Example 4, but applying the new rules.

	£
Value transferred	450,000
Less reduced value of specific gifts of business or agricultural property	100,000
Numerator	£350,000
Unreduced value transferred	750,000
Less unreduced value of any specific gifts of business or agricultural property	200,000
Denominator	£550,000
The 'appropriate fraction' is, therefore	350,000
	550,000

The amount of the transfer attributable to the bequest to the widow is calculated as follows:

$$\frac{350,000}{550,000} \times £300,000 \qquad = \qquad £190.909$$

The exempt part of the estate is, therefore, £190,909, and the chargeable estate becomes:

	450,000
Less exempt bequest to widow	190,909
	£259,091

The IHT payable will be as follows:

On the first £257,000 @ Nil to 50%	=	77,500.00
On the next £ 2,091 @ 55%	=	1,150.05
		£78,650.05

2. *Additional requirements for business and agricultural property relief*

The conditions for these reliefs, as described in Chapter 11, continue to apply for IHT purposes, in respect of transfers made on or after 18 March 1986, but additional conditions now have to be satisfied before relief is due in respect of gifts of business or agricultural property which, when made, were potentially exempt transfers, but which become chargeable transfers as a result of the death of the donor within seven years of the date of the gift.

Relief will continue to be available in calculating the IHT payable, provided the donee has continued to own the property throughout the period from the date of the gift to the date of the donor's death, or the date of the donee's death if earlier, and on the assumption that, had the donee made a transfer of the property immediately prior to the donor's death, or his own death if he pre-deceases the donor, the donee would qualify for business or agricultural property relief.

If only part of the property can satisfy these additional conditions, then relief is only allowed on that part of the property that satisfies these additional conditions.

Special rules are introduced to deal with replacement property, which allow property acquired within 12 months of the disposal of part or all of the original property, where both the sale and purchase are at arm's length, to be treated in substitution for the original gifted property.

(Paras 21 and 22, Sch. 19, FA 1986)

One of the general exclusions from business property relief under the original provisions (see Chapter 11) was the business of dealing in or holding investments. There is an exception for stock-jobbing businesses in the UK (Section 105(3), CTTA 1984). As a result of the recent Stock Exchange reforms — 'the Big Bang' — there will be no distinction between brokers and jobbers. It is provided that, following this reform, the relief previously available to stock-jobbers will now be available to 'marketmakers', although it is possible for the Inland Revenue to add further categories by Statutory Instrument.

(Section 106, FA 1986)

A similar amendment has been made in relation to the provisions dealing with payment by interest-free instalments.

(Section 107, FA 1986)

SETTLED PROPERTY

The old CTT rules in relation to settled property remain virtually intact under the new IHT regime. These were fully described in Chapter 13. The important points to note are as follows:

a. Gifts into settlements remain chargeable transfers, i.e. not PETs, but are chargeable initially at half the death-rate scale. Example 1 demonstrated the way in which additional IHT could become payable if the transferor should die within seven years of making the gift.

b. Only gifts to the favoured settlements, accumulation and maintenance settlements, and disabled trusts are treated as PETs.

c. The termination of an interest in possession remains chargeable to IHT, but at 50% of the death-rate scale initially.

d. The only significant change as far as discretionary trusts are concerned is the reduction of the aggregation period for previous transfers made by the settlor from ten years to seven years. The periodic charge remains at every ten years.

(Para. 43, Sch. 19, FA 1986)

e. Exit charges arising in the early years of a settlement may have to be revised if the settlor dies soon after making the settlement, such that PETs made within seven years before the settlement was created become chargeable transfers.

INSURANCE SCHEMES

During recent years, many CTT avoidance schemes were marketed by insurance companies, such as PETA plans, inheritance trusts and discounted gift schemes. The new 'gifts with reservation' rules have put an end to such schemes, with effect from 18 March 1986, although policies entered into before that date are not affected.

Gifts involving insurance policies that reserve a benefit to the donor effected on or after the 18 March 1986 will be treated in exactly the same way as any other gift. Gifts made to an individual will give rise to no immediate charge to IHT, but gifts to companies or trusts, other than the favoured trusts, will give rise to an immediate charge to IHT.

When the donor dies, special rules will apply. The gift will be treated for the purposes of the charge to IHT on death as having been made when the reservation was released, or if later, the enjoyment ceased, as follows:

a. If the reservation was released *more* than seven years prior to the death of the donor, no charge to IHT arises.
b. If the reservation was released *less* than seven years prior to the death of the donor, the gift will be taxed as if it had been made at the time of the release at its value at that time. Any tax paid at the time of the original gift will be allowed as a credit against this tax charge.
c. If the reservation is not released in the lifetime of the donor, the gift will be taxed as part of the donor's estate at the date of death value. As in (b), credit will be given for any tax paid on the original gift.

Exercise 14

1. How long is the cumulation period under inheritance tax?
2. What do you understand by the term 'taper relief'?
3. What gifts can be treated as 'potentially exempt transfers', and what gifts remain as 'chargeable transfers'?
4. What annual or other exemptions available for CTT purposes remain available for inheritance tax?
5. What do you understand by the term 'gifts with reservation of benefit'?
6. Has the Inland Revenue given any examples of the 'gifts with reservation of benefit', and, if so, what are these?
7. Under what circumstances can a donor continue to occupy a property which he has gifted without this being treated as a gift with reservation?
8. Describe the tracing procedure which applies in connection with gifts with reservation of benefit.
9. What new rules have been introduced to deal with debts outstanding at the date of death?
10. How have the rules in relation to partially exempt estates been changed?
11. What additional conditions now have to be satisfied in relation to business and agricultural property reliefs?

15
Capital Gains Tax

A full description of the provisions relating to capital gains tax is outside the scope of this book. A basic knowledge of capital gains tax has been assumed and this chapter will concentrate upon the provisions as applied to personal representatives and trustees. The method of computation of gains and losses will not be described, except where this is relevant to the tax payable by the personal representatives or trustees.

RATE OF TAX PAYABLE AND EXEMPTIONS

The rate of capital gains tax (CGT) is currently 30 per cent of the taxable gains for the year of assessment. The taxable gains represent the chargeable gains for the year of assessment less the available exemption for that year. The chargeable gains for any year of assessment are the total gains for that year less the total losses for that year or losses unused from an earlier year. The position regarding losses and exemptions is best explained separately for personal representatives and trustees.

Personal representatives

The personal representatives will be responsible for the agreement and payment of any CGT liability due up to the date of death. The normal rule that losses unrelieved for an earlier year can be set off against gains for a later year applies, but also, losses sustained in the year of death may be carried back and be set against any taxable gains arising in the three years of assessment prior to the year in which the deceased died, taking later years of assessment first. (Section 49(2), CGTA 1979)

Losses carried forward or back under the above rules are only set off to the extent required to reduce the taxable gains for the year to an amount equivalent to the exempt amount for the year of assessment. (Section 5(4), CGTA 1979)

Example 1

Mr A died on 1 August 1985. His chargeable gains or allowable losses for the relevant years of assessment were as follows:

1985/86 — to date of death	Loss	£5,000
1984/85	Gains	£7,600
1983/84	Gains	£12,500
1982/83	Gains	£8,000

Mr A had unrelieved losses at 5 April 1982 of £4,500.

The taxable gains of Mr *A* deceased for the four years of assessment to the date of death are as follows:

	£	£
1985/86 Allowable loss		5,000
Less Carried back		5,000
Taxable		Nil
1984/85 Chargeable gains		7,600
Less Exempt amount	5,600	
Losses brought back	2,000	7,600
Taxable		Nil
1983/84 Chargeable gains		12,500
Less Exempt amount	5,300	
Loss carried back	3,000	
Loss carried forward	1,500	9,800
Taxable		£2,700
1982/83 Chargeable gains		8,000
Less Exempt amount	5,000	
Losses brought forward	3,000	8,000
		Nil

If there were losses unrelieved at the date of death, either sustained in the year or brought forward from earlier years, these cannot be carried forward to future years.

If the personal representatives make chargeable gains during the course of administering the estate (see later in this chapter) they are entitled to the exempt amount applicable to individuals for the year of death and the following two years of assessment. In the above example, the personal representatives of Mr *A* would be entitled to an exempt amount of £5,900 for the year 1985/86 and the exempt amount applicable to individuals for the years 1986/87 and 1987/88. Thereafter, if the estate is still in the course of administration and the personal representatives make chargeable gains they will be wholly taxable at 30 per cent as no exempt amount is available. It is advantageous for personal representatives, therefore, to realize chargeable gains before the beginning of the year of assessment for which no exempt amount is due in order to minimize the CGT payable out of the estate.

(Paragraph 4, Schedule 1, CGTA 1979)

Trustees

Losses sustained by trustees on actual or deemed disposals (see later in this chapter) can be set off against gains arising in the same year of assessment, or if there is a loss overall for a year of assessment, the loss can be carried forward for set off against gains arising in subsequent years. As with personal representatives above, a loss carried forward is only set off to the extent necessary to reduce the taxable gains for the year of assessment to an amount equivalent to the exempt amount for that year.

(Section 5(4), CGTA 1979)

The exempt amount available to trustees depends upon the nature and number of settlements, as follows:

Type of settlement	*Exempt amount*
a. Single settlement for mentally disabled person or a person in receipt of an attendance allowance	As for individuals

b. More than one qualifying settlement within (a) above, i.e. settlements made by the same settlor	Amount for individuals divided by number of qualifying settlements. Minimum amount = 1/10 × amount for individuals.
c. Settlements generally:	
i Settlements made before 7 June 1978	½ × amount for individuals
ii. Single settlement made after 6 June 1978	½ × amount for individuals
iii. More than one qualifying settlement made after 6 June, i.e. settlements made by the same settlor	As for (b) above

PERSONAL REPRESENTATIVES AND TRUSTEES

The remainder of this chapter concentrates on capital gains tax as it affects personal representatives and trustees. Since it was first introduced in 1965 capital gains tax as it is applied to personal representatives and trustees has been amended significantly by successive Finance Acts and it should therefore immediately be stated that this chapter states the law as it is now in force. In many situations the law was quite different formerly, but the present chapter is concerned only with the position which obtains at the present time.

It is of crucial importance to distinguish firstly in considering the effect of capital gains tax between personal representatives, trustees, and bare trustees. Personal representatives, are of course, executors and administrators and they are to be considered for capital gains tax purposes as personal representatives for so long as they are acting in the actual administration of a deceased's estate. Where such an estate is immediately distributable there comes a point during the administration at which personal representatives are merely holding assets which can be released to the beneficiaries. At this point the personal representatives become bare trustees for capital gains tax purposes.

'Bare trustees' are those who hold property as mere nominees for other persons. Thus where an individual transfers his investments to an institution which undertakes to manage them under an investment management agreement or a deed of declaration of trust, the institution holds the investments as bare trustee for the original owner who remains the equitable (though not the legal) owner. Trustees and personal representatives become bare trustees at all times during the administration of estates, trusts and settlements when they are merely holding trust property on behalf of persons who are absolutely entitled to it. Thus personal representatives and trustees are in fact bare trustees in all the following circumstances:

a. where they have appropriated the residue of a distributable estate to a residuary beneficiaries' account;
b. where they hold trust property on behalf of a beneficiary whose interest is vested but whose legacy or other interest is not payable until he attains a specified age;
c. where they hold property on behalf of a minor who is unable to give a valid receipt and must therefore wait until he attains the age of majority;
d. where trustees hold trust property on behalf of residuary beneficiaries when a life interest has terminated.

Examples (a), (b) and (c) are clear enough but some difficulty may be experienced in relation to (d). The important point here is that immediately a life tenant has died and provided that no legacies (as distinct from shares of residue) then become payable, the trustees then become bare trustees for the beneficiaries. To the extent that legacies are payable they remain trustees so far as the sale of chargeable assets to satisfy the legacies is affected, but they are bare trustees so far as all other disposals are concerned. The capital gains tax legislation provides that this rule applies notwithstanding the fact that there may arise the necessity to raise money out of the trust assets to pay capital transfer tax and administration expenses. Whilst this may be illogical, it certainly simplifies the position (as will be appreciated below when the taxable status of personal representatives, trustees and bare trustees is compared).

Broadly speaking, the term 'trustees' for capital gains tax purposes applies to all trustees who do not fall within the definitions of personal representatives or of bare trustees outlined above. It will be appreciated that at the point where personal representatives become bare trustees in a distributable estate, they become trustees in an estate which is not immediately distributable but involves a life or other interest which does not immediately vest in possession. The fact that the personal representatives have become trustees of such an estate should be evidenced by a bookkeeping entry whereby assets are transferred from the general estate to a residuary trust fund. Similarly, bookkeeping entries of this type are required when personal representatives become bare trustees in a distributable estate to effect the transfer of assets from the general estate to a residuary beneficiaries' account. It is thought that where bookkeeping entries of this type are not made, the Inland Revenue could argue that disposals were made in the general estate by personal representatives, and there are occasions when this would involve the charging of capital gains tax which would not otherwise be payable.

Notional disposals

At the beginning of this chapter reference was made to disposals for capital gains tax purposes. In the case of personal representatives and trustees notional disposals must also be considered. A notional disposal is a disposal which is deemed to take place for capital gains tax purposes although there is no actual sale of chargeable assets. Some notional disposals give rise to taxable gains and allowable losses whilst others are considered as giving rise to gains and losses which are non-taxable or non-allowable as the case may be. Most of the remainder of this chapter will be concerned with the capital gains tax considerations which are applicable to personal representatives, bare trustees and trustees, and these considerations will include the occasions on which notional disposals occur

PERSONAL REPRESENTATIVES

Actual disposals of deceased

It is of course the duty of the personal representatives to settle the capital gains tax position of the deceased for the tax year in which he died and for all earlier years where assessments may be outstanding. In this respect the personal representative stands in the shoes of the deceased and therefore ranks as an individual for capital gains tax purposes with the result that the reliefs applicable to individuals are available. This, however, only applies to disposals effected by the deceased personally prior to his death (see also the paragraph on personal representatives on p. 234).

Actual disposals of personal representatives

The personal representatives of a deceased person become a separate taxable body from the date of death of the deceased. Personal representatives are always liable to capital gains tax at the rate of 30 per cent, except in the year of death and the next two years, when the method of computing capital gains tax for individuals may be used as illustrated in Example 1 above.

During the administration of an estate sales of chargeable assets carried out by the personal representatives will give rise to capital gains and losses in the normal way. At 5 April each year the personal representatives must calculate the net overall gain or loss for the tax year in question. Any net gain so calculated will be liable to tax whilst any net overall loss is carried forward to future years. It is no longer possible for personal representatives to carry losses back either before the death of the deceased or to earlier tax years falling within the administration of the estate. If, at the completion of the administration period, there is an overall net loss for the year in which the administration is completed, then that loss remains unrelieved and is simply 'lost'. Under no circumstances can such a loss be carried forward either to residuary beneficiaries (in a distributable estate) or to trustees of the residue (in an estate where there is a life or other limited interest).

Where investments are sold by personal representatives, following the decision in *IRC* v. *Exors. of Dr Robert Richards* (1971), the personal representatives may add to the probate value of such investments an appropriate part of the cost of obtaining representation and title to the assets of the estate. This addition will, by increasing the probate value, serve to reduce capital gains or increase capital losses on sales of investments.

Following discussions between the Inland Revenue and representative bodies, the Inland Revenue issued a statement of practice, SP7/81, in which it was indicated that in relation to estates of up to £400,000 the Inland Revenue will accept additions to the probate value of assets sold for the costs of establishing title based on the scale shown below or the actual expenditure incurred. For estates of over £400,000 the allowable costs must be separately negotiated with the Inland Revenue.

Gross value of estate	*Allowable expenditure*
a. Up to £20,000	1.5% of the probate value of the assets sold by the personal representatives.
b. Between £20,001 and £30,000	A fixed amount of £300 divided between all the assets in the estate in proportion to their probate values.
c. Between £30,001 and £150,000	1% of the probate value of the assets sold by the personal representatives.
d. Between £150,001 and £200,000	A fixed amount of £1,500 divided between all assets as in (2) above.
e. Between £200,001 and £400,000	0.75% of the probate value of the assets sold by the personal representatives.

Losses on investments can in some circumstances be claimed as a deduction from the value of the estate for capital transfer tax purposes. Where such a deduction is claimed, the realized value of the investments sold becomes their probate value for capital gains tax purposes. Such a loss will normally only arise in respect of brokerage and the 'Richards' allowance.

Notional disposals

Personal representatives are never involved in any situation where a notional disposal can occur provided that they remain personal representatives as defined earlier in this chapter for capital gains tax purposes. They do, however, acquire all chargeable assets held by a deceased person at their probate values so that the capital gains and losses on the disposals effected by the personal representatives are calculated by reference to the values of the assets concerned at the date of death of the deceased. The cost of the chargeable assets still held by the deceased at the time of his death is therefore totally irrelevant. The death of an individual is no longer a chargeable event for capital gains tax purposes. (Section 49(2), CGTA 1979)

BARE TRUSTEES

Actual disposals

Where chargeable assets are disposed of by bare trustees, the capital gain or loss is considered to be the capital gain or loss for tax purposes of the beneficiary or beneficiaries concerned. There is thus no question of the bare trustees having any liability as such to capital gains tax. This follows from the general rule that where trustees are effectively nominees (and therefore bare trustees) they are merely acting as agents of the beneficiaries in effecting sales of chargeable assets. Any capital gains tax payable will be the liability of the beneficiaries concerned and will be assessed by reference to the circumstances of the beneficiaries. (Section 46, CGTA 1979)

There is one case, however, where the bare trustees, although the capital gains tax is not assessable on them, may be called upon to meet the capital gains tax liability. This is the case where the trustees are holding trust property for a minor who is absolutely entitled and who is unable to have the trust property transferred into his name since he cannot give a receipt. In such circumstances it is the duty of the trustees to supply the beneficiary each year with full details of all transactions carried out on his behalf so that any capital gains tax payable by the beneficiary can be calculated by reference to the circumstances of the beneficiary. Any tax which is so payable may be paid by the trustees out of the trust funds which they are holding for the beneficiary.

Notional disposals

There are no circumstances under which bare trustees are involved in a notional disposal. As bare trustees they are merely the nominees of the true owner, and none of circumstances under which trustees are involved in a notional disposal is applicable to bare trustees. Frequently, however, the event which converts trustees to bare trustees is itself a notional disposal, but this disposal is a disposal of the trustees (see below).

TRUSTEES

Actual disposals

The trustees of an estate or settlement represent one continuing body for tax purposes notwithstanding the fact that individual trustees may retire and others may be appointed. That body is treated as being resident and ordinarily resident in the UK unless the general administration of the trust is normally carried on outside the UK *and* the trustees (or a majority of them) are not resident or not ordinarily resident in the UK.   (Section 52(1), CGTA 1979)

If the trustees dispose of assets during the normal course of administering the trust, a charge to capital gains tax may arise. There are three possible rates of charge as described in the paragraph on trustees on pp. 235 and 236.

Where a notional disposal occurs which gives rise to a taxable gain or an allowable loss (see below), that gain or loss is to be aggregated with the gains and losses arising from actual disposals in the tax year in question in order to arrive at a net overall capital gain or loss for the year. If trustees are carrying forward a net loss when their trusteeship ends and beneficiaries become absolutely entitled to the trust assets, that loss may be carried forward to the beneficiaries themselves. The position of trustees in this respect is to be contrasted with that of personal representatives who can never carry losses forward except for their own benefit.   (Section 54(4), CGTA 1979)

Notional disposals

There are certain occurrences which give rise to notional disposals of trustees and these are considered in some detail below.

(a)   On the death of a life tenant

At the date of death of a life tenant who is in receipt of trust income there is a notional disposal of the trust assets. Where the life tenant concerned is one of several life tenants who are in receipt of the income of an undivided trust fund, the notional disposal is restricted to that fraction of the trust assets which corresponds to the fraction of the trust income which the life tenant has enjoyed. Thus on the death of a life tenant who has during his life received a one-quarter share of the income of an undivided trust fund, there is a notional disposal as to a one-quarter share of each chargeable asset comprised within the fund.

The whole of any gain or loss which arises as a result of the notional disposal which occurs on the death of a life tenant is, however, in all circumstances non-taxable or non-allowable as the case may be. To all intents and purposes, therefore, the notional disposal merely serves to provide new acquisition values for the assets which are subject to the disposal.   (Section 55(1), CGTA 1979)

The following brief examples conveniently summarize the rules outlined above:

(i)   *A* who is sole life tenant of a trust fund dies and the fund then passes to *Z* absolutely. The death of *A* gives rise to a notional disposal but the gain or loss which accrues to the trustees is entirely non-taxable or non-allowable. *Z* acquires the trust assets at their values on the date of death of *A*.

(ii)   *B* is life tenant as to a one-third share of an undivided trust fund of which there are two other life tenants. On the death of *B* the income of the undivided fund is to be paid in equal shares to the surviving life tenants. *B*'s death gives rise to a notional disposal of a one-third share of each trust asset, but again the net gain or loss produced on the disposal is totally non-taxable or non-allowable. The acquisition value of each trust asset for the purpose of future capital gains tax calculations required of the trustees will be the sum of:

1.   a one-third share of the value of the total asset as at the date of death of *B*, and

2.   a two-thirds share of the original acquisition value or cost of the total asset.

(iii) *C* is life tenant of a trust fund which on his death is distributable as to a one-half share to *Y* absolutely and is to be held in trust as to the remaining one-half share for *X* for life. There is therefore a notional disposal of the trust assets at *C*'s death but, as usual, the resulting net gain or loss is entirely non-taxable or non-allowable. *Y* will acquire his one-half share of the trust assets at their values on *C*'s death, and the trustees will use the values of the assets which remain in trust as at the date of *C*'s death for all future capital gains tax calculations.

For the purpose of all the above rules, the term 'life tenant' includes an annuitant, a person who is entitled to trust income *pur autre vie* (for the life of another) and a person who is the assignee of a life tenant. The rules outlined above apply to all such persons, and it follows therefore that on the death of an annuitant whose annuity is paid from the general income of the residue of an estate, there will be a notional disposal of that fraction of the trust assets which corresponds to the fraction of the trust income which the annuitant is receiving at the date of his death. This is, of course, the 'slice' principle again, and of course in accordance with the normal rules the notional disposal so arising will give rise to a non-taxable gain or a non-allowable loss.

(Section 57, CGTA 1979)

(b) On the termination of a life interest other than by the death of a life tenant

There are various sets of circumstances which can arise under which, although a life tenant does not die, his life interest in a trust fund is terminated. In general, the circumstances envisaged here will arise on the breaking of a settled trust fund either by release of the life tenant's interest to the remainderman, or by a partition of the trust fund between life tenant and remainderman, or by other deeds of family arrangement.

In such circumstances a notional disposal will arise on the date of termination of the life interest. The net gain or loss which accrues to the trustees will be taxable in the normal way.

(Section 55(1), CGTA 1979)

(c) When persons become absolutely entitled to trust property as against the trustees

There is a notional disposal whenever a person becomes absolutely entitled to trust property as against the trustees. On many occasions, of course, beneficiaries will become absolutely entitled to trust assets on the death of a life tenant, and accordingly under the rules outlined in (a) above such a disposal will give rise to a non-taxable gain or a non-allowable loss. There are, however, other occasions when a beneficiary might become absolutely entitled to trust assets by reason of the happening of some event other than the death of a life tenant. Thus a beneficiary's interest may be contingent on his attaining the age of majority or some other specified age.

In all cases where a person becomes absolutely entitled to trust assets otherwise than by death of a life tenant, the notional disposal which will take place at the effective date will give rise to a gain or a loss which will be taxable or allowable in the normal way. The person who acquires the trust assets acquires them at their values as at the date of the notional disposal (and this applies whether or not the notional disposal produces taxable gains or allowable losses).

(Section 54, CGTA 1979)

(d) Held-over gains

Section 79, FA 1980, introduced provisions whereby gains arising on, broadly, gifts of assets could be held over against the base cost of the asset as far as the donee was concerned. The original provisions applied to transactions between individuals only, but section 82, FA 1982, extended the availability of hold-over relief to transfers to and from trustees. A combination of a hold-over relief claim when assets are transferred to trustees followed by the settled property passing to an ultimate beneficiary absolutely on the termination of a life interest on the death of a life tenant would result in the original gain, i.e. the gain of the settlor, and the gain arising between the date the property was transferred to the trustees and the date of death of the life tenant escaping liability to CGT completely.

Section 84(3), FA 1982, introduced a new section 56A, CGTA 1979, to deal with this situation. This now provides that, where:

i. a claim for relief was made under section 79, FA 1980, on the disposal of an asset to a trustee, and
ii. the trustee is deemed to have disposed of the asset when a person becomes absolutely entitled to the asset (section 54(1), CGTA 1979) or on the termination of a life interest on the death of the life tenant (section 55(1)(a), CGTA 1979), the normal exemption which applies where these deemed disposals arise on the death of the life tenant do not apply, but the charge to CGT is limited to the amount of the gain previously held over.

Example 2

Mr *B* transfers property to trustees to be held in trust for the life of Mrs *C* with remainder to *D* on her death. The value of the property transferred was £10,000 in 1982, in respect of which Mr *B* had a gain of £3,000 which he held over. Mrs *C* died in 1985 when the property was valued at £15,000. At this point the trustees would be liable to CGT on £3,000, the amount of the held-over gain.

It is arguable that in this example the trustees and *D* could jointly elect to hold over the gain of £3,000 arising.

Capital gains tax, as it is applied to personal representatives and trustees, represents a formidable bulk of legislation which, however, must be fully understood if estates and trusts are to be properly administered. By way of conclusion to this chapter it might perhaps be suggested that the very existence of capital gains tax has necessarily complicated and delayed the whole business of trust administration which is increasingly becoming a sphere requiring professional advice and, in many cases, a professional trustee.

ALTERATION OF DISPOSITIONS TAKING EFFECT ON DEATH

The provisions relating to alteration of dispositions taking place on death have already been explained in relation to capital transfer tax pp. 154 and 155. The regulations in section 24(11), FA 1965, in relation to capital gains tax were amended by section 52, FA 1978, to bring them into line with those on capital transfer tax. These provisions are now to be found in section 49(6) to (10), CGTA 1979. It is worth noting that there are, as yet, no comparable provisions relating to the income tax liability from the date of death to the date of the instrument effecting the rearrangement.

Exercise 14

1. Distinguish between the exempt amount due to personal representatives and trustees.
2. What special rule regarding losses is available to personal representatives in dealing with the agreement of the capital gains tax affairs of a deceased person?
3. Explain what is meant by a 'notional disposal' and indicate occasions when notional disposals give rise to a charge to capital gains tax and when no such charge arises.

4. Would your answer to (3) be different if you were advised that a claim to hold-over relief had been made when the assets had been transferred to the trustees?
5. When personal representatives make actual disposals of assets during the course of administering an estate the allowable cost of the assets disposed of can be increased over and above the probate value by an amount equivalent to the costs of establishing title to the assets. How is this amount normally computed?

16
Introduction to Executorship Accounts

INTRODUCTION

An important part of the duties of an executor or administrator is that of keeping a detailed and accurate record of his dealings with the estate being administered, as those who are interested in the distribution of the assets (e.g. beneficiaries, the Inland Revenue) may call upon the personal representative to give an account of his actions and dealings.

There is no rigid uniformity as to the best method of recording the conduct of an administration, and it must be borne in mind that although the system which is contained in this book is the one which appears most suitable for examination purposes and is most commonly employed in practice there are other systems in regular use which should not be entirely condemned.

The method of accounting adopted by the accountancy profession is based upon double entry book-keeping principles. In the case of the legal profession, however, the method usually adopted is designed on a 'cash' basis, and does not follow double entry principles or produce accounts in terms of profit or loss, but deals only with current receipts and payments. Where specific assets are transferred to beneficiaries a memorandum note is made without any reference to the cash value, and when investments are transferred other than by way of purchase or sale, only the nominal value is recorded.

Whatever system is employed must provide for adequate protection for the executor or administrator concerned, and must show clearly the property which came into his hands at the commencement and during the course of the administration; how it has been dealt with; what payments have been made out of the estate; the income that has arisen; the property presently owned by the estate or to whom the residue has been distributed.

Difficulties may arise where life interest are created by will or intestacy, for in such cases the *income* of the estate has to be given to one person, while the *capital* has to be retained intact for another person who will not receive his share until the death of the life tenant. In these circumstances, the personal representative must endeavour to weigh equally the conflicting interests of the *life tenant*, who is entitled to the income, and naturally hopes to receive as much as possible, and the *remainderman*, who is entitled to the capital and whose interest lies in adding thereto, if possible. With this consideration in view, rules have been established as to the apportioning of receipts and payments equitably between the life tenant and the remainderman, which maintain a balance between the two conflicting interests.

Apart from these rules it must be borne in mind that the ordinary principles of double entry book-keeping are applied to the requirements and necessities of the situation.[1]

BOOKS EMPLOYED

The three books most commonly kept by the personal representative are a *journal*, a *cash book* and a *ledger*. In addition, it will often be found necessary to keep *rent records*, a *minute book* and an *investment register*.

The journal

This book is advisable for recording opening entries of the assets and liabilities of the estate, transfers between the accounts within the ledgers, adjustments in respect of profits and losses on the sale of investments, etc., and other items not entered directly into the cash book, e.g. specific legacies and devises. It is important that the narration should be adequate and self-explanatory. In addition, it is common to include an epitome of the will (if any) in the journal, particularly those provisions that will affect the accounts of the estate, although it should be borne in mind that the epitome will not indicate the assets of the estate or the capacity of the estate to pay the legacies and devises stated in the will. The usual ruling for a journal is as follows:

Journal

Date	Particulars	Folio	Dr	Cr
			£	£

It is often contended that the journal can be dispensed with, transfers being made direct from one ledger account (including the cash book) to another, provided full narrations are shown in both accounts. Much will depend on the nature and number of the transactions in the particular estate.

The cash book

This book is ruled with three columns, for income, capital and bank. The personal representative's first step should be to open a bank account on behalf of the estate, and it is advisable to place all receipts into this account immediately and pay all disbursements by cheque. If small payments have to be made, it may be advisable to employ a *petty cash book*, this being kept on the imprest system using the columnar method. Alternatively, these minor disbursements can be made by one of the personal representatives and refunded to him periodically by drawing a cheque on the estate banking account.

1. Reference should be made to the Recommendations of the Council of the Institute of Chartered Accountants on 'Trust Accounts' reproduced in Appendix II of this work.

The income and capital columns enable the personal representative to record any necessary apportionments between the life tenant and the remainderman, and consequently to ascertain at a glance the proportion of the balance at the bank which relates to income, and which to capital. It is advisable that all entries be supported by detailed narrations. A specimen ruling of the cash book is shown below.

Cash Book

Date	Particulars	Folio	Income	Capital	Bank		Date	Particulars	Folio	Income	Capital	Bank
			£	£	£					£	£	£

The ledger

This should be ruled with two columns, for income and capital, thus facilitating apportionments and adjustments between income and capital. In certain accounts, however, only one column need be provided, e.g. a capital column in the estate account and an income column in the income account. In the case of investment accounts a third column for 'Nominal value' is usually also provided.

Adequate narrations should accompany all entries in the ledger.

The usual ledger accounts are as follows:

a.   estate account (alternatively termed the estate capital account);
b.   separate accounts for each investment;
c.   household furniture account;
d.   funeral expenses account;
e.   testamentary expenses account;[1]
f.   debts due *by* deceased account;
g.   debts due *to* deceased account;
h.   executorship expenses account;[1]
i.   legacies account;
j.   devises account;
k.   income account;

Ledger Account*

Date	Particulars	Folio	Income	Capital		Date	Particulars	Folio	Income	Capital
			£	£					£	£

*In the case of investment accounts an additional column for 'nominal value' is inserted immediately before the income column on each side of the account.

1.   In practice, a single testamentary and executorship expenses account is sometimes used.

l. separate accounts for each annuitant and for each life tenant;
m. separate accounts for each residuary legatee.

The estate account and income account are the most important accounts kept in the ledger as they have a material bearing on the distribution of the funds of the estate.

The *estate account* (or estate capital account) is the equivalent of the capital account of a sole trader, and is credited with the assets of the deceased as at date of death, at probate values (corresponding asset accounts being debited) and debited with the liabilities of the deceased as at date of death (liability accounts being credited). The official tax account and corrective account furnish the information from which the estate account and the various asset and liability accounts are thus written up, so that, on balancing the estate account, the balance carried down will reveal the net value of the estate for tax purposes. The estate account is subsequently debited with losses on realization of assets, expenses charged to capital, and legacies and devises, and credited with profits on realization, the balance thereon thus representing, at any time, the capital value of the estate (unrealized profits and losses being ignored). In this way the principles of double entry are maintained throughout. It should be noted that included in debits to this account will be any tax payable on capital gains; any adjustments of book figures to capital gains tax base values will also appear in this account as well as statutory or equitable apportionments.

The *income account* is credited with transfers of income from the income columns of the various asset accounts, and is debited with payments to the life tenant and with other payments (e.g. interest on capital transfer tax) that are chargeable against income.

The books of account are kept on exactly the same lines as those of an ordinary business, apart from the fact that accrued or accruing income is not taken into account until received except where interest has accrued due on (a) loans made out of the estate funds to the personal representative, or (b) advances to beneficiaries upon which interest is payable. On the other hand, full provision should be made for accrued liabilities in order to avoid an over-distribution of income to the life tenant.

The books of account of the estate should be balanced and reconciled with the inheritance tax assessments and then a balance should be struck at least annually on each anniversary of the date of death, and a special balance taken at the date of termination of a life interest and similar occasions.

The minute book

This book is necessary only where there are two or more executors or administrators. Particulars of discussions and decisions taken should be recorded and signed by the personal representatives. In this manner evidence of all decisions is obtained.

Rent records

It is advisable to keep adequate records where the estate includes a number of small properties which are rented by tenants on short-term leases, e.g. small house property. In the case of large landed estates it may be advisable to keep separate ledger accounts for each tenancy.

Rent Record

No.	Particulars of property	Rental	When payable	Date	Arrears brought forward	Current rent due	Total amount due	Amount received	CB folio	Arrears carried forward
		£			£	£	£	£		£

Investments register

This book, though not essential, will be found useful where there are a substantial number of investments. Suitable distinction should be made between narrower-range and wider-range investments, where necessary.

Investments Register

No.	Date	Particulars	Nominal value	Probate value	Market value	How acquired	How disposed of	Interest and dividends					
								When payable	Date received	Gross amount	Income tax deducted	Net amount received	CB folio
			£	£	£					£	£	£	

Business books

In addition to the books described above, if it is necessary for the personal representatives to carry on the business of the deceased, ordinary business books will have to be kept according to the requirements of the deceased's trade or profession. Transactions effected after the date of death should clearly be distinguished from those prior to the date of death. The business accounts should be written up to the date of death and a balance sheet prepared as at that date, the transactions of the personal representative being recorded on subsequent pages or in a new set of books.

Documentary evidence

As in the case of an ordinary commercial undertaking, it is most important that a personal representative should preserve carefully all documents which will serve to verify the entries in his books, so that an auditor may be able to check the items by means of such evidence. Accordingly, all vouchers, receipts, etc., should be carefully filed and numbered, the filing number being entered in the cash book opposite the item concerned, in order to facilitate reference thereto. In addition, all brokers' contract notes received in respect of sales and purchases of investments should be retained for production at the audit.

In this connection, it must be borne in mind that the personal representative may be called upon, by the court or by a beneficiary, at any time to substantiate his accounts, even after the lapse of many years. Every book entry should therefore be self-explanatory and supported, where possible, by documentary evidence.

OFFICIAL ACCOUNTS

The basis of all executorship accounts is one of the official accounts for inheritance tax purposes. These vary according to the nature of the estate, the ones having the most general application are Inland Revenue affidavits and corrective affidavits. The forms may be obtained on application at the Capital Taxes Office, Minford House, Rockley Road, London, or at a Head Post Office. As neither probate nor letters of administration will normally be granted until at least a portion of the inheritance tax for which the estate is liable has been paid, one of the first steps to be taken by the personal representative is the preparation of the official account upon which the value of the estate is declared, so that the tax to be paid may be assessed.

Before preparing this account, the personal representative must ascertain the value of the estate, and make an inventory from which the items in the official form may be inserted. In making this inventory the following steps should be taken.

a. The deceased's private and business documents and books of account should be examined and, where necessary, his books (if any) should be written up to the date of death.

b. Enquiry should be made of all agents who acted for the deceased with regard to all documents they may hold on his behalf, together with any other information they may be able to give regarding his affairs. The deceased's bank statement will probably show most of his income and this, together with the paying-in counterfoils, will form a valuable clue to his assets.

c. All creditors of the deceased should be asked to confirm the amounts of their accounts and a preliminary advertisement may be inserted in a local paper to this end.

RIGHTS AND DUTIES IN RELATION TO ACCOUNTS

Action for an account

Where any person possess a right to have an uncertain sum of money paid to him, e.g. the residue of an estate, he is entitled to bring an action in the Chancery Division for an account against the person responsible for the payment. The court will in such a case order an account of the dealings of the person responsible to be taken at the judge's chambers, the account being supported by an affidavit and vouchers of all items.

Audit under Public Trustee Act 1906

By section 13, Public Trustee Act 1906, any trustee or beneficiary may demand an investigation and audit of the accounts of any trust by a solicitor or public accountant, to be agreed upon by the applicant and the trustee, or in default of agreement, by the public trustee. Application is made to the public trustee and notice thereof must be given by the applicant to every other person who is either a trustee of, or beneficiary under, the trust. If within one month of such notice no solicitor or public accountant has been appointed, the applicant may apply to the public trustee to appoint a person to conduct the audit.

Except with the leave of the court, an audit cannot be demanded within twelve months of a previous audit, nor is a trustee or beneficiary capable of appointment to conduct the audit.

The auditor has a right of access to the books, accounts and vouchers of the personal representatives, and to any securities and documents of title held by them on account of the estate, and may require from them such information and explanation as may be necessary for the performance of his duties.

Upon completion of the audit, a copy of the accounts, with a report and certificate as to their state, must be forwarded by the auditor to the applicant and to every trustee. The Act does not specify exactly what accounts are necessary but presumably summarized accounts are intended. The certificate must state that the accounts exhibit a true and correct view of the state of the affairs of the estate, and that the auditor has had the securities of the estate investments produced to him, or that such accounts are deficient in such respect as may be specified in the certificate. The remuneration of the auditor and the expenses of investigation are to be determined by the public trustee, and shall be borne by the estate unless the public trustee directs that such charges shall be borne by the applicant or by the trustees personally (or partly by each).

Every beneficiary is entitled at all reasonable times to inspect and take copies of the accounts of the trust, the report and auditor's certificate and, at his own expense, to be furnished with copies or extracts.

Audit under Trustee Act 1925

By section 22, Trustee Act 1925, trustees may at their discretion from time to time, but not more than once in every three years unless the nature of the trust or any special dealings with the trust property makes a more frequent audit desirable, cause the accounts of the trust property to be audited by an independent accountant. The trustees must, for that purpose, produce such vouchers and give such information to the auditor as he may require. The costs of such an audit are to be paid out of the capital or the income of the trust property, or partly out of each, as the trustees think fit, but, in default of any direction by the trustees to the contrary in any special case, costs attributable to capital shall be borne by capital and those attributable to income by income.

This audit may be held *in addition to* that held under the Public Trustee Act 1906.

Audit under Judicial Trustee Act 1896

Under the Judicial Trustee Act 1896, the court may, upon the application of any person interested in a trust estate, appoint some person as an officer of the court to act as judicial trustee. In such cases the court will fix a date to which the accounts of the trust are to be made up and audited each year. In ordinary cases, the audit is carried out by the officer of the court, but where questions of difficulty arise the court may refer them for report to a professional accountant, whose fees, as fixed by the court, may be paid out of the estate.

Duties of personal representatives in relation to accounts

The duties of personal representatives in regard to accounts may be summarized as follows:

a. to keep proper, regular, distinct and accurate accounts of the estate;
b. to produce the accounts in which he is interested to any beneficiary at his request, and to keep such accounts up to date;
c. to render to all beneficiaries without requisition a statement of income at reasonable intervals, e.g. annually, and of capital when it falls into possession, e.g. on the death of a life tenant;
d. to allow inspection and investigation of the accounts by beneficiaries (or their solicitors) and allow them to examine and take copies of the vouchers, title deeds, etc., relating to the affairs of the estate;
e. to render to every beneficiary a satisfactory explanation of the state of the trust assets;
f. to employ a competent person to keep the accounts if they do not wish to do so themselves;
g. to employ an agent when such is necessary to facilitate the administration of the estate.

Personal representatives must at all times be in a position to furnish on request to every beneficiary (or to the parent or guardian of a minor beneficiary):

a. full and accurate information as to the amount and condition of the estate property;
b. all reasonable information with reference to all matters relating to the estate generally, and the manner in which the estate property has been dealt with by the personal representatives;
c. proper facilities to enable the beneficiary to verify the estate investments;
d. proper facilities to examine the trust deeds and title deeds of the assets of the estate;
e. the information which the public trustee must give when acting as trustee (see the Public Trustee Rules 1912) as to (i) inspection of the register and documents in his possession, (ii) supplying copies of entries in the register and other documents at the expense of the applicant, and (iii) affording access to all reasonable information.

Exercise 16

1. Enumerate the essential books of account for the use of a personal representative.
2. Give a ruling for and explain the use of an investments register.
3. For what purpose and in what circumstances should a minute book be kept by personal representatives?
4. Answer each of the following questions by means of a short paragraph:
   a. What is the general duty of a trustee in regard to accounts?
   b. What are the objects of trust accounts?
   c. To whom will the trustee account if the beneficiary is a minor?
   d. When should trust accounts be rendered?
   e. To what audit are trust accounts subject?
   f. What are the rights of trustees in regard to the employment and payment of accountants to prepare accounts?
   g. What are the rights and obligations of beneficiaries and trustees in relation to the inspection of the trust books?
5. You are asked to open the books of the executors of a testator who died about a year ago leaving a widow and children. You are told that in his will he left a life interest to the widow with remainder to the children, and that he left a house, furniture, a business and investments.

    a. List the documents and additional information for which you would ask to enable you to write the books up to date.

    b. List the accounts you would expect to open in the books.

17
Accounts of Personal Representatives: General System of Accounts

Chapter 16, on the Introduction to Executorship Accounts, dealt with the various books of account which are usually employed by executors and administrators, and it was pointed out that these accounts should be designed to show clearly:

a. the whole of the property of which the deceased died possessed;
b. the manner in which such property has been administered;
c. particulars of the debts which have been paid; and
d. the manner in which the residue has been distributed.

The basis upon which all executorship accounts are compiled is supplied by the official account, which is filed on applying for probate or administration. The balance shown by this account should equal the net principal value of the estate (provided it does not include any property exempt from the inheritance tax) and will represent the net capital available for the payment of tax, expenses and bequests.

It is advisable to open the journal by inserting an epitome of the will in so far as its contents are likely to affect the accounts or the general administration of the estate. In this way continual reference to the will may be avoided.

The opening entries will consist of:

- *sundry assets*, followed by
- *sundry liabilities*, details of which will be supplied by the official account, the balance being the capital of the estate.

CASH BOOK AND LEDGER

Cash book

As already explained, the cash book is ruled with three columns for income, capital and bank. By this means cash items, which require to be apportioned between income and capital, may be dealt with in a very convenient way by being entered in the appropriate income and capital columns, the total of the two being entered in the bank column on the assumption that all money is banked the same day as received. Detailed narrations should be given for all entries (particularly those involving apportionments) and all deductions by way of income tax etc., should be shown.

It is advisable for the personal representative to open an account at a bank in the name of the estate. Any cash standing to the credit of the deceased's private accounts should be transferred into this account upon receipt of the grant, and any cash held by the deceased should be deposited. All receipts should thereafter be paid into this account and all payments made by cheque.

The balances of the cash book should be reconciled periodically (say monthly in the case of a large estate) with that of the bank statement.

Ledger

By means of the opening entries in the journal, the accounts for the various assets and liabilities may be opened in the ledger.

The first and most important account is the *estate account*, which takes the place of the capital account of an ordinary commercial concern. This account will be credited with the assets at their probate values, including any items of accrued rent and interest, and debited with liabilities due at or accrued to the date of the death, and funeral expenses.

It is advisable to rule off the account at this stage and bring down a balance, which will equal the aggregate value of the estate for tax purposes and will represent the net capital available to meet inheritance tax, expenses and bequests.

In addition to the estate account, separate accounts should be opened for each asset and each liability, except that, in practice, separate ledger accounts are not usually opened for each individual creditor and debtor. (Instead, a 'sundry creditors account' and a 'sundry debtors account', or accounts bearing similar titles, would be opened.)

MORTGAGES

Where an asset is subject to a mortgage or charge, two separate accounts should be opened, namely:

a. an asset account, which will be debited with the gross value of the asset concerned and rent accrued (if any) to the date of death and credited with any accrued ground rent (in the case of leaseholds);
b. a liability account in the name of the mortgagee, to which will be credited the mortgage debt and interest accrued to the date of the death.

When a payment of mortgage interest is made, this will be credited to cash, any necessary apportionment being made in the income and capital columns of the cash book, and debited to the liability account in the name of the mortgagee.

Where, on the other hand, the deceased is mortgagee of certain property, the mortgage debt and accrued interest due to the estate will be treated as a secured loan, an asset account being opened for the purpose. To this account the mortgage debt and accrued interest will be debited, and upon receipt of the interest any apportionment necessary will be made between income and capital and entered in the appropriate columns.

Example 1

Part of the estate of Alfred Mayes, who died on 30 June, consisted of the following.

a. Freehold land valued at £15,000, subject to a mortgage of £6,000 to Thomas Bright, at 10 per cent per annum, interest payable each 31 July and 31 January. The freehold land was occupied by the deceased.

b. A sum of £8,000 loaned to his son, Albert Mayes, secured upon a mortgage of a house, at 7 per cent per annum interest payable each 31 March and 30 September.

The ledger entries in the books of Alfred Mayes' estate would appear as follows:

THE ESTATE OF ALFRED MAYES, DECEASED

Freehold Land Account

			Income	Capital			Income	Capital
			£	£			£	£
19–								
June 30	Estate account			15,000				

Thomas Bright Mortgage Account

			Income	Capital			Income	Capital
19–		£	£	£	19–		£	£
July 31	Cash:				June 30	Estate account		6,000
	Interest for					Do. Accrued		
	half-year	300				Interest:		
						5 months at 10%		
						per annum		250
	Capital							
	(5 months)			250				
	Income							
	(1 month)		50					

Loan to Albert Mayes Account

			Income	Capital			Income	Capital
19–			£	£	19–		£	£	£
June 30	Estate account			8,000	Sept 30	Cash:			
	Do. Accrued					Interest for			
	interest:					half-year	280		
	3 months at 7%			140					
	per annum								
						Capital			
						(3 months)			140
						Income			
						(3 months)		140	

BUSINESS INTERESTS

Business of sole trader

In those cases in which part of the assets consists of the stock-in-trade, book debts and goodwill of a business which was carried on by the deceased as a sole trader, separate accounts should be opened for each type of business asset or liability, as these are assets or liabilities of the deceased equally with those which are in no way connected with his business. Thus, *A* died on 1 January, and the balance sheet of a business carried on by him as a sole trader as at 31 December was as follows:

Balance sheet as at 31 December 19—

	£		£
Capital	9,100	Office furniture	1,000
Sundry creditors	400	Stock-in-trade	5,000
		Sundry debtors	2,000
		Cash at bank	1,500
	£9,500		£9,500

Separate ledger accounts in the books of the estate would be opened as follows:

(1) Office furniture	(4) Goodwill (at valuation)
(2) Stock-in-trade	(5) Sundry creditors
(3) Sundry debtors	

The cash at bank would be entered in the same cash book as the other cash of the estate, unless a separate account is kept at the bank for the business cash.

Should the business subsequently be sold by the personal representative as a going concern, the accounts affected would be closed, the balances being transferred to a *sale of business account*, which would be credited with the purchase price. The profit or loss on sale would then be transferred to the estate account.

Share in a partnership

Where, on the other hand, the deceased was a member of a partnership, the value of his interest in the firm, as ascertained in accordance with the partnership agreement, should be entered in the accounts of the estate as one item in one amount. The method of arriving at the value of such an interest varies considerably according to the provisions of the agreement, but it is usually provided that a deceased partner is entitled to his share of the capital as shown by the last balance sheet, with interest upon that amount from the date of the balance sheet to the date of death.

Thus, the last balance sheet of a firm of which a deceased person A was a member would be as shown below.

Balance sheet of AB & Co. as at 31 December 19—

	£	£		£
Capital			Goodwill	8,000
	£		Furniture and equipment	1,000
A	9,600		Stock-in-trade	5,000
B	3,200		Sundry debtors	2,000
C	3,200		Cash at bank	2,000
		16,000		
Sundry creditors		2,000		
		£18,000		£18,000

One account would be opened in the books of A's estate for *capital in partnership*, to which A's share, namely £9,600, would be debited. Interest from the date of the balance sheet to the date of death would also be debited in the capital column; but where further interest is payable after the death, as under section 42, Partnership Act 1890, this will be treated as *income* and must be entered in the appropriate column.

It may happen, therefore, that when the amount due from the surviving partners is received, an apportionment of interest will be necessary.

Where necessary, account should also be taken of the deceased's share of profits from the date of the last balance sheet to the date of death and of any adjustment in the value of goodwill, together with the deceased partner's share of any undisclosed or undervalued assets, e.g. assurance policies etc.

INVESTMENTS

Cum-div. and *ex-div.* quotations

A *cum-div.* quotation includes interest or dividends earned or accrued up to the date of the quotation. For the purposes of IHT on death, values must be *cum-div.*, so the *cum- div.* quotation will be used for valuation purposes without any adjustment being necessary.

On the other hand, quotations become *ex div.* from about a month before the dividend or interest payment date, which effectively means that the value is *cum div.* less the full amount of the impending dividend or interest, to make it an *ex-div.* valuation. As values for IHT must be *cum div.*, to the *ex-div.* valuation the amount of the full impending dividend or interest is added. The amount to add is the cash amount of the dividend etc, excluding the tax credit.

Accounting for investments

The above has accounting consequences. If the quotation is *cum div.*, that value is credited to the estate accounts and debited to the capital column of the investment account. If the quotation is *ex div.*, then the full value, including the addition of the full impending dividend, is credited to the estate account, but the debits should be split. The *ex div.* value should be debited to the capital column of the investment account, the amount of the adjustment for the impending dividend should, in accordance with best practice, be debited to a separate account. This separate account could be called an '*Ex div.* adjustment account' or something similar. After subsequent transactions have been recorded, the balance on this latter account is transferred to the debit of the estate account. An example of the treatment is given shortly.

THE APPORTIONMENT ACT 1870

The term 'apportionment' is used to denote the division of the income and expenditure of an estate between those interested in the income and those interested in the capital. In the absence of a contrary provision in the will, receipts and payments are apportioned on a day-to-day basis over the period that they cover, the part relevant to the period after death being 'income', and the part apportioned to the period up to and including the day of death being part of the capital of the estate.

Thus, if the date of death is 3 November and on 1 December following interest is received gross for the half-year to that date of £350, the apportionment will be:

Capital: 2 June to 3 November	154 days	$154/182 \times £350 = £296.15$
Income: 4 November to 1 December	28 days	$28/182 \times £350 = £\ 53.85$
	182	£350.00

Note: In examinations it is usual to calculate the apportionment in months rather than days, and only use round £s.

The £296.15 above is debited to the cash book capital column, and credited to the estate account, whilst the £53.85 is debited to the cash book income column, and credited to the income account. It may, however, be preferable to make intermediary credit entries in the capital and income columns of the appropriate investment account and transfer the items from there to the credit of the estate account and income account. Crediting the capital portion of dividends ultimately to the estate account has the effect of maintaining the investment account at its original value.

Interim and final dividends

Apportionment is usually a straightforward arithmetical process, but difficulties tend to arise with dividend income from quoted investments.

Normal position

Where an interim payment is paid during the life of the deceased and a final is paid after the death, the interim dividend will have been included in the deceased's assets, but when the final dividend is received it will be necessary to ascertain what proportion of it, if any, relates to the period prior to the date of death. This is done by taking the actual dividend for the whole year (for the interim dividend is merely a payment on account for the whole year) and apportioning it between the periods which have elapsed before and after the death: the whole apportionment revolving around the company's financial year in respect of which the dividends are expressed to be paid.

Thus, *A* held 10,000 fully paid shares of £1 each in the *XYZ* Plc valued at par. An interim dividend of 2 per cent was paid on 30 June and a final dividend of 8 per cent was paid in the following January, making the full dividend for the year to 31 December the sum of £1,000. *A* died on 30 September.

	£
Dividend accrued to death, 9 months	750
Dividend earned after death, 3 months	250
Total dividend	£1,000

It is therefore clear that £750 of the dividend for the whole year is the capital portion of the dividend, having accrued up to the date of the death.

Of this sum, £200 had already been received by the deceased and would therefore be already included in some form in his estate; the remaining £550 is not receivable until the final dividend is paid after the death, but nevertheless this sum must be regarded as part of the capital of the estate.

In order, therefore, to ascertain what portion of the final dividend belongs to capital, the amount of the *interim dividend* must be deducted from that portion of the *total* dividend which has accrued up to the date of the death, the resulting difference being the proportion of the *final dividend* which is to be treated as capital.
Thus:

	£
Interim dividend of 2 per cent	200
Final dividend of 8 per cent	800
Total dividend for year	£1,000

Proportion of total dividend accrued to date of	
death, three-fourths	750
Less Interim dividend	200
Capital portion of final dividend	£550

The ledger entries on receipt of the final dividend, income tax ignored, would be as in No. 1 Account (see overleaf).

Deficiency of income proportion

It sometimes happens, however, that capital has already received more in the form of the interim dividend than its proper proportion of the full dividend for the year. Thus, if A died on 30 September, owning 10,000 fully paid shares of £1 each valued at par, upon which an interim dividend of 5 per cent had been declared and paid, and a final dividend of 1 per cent per annum was declared for the year ending 31 December, the total dividend for the whole year would be £600. The proportion accrued due to date of death would be three-fourths, or £450. From this sum the interim dividend of £500, the amount actually received before death, cannot be deducted.

In such a case the whole of the interim dividend will be treated as capital, as it was actually received before the date of death, whilst the whole of the final dividend will be treated as income, the entries in the ledger being as recorded in No. 2 Account (see page 261). Again income tax has been ignored for the sake of simplicity.

In both the foregoing examples it must be remembered that the interim dividend is merely a payment on account of the full financial year of the company, and that it has already been definitely capitalized and included in the deceased's estate. Thus, if capital has been over-credited, no adjustment is possible, for capital cannot receive less than the amount of the interim dividend received prior to death. Similarly, where no final dividend is received, since no apportionment of the interim dividend can be made, income receives nothing: *Ellis* v. *Rowbotham* (1900).

No. 1 Account: XYZ Plc

Date	Particulars	Nominal £	Income £	Capital £	Date	Particulars	Nominal £	Income £	Capital £
19— Sept 30	Estate account: 10,000 fully paid £ shares at par	10,000		10,000	19— Jan 31	Cash: Final dividend of 8%, making with interim dividend declared and paid on 30 June, 10% for the full year, £1,000 Capital, £750 (9 months) Income, £250 (3 months) Proportion of total dividend to Capital £750 *Less* Interim dividend £200 Proportion of total dividend to income			
19— Jan 31	Income account		250						
Jan 31	Estate account			550					
									550
								250	
					Jan 31	Balance c/d	10,000		
		£10,000	£250	£10,550			£10,000	£250	£10,550
Feb 1	Balance b/d	10,000		10,000					

Note: Income tax has been ignored.

No. 2 Account: Blank Plc

19–		Nominal £	Income £	Capital £	19–		Nominal £	Income £	Capital £
Sept 30	Estate account: 10,000 fully paid £1 shares at par	10,000		10,000	Dec 31	Cash: Final dividend of 1%, making with interim dividend declared and paid on 30 June, 6% for the full year, £600 Capital, £450 (9 months) Income, £150 (3 months) Proportion of total dividend to Capital £450 *Less* Interim dividend £500 Nil			
Jan 31	Income account		100						
					Dec 31	Total dividend to income		100	
						Balance c/d	10,000		10,000
		£10,000	£100	£10,000			£10,000	£100	£10,000
19–									
Jan 1	Balance b/d	10,000		10,000					

Note: Income tax has been ignored.

Interim dividends received after death

Where an interim dividend is received *after* the date of death and it covers the period in which the death occurred, both the interim and final dividends must be apportioned on the basis of the financial year of the company to which they relate.

Since interim dividends are normally paid *during* the financial year rather than after its close, care must be taken to ensure that they are not apportioned in such a way that a life tenant receives any element of future income, for he might die before ever becoming fully entitled to it. One convenient way of dealing with such a dividend is to credit it temporarily to capital.

Thus if *A* died on 31 March 19. ., owning 10,000 fully paid shares of £1 each in MC Plc valued at par, upon which an interim dividend of 5 per cent was paid on 30 June following the death and final dividend of 10 per cent was paid on the following 31 December in respect of the year to that date, the total dividend for the whole year would be £1,500.

If the interim dividend of £500 is credited to capital, then when the final dividend is received, the total dividend for the year will be apportioned as to one-quarter capital, £375, and three-quarters income, £1,125. As, however, capital has received more in the form of the interim dividend than its proper proportion of the whole dividend for the year adjustment is necessary as shown in No. 3 Account opposite. A corresponding adjustment will be necessary in the cash book, the income column being debited with £125 and the capital column being credited with a like amount.

An alternative method of dealing with the problem is to credit to income at the time of receipt or at each anniversary of the death only such part of the year's dividend as represents the minimum to which the life tenant could possibly be entitled. Thus, on 30 June 19. . it is known that the life tenant has lived for half the year, i.e. for three months after *A*'s death, and it is known that the total dividend for the year cannot be less than £500, for that amount has already been received. No question of overpayment could possibly arise, were the life tenant to be credited with: ³⁄₁₂ths of £500 = £125. The position would be adjusted on receipt of the final dividend as shown in No. 4 Account on page 264.

Cumulative preference dividends

In certain cases it may happen that after death a dividend is declared upon cumulative preference shares, which includes arrears of dividend accrued over a number of years in which no dividend was declared. In such cases, the only point to be considered when deciding whether it is necessary to make an apportionment is the date of death in relation to the period of the profit and loss account *from the credit balance of which the arrears were paid*. If the deceased died before or after that period, no apportionment is required, the whole dividend being income in the former case and capital in the latter. If, however, the deceased died during the period, an apportionment will be required, the payment being treated as one dividend for the period covered by the profit and loss account out of the credit balance of which the dividend was declared and *not* as a series of dividends: *Re Wakley; Wakley* v. *Vachell* (1920).

Thus, suppose that *A* held 10,000 fully paid 5 per cent preference shares of £1 each in the OBE Company Ltd, valued at par, and died on 30 September 1986, no dividend having been declared for the years 1984 and 1985, and that, out of the company's credit balance on profit and loss account for the year ended 31 December 1986, a dividend of 15 per cent was paid on the shares, being the current year's dividend, together with all arrears. Since the dividend was paid out of the credit balance shown by the account for the year ended 31 December 1986, and since the deceased died during this period,

No. 3 Account: MC Plc

Date	Particulars	Nominal £	Income £	Capital £	Date	Particulars	Nominal £	Income £	Capital £
19— Mar 31	Estate account: 10,000 fully paid £1 shares at par	10,000		10,000	19— June 30	Cash: Interim dividend of 5%, £500			500
Dec 31	Transfer to income (contra) Income account		1,125	125	Dec 31	Cash: Final dividend of 10%, £1,000, making with interim dividend, 15% for the year to date, £1,500 Capital, £375 (3 months) Income, £1,125 (9 months)		1,000	
Dec 31	Estate account: Capital portion of dividends received			375		Final dividend to income Transfer from capital of excess of interim dividend credited to capital (contra)		125	
					Dec 31	Balance c/d	10,000		10,000
		£10,000	£1,125	£10,500			£10,000	£1,125	£10,500
19— Jan 1	Balance b/d	10,000		10,000					

Note: Income tax has been ignored.

No. 4 Account: MC Plc

Debit side

Date		Nominal £	Income £	Capital £
19– Mar 31	Estate account: 10,000 fully paid £ shares at par	10,000		10,000
Dec 31	Income account		1,125	
Dec 31	Estate account: Capital portion of dividends received			375
		£10,000	£1,125	£10,375
19– Jan 1	Balance b/d	10,000		10,000

Credit side

Date		Nominal £	Income £	Capital £
19– June 30	Cash: Interim dividend of 5%, £500, provisionally apportioned:			
	Capital (9 months)			375
	Income (3 months)		125	
Dec 31	Cash: Final dividend of 10%, £1,000, making with interim dividend 15% for the year to date:			
	Capital (3 months) £375			
	Less Provisional apportionment 375			
	Nil			
	Income (9 months) £1,125			
	Less Provisional apportionment 125			
	£1,000			
			1,000	
Dec 31	Balance c/d	10,000		10,000
		£10,000	£1,125	£10,375

Note: Income tax has been ignored.

the dividend must be apportioned in the ordinary manner as if it were in fact a single dividend of 15 per cent for the year. It will therefore be divisible as follows:

		£
Proportion accrued to date of death, three-fourths		1,125
Proportion accrued after death, one-fourth		375
		£1,500

The fact that some portion of the profits out of which the dividend was declared may have been earned in an earlier year does not affect the above apportionment. In such a case, the dividend will be apportioned by reference to the period covered by the profit and loss *appropriation* account out of the credit balance of which the dividend is declared.

Ex-div. *Investments*

Where the dividend received is from an investment which was *ex div.* at the date of death, apportionments are made as described above. However, it was stated earlier that the full impending dividend should be credited to the estate account but should be debited to an '*ex-div.* adjustment account'. The capital portion of the dividend received should be credited to the adjustment account, and the final balance on this account should then be transferred to the debit of the estate account.

Purchase and sale of investments

It is likely that during the course of the administration of the estate, investments will be sold to raise cash to meet the estate liabilities, to pay IHT, etc. Sales could be *cum div.* or *ex div.* If the sale is *cum div.*, the purchaser will receive the next dividend and the price that he pays will include a sum on account of the dividend accrued up to the time that he buys the shares. From the executor's point of view, even though the proceeds include income accrued, the entire proceeds are treated as being capital, i.e. the income in the proceeds is not separated: *Scholefield* v. *Redfern* (1863).

Likewise, if the executor purchases investments *cum div.*, even though capital monies have effectively been used to acquire the income included in the purchase price, the next dividend, when received, will not be apportioned but will be treated as being entirely income: *Clark, Barker* v. *Perowne* (1881). However, should the purchase by the executor be *cum div.* but be made after the dividend has been declared, the dividend will be treated as being entirely capital: *Re Peel's Estates* (1910).

These rules are essentially rules of convenience to relieve executors of onerous and time-consuming calculations which would really be of little benefit to the parties involved.

It should also be noted that it follows from *Clark, Barker* v. *Perowne* that the Apportionment Act only applies to assets and investments held by the deceased at his death. Dividends etc. received from purchases made by the executor on behalf of the estate after the death are not apportioned; the whole receipt is treated as being income.

Where investments of the estate are sold, the proceeds are debited to the cash book capital column and credited to the relevant investment account capital column. The profit or loss on the disposal is then transferred from the capital column of the investment account to the credit or debit, respectively, of the estate account.

Expenditure and receipts — capital or income

Broadly, expenses of obtaining probate or letters of administration, collecting and realizing the assets etc. will be chargeable to capital, whilst expenses incurred in administering the estate will properly be chargeable to income.

In particular, expenditure to be allocated to capital will include:

a. funeral expenses;
b. IHT;
c. costs of obtaining probate etc. and of valuing the estate assets;
d. expenses of realizing the estate assets, or of changing investments;
e. the outlay on meeting calls on shares;
f. costs of appointing new trustees;
g. satisfaction of legacies.

Expenditure to be allocated to income will include:

a. interest payable on IHT;
b. interest on loans and overdrafts raised to pay IHT;
c. expenses of keeping the books of account;
d. expenses of getting in the estate income;
e. costs of maintaining estate assets;
f. interest on legacies;
g. expenditure such as rates payable on estate properties.

Where there is doubt as to whether an item of expenditure should be capital or income, it may be wise to charge it to income, whilst crediting doubtful receipts to capital. In this way, when the final outcome is known, it can, if necessary, be adjusted with the minimum of inconvenience, and an overdistribution of income is avoided.

In the context of receipts, the distinction between capital and income can be problematic where distributions by companies are involved. The exercise by a company of a power either to distribute profits as dividend or to convert the profits into capital has been held (in *Bouch* v. *Sproule* (1887)) to be binding on those interested in the shares, so that if a distribution is paid as capital it is a capital receipt, whilst if paid as a dividend it is income. The intentions of the company are therefore very relevant. A bonus issue on shares held as estate capital will be capital, and in *Re Doughty* (1947) a distribution of what were realized capital profits was held to income to the extent that it applied to the post-death period, but in the year of death was apportionable between capital and income. On the other hand, a distribution of the balance of a share premium account is capital: *Re Duff's Settlements* (1951).

If a company gives an option to take a distribution either in cash or in shares, any shares so issued will be treated as being income. Where rights are sold by the executor, the proceeds will be capital by the authority of section 10, Trustee Act 1925.

FINAL ACCOUNTS

Income account

Except in those cases in which the administration of an estate involves no complications or delay or where the residue is left absolutely to one or more persons (without the creation of a life interest), an income account should be opened. To this will be transferred periodically the balances of the income columns of the various asset accounts and of the income column of the testamentary and executorship expenses account. In this manner it is possible to ascertain what income is available for distribution among the beneficiaries at a given date. These transfers may be made at any time, but in practice it is usual to make them yearly, half-yearly or quarterly, as the case may require. The balance of the income account should correspond with the balance of the income columns of the cash book, subject to adjustment in respect of any accrued expenditure or income taken into account (see below).

Income accrued, but not yet received, must not be taken into account, otherwise the personal representative may distribute more income than is eventually received and may thus become personally liable to refund the amount overdistributed.

There are two exceptions to this rule, however. Where the personal representative has borrowed money from the estate, the amount of accrued interest must be taken into account, as the personal representative is under a definite obligation to account for such interest. Similarly, where beneficiaries have received advances from the estate and interest is payable on such advances, the amount of interest accrued to date is taken into account and set off against the estate income due to the beneficiaries.

On the other hand, it is usual to take into account all accrued expenditure in order to avoid an over distribution of *net* income.

Balance sheet

The balance sheet will be based on the usual accounting principles, but for an estate or a trust is likely to fall into two self-balancing parts, one for capital and one for income. If two-sided balance sheets are produced, the estate account balance on one side will be represented by the assets held as capital shown on the other side. The income account balance will be shown beneath the capital, with the assets, probably only consisting of a bank balance, on the other. Alternatively, the detailed assets can be shown in an accompanying schedule, only the total being shown on the balance sheet. It may be considered better presentation to produce the balance sheet in columnar form, one column for capital and one for income. Either way, creditors should be deducted from total assets rather than being shown on the opposite side. If this layout is followed, the liabilities side will only show the capital and income funds, and the assets side, the net assets represented by the funds. An example of the presentation of a balance sheet is included as part of the answer to the following example.

Example 2

Fred Green died on 1 January 1987, and his will directed that particular investments should be placed in trust, the income to be paid to his niece, Violet Blue, for life, and on her death, the assets are to pass to a charity absolutely. The trustees have the power to change the investments and reinvest the proceeds as they deem fit.

The particular investments are:

8,000 5% cum. pref. shares of £1 in Yellow Plc; probate value £1
3,000 £1 ords in Orange Plc, quoted on 1 January 1987 at 73½p to 83½p each
£12,000 6% Red County loan stock. The price on 1 January 1987 was 98 to 102 *ex div*. The interest is payable on 31 January and 31 July

The transactions of the trust were:

31 January   Red County loan stock: interest received net.
25 February   Red County loan stock: proceeds of sale of £6,000 stock, £6,100.
26 February   Yellow Plc: £6,050 spent on acquiring 6,000 further pref. shares.

10 May	Yellow Plc: dividend of 10% on 14,000 shares being two years dividend paid out of the profit and loss account of the year to 31 March 1987.
30 June	Violet Blue paid £650 on account of income to date.
31 July	Red County loan stock: interest received for the half year.
30 September	Orange Plc: final dividend of 8% for the year to 30 June 1987. An interim of 2% had been paid on 1 December 1986.
11 October	Orange Plc: a bonus issue of one £1 ordinary share was made for every five shares held.
21 December	Orange Plc: 600 shares were sold for £500.
31 December	Orange Plc: interim of 2% received on 3,000 shares for the year to 30 June 1988.

Write up the investment accounts for the year to 31 December 1987 and prepare a balance sheet at that date. Assume that the standard rate of income tax is 50p in the £.

Yellow Plc 5% Cum. pref. £1 shares

1987		Nominal £	Capital £	Income £	1987		Nominal £	Capital £	Income £
1 Jan	Estate A/C	8,000	8,000		10 May	10% on 8,000 = 800		600	200
26 Feb	Acquisition	6,000	6,050			Capital (9 months)			
31 Dec	Estate A/C		600			Income (3 months)			600
31 Dec	Income A/C			800		10% on 6,000 = 600			
						C/fwd	14,000	14,050	
		£14,000	£14,650	£800			£14,000	£14,650	£800
1988									
1 Jan	B/fwd	14,000	14,050						

Note that the Apportionment Act only applies to investments held at the death, so only the dividend on 8,000 shares will be apportioned. The dividend on the 6,000 acquired after the death will be income.

Orange Plc £1 ordinary shares

1987		Nominal £	Capital £	Income £	1987			Nominal £	Capital £	Income £
1 Jan	Estate A/C	3,000	2,280		30 Sept	10% = 300				
31 Oct	Bonus issue	600	—			Capital (6 months)	150		90	
31 Dec	Estate A/C		110			Less Interim income (6 months)	60			150
31 Dec	C/Fwd			30		Income (6 months)				
31 Dec	Income A/C			180	21 Dec	Proceeds			500	60
					21 Dec	2% = 60				
						C/fwd $\frac{3,000}{3,600} \times 2280$			3,000	1,800	
		£3,600	£2,390	£210				£3,600	£2,390	£210
1988					1988					
1 Jan	B/fwd	3,000	1,800		1 Jan	B/fwd				30

Note that it would be unwise to transfer the whole income to the income account as the interim received on 31 December is for the year to 30 June 1988. The life tenant is only entitled to receive the full amount if she is alive at that date. One half has therefore been carried forward to the next period.

The probate value using the 1/4 up method is 73 1/2 p plus 1/4 (83 1/2 − 73 1/2) = 76p.

£12,000 6% Red County Loan Stock

Date	Particulars	Nominal £	Capital £	Income £	Date	Particulars	Nominal £	Capital £	Income £
1987					1987				
1 Jan	Estate A/C	12,000	11,880		31 Jan	Interest 6 months net £180			
31 Jan	Interest on *ex div*. A/C		150			Capital (5 months)		150	
31 Dec	Income A/C			120		Income (1 month)			30
31 Dec	Estate A/C				25 Feb	Proceeds	6,000	6,100	
	Profit on sale		160		31 July	Interest on £6,000			90
					31 Dec	C/fwd			
						$\dfrac{6,000}{12,000} \times 11,880$	6,000	5,940	
		£12,000	£12,190	£120			£12,000	£12,190	£120
1988									
1 Jan	B/fwd	6,000	5,940						

The carry forward of £5,940 is 6,000/12,000 × 11,880, i.e. a proportion of the opening balance. The profit on sale is the balancing figure on the capital column.

Interest on ex div. Investments Account

1987		£	1987		£
1 Jan	Estate A/C	180	31 Jan	Investment A/C	150
			31 Dec	Transfer to estate A/C	30
		£180			£180

The estate account will be:

Estate Account

1987		£	1987		£
			1 Jan	Probate values:	
				Yellow Plc at £1	8,000
				Orange Plc at 76p	2,280
				Red County Stock at 99p	11,880
				Interest on *ex div.* A/C	180
					22,340
31 Dec	Interest on *ex div.* A/C	30	31 Dec	Yellow Plc	600
			31 Dec	Orange Plc	110
31 Dec	C/fwd	23,180	31 Dec	Red County	160
		£23,210			£23,210

The cash book and income account will be:

Cash Book

Date		Capital (£)	Income (£)	Date		Capital (£)	Income (£)
1987				1987			
31 Jan	Red County Stock	150		26 Feb	Yellow Plc	6,050	
25 Feb	Red County Stock	6,100	30	30 June	Violet Blue		650
10 May	Yellow Plc	600		31 Dec	C/fwd	1,390	480
31 July	Red County Stock		800				
30 Sept	Orange Plc		90				
21 Dec	Orange Plc	90	150				
31 Dec	Orange Plc	500	60				
		£7,440	£1,130			£7,440	£1,130
1 Jan	B/fwd	1,390	480				

Income Account

1987		£	1987		£
31 Dec	Violet Blue	650	31 Dec	Red County Stock	120
31 Dec	C/fwd	450	31 Dec	Yellow Plc	800
			31 Dec	Orange Plc	180
		£1,100			£1,100
			1 Jan	B/Fwd	450

If it is considered advisable to show the taxation separately, the income account would be:

Income Account

1987		£	1987		£
31 Dec	Tax suffered at source		31 Dec	Red County Stock	240
	at 50%	1,100	31 Dec	Yellow Plc	1,600
31 Dec	Violet Blue	650	31 Dec	Orange Plc	360
31 Dec	C/fwd	450			
		£2,200			£2,200

Note that the percentage rate of a dividend gives the cash amount to be received which has to be grossed up for the tax to give the 'gross' amount. In the case of loan interest, the percentage rate is the full amount from which tax has to be deducted to give the actual cash received.

The balance sheet at 31 December 1987 could be presented as follows:

THE FRED GREEN TRUST
Balance Sheet as at 31 December 1987

	£		£
Estate account	23,180	*Investments of capital*	
		14,000 5% Yellow Plc prefs	14,050
		3,000 £1 Orange Plc ords	1,800
		£6,000 6% loan stock	5,940
		Bank balance	1,390
	23,180		23,180
Income account		*Investments of income*	
Balance due to		Bank balance	480
life tenant	450		
Income c/fwd	30	480	
	£23,660		£23,660

Example 3

John Smith died on 1 June 19.. leaving the following property as valued for IHT purposes:

	£
£1,000 6% corporation stock *ex div.*	626
£1,000 Utopia 8% registered stock	935
Cash in house	56
Cash at bank	562
Life assurance policies	5,250
Household furniture	2,750
Loan on mortgage of freehold property (interest at	
12% half-yearly on 1 January and 1 July)	3,000
Freehold house (occupied by testator)	32,250

The liabilities at date of death amounted to £340 and the funeral expenses were £650.

The whole of the estate was bequeathed absolutely to his wife, subject to a legacy of £275 to a nephew.

The life assurance money was received on 8 September 19..; on 31 October the investments were sold, the corporation stock realizing £645 net and the Utopia stock £984 net. Interest on the corporation stock (quarterly) was received on 5 July and 5 October, and on the Utopia stock (half-yearly) on 1 August. The mortgage interest was received on the due date.

The furniture, freehold house and mortgage were not realized, but were transferred to the widow.

The liabilities, including funeral expenses, were paid on 30 September 19.. and on the same day the legacy was paid to the nephew.

Administration expenses amounting to £127 (chargeable to capital) were paid on 30 December 19..

On 31 December 19.. the balance of the estate was transferred to the widow.

You are required to prepare complete accounts of the estate, with apportionments. Ignore income tax and capital gains tax; work in months and to the nearest £ (see following pages).

THE ESTATE OF JOHN SMITH, DECEASED
Estate Account

19–		£	19–		£
June 1	Sundry liabilities	340	June 1	£1,000 6% corporation	
	Funeral expenses	650		stock *ex div.*	626
	Balance c/d	44,604		Do. – Quarter's interest	15
				£1,000 Utopia 8% registered	
				stock *ex div.*	935
				Cash in house	56
				Cash at bank	562
				Life assurance policies	5,250
				Household furniture	2,750
				Loan on mortgage	3,000
				Do. – Five months' interest	150
				Freehold house	32,250
		£45,594			£45,594
Sept 30	Legacy to nephew	275	June 1	Balance b/d	44,604
Oct 31	Transfer from interest on		Oct 31	Utopia stock – interest	
	ex div. investments A/C	5		transferred	26
Dec 30	Administration expenses	127		Profit on Utopia stock	49
Dec 31	Balance to widow's A/C	44,291		Profit on corporation stock	19
		£44,698			£44,698

Life Assurance Policies

19–		£	19–		£
June 1	Estate account	5,250	Sept 8	Cash	5,250

Household Furniture

19–		£	19–		£
June 1	Estate account	2,750	Dec 31	Balance to widow	2,750

Freehold House

19–		£	19–		£
June 1	Estate account	32,250	Dec 31	Balance to widow	32,250

Sundry Liabilities and Funeral Expenses

19–		£	19–		£
Sept 30	Cash – Sundry liabilities	340	June 1	Estate account – Sundry liabilities	340
	Cash – Funeral expenses	650		Estate account – Funeral expenses	650
		£990			£990

Income Account

19–		£	19–		£
Dec 31	Balance to widow	64	Dec 31	Corporation stock	20
				Utopia stock	14
				Mortgage	30
		£64			£64

Widow's Account

19–		Income £	Capital £	19–		Income £	Capital £
Dec 31	Furniture		2,750	Dec 31	Estate account		44,291
	Mortgage		3,000		Income account	64	
	Freehold house		32,250				
	Cash	64	6,291				
		£64	£44,291			£64	£44,291

6% Corporation Stock

19—		Income £	Capital £		19—		Income £	Capital £
June 1	Estate account – £10,000 stock at probate value ex div.		626		July 5	Cash – Interest for quarter to date	5	10
Oct 31	Interest on ex div. investments account		10		Oct 1	Cash – Do.	15	
Oct 31	Estate account – Profit on realization		19		Oct 31	Cash – Proceeds of realization		645
Dec 31	Income account	20						
		£20	£655				£20	£655

Utopia 8% Registered Stock

19—		Income £	Capital £		19—		Income £	Capital £
June 1	Estate account – £1,000 stock at probate value		935		July 1	Cash – Interest for half-year to date	14	26
June 1	Estate account – Interest transferred		26		Oct 31	Cash – Proceeds of realization		984
Oct 31	Estate account – Profit on realization		49					
Dec 31	Income account	14						
		£14	£1,010				£14	£1,010

Loan on Mortgage at 12%

19—		Income £	Capital £		19—		Income £	Capital £
June 1	Estate account		3,000		July 1	Cash – Interest for half-year to date	30	150
June 1	Estate account – Interest accrued to date		150		Dec 31	Balance to widow		3,000
Dec 31	Income account	30						
		£30	£3,150				£30	£3,150

Interest on ex. div. Investments Account

		Capital				Capital
19–		£	19–			£
June 1	Estate account (corporation stock)	15	Oct 31	Capital portion of interest received		10
			Oct 31	Transfer to estate capital account		5
		£15				£15

Cash Book

		Income	Capital	Bank			Income	Capital	Bank
19–		£	£	£	19–		£	£	£
June 1	Estate account		618	618	June 1	Sundry liabilities		340	340
July 1	Mortgage – interest for half-year to date:				Sept 30	Funeral expenses		650	650
	Capital (5 months)		150	180	Dec 30	Legacy to nephew		275	275
	Income (1 month)	30			Dec 31	Administration expenses		127	127
July 5	Corporation stock: Interest for quarter to date:				Dec 31	Balance to widow	64	6,291	6,355
	Capital (2 months)		10	15					
	Income (1 month)	5							
Aug 1	Utopia stock Interest for half-year to date:								
	Capital (4 months)		26	40					
	Income (2 months)	14							
Sept 8	Life assurance policies		5,250	5,250					
Oct 5	Corporation stock – Interest for quarter to date	15		15					
Oct 31	Corporation stock – Proceeds of sale		645	645					
	Utopia stock – Proceeds of sale		984	984					
		£64	£7,683	£7,747			£64	£7,683	£7,747

Example 4

A died on 1 April 1987 and the liability for IHT was:

	£
Realty	1,300
Personalty	24,700

The will was proved on 30 April 1987.

Arrangements were made with the bank to allow a temporary overdraft to meet the tax payable.

The freehold property was subject to a mortgage of £2,000 at 10 per cent per annum, interest on which was paid quarterly on 31 March, 30 June, 30 September and 31 December. The property was let at £500 per annum payable on 30 June and 31 December. The property was sold by the executors on 30 September 1987 for £38,000, with due apportionment of rent, and the mortgage was repaid on that date. Inheritance tax on realty was paid on the date of the sale.

Included among the assets were the following investments:

a. £24,000 3½% government stock (interest receivable 1 June and 1 December). The investment was sold on 30 June 1987 and realized £16,840.
b. 5,000 ordinary shares of £1 each fully paid in AB Plc. An interim dividend of 5% for the year to 31 May 1987 had been received on these shares on 31 December 1986, and a final dividend of 7½% was received on 31 July 1987. These shares were sold on 31 August 1987 and realized £7,500.
c. 5,000 6% cumulative preference shares of £1 each fully paid in XY Plc. The dividend had been received by *A* up to 31 December 1984. A dividend for the half-year to 30 June 1985 was received on 30 June 1987 out of the profits of the year to 31 May 1987. These shares were sold on 31 July 1987 and realized £4,000.

The executors made the following payments on 30 June 1987:

	£
Debts of deceased	1,250
Funeral expenses	550
Executorship expenses (of which £50 related to income)	200
Bank interest on temporary overdraft	120

You are required to write up the estate cash book for the period to 30 September 1987. Ignore income tax and capital gains tax and apportion in months. Calculations to be made to the nearest £.

THE ESTATE OF A, DECEASED
Cash Book

Dr (Receipts)

Date	Particulars	Income £	Capital £	Bank £
1987				
June 1	3½% government stock, interest for half-year to date			420
	Capital (4 months)		280	
	Income (2 months)	140		
June 30	3½% government stock, proceeds of realization		16,840	16,840
	Rent of freehold property for half-year to date:			250
	Capital (3 months)		125	
	Income (3 months)	125		
	Shares in XY Plc, dividend for half-year to 30 June 1985 out of profits of year to 31 May 1987:			150
	Capital (10 months)		125	
	Income (2 months)	25		
July 31	Shares in AB Plc, final dividend of 7½%, making with interim dividend of 5%, 12½% for year to 31 May 1987 (£625) –			375
	Capital (10 months) £521			
	Less Interim dividend, £250		271	
	Income (2 months)	104		
Aug 31	Shares in XY Plc, proceeds of realization		4,000	4,000
	Shares in AB Plc, proceeds of realization		7,500	7,500
Sept 30	Freehold property, proceeds of realization		38,000	38,000
	Freehold property, rent to date of sale (3 months)	125		125
		£519	**£67,141**	**£67,660**

Cr (Payments)

Date	Particulars	Income £	Capital £	Bank £
1987				
April 30	Inheritance tax on personalty		24,700	24,700
June 30	Mortgage, interest on £2,000 at 10% per annum for quarter to date	50		50
	Debts		1,250	1,250
	Funeral expenses		550	550
	Executorship expenses	50	150	200
	Bank interest on overdraft	120		120
Sept 30	Inheritance tax on realty		1,300	1,300
	Repayment of mortgage		2,000	2,000
	Interest on mortgage for quarter to date	50		50
	Balances c/d	249	37,191	37,440
		£519	**£67,141**	**£67,660**

EXAMINATION TECHNIQUE

In an examination it would be rare for you to have the time to produce accounts for all assets and liabilities of the estate and you should not attempt to do so. It will only be necessary to prepare the particular accounts asked for, and other key accounts needed as workings to enable, say, a balance sheet to be produced.

To enable a problem to be worked through speedily and accurately, the following procedure may be useful.

1. From the question details write up the estate account showing each specific asset and liability, carrying forward the balance being the net value of the estate.
2. When accounts are opened for particular assets etc. tick the entry on the estate account in pencil.
3. If assets are disposed of where no account has been opened, take the profit and loss to the estate account and again tick the entry for the asset disposed of.
4. Write up the cash book as normal, taking the capital apportionments directly to the estate account if no account has been opened for the asset.
5. Where liabilities at death are paid, simply tick the item on the estate account.
6. The income account will be the income column of the cash book reversed, i.e. cash book debits are credited, ultimately to the income account. The income account can therefore be written as a summary of the cash book so avoiding writing up the account on double-entry principles. If an income account is not asked for, the balance on it will normally be equal to the balance in the income column of the cash book.
7. Having balanced off the estate account, a balance sheet can be produced. The items will consist of the balances on the accounts in your workings plus items still unticked on the estate account.

The above procedure should help you to prepare a balance sheet that balances without an undue amount of time being spent.

Exercise 17

1. *A. B.* died on 1 May leaving the following estate:

	£
Cash at bank on current A/c	778
Cash on deposit	1,000
Interest thereon to date	12
Cash in house	20
Furniture etc. valued at	2,000
2,000 shares of £5 each in AB Plc quoted at 550p	
£12,000 5% debentures in XY Plc quoted at 90 *ex div.*	
Loan on mortgage, £4,000, at 6% per annum interest, payable 30 June and 31 December	
Freehold property, in own occupation, valued at £4,000, subject to a mortgage of £2,000 at 6% per annum interest, payable on 31 March and 30 September	
Life assurance policy	2,000
Sundry debtors	400
Sundry creditors	320
Funeral expenses	60

You are required to write up the cash book of the estate, incorporating the following particulars:

May 15 Received assurance policy moneys.
June 1 Received interest for half-year on debentures.
June 16 Realized debtors £350, remainder being a bad debt.
June 18 Paid creditors and funeral expenses.
June 30 Received £15 interest on deposit account. Transferred deposit to current account.
July 10 Received mortgage interest for half-year to 30 June.
July 29 Sold furniture etc. for £1,900, less commission £100.
Aug 22 Received dividend of 10% for the year ended 30 June on the shares in AB Plc.
Aug 24 Paid executorship expenses, £50 (income).
Aug 31 Realized loan on mortgage, with interest to date. Sold the shares in AB Plc at 525p.

Apportionments are to be made in months, and income tax and capital gains tax are to be ignored. Round figures to nearest £.

2. A testator *X* died on 30 September leaving, among other things, cash at the bank, £1,500.
   During the half-year ending 31 March the following payments and receipts were made:

Oct 5 Received on quarter's interest, less tax, on £3,000 government 3% stock.
Nov 1 Received half-year's interest, less tax, due this day, on £5,000 6% debentures in A Plc.
Received quarter's rent of house (let at £300 per annum), for quarter to date.
Nov 10 Proceeds of life policy £1,000 received.
Nov 15 Paid funeral expenses, £100, debts due at death £250, and inheritance tax £2,000.
Dec 1 Received half-year's interest on £4,000 3½% war loan without deduction of income tax.
Dec 23 Received final dividend of 7½% on £10,000 shares in B Plc, making, with interim dividend paid before death, 12½% for the year ended 31 October.
Jan 1 Proceeds of sale of shares in B Plc, £12,500.
Jan 4 Invested £13,000 in 5% municipal loan at 100.
Jan 4 Received quarter's interest, less tax, on £3,000 government 3% stock.
Feb 1 Received quarter's rent of house.

You are required to write up the cash book of the estate and to bring down the balances as at 31 March, taking income tax into account at 29 per cent. Apportion in days.

3. The late Thomas Shannon died on 31 December 19.. and by his will appointed his brother, Charles Shannon, and his solicitor, Horace Jones, his executors and trustees. He bequeathed the residue of his estate to his mother for life, with remainder over to his two children.
   The following is a trial balance extracted from the books of the executors as at one year from the date of death.

	£	£
Estate account, as shown for probate		53,143
6% Universal loan (£20,000 nominal) – Probate value	23,325	
Interest on *ex div.* value	600	
Interest:		
Income proportion		600
Capital proportion		600
Northern Electric ordinary shares of £1 each		
– 3,000 Shares –		
Probate value	7,406	

Dividend:		
Capital proportion		300
Proceeds of sale		9,721
Inheritance tax on personalty and realty	6,960	
Interest on inheritance tax	19	
Testamentary and executorship expenses:		
Capital proportion	200	
Income proportion	30	
Furniture	600	
Legacies paid	200	
Freehold property	24,000	
Rent received		150
Mrs Shannon, on account of income	200	
Cash at bank:		
Income	501	
Capital	473	
	£64,514	£64,514

Provision should be made for outstanding executorship expenses of £40 in respect of legal and accountancy charges (chargeable to income). A quarter's rent of £50 had accrued in respect of the freehold property, but had not been received. Income tax and capital gains tax are to be ignored.

You are required to prepare a balance sheet, estate account, income account and life tenant's account as at one year after the date of death.

4. Set out in tabulated form items which would normally be treated in executorship accounts (a) as capital and (b) as income, and state what course an executor should adopt when he is in doubt as to the nature of a particular receipt or payment.

5. To what accounts should the following items be posted:
   a. inheritance tax?
   b. interest on inheritance tax?
   c. cost of advertising for creditors?
   d. fees of counsel incurred in obtaining probate in solemn form?
   e. cost of warehousing the deceased's furniture, pending its sale?
   f. cost of garaging a car bequeathed to X, pending his return from abroad?
   g. auctioneer's fees for selling the furniture?

18
Accounts of Personal Representatives: Distribution Accounts

In Chapter 17 we have dealt with the general accounting system applicable to executors and administrators. It is now proposed to consider that section of the accounting system which deals with the distribution of an estate.

LEGACIES

Where legacies are payable under the will of the deceased, it is usual to open a *legacies account* in the ledger.

In the case of a specific legacy, the appropriate asset account will be credited and the legacies account debited, while in the case of a *general* or a *demonstrative legacy*, the cash book will be credited and the legacies account debited.

The balance of the legacies account is subsequently transferred to the debit of the estate account.

Where bequests are made of freehold property a separate devises account can be opened on similar lines to the legacies account, but where such bequests are few in number the devises can be incorporated in a combined legacies and devises account.

Example 1

A dies on 31 March. After payment of all debts and expenses his estate consisted of £10,000 in cash, chattels worth £5,000, and a freehold house valued at £53,000. By will, *A* made the following bequests:

a. to his wife, the freehold house and £4,000;
b. to his brother, his personal chattels and £2,000;
c. to his friend *X*, the residue of his estate absolutely.

The legacies and devise were paid or transferred to the legatees and devisee on 2 November.

Show the entries in the books in order to record these transactions.

Cash Book

19–		£	19–		£
Oct 22	Balance b/d	10,000	Nov 2	Legacies:	
				Widow	4,000
				Brother	2,000
				X Residue	4,000
		£10,000			£10,000

Estate Account

19–		£	19–		£
Nov 2	Legacies and devises account	68,000	Mar 31	Balance b/d	68,000
		£68,000			£68,000

Personal Chattels Account

19–		£	19–		£
Mar 31	Estate account	5,000	Nov 2	Legacies and devises account	5,000

Freehold House Account

19–		£	19–		£
Mar 31	Estate account	53,000	Nov 2	Legacies and devises account	53,000

Legacies and Devises Account

19–		£	19–		£
Nov 2	Personal chattels left to brother	5,000	Nov 2	Estate account	68,000
	Freehold house left to widow	53,000			
	Cash:				
	To widow	4,000			
	To brother	2,000			
	To X residue	4,000			
		£68,000			£68,000

Abatement of legacies

Where the assets remaining after the payment of debts and expenses are not sufficient to pay all the legacies in full, abatement will take place.

The entries necessary to record such abatements are illustrated in the cash book and legacies account in the following example.

Example 2

A died leaving the following estate after the payment of debts and expenses: personal chattels valued at £6,000; £3,000 3½% war loan valued at £2,000; £1,000 2½% consols valued at £500; cash £10,000.

By *A*'s will the following legacies were made: to *Y*, my personal chattels; to *P*, £2,000

2½% consols; to Z, £5,000, payable out of my 4% consols; to B, £9,000, payable out of my 3½% war loan; and to C, £8,000.

Show the cash book and legacies account.

Note: The legacy of the personal chattels, being of a specific nature, will not suffer from abatement, as the rest of the personalty is more than sufficient for the payment of the debts. Nor will the specific legacy to P, though since A had disposed of most of his holding of 2½% consols, it will be partially adeemed.

On the other hand, the legacies to Z, B and C must abate (those to Z and B ranking as ordinary pecuniary legacies in so far as the demonstrated fund has ceased to exist or is insufficient to cover the payment), as only £10,000 is available for their payment. The amount required to pay these legacies in full is £20,000, and each legatee will consequently receive 10,000/20,000ths of the the the amount bequeathed.

Cash Book

	£		£
Balance	10,000	Legacies after abatement *pro rata:*	
		Z proportion of £5,000	2,500
		B proportion of £7,000	3,500
		C proportion of £8,000	4,000
	£10,000		£10,000

Legacies Account

	£		£
Personal chattels to Y	6,000	Estate Account	18,500
2½% consols to P	500		
Cash – B (out of 3½ war loan)	2,000		
Z proportion of £5,000	2,500		
B proportion of £7,000	3,500		
C proportion of £8,000	4,000		
	£18,500		£18,500

ANNUITIES

Where annuities are bequeathed by will, the method of accounting to be employed will vary with that adopted for providing the annual sum required.

Annuity purchased in cash

Where an annuity is purchased, the lump sum required for this purpose will be treated as a legacy by a credit entry in the cash book and a debit entry in the legacies account.

The capital value of an annuity is treated as a general legacy and, in the case of a deficiency of assets, an annuity abates proportionately with other general legacies.

Annuity paid from interest on specific investments appropriated

Where investments are appropriated either by the testator's instructions or under the powers given to the personal representative by section 41 of the Administration of Estates Act 1925, it will be necessary to open an *annuity fund account* and an account in the name of the annuitant.

In making the entries consequent upon such an appropriation, four stages may be observed.

a. When the particular investment is appropriated, its value should be credited to an *annuity fund account* and debited to the *estate account*, while a note should be made at the head of the *investment account* to the effect that it is earmarked for the particular annuity.
b. As income from the investment is received, it should be debited to *cash* and credited to the income column of the *investment account*.
c. Periodically, the balance of the income column of the *investment account* will be transferred to an *account opened in the name of the annuitant*.
d. Upon payment of the annuity, *cash* will be credited and the *annuitant's account* debited.

Example 3

A died on 6 January, leaving *inter alia* £21,600 2½% government stock valued at 50 on the date of his death, and instructed his executors to appropriate this stock in order to produce an annuity of £540 per annum for *Q*.

The entries in the executor's books for the first year would be as shown on the following pages. Income tax is taken at 29 per cent.

Estate Account

		£				£
19– Jan 6	Annuity fund account: Transfer of £21,600 2½% government stock at 50 appropriated for annuity to X	10,800		19– Jan 6	2½% government stock, £21,600 at 50	10,800

Annuity Fund Account

		£				£
				19– Jan 6	Estate account: Transfer of £21,600 2½% government stock at 50 appropriated for annuity to X	10,800

Government Stock (appropriated for annuity of £540 per annum to X)

		Income	Capital				Income	Capital
		£	£			£	£	£
19– Jan 6	Estate account: £21,600 as per estate duty account, valued at 50		10,800	19– April 5	Cash Interest for quarter *Less* Tax at 29%	135.00 39.15 95.85	95.85	
19– Jan 6	X's annuity account	540.00		July 5	Cash: Interest for quarter less tax		95.85	
				Oct 5	Do.		95.85	
				19– Jan 5	Do.		95.85	
				19– Jan 6	Income tax account: Tax on £540 at 29%		156.60	
					Balance c/d			10,800
		£540.00	£10,800				£540.00	£10,800
19– Jan 7	Balance b/d		10,800					

Cash Book

19—		Income £	Capital £	19—		Income £	Capital £
April 5	2½% government stock: Quarter's interest, *less* Tax	95.85		Jan 6	X's annuity: 1st year's payment, *less* Tax	383.40	
July 5	Do.	95.85					
Oct 5	Do.	95.85					
19—							
Jan 5	Do.	95.85					
		£383.40				£383.40	

X's Annuity Account

19—		£	19—		£
Jan 6	Cash: Year's annuity, *less* Tax	383.40	Jan 6	2½% government stock	540.00
	Income tax, tax thereon	156.60			
		£540.00			£540.00

Income Tax

19—		£	19—		£
Jan 6	2½% government stock	156.60	Jan 6	X's annuity	156.60

Note: A claim for repayment of income tax may be made by the annuitant where he is not liable to income tax.

Upon the death of the annuitant the amount to the credit of the annuity fund account should be transferred back to estate account.

Annuity payable out of residuary estate

Where neither of the foregoing methods of providing for the annuity is employed, and the annual payments are made out of the residuary estate, it will be necessary to open an income account to which income earned by the residue will be credited, and an account in the name of the annuitant to which the net payments made, together with the income tax deducted therefrom, will be debited. At the end of each accounting period, the income account will be debited and the annuitant's account credited with the gross amount of the annuity. This course should be adopted in the absence of any contrary instructions in the will, or if no appropriation has been made under section 41, Administration of Estates Act 1925.

Thus, if *B*, who died on 6 April, instructed his executors to pay an annuity of £600, less tax, to his widow out of the general residue of his estate, which residue consisted of £60,000 2½% consols, the income, income tax and widow's annuity accounts would appear as follows, taking income tax at 29 per cent.

Income Account

	£		£
Annuity to Mrs *B*	600	Interest:	
Net income before tax, c/d	900	£60,000 2½% consols (gross)	1,500
	£1,500		£1,500
Income tax	261	Net income before tax, b/d	900
Net income after tax, c/f	639		
	£900		£900

Income Tax

19–		£	19–		£
Apr. 6	2½% consols	435	Apr. 6	Annuity to Mrs *B*	174
				Income account	261
		£435			£435

Annuity to Mrs B

19–		£	19–		£
Apr. 6	Cash	426	Apr. 6	Income account	600
	(Annuity, £600 *less* tax)				
	Income tax account:				
	Tax deducted therefrom	174			
		£600			£600

If the widow were not liable to income tax, she would be able to claim a repayment of income tax beyond what was actually due from her.

Where the residuary income is insufficient for the payment of the annuity, residuary capital should be employed, provided the annuity is charged on the general residue of the estate. If the will directs that the annuity is to be paid out of income without any resort to capital, arrears will of course be made good out of the surplus income of future years, and not out of capital.

INTESTACY

Where the administration of an estate is carried on under the rules of intestate succession, a similar method of accounting should be employed to that already illustrated, except that no questions concerning legacies will of course arise.

After the payment of debts and expenses, and when the moment for distributing the residue among those entitled by the laws of intestate succession arrives, it is usual in such cases to open a distribution account to show how the property is to be distributed.

Under the rules of intestate succession laid down by the Administration of Estates Act 1925 as amended by subsequent legislation, no distinction is made between the devolution of real and personal property, so that it is unnecessary to have a separate account for each type of property.

The entries in the books of the estate will be similar to those involved where a will is left, but a legacies account will not be necessary. Where all the beneficiaries are of full age and no trusts are involved an *account of the final distribution,* similar in form to a legacies account, may be opened to show the distribution of the residue, but where trusts are involved the methods discussed in Chapter 18 will need to be employed. For the purpose of the following examples it is assumed that no inheritance tax is payable. Were inheritance tax payable it would be charged against other beneficiaries to the exclusion of the widow, because of the spouse exemption.

Example 4

A died intestate on 5 January leaving freehold land valued at £74,000, personal chattels valued at £1,000 and cash assets £50,000. Debts due at the date of death amounted to £400, funeral expenses absorbed £550 and administration expenses £50 which were capital.

It is proposed to show the basis of the final distribution in the following cases:
a. where *A* leaves a widow, no issue, one sister and a mother;
b. where *A* leaves a widow, a son *X*, a daughter *Y*, and two grandchildren *L* and *M*, who are sons of *A*'s deceased daughter *Z*.

a. *A leaves a widow, no issue, one sister and a mother*
In this case *the widow* would receive all the personal chattels and £85,000 free of costs and inheritance tax, with interest (payable primarily out of income) from the date of death to the date of distribution. One-half of the balance would pass to the widow absolutely and the other half to the mother absolutely.

Statement of Final Distribution

	£	£
Estate valued at		125,000
Less Debts due at death	400	
Funeral expenses	550	
Administration expenses	50	1,000
Amount available for distribution		124,000
Widow: Personal chattels	1,000	
Net sum	85,000	86,000
Balance available		£38,000
One-half for widow absolutely		19,000
One-half for mother absolutely		19,000
		£38,000

b. A *leaves a widow, a son* X, *a daughter* Y, *and two grandchildren* L *and* M, *who are sons of* A*'s deceased daughter* Z.

Statement of final distribution

	£	£
Balance to be distributed		124,000
Widow: Personal chattels	1,000	
Net sum (free of tax)	40,000	41,000
Balance available		£83,000
One-half in trust for issue, subject to widow's life interest		41,500
Balance upon the statutory trusts as follows:		
In trust for X, one-third	13,833	
In trust for Y, one-third	13,834	
In trust for L, one-sixth	6,916	
In trust for M, one-sixth	6,917	41,500
		£83,000

Upon the death of the widow, the sum in which she enjoyed a life interest will be distributed to those entitled. In the meantime, accumulations of income will be dealt with in the manner described in Chapter 18.

Note: Interest on the net sum payable to the widow is payable primarily out of income.

HOTCHPOT

It has already been shown that children wishing to share in the distribution of the estate of an intestate father or mother must bring into hotchpot any advances made to them by the deceased parent during his or her lifetime.

Unless the advances were made more than seven years prior to the death of the deceased, they were under the former legislation liable to estate duty as a gift *inter vivos*, the donee being liable for payment of such duty. Where this was the case, the amount to be brought into account was the advance less the estate duty thereon: *Re Beddington* (1900). It is submitted that the principle in *Re Beddington* applies to capital transfer and inheritance tax payable by the donee by reason of the death, on an advance made within three years of the death.

Example 5

A, a widower, died intestate on 5 January 1986 leaving a net estate valued at £40,000. A was survived by a daughter X, and *four* grandchildren, P, Q, R and S who were the children of a deceased son Y. Two years before his death A had made by way of advance a cash gift of £8,000 to Y and six months before he died he had made a further cash advance of £2,000 to X. Inheritance tax liabilities of £9,400, of £1,880, and of £470 were incurred respectively by the estate, by Y and by X on the death.

Statement of final distribution *(ignoring interest on advances)*

	£
Net estate (excluding advances)	40,000
Less Inheritance tax	9,400
Balance to be distributed	30,600

Add Advances:	£		
Y	8,000	£	
Less Inheritance tax	1,880	6,120	
X	2,000		
Less Inheritance tax	470	1,530	7,650
			38,250

Issue of Y – one-half	19,125	
Less Net advance	6,120	
	£13,005	

Divisible as follows:		
P – one-quarter	3,251	
Q – one-quarter	3,251	
R – one-quarter	3,251	
S – one-quarter	3,252	£13,005
X – one-half	19,125	
Less Net advance	1,530	
		£17,595

The effect of the rule in *Re Tollemache, Forbes* v. *Public Trustee* (1930) is important where advances are not liable to capital transfer tax. Such advances are brought into hotchpot; the gross fund before deduction of inheritance tax must be taken for the purposes of division and the tax must then be borne by the beneficiaries in proportion to their net shares (i.e. after deducting advances) in the estate.

Example 6

A died leaving a net estate of £17,375 after payment of inheritance tax equally divisible between his two sons, B and C. Inheritance tax on death amounted to £2,625 and A had advanced £4,000 to B and £8,000 to C, which being within the nil rate band had borne no IHT.

Under the rule in *Re Tollemache* the net estate would be divided between B and C as follows:

		B £	C £
Net value of estate	17,375		
Add Inheritance tax	2,625		
Advance to B	4,000		
Advance to C	8,000		
	32,000	16,000	16,000
Less Advances	12,000	4,000	8,000
	20,000	12,000	8,000
Less Inheritance tax	2,625		
B $\frac{12,000}{20,000}$ of £2,625		1,575	
C $\frac{8,000}{20,000}$ of £2,625			1,050
Division of residue	£17,375	£10,425	£6,950

Cases arise in which some advances are liable to tax and some are not. The true benefit of an advance is the net amount the beneficiary receives, and so the net amount should be regarded as the amount of the advance for the purpose of applying *Re Tollemache: Re Slee* (1962)

Example 7

F died leaving a net estate of £14,560, after payment of legacies, debts, etc., and of inheritance tax, £21,840, divisible equally between his two sons *G* and *H*. *F* had made advances as follows:

	£
G, five years before death	12,000
H, one year before death	10,000

Applying the method suggested above, the net estate would be divided as follows if *H* incurred an inheritance tax liability of £4,000 on the gift, being the tax he had paid plus the tax under the seven-year rule. The advance to *G* had borne no tax at all.

	£	£	*G* £	*H* £
Net value of estate		14,560		
Add: Inheritance tax		21,840		
Advance to *G*		12,000		
Advance to *H*	10,000			
Less: Tax thereon	4,000	6,000		
		54,400	27,200	27,200
Less: Advances		18,000	12,000	6,000
		36,400	15,200	21,200
Less: Inheritance tax		21,840	9,120	12,720
		£14,560	£6,080	£8,480

In the *Tollemache* case the court was concerned with a fund which had to bear its own duty. This case was distinguished in *Re Turner's Will Trusts; Westminster Bank Ltd* v. *Turner and Others* (1968) where a testator had made gifts (portions) during his lifetime to his son and daughter, which had to be brought into account in the distribution of the residuary estate. Testamentary portions were bequeathed from the net residuary estate after, *inter alia*, payment of estate duty. This being so the court decided that to add back the estate duty would be to treat that duty as part of the testamentary portions and this was not the true position. Similar principles must therefore be applied to the inheritance tax, and the application of *Re Tollemache* will be avoided when residue is bequeathed after payment of inheritance tax.

Hotchpot and partial intestacy

In the case of a partial intestacy, legacies to the issue of the deceased must be brought into account as if they were advances, and the widow or widower is entitled to a further £40,000 (or £85,000, as the case may be) *net* out of the unbequeathed residue less any beneficial interest (other than personal chattels) received under the will, together with the personal chattels, in so far as they have not been disposed of by the will.

Example 8

A died on 5 January 1987 leaving the following estate: sundry assets £59,750, personal chattels £1,000. By will *A* bequeathed the following legacies:

'To my wife all my personal chattels and £3,000;
'To my son *X*, £2,500;
'To my son *Y*, £3,500;
'To my daughter *Z*, £3,000.'

Debts amounted to £100, Funeral expenses £920, testamentary expenses £148.

Estate Account

1987		£	1987		£
Jan 5	Debts due at death	100	Jan 5	Sundry assets	60,750
	Funeral expenses	920			
	Testamentary expenses	148			
	Legacies account	13,000			
	Balance c/d	46,582			
		£60,750			£60,750
			Jan 6	Balance b/d representing residue	£46,582

Legacies Account

1987		£	1987		£
Jan 5	Personal chattels	1,000	Jan 5	Estate account	13,000
	Cash:				
	Widow	3,000			
	X	2,500			
	Y	3,500			
	Z	3,000			
		£13,000			£13,000

Statement of final distribution

		£	£
Residue available			46,582
Widow: Net sum		40,000	
Less Legacy		3,000	37,000
Balance available			£9,582
Proportion subject to widow's life interest			4,791
			£
Balance subject to statutory trusts			4,791
Add Legacies to issue			9,000
			£13,791
X: one-third		4,597	
Less Legacy		2,500	2,097
Y: one-third		4,597	
Less Legacy		3,500	1,097
Z: one-third		4,597	
Less Legacy		3,000	1,597
			£4,791

The amount of £4,791, in which the widow had a life interest, would pass on her death in equal shares to the issue subject to the statutory trusts, as follows:

Statement of total distribution

	£	X £	Y £	Z £
Residue available	46,582			
Less Widow's share	37,000			
	9,582			
Add Legacies	9,000			
	18,582	6,194	6,194	6,194
Less Legacies	9,000	2,500	3,500	3,000
	9,582	3,694	2,694	3,194
Less Previous distribution				
(see above)	4,791	2,097	1,097	1,597
Distribution on death of widow	£4,791	£1,597	£1,597	£1,597

Note: Any inheritance tax payable on the death of the widow is ignored above.

Interest on advances

The questions as to whether interest shall be charged on advances brought into hotchpot, and as to how the income of an estate shall be divided among advanced and unadvanced beneficiaries, depend on the exact circumstances of the estate under review. Thus, in *Re Hargreaves* (1903), where a testator left the residue of his estate between his children, and provided that certain advances made to some of his children should be treated as a payment on account of their share and accounted for accordingly, it was decided that such advances must be added to the value of the residuary estate on the date of death, that the augmented trust fund must then be divided between the children in the trust ratio, and that from each child's share must be deducted his or her own advance. Each child would then divide the income derived from the residue of the estate in proportion to his or her net share of the estate as computed after the advances have been taken into account in the manner outlined above.

Example 9

A, B and *C* are entitled to the income from the estate of their father in equal shares, and are ultimately entitled to the residuary capital equally, subject to a hotchpot clause. The beneficiaries had received advances of *A* £6,000, *B* £4,000, and *C* £3,000, while the residuary estate, exclusive of such advances, was valued at the date of death at £20,000. The income of the estate for the first year amounted to £1,200 before tax.
Applying the rule in *Re Hargreaves*:

	£	£
Residuary estate		20,000
Add: Advances A	6,000	
B	4,000	
C	3,000	13,000
		£33,000
Capital shares:		
A, one-third of £33,000	11,000	
Less: Advance	6,000	5,000
B, one-third of £33,000	11,000	
Less: Advance	4,000	7,000
C, one-third of £33,000	11,000	
Less: Advance	3,000	8,000
		£20,000

Division of first year's income:

A $\frac{5,000}{20,000}$ of £1,200   300

B $\frac{7,000}{20,000}$ of £1,200   420

B $\frac{8,000}{20,000}$ of £1,200   <u>480</u>
                                                                        <u>£1,200</u>

It seems clear, however, the the courts do not contemplate that the rule in *Re Hargreaves* should be in the nature of a general one, and that they would be unwilling to employ it in any case where its adoption would give rise to an inequitable division of the income between the beneficiaries. Thus, in *Re Poyser* (1905), it was decided that where a testator left the residue of his estate between his children, and provided that certain advances made to some of his children should be brought into account together with interest at 4 per cent per annum from the date of death, then the income derived from the residue of the estate, together with the interest on such advances, must be divided between the children in the trust ratio, exclusive of advances, subject to a deduction from the share of each child of the interest on his or her own advance.

Thus, taking the facts shown in the above example, the rule in *Re Poyser* will be applied as follows:

		£	
First year's income of the estate			1,200
Add: Interest on advances:	£		
A, £6,000 at 4%	240		
B, £4,000 at 4%	160		
C, £3,000 at 4%	<u>120</u>		<u>520</u>
Total income to be divided			<u>£1,720</u>
Division of total income:			
A, one third of £1,720	573.37		
Less: Interest on advance	<u>240.00</u>		333.37
B, one-third of £1,720	573.37		
Less: Interest on advance	<u>160.00</u>		413.37
C, one-third of £1,720	573.36		
Less: Interest on advance	<u>120.00</u>		<u>453.36</u>
			<u>£1,200.00</u>

In view of the general rule that interest is chargeable at 4 per cent per annum, as from the date of death, on advances brought into hotchpot, it would seem that the rule in *Re Poyser* should be applied unless the facts of the case definitely point to an application of the rule in *Re Hargreaves*.

Re Poyser was followed both in *In Re Wills, Dulverton* v. *MacLeod* (1939) and in *In Re Hillas-Drake* (1944). In the latter case it was held that the rights of beneficiaries were to be adjusted upon the basis of the value of the assets at the date of distribution, not that at the testator's death.

DISTRIBUTION *IN SPECIE*

As regards the actual distribution of the residue the terms of the will, if any, or the laws of intestate succession must be carried out, but if several persons are each entitled to a proportion of the residue, they may agree among themselves to take specific assets instead of insisting upon a realization of the whole and a proportionate distribution of the proceeds. This involves a revaluation of the estate investments at the date of distribution in order that the beneficiaries may share the ultimate profit or loss on revaluation.

The following is an example of the method of accounting for a distribution *in specie*.

Example 10

A, B and *C* were entitled in equal shares to the residue of a trust fund, the life tenant of which died on 18 February. They had had advances, to be brought into hotchpot, as under:

A, £2,000;   *B*, £1,000;   *C*, £2,500.

On the death of the life tenant the trust consisted of the following investments:

£5,300 5% government stock, valued at 103¾
£1,000 6% corporation loan, valued at 111⅕
£700 blank 5% debentures, valued at 80
500 Phoenix Ltd shares, valued at 104p
360 Manufacturers Ltd shares, valued at 100p

The several remaindermen agree to take over investments as follows, at the prices given, towards their respective shares:

A	£500	Corporation loan
	£700	Blank debentures
	180	Manufacturers' shares
B	£3,000	Government stock
C	£500	Corporation loan
	180	Manufacturer's shares

The balance of the government stock was sold, realizing £2,390, and the Phoenix shares realized £508. The sum of £172.50 was due to the representatives of the life tenant in respect of accrued income.

Prepare an account of the distribution, ignoring income tax.

Statement of trust funds

Stocks:	£	£
£3,000 government stock at 103¾	3,112.50	
£1,000 corporation loan at 111⅕	1,118.00	
£700 blank debentures at 80	560.00	
360 Manufacturer's shares at 100p	360.00	5,150.50
Cash:		
Proceeds of Sale of £2,300 government stock	2,390.00	
Proceeds of Sale of 500 Phoenix shares	508.00	
	2,898.00	
Less Amount due to life tenant	172.50	2,725.50
Value of residue		7,876.00
Add Advances		5,500.00
		£13,376.00

Amount due to *A* – one-third	4,458.67	
Less Advance	2,000.00	2,458.67
Amount due to *B* – one-third	4,458.67	
Less Advance	1,000.00	3,458.67
Amount due to *C* – one-third	4,458.66	
Less Advance	2,500.00	1,958.66
		£7,876.00

Distribution of Trust Fund Account

19–	£	£	19–		£
A:			Estate account		7,876.00
£500 Corporation loan at 111⅞	559.00				
£700 Blank debentures at 80	560.00				
180 Manufacturers' shares at 100p	180.00				
Cash	1,159.67	2,458.67			
B:					
£3,000 Government stock at 103¾	3,112.50				
Cash	346.17	3,458.67			
C:					
£500 Corporation loan at 111⅘	559.00				
180 Manufacturer's shares at 100p	180.00				
Cash	1,219.66	1,958.66			
		£7,876.00			£7,876.00

Exercise 18

1. *A* died on 30 June. After the payment of all debts and expenses, property valued at £10,000 remained for distribution, £1,000 of which consisted of household furniture and jewellery.
   By his will *A* made the following bequests:

   'To my widow, my household furniture and jewellery, and £2,000;
   'To my cousin Charles, £1,000;
   'To my executor, £1,000;
   'To my aunt Jane, my gold watch given to me by my father;
   'To my brother, £500 payable out of my holding of war loan;
   'To my son, the residue of my estate.'

   At the date of *A*'s death his gold watch had already been sold, and he owned no war loan.
   You are required to give the entries in the cash book showing the distribution of this property.
2. A testator died leaving an estate which, after payment of liabilities and all expenses, realized £16,542, excluding furniture valued at £500. He bequeathed the following legacies:

   To his widow, the furniture and £10,000;
   To his three sons, £5,000 each;
   To his sister, £1,000;
   To his gardner, £60;
   To various charities, £1,510;
   The residue to be divided equally among his sons.

   You are required to show the distribution of the estate.
3. *A, B* and *C*, who were all over 18 years of age, were entitled to share equally the property of their intestate mother, there being no surviving spouse. The residue of the estate, after payment of debts and expenses, consisted of the following:

	£
Land valued at	9,000
Shares valued at	1,000
Furniture and chattels valued at	2,000
Cash	15,000

   By agreement between the beneficiaries the tax on realty had been charged against the residuary personalty.
   A agreed to accept the land at its probate value towards his share, while *B* agreed to accept the shares, furniture and chattels. An advance of £3,000 which had been made to *C* had to be brought into hotchpot.
   Show the ultimate distribution of the estate.
4. An estate consisted of the following assets:

	£
Furniture, book value	100
9,000 shares in Commas Plc, book value	31,400
9,000 shares in Full Stops Plc, book value	6,000
Freehold house, book value	2,300
Cash (including £480 on income account)	680
	£40,480

   The estate was left in trust, the income to go to Miss *X*, who died on 31 December 1986, and the capital equally to *A, B* and *C*. *C* was fourteen years of age on 31 December 1986.
   It was agreed that in the distribution following the death of Miss *X*:

   a. *A* should take the remaining furniture and *B* the freehold house, both at book values;
   b. the shares in Full Stops Plc should be transferred to *A* at a value of £5,500;

c. the shareholding in Commas Plc should be divided equally between the three remaindermen at a value of £27,900.

d. Differences on beneficiaries' account were to be adjusted in cash.

After paying legal costs, £120, these agreed steps were carried out on 31 March 1987. Write up the estate capital account and the personal accounts of A and B: ignore inheritance tax.

5. Bertram died intestate on 1 January 1987, survived by his widow, Honoria, and by his infant children, Roderick and Roberta. The estate, as valued for IHT purposes on 1 January was:

	£
Freehold house	30,000
Life assurance policies	11,000
£12,000 Wickham Plc 12% loan stock (interest	
due 30 June and 31 December) at par	12,000
Chattels	3,700
Bank balances	11,300
	68,000
Debts and funeral expenses	3,000
	£65,000

The transactions during the year to 31 December 1987 were:

Receipts:	Freehold house sold for	£31,000
	Life assurance policies	£11,000
	(The loan stock interest was received on the due dates)	
Payments:	Debts and funeral expenses	3,000
	Purchase of a further £40,000 Wickham 12% stock on	
	1 July 1987	£40,400
	Administration costs (all income)	£20
	Maintenance of Roderick and Roberta	£100
	IHT including £28 interest	£1,628

Honoria decided not to take the freehold house but requested that her life interest should be redeemed on 31 December 1987. The value of the life interest was agreed at that date at £8,700, to be satisfied by a transfer to her of 12% Wickham Plc loan stock (to the nearest £100 of nominal stock) revalued at 101 *ex div*. The balance of Honoria's entitlements were paid on 31 December 1987 by means of a bank overdraft pending sale of the balance of the loan stock.

Write up the cash account and the estate capital account for the year. Prepare a statement of the division of the estate residue on 31 December 1987 and a balance sheet on that date after the agreed distributions had been made. (Income tax is to be taken at 29 per cent.)

19

Accounts of Personal Representatives: Trust Accounts and Apportionments

A *life tenant* is entitled to the *income* arising from the trust property for the duration of his life, and upon his death the *remainderman* will receive the *capital*. The trustee therefore has to distinguish carefully between that portion of the property which is income and that portion which is capital, in order that an equitable balance may be maintained between the conflicting interests of life tenant and remainderman. In determining what is income and what is capital there exist a number of judicial decisions which have established rules which may be applied with confidence in the majority of cases.

EQUITABLE APPORTIONMENT

These rules are known as the *rules of equitable apportionment* by reason of the fact that they have been formulated by the decisions of the Chancery judges in the exercise of their equitable jurisdiction. Each decision aims at bringing about a fair and equitable distribution of the trust funds between the life tenant and the remainderman, but it should be noted that where the will directs a particular form of distribution, this must be carried out, the terms of the will being paramount. Many professionally drawn up wills exclude the rules of equitable apportionment but where the will is silent, the rules will apply. The rules have become established through case law, and are given effect to by the courts in the same way that a statute would be enforced. They are deemed to carry out the unexpressed intentions of the testator, in order to give effect to and protect the respective rights of the life tenant and the remainderman.

Equitable apportionments differ from statutory apportionments in the following respects.

a. *Equitable apportionments apply only where not expressly excluded or modified by the terms of the will itself,* whereas statutory apportionments cannot be excluded or modified by contrary provisions in the testamentary dispositions of a deceased person, in so far, at least, as the liability to inheritance tax is concerned.

b. *Equitable apportionments apply only where residuary personalty is left to persons in succession*, whereas statutory apportionments apply in all cases, although there is not strictly any need to give effect to them in the estate accounts (apart from, in certain circumstances, the computation for inheritance tax) in cases where the residue is left absolutely to one or more persons without the creation of a prior life interest.

In the case of the majority of these equitable apportionments the life tenant receives income calculated on a 4 per cent per annum basis. This rate is not permanently fixed and it is quite probable that the courts might direct a higher rate of interest, if that rate were more representative of the current interest yield on trustee securities.

Howe v. Lord Dartmouth (1802)

The rule established in this case is as follows:

Where by will a bequest of residuary personalty is left to persons in succession, any property included in such residue which is of a wasting or hazardous nature must be realized and after payment of debts, legacies, etc., the balance must be invested in authorized securities.

This general duty may also be contained in the will, or implied by statute (e.g. the Administration of Estates Act 1925 provides for this on the death of a person intestate). On the other hand, in all cases of testate succession the real intention of the testator must be carried out as far as possible; therefore, where the testator has expressly or impliedly so directed, the trust must be allowed to take its natural course, to the detriment of the remainderman's interest.

If *residuary personalty* is left by will to persons in succession, it is presumed, in the absence of a contrary intention in the will, that the testator intended an equitable balance to be maintained between the life tenant and the remainderman, so that it becomes necessary for the trustee to convert any property that is of a wasting or hazardous nature into authorized investments. In other words, there is, in such cases, an implied trust to convert unless the will shows a contrary intention: *Howe* v. *Lord Dartmouth* (1802).

Thus, if part of the residue consists of, say, certain copyright royalties, by the time the remainderman's interest falls into possession upon the death of the life tenant the royalties may be of little or no value. Such property is of a *wasting* nature.

Similarly, shares in a trading company carrying on a speculative undertaking may be yielding 20 per cent dividend, which would normally go to the life tenant, but this may not last until the remainder falls into possession. Such shares are therefore of a hazardous nature. In fact, any investment which is not a trustee security or authorized by a will should be regarded as being hazardous by nature.

The rule aims at carrying out the presumed wishes of the testator by preserving an equitable balance between the life tenant and the remainderman, so that if the will shows an expressed or implied intention that existing securities are to be retained, or gives instructions to the personal representative as to the course which he is to pursue, those intentions or instructions must be carried out, even if they are contrary to the rule, and for this reason the rule applies only where *residuary personalty* is settled, and not to residuary realty (freeholds), general legacies, specific bequests or devises.

The rule will not apply to an otherwise unauthorized security if this has been allocated to the *wider range* under the Trustee Investments Act 1961 because it has then become *authorized*. Where a division under TIA 1961 has been carried out, the rule will apply only to securities held in *special range*.

Where *Howe* v. *Lord Dartmouth* applies, the court endeavours to secure that the life tenant shall enjoy the income from the fund that will ultimately go to the remainderman as capital. Thus, pending the actual realization of the unauthorized property and its conversion into authorized securities, an equitable apportionment is required of all income produced pending conversion (with resort to capital in certain circumstances). The principles of this form of equitable apportionment have been clarified by *In Re Fawcett, Public Trustee* v. *Dugdale* (1940), which may be summarized as follows:

a. Where unauthorized property is unsold at the end of the executor's year, the life tenant is entitled to receive interest at 4 per cent per annum (less tax) from the date of death until ultimate realization on the value of the property at the end of the year.[1] In calculating the interest payable to the life tenant the unsold investments are taken *en bloc* as one aggregate fund and are not considered individually.

b. Where unauthorized property is realized during the executor's year, the life tenant receives interest at 4 per cent per annum (less tax) on the net proceeds of realization from the date of death to the date of realization.

c. Statutory apportionments should not be applied, either at the date of death or at any other date with reference to the income from unauthorized investments, i.e. all such income received after death should be deemed to be available for payment of the income to the life tenant.

d. If the actual income produced by the unauthorized property exceeds the amount due to the life tenant under (a) and (b) above, the excess should be invested in authorized securities, the subsequent income from which is payable to the life tenant.

e. If the actual income produced by the unauthorized property is less than the amount due to the life tenant, the deficiency should be paid out of the proceeds of sale of any unauthorized securities during the same accounting period, whether the sale relates to the particular unauthorized security which yields insufficient income or any other unauthorized security sold during the same period.

f. If the deficiency of income cannot be made good as in (e) above, the balance still due to the life tenant must be made good out of:
    i. future excess income, and
    ii. proceeds of future sales of unauthorized securities. Until such future amounts become available, the life tenant cannot be paid more than the income available during the current accounting period.

g. A deficiency of income in any period cannot be made good out of past excess income from unauthorized securities or past realizations of such securities, as such sums should have been invested in authorized securities.

The principles established by *Re Fawcett* may be briefly summarized as follows:

a. *at the end of the executor's year*, the life tenant is entitled to 4 per cent per annum (less tax) on the net proceeds of sale of unauthorized investments during that year (calculated to the date of sale) and on the aggregate value of unsold unauthorized investments at the end of the year (calculated for the full year), *and*

b. *after the end of the executor's year*, the life tenant is entitled to 4 per cent per annum (less tax) on the value of the unsold unauthorized investments at the end of the executor's year (calculated from the end of the year to the date of ultimate realization).

1. Different rules apply where the trustees have full power to postpone conversion, see p. 317.

Example 1 *(Howe* v. *Dartmouth* (as amended by *Re Fawcett*)

X died on 1 July 1985 leaving the residue of his estate to *Y* for life with remainder to *Z* absolutely. Part of *X*'s residuary estate consisted of 20,000 ordinary shares of £1 each, fully paid, in Sandridge Shipping Ltd, and £5,000 3% debentures in Selected Metals Ltd. Both these securities were unauthorized investments. A regular dividend of 10% per annum was received each 31 December from the holding of ordinary shares in respect of the year ended to the previous 30 September, while Selected Metals Ltd defaulted in payment of interest on its debentures for the two years subsequent to death. The ordinary shares were valued at 150p each for probate purposes and were sold at 140p each (net) on 31 March 1986, and the available proceeds were invested in 3% government stocks at 96 *ex div.*, interest payable quarterly on 5 April, etc. The debentures were valued at 90 for probate purposes and at 80 one year after the death, and were then sold at 75 (net) on 31 December 1986, and the available proceeds were invested in 3% government stock at 96 *ex div.*

Prepare a statement showing the income from the date of death to 5 July 1987 payable to the life tenant, and write up the investment accounts for that period. Calculations are to be made in months and income tax and capital gains tax are to be ignored.

Statement of Income for Life Tenant

Unauthorized investments	Available income	Equitable income	Remarks
Ordinary shares in Sandridge Shipping Ltd	£ 2,000	£ 840	Life tenant entitled to 4% per annum on £28,000 (proceeds of sale) for 9 months.
Debentures in Selected Metals Ltd	Nil	160	Life tenant entitled (a) at 30 June 1986 to 4% per annum on £4,000 (£5,000 at 80) which is taken from the excess income from the ordinary shares in Sandridge Shipping Ltd, and (b) at 31 December 1986 to 4% per annum for 6 months on £4,000 taken out of the proceeds of sale.
		1,000	
		80	
	£2,000	£1,080	

Authorized investments	Available income	Life tenant's income	Remarks
3% government stock (5 quarters)	£ 1,132.80	£ 1,132.80	The proceeds of sale of the ordinary shares (£28,000) plus the surplus income (£1,000, i.e. £2,000 less £840 and £160) are invested in £30,208.33 government stock at 96 *ex div.* at 31 March 1986.
3% government stock (2 quarters)	57.34	57.34	The proceeds of sale of the debentures (£3,750) less the amount paid to the life tenant (£80) are invested in £3,822.92 government stock at 96 *ex div.* on 31 December 1986.
	£1,190.14	£1,190.14	

Income from Unauthorized Investments

1986		£	1986		£
June 30	Life tenant (see above: the £80, being taken from sale proceeds, will not appear in this account)	1,000	June 30	Sandridge Shipping Ltd	2,000
	Estate capital account	1,000			
		£2,000			£2,000

(For the other accounts, see following pages.)

In all cases the life tenant will be entitled to the full interest received from the securities into which the capitalized portion of the income from the original capital has been converted, together with the income from the securities into which the proceeds of sale of the original capital are ultimately converted.

The rule in *Howe* v. *Lord Dartmouth* (and *Re Fawcett*) does not apply in the following circumstances.

a. *Where there is no trust for conversion but an express power is given to retain existing investments.* No apportionment of income is necessary, and the life tenant is entitled to the whole of the net income produced by the property until sale: *Re Bates* (1907).
b. *Where there is a trust for conversion and an express power is given to retain existing investments.* Then, if the power to retain is independent of the trust to convert, the life tenant is entitled to the net income arising from the assets retained: *Re Inman* (1915). If, however, the power to retain is ancillary or subsidiary to the trust to convert, the court will apportion the income: *Re Chaytor* (1905).
c. *Where there is a trust for sale and the trustees have full, absolute and unrestricted power to postpone sale at their discretion.* The value of unauthorized investments is to be taken at the date of the testator's death: *Re Parry* (1946).
d. *To long leaseholds* which are authorized securities: *Re Gough* (1957).

It was at one time thought that there would be no equitable apportionment of income on an intestacy, but *Re Fisher* (1943) shows that it is not true to say that the rule in *Howe* v. *Lord Dartmouth* cannot be applied on intestacy, since successive interests may arise thereunder.

Leasehold property

Although leaseholds are examples of wasting personalty, section 28 of the Law of Property Act 1925 provides that where land (defined to include 'land of *any* tenure') is held on trust for sale, the net income until sale shall be applied in the same manner as the income from investments representing the purchase money would be applied if the land had been sold and the proceeds invested in authorized securities. Pending conversion of the property the life tenant is entitled to the whole of the net income arising therefrom *Re Brooker: Brooker* v. *Brooker* (1926). This decision does not relieve the legal personal representative of his duty to convert the property and invest the proceeds in authorized securities; it merely renders inapplicable to leaseholds the rule in *Re Fawcett* as to the *application of the income* received pending conversion.

Re Earl of Chesterfield's Trusts (1883)

This rule is an extension of *Howe* v. *Lord Dartmouth*.

Sandridge Shipping Ltd

Date		Income £	Capital £	Date		Income £	Capital £
1985 July 1	Estate account: 20,000 ordinary shares of £1 each, fully paid, at 150p each		30,000	1985 Dec 31	Cash: Dividend at 10% per annum for year to 30 September 1985		2,000
1986 June 30	Transfer to income from unauthorized investments account		2,000	1986 Mar 31	Cash: Sale of 20,000 shares at 140p each		28,000
				June 30	Estate account: Loss on realization		2,000
			£32,000				£32,000

Selected Metals Ltd

Date		Income £	Capital £	Date		Income £	Capital £
1985 July 1	Estate account: £5,000 3% debentures at 90		4,500	1986 June 30	Balance c/d		4,500
			£4,500				£4,500
1986 July 1	Balance b/d		4,500	1986 Dec 31	Cash: Sale of £5,000 debentures at 75		3,750
				1987 June 30	Estate account: Loss on realization		750
							£4,500

Government Stock

Date		Income £	Capital £	Date		Income £	Capital £
1986 Mar 31	Cash: £30,208.33 stock at 96 *ex div.* purchased from proceeds of sale of ordinary shares in Sandridge Shipping Ltd and surplus income therefrom	226.56	29,000.00	1986 July 5	Cash: Interest for quarter to date on £30,208.33 stock Balance c/d (£30,208.33 stock)	226.56	29,000.00
July 5	Income account	£226.56	£29,000.00			£226.56	£29,000.00
July 6	Balance b/d (£30,208.33 stock);		29,000.00	Oct 5	Cash: Interest for quarter to date on £30,208.33 stock	226.56	
Dec 31	Cash £3,822.92 stock at 96 *ex div.* purchased from proceeds of sale of debentures in Selected Metals Ltd less part proceeds paid to life tenant		3,670.00	1987 Jan 5	Do.	226.56	
				April 5	Cash: Interest for quarter to date on £34,031.25 stock	255.23	
1987 July 5	Income account	963.58		July 5	Do. Balance c/d (£34,031.25 stock)	255.23	32,670.00
		£963.58	£32,670.00			£963.58	£32,670.00
July 6	Balance b/d (£34,031.25 stock)		32,670.00				

Note: For convenience, this account has been balanced annually at 5 July.

Where part of the settled residue consists of a reversionary interest under the rule in *Howe* v. *Lord Dartmouth* the property should be converted into authorized securities. Until conversion takes place (or until the reversionary interest falls into possession, if there is no conversion), the position of the life tenant will not be regulated by any of the above rules as a reversionary interest produces no income. It is therefore impossible to apportion the interests of the life tenant and the remainderman until conversion has taken place or the interest falls into possession, and when one of these events occur, the proceeds will be apportioned under the rule in *Re Earl of Chesterfield's Trusts*, subject to any contrary indication in the will of the testator.

The rule established in this case is as follows:

Ascertain the sum which, if put out at 4 per cent compound interest with yearly rests, at the date of the testator's death would have produced the amount actually realized. This sum is capital. The balance and future interest on the capital go to the life tenant as income.

An apportionment of this nature will be necessary where, for example, A dies and leaves his residuary estate to B for life with remainder to C. Part of A's residuary estate consisted of a reversionary interest in the estate of X, left for life to Y with remainder to A. On the death of Y, the estate of X which comes to A's estate is apportioned between capital and income as explained above; the income goes to B, while the capital is invested by A's trustees, the income it earns going to B, while on B's death, the capital will vest, together with the remainder of A's estate, in C.

Example 2 *(Re Earl of Chesterfield's Trusts)*

X died on 30 September. Part of his residuary personal estate consisted of a reversionary interest, valued at £600. This was bequeathed to Y for life, with remainder over to Z. It was retained until the second anniversary of the death, when it fell into possession, and consisted of £700 3½% stock valued at 90, and £70 cash.

The resulting ledger entries would be as shown on p. 000.

In order to ascertain the sum which, if invested at 4 per cent compound interest at the date of the testator's death, would have produced the sum actually received, the following formula may be applied.

Let x be the amount to be received by capital:

$$\therefore x = \text{value of reversion when it falls in} \ \times \ \frac{100}{108.16}$$
$$= \pounds700 \ \times \ \frac{100}{108.16} \ = \pounds647.19$$

The £108.16 is £100 plus 4% p.a. = £104 plus 4% p.a. = £104 plus 4% × £104 for the second year, i.e. £108.16.

Thus, of the £700 received upon the falling in of the reversion:

	£
Capital will receive	647.19
Life tenant	52.81
	£700.00

The accuracy of the formula can be checked by calculating 4 per cent compound interest for two years upon the sum apportionable to capital, thus:

	£
1st year: 4% on £647.19	25.89
Add Capital	647.19
	673.08
2nd year: 4% on £673.08	26.92
Total at end of 2nd year	£700.00

Actually, the life tenant will receive less than £52.81 as his interest is subject to income tax, but the tax deducted will not be paid to the Inland Revenue authorities. It is only notional tax, which cannot form the basis of a repayment claim by the life tenant, for, as the whole £700 is of a capital nature, no income tax is actually payable, the object being merely to give to the life tenant, as far as possible, the *net* income which he would have received if the property had been sold at the testator's death and the proceeds invested in authorized securities. Thus the rate of interest employed in the calculation should be taken as 4 per cent per annum less income tax at the basic rate in force during the period from the date of death to the date of realization, i.e. 2.84 per cent if the rate of tax is 29 per cent. The true apportionment should, therefore, be stated as follows, and this method is usually adopted in practice:

$$\text{Capital} = £700 \times \frac{100}{105.76} = \qquad 661.87$$

	£
Income	38.13
	£700.00

The above formulae apply when the rate of tax remains constant throughout the period. When it differs from year to year, separate fractions should be introduced in respect of each change.

Another method giving the same result which some may find to be more speedy is illustrated below:

Value of reversionary interest when falling into possession £700.

Calculation on £100 basis:

	£	£
1st year:		
Interest	4.00	100.00
Less Tax at 29%	1.16	2.84
		102.84
2nd year:	£	
Interest	4.11	
Less Tax at 50%	1.19	2.92
		£105.76

£105.76 is yielded by	£100
∴ £700 is yielded by £ $\frac{700}{105.76} \times 100 =$	£661.87

Therefore capital receives £661.87 and income £38.13.

In practice, realization will rarely take place exactly one or more years after the death, so that an odd number of days will have to be accounted for, which will complicate the formula to be employed. If, however, it is observed that the formula is based on the yield on £100 at compound interest with yearly rests, no real difficulty should be experienced.

The effect of the application of the rule in *Re Chesterfield* is to place the life tenant in the same position as he would have been if the reversion had been sold at the date of death and the proceeds invested in authorized securities, while compound interest is taken into account in order to compensate for the loss of the use of the money.

The principle is not confined to reversionary interests, as the rule was applied in a case where a testator had sold his business for a consideration to be paid by ten half-yearly instalments and the testator's widow was life tenant of the residue. Each instalment when received was therefore apportioned in the above manner: *Re Hollebone* (1919).

Where there is a direction in the will to retain the reversionary interest, the rule in *Re Chesterfield* should not be applied. The life tenant is entitled to the actual income arising from the property which, until the reversionary interest falls into possession, will be nil.

It should now be evident that the object of *Howe* v. *Dartmouth* is to safeguard the interest of the remainderman (subject to the payment of a reasonable income to the life tenant under *Re Fawcett*), while that of *Re Chesterfield* is to safeguard the interest of the life tenant (see overleaf).

③ *Allhusen v. Whittell* (1867)

The residue of an estate is that which remains after the payment of all debts, legacies and expenses. Where the residue is left in trust for persons in succession, the life tenant is normally entitled to the income arising from the residue from the date of the testator's death. If the executors postpone the payment of the testator's debts, legacies, etc., until, say, one year after the death, considerable benefit might be obtained by the life tenant, for he would take the income yielded by that portion of the estate which will have to be applied to the payment of the debts, etc. It must not be supposed that this result would be obtained only by a deliberate postponement of the payment of debts, etc., for it is never possible to pay all debts immediately after the death, and frequently a lengthy period must elapse during which those assets which will eventually be required for the payment of debts, etc., will be earning income.

In *Allhusen* v. *Whittell* (1867) it was decided that the whole of this surplus income should not go to the life tenant, and that the payments of debts, legacies, etc., should be apportioned between capital and income. The apportionment is made by ascertaining 'what part, together with the income of such part for a year, will be required for the payment of debts, legacies, and other charges during the year', and the proper necessary fund must be ascertained by including the income for one year which may arise from the fund which may be so wanted.

Thus, if the capital of the testator is £20,000, producing an annual income of £1,200, and debts, legacies, etc., amount to £3,000, the apportionment would be as follows:

				£
Proportion of debts to be borne by capital:	$£3,000 \times \dfrac{20,000}{21,200}$	=		2,830.19
Proportion of debts to be borne by income:	$£3,000 \times \dfrac{1,200}{21,200}$	=		169.81
				£3,000.00

The life tenant will, therefore, receive £1,200 less £169.81 = £1,030.19.

RULE IN *EARL OF CHESTERFIELD'S TRUSTS*

Reversionary Interest

Date		Income £	Capital £	Date			Income £	Capital £
19– Sept 30	Estate account	38.13	600.00	19– Sept 30	£700 3½% stock at 90	£630		
19– Sept 30	Income account					70		
	Estate account: Profit on realization		61.87			£700		
					Cash			
					Apportioned between capital and income in accordance with the rule in *Re Chesterfield's Trusts*:			
					Capital			661.87
					Income		38.13	
		£38.13	£661.87				£38.13	£661.87

The rule as stated in *Allhusen* v. *Whittell* assumes that the debts and legacies are all paid one year after the testator's death. In practice, this will not be the case, and the rule frequently operated to the detriment of the life tenant, until it was modified by *Re McEuen* (1913). This modification was confirmed in *Re Wills* (1915).

In *Re Oldham* (1927), it was held that where the rule in *Allhusen* v. *Whittell* is applied, income must be calculated on the basis of the net amount after deduction of income tax.

Re McEuen (1913)

It was held that where debts, etc., are paid within the year following the death, the income yielded during that year should be charged with interest at 4 per cent per annum upon the capital sum which would, with the interest, make up the amount paid in respect of debts, but that interest was only to be calculated from the date of death to the date upon which the debts were actually paid. Thus this decision overcomes the inequity by which under *Allhusen* v. *Whittell* the life tenant was debited with a full year's interest whereas he was only credited with income for a shorter period.

Re Wills (1915)

It was held that the principle applies also in respect of debts paid more than one year after the testator's death, and that the average rate of net interest actually earned by the estate should be adopted as the basis of the apportionment, if a definite rate cannot be agreed upon between the parties. It is doubtful whether simple or compound interest should be taken, but it is suggested that simple interest should be used for examination purposes.

To apply this rule it is therefore necessary to make a calculation similar to that under *Re McEuen* (1913), substituting the average interest earned by the estate over the period from the date of death to date of payment for the 4 per cent agreed upon in *Re McEuen*.

Example 3 *(Re McEuen)*

A died on 1 July, leaving the residue of his estate in trust for *Y* for life, with remainder to *Z* absolutely. Inheritance tax of £3,627 was paid on 1 October. Debts amounting to £4,000 were paid on 12 September, and legacies to the amount of £4,000 on 1 April following. The income for the year after the death amounted to £1,500, and an agreed rate of 4 per cent was adopted for apportionment purposes. The value of the assets before deducting debts, at the date of death, was £28,000.

Apportionment under the rule in *Re McEuen* would be as follows:

1. *Inheritance tax* = £3,627
   The sum which invested at 4 per cent interest at the date of death would produce £3,627 on 1 October is:

$$\frac{100}{100 + \left(4 \times \frac{3}{12}\right)} \times \text{£3,627} = \text{£3,591.09}$$

2. *Debts* = £4,000
   The sum which invested at 4 per cent interest at the date of death would produce £4,000 on 12 September is:

$$\frac{100}{100 + \left(4 \times \frac{73}{365}\right)} \times \text{£4,000} = \text{£3,968.25}$$

3. *Legacies* = £4,000
   The sum which invested at 4 per cent interest at the date of death would produce £4,000 on 1 April following death is:

$$\frac{100}{100 + \left(4 \times \frac{9}{12}\right)} \times \text{£4,000} = \text{£3,883.49}$$

. The payments would therefore be apportioned as follows:

	Capital	Income
	£	£
1. Inheritance tax	3,591.09	35.91
2. Debts	3,968.25	31.75
3. Legacies	3,883.49	116.51
	£11,442.83	£184.17

For the first year the life tenant would therefore receive:

	£
Total income	1,500.00
Less Adjustment under *Re McEuen*	184.17
	£1,315.83

The necessary adjustments in the accounts would be made as shown on p. 000.

Estate Account

19–		£	19–		£
July 1	Sundry debts	4,000.00	July 1	Sundry assets	28,000.00
	Balance c/d	24,000.00			
		£28.000.00			£28,000.00
Oct 1	Inheritance tax	3,627.00	July 1	Balance b/d	24,000.00
19–			19–		
April 1	Legacies	4,000.00	April 1	Income account:	
	Balance c/d	16,557.17		Adjustment under rule	
				in *Re McEuen*	184.17
		£24,184.17			£24,184.17
			April 1	Balance b/d	16,557.17

Legacies Account

19–		£	19–		£
April 1	Cash	4,000.00	April 1	Estate account	4,000.00

Income Account

19–		£	19–		£
April 1	Estate account:		April 1	Sundry investments	1,500.00
	Adjustment under the				
	rule in *Re McEuen*	184.17			
	Life tenant for year	1,315.83			
		£1,500.00			£1,500.00

Although interest on inheritance tax is normally a charge against income, in applying the rule in *Allhusen* v. *Whittell* (as modified by *Re McEuen*, etc.) it should be treated as the payment of a liability, and the combined sum of tax and interest thereon apportioned between capital and income.

The rule in *Allhusen* v. *Whittell* does not apply to specific legacies, as such legacies carry the income accrued from the date of death; and the life tenant does not gain by the postponement of payment. It is also thought that the rule does not apply when non-income producing assets are sold for the payment of debts, etc. The operation of the rule is frequently excluded by the will, and is often disregarded in practice because of its complexity and because of the small difference it would make.

In *Re Shee, Taylor* v. *Stoger* (1934) a similar apportionment was authorized in connection with the assignment of leases subject to onerous convenants, on the grounds that had they not been so assigned the rent and outgoings would have fallen on the life tenant (and not on capital).

Re Perkins (1907)

In this case, a testator had, during his lifetime, contracted to pay an annuity to X, and by will settled the *residue* of his estate upon persons in succession, subject to the payment of the annuity. The court held that in such circumstances the annuity was not payable wholly out of the income of the residue, but must be apportioned between the life tenant and remainderman.

As each payment of the annuity becomes due, it is necessary to ascertain the sum which, if invested at 4 per cent *simple* interest at the date of the testator's death, would, with such interest, produce the instalment due in respect of the annuity. This sum is chargeable to *capital* and the balance of the instalment to *income*.

Example 4 *(Re Perkins)*

A died on 30 June, having contracted during his lifetime to pay an annuity of £250 to *X* for life, and charged this annuity upon the residue which is settled upon *L* for life with remainder to *M* absolutely. Apportion the first two annual payments, ignoring income tax.
These apportionments would be made as follows:

First year:
    Instalment due 30 June   £250

$$\text{Capital} = \frac{100}{104} \times £250 = £240.38$$

	£
Proportion payable out of capital =	240.38
Proportion payable out of income =	9.62
	£250.00

Second year:
    Instalment due 30 June   £250

$$\text{Capital} = \frac{100}{108} \times £250 = £231.48$$

	£
Proportion payable out of capital =	231.48
Proportion payable out of income =	18.52
	£250.00

As the years proceed, less will be payable out of capital and more out of income. The equity of this results from the fact that the liability for all instalments existed at the date of death of the testator, and it is assumed that the capital sum required, with interest, to meet future instalments will be less the more distant the actual date of each instalment. In other words, the annuity is regarded as a liability rather than as a legacy.

The rule applies where the *residue* upon which the annuity is charged has been *settled upon persons in succession*; but if there is a definite bequest of the residue, or a partial intestacy in which no life tenancy is involved, the ordinary rules as to the payment of annuities charged upon the residue apply. Further, the rule does not apply to an annuity bequeathed by will, but only where there was a prior contract to pay such annuity, e.g. under a separation agreement, and the annuity has been charged on residuary personalty left in succession.

The personal representative should deduct income tax from the whole of the annuity instalments at the basic rate.

Loss of trust funds

Where a loss of income occurs on realization of the trust property, the life tenant is not entitled to have such loss made good out of capital, so that if trust funds are invested in shares which pay no dividends and are finally realized by the trustee, no portion of the proceeds can be claimed by the life tenant. Similarly, losses incurred in carrying on a business which forms part of the authorized trust fund must be borne by the life tenant. In connection with the subject of losses of trust property invested on mortgage, however, the rule in *Re Atkinson* (1904) must be considered.

⑦ *Re Atkinson* (1904)

Where trust funds settled upon persons in succession are invested in an authorized mortgage security, and upon a realization the mortgaged property proves insufficient to pay principal and interest in full, the sum realized must be apportioned between the life tenant and the remainderman in the proportion which the amount due for arrears of interest bears to the amount due in respect of the capital debt. This rule recognizes the fact that the security afforded by a mortgage is a joint charge in respect of both principal and interest, each of which must abate proportionately in the event of a loss on realization.

Where arrears of interest exist prior to the date of death of the testator, these are added to the capital debt before the apportionment is calculated. The cost of advertising the property for sale and similar capital expenses should be deducted from the gross proceeds of realization before the apportionment is made.

Example 5 *(Re Atkinson)*

A died on 1 January, leaving the residue of his estate in trust for *X* for life, with remainder to *Y* absolutely. He authorized the trustees to retain the existing investments, and part of the residue consisted of a loan of £20,000 at 5 per cent per annum upon the security of a mortgage, interest being payable each 30 June and 31 December. Interest was in arrear from the six months prior to the date of death, and upon sale on 30 June, eighteen months after the date of death, the property realized only £15,000.

The apportionment of this sum would be as follows (ignoring income tax):

Amount due:	£	£
Capital debt	20,000	
Add Arrears of interest to date of death, 6 months	500	20,500

Arrears of interest from date of death to date of sale, 18 months	1,500
	£22,000
	£15,000

Amount realized:

Proportion due to *capital:*

$$\frac{20,500}{22,000} \times £15,000 = £13,977.27$$

Proportion due to *income:*

$$\frac{1,500}{22,000} \times £15,000 = \frac{£\ 1,022.73}{£15,000.00}$$

On default of payment of interest by the mortgagor, the mortgagee may, instead of exercising his power of sale, apply to the court for a foreclosure order, which is an order of the court extinguishing the mortgagor's equity of redemption and which, in effect, makes the mortgagee the absolute owner of the mortgaged property.

Consequently, if trustees, in exercise of their powers, have invested trust funds on the security of property and on default by the mortgagor have foreclosed, the trustees become the owners of the property and the law treats the property as if it had originally formed part of the testator's estate. Pending the sale of the property, the life tenant is entitled to the whole of the net rents received from the letting of the property. Even if this rent amounts to more than the interest which would otherwise have accrued on the mortgage, the remainderman cannot claim the excess, and similarly, if the net rents received during the period pending the sale of the property amount to less than the interest which would otherwise have accrued on the mortgage from the date of foreclosure, the life tenant cannot claim any part of the proceeds of the sale to reimburse him for the amount of his deficiency: *Re Horn's Estate* (1924).

The decision in *Re Horn* applies only from the date of foreclosure. The life tenant is, however, entitled, upon the sale of the property, to an apportionment under *Re Atkinson*, in respect of the interest accrued up to the date of foreclosure.

Where the testator had gone into possession prior to his death and had continued in possession up to the date of death, rents received should be applied first in discharge of any interest in arrear at the date of death, and secondly in discharge of any interest in arrear since the date of death, while any further excess should be applied as capital: *Re Coaks* (1911). The position would appear to be the same where the trustees went into possession after the testator's death.

The apparent contradiction between the decision in *Re Horn* and that in *Re Coaks* arises out of the distinct legal processes of 'foreclosure' and 'taking possession'. Where the trustees 'foreclose', the mortgaged property becomes part of the trust property, and section 28 of the Law of Property Act 1925 applies, whereas if the trustees 'take possession' the mortgagor still has the right to recover the property on payment of principal and arrears of interest. In other words, under *Re Horn* the trust asset consists of the foreclosed property, whereas under *Re Coaks* the asset is still the mortgage.

SPECIFIC SETTLEMENTS

It must be remembered that the rules of equitable apportionment apply only where a *residuary* bequest is settled. If a specific bequest of wasting, hazardous or reversionary property is settled upon persons in succession, and the will shows no intention to convert the property into authorized securities, the life tenant will be entitled to any income actually produced by the property.

On the other hand, where property is settled specifically, upon trust to be sold, the equitable rules of apportionment will apply.

APPORTIONMENT OF DISBURSEMENTS *for life tenant & remainderman*

As a general rule payments which effect a permanent benefit to property should be capital, while payments of a transitory nature should be income; but this rule is of a rough and ready nature only, and the following items call for more consideration.

Repairs

The life tenant of settled land is not normally personally liable for repairs, unless the settlement so provides. Nevertheless he cannot have them paid for out of capital. If he executes repairs he is not entitled to charge the estate, and repairs carried out by the trustees must be paid out of income.

A life tenant of leaseholds is bound to perform any repair covenant contained in the lease, and liable for any breach of the covenants occurring in his lifetime. His estate is not, however, liable for the repairs made necessary by any non-fulfilment of those convenants during his life tenancy.

Improvements

Under the Settled Land Act 1925 certain improvements to trust property specified in the Third Schedule to that Act may be made out of *capital*, but the trustees of the settlement or the court *may* (where the improvement falls within Part II of the Schedule, e.g. the development of the land as a building estate), or *must* (where it falls within Part III of the Schedule, e.g. the installation of movable machinery for farming purposes) require the cost to be replaced out of the income of the settled land by not more than fifty half-yearly instalments. The maintenance and insurance of any such improvements must be borne by the life tenant out of *income*.

No right of recoupment exists in regard to improvements falling within Part I of the Schedule, i.e. those necessarily of permanent value to the land, e.g. drainage works.

When the life tenant has obtained relief from income tax under section 68, Capital Allowances Act 1968, in respect of expenditure on improvements payable out of capital moneys he is not liable to account therefor to the trustees of the settlement: *Re Pelly's Will Trusts, Ransome v. Pelly* (1956).

TRUSTS FOR MINORS

That portion of the income which is not applied to the maintenance of the minor, and is not bequeathed to another person, must be accumulated for the benefit of the minor, and invested from time to time by the trustees. As income is received from the investments it will be credited to the estate income account and the proportions due to the various beneficiaries will be transferred to their accounts in accordance with the ratios set out in the trust instrument. To these accounts will be debited any payments made in respect of maintenance. The balances of such accounts should then be invested from time to time by the trustees, the investments being earmarked as accumulations, and the income arising therefrom being credited to an account known as accumulations income. The income derived each year from these accumulations investments is apportioned between beneficiaries on the basis of the balances, as at the commencement of the year in question, on their separate accumulations accounts. Where, however, accumulations income is reinvested during the course of the year, the first income yielded by such investments should be apportioned between the beneficiaries in the ratio of their credit balances on accumulations accounts at the date of the re-investment.

Example 6

A, B, C and *D* are beneficiaries under a trust, and share the income in the proportions of 9, 7, 5 and 4 respectively. All the beneficiaries are minors. From the following trial balance, extracted from the books of the trust as on 3 October, you are required to prepare statement showing the beneficiaries' accumulations accounts for the year and a balance sheet as at 3 October.

Trial Balance

		£	£
Estate capital account			31,754
Beneficiaries' maintenance accounts:	A	196	
	B	217	
	C	154	
	D	146	
Estate income account			2,500
Accumulations income account			200
Estate capital investments at cost		31,754	
Accumulations account investments at cost		3,520	
Beneficiaries' accumulations accounts at beginning of year:	A		352
	B		528
	C		704
	D		1,936
Cash at bank		1,987	
		£37,974	£37,974

Balance Sheet as at 3 October 19–

	£	£		£	£
Estate capital A/c		31,754	Estate investments		
Accumulations A/cs:			at cost		31,754
	£		Accumulations	£	
A	1,076		Investments at cost	3,520	
B	1,041		Cash at bank	1,987	5,507
C	1,090				
D	2,300	5,507			
		£37,261			£37,261

Estate Income Account

19–		£	19–		£
Oct 3	Transfer to accumulations A/cs:		Oct 3	Balance	2,500
	A: $9/25$	900			
	B: $7/25$	700			
	C: $5/25$	500			
	D: $4/25$	400			
		£2,500			£2,500

Accumulations Income Account

19–		£	19–		£
Oct 3	Transfer to accumulations A/cs:		Oct 3	Balance	200
	A: $\frac{£\ 352}{£3,520}$ of £200	20			
	B: $\frac{£\ 528}{£3,520}$ of £200	30			
	C: $\frac{£\ 704}{£3,520}$ of £200	40			
	D: $\frac{£1,936}{£3,520}$ of £200	110			
		£200			£200

A's Accumulations Account

19–		£	19–		£
Oct 3	Cash: Maintenance	196	Oct 3	Balance	352
	Balance c/d	1,076		Estate income account	900
				Accumulations income account	20
		£1,272			£1,272
			Oct 4	Balance b/d	1,076

B's Accumulations Account

19–		£	19–		£
Oct 3	Cash: Maintenance	217	Oct 3	Balance	528
	Balance c/d	1,041		Estate income account	700
				Accumulations income account	30
		£1,258			£1,258
			Oct 4	Balance b/d	1,041

C's Accumulations Account

19–		£	19–		£
Oct 3	Cash: Maintenance	154	Oct 3	Balance	704
	Balance c/d	1,090		Estate income account	500
				Accumulations income account	40
		£1,244			£1,244
			Oct 4	Balance b/d	1,090

D's Accumulations Account

19–		£	19–		£
Oct 3	Cash: Maintenance	146	Oct 3	Balance	1,936
	Balance c/d	2,300		Estate income account	400
				Accumulations income	
				account	110
		£2,446			£2,446
			Oct 4	Balance b/d	2,300

Upon the coming of age of one of the beneficiaries his share of the trust property would be transferred to him, at a valuation made at the date of the distribution. Thus upon attaining full age, the beneficiary will be entitled to his share of the value of the capital investments in addition to any balance outstanding upon his accumulations account (plus or minus his share of any profit or loss on revaluation of the accumulations investments), and his share of the accrued income on the estate investments and the accumulations investments from the date of the last account, less any amounts paid in respect of his maintenance.

Any profit or loss shown by the revaluation of investments for distribution purposes should be divided between the beneficiaries on a similar basis to that for the division of the trust income, i.e. profits or losses on the capital investments are divided in the ratio laid down by the trust instrument, while profits or losses on accumulations investments are divided in proportion to the balances standing to the credit of the minors' accumulations accounts at the date of revaluation. When revaluing investments for this purpose the mean price at the date of revaluation should be taken, i.e. the lower quoted price plus half the difference between the lower and higher quoted prices.

The actual division of the property would usually require adjustment between the parties concerned, as it is not always possible to divide the property *in specie* and accordingly the trustees must be guided principally by the circumstances of each case.

Any necessary adjustment may be effected by payment of cash to the beneficiary concerned.

INCOME TAX ON TRUST FUNDS

The income derived from an estate or trust is liable to income tax which is normally borne by the estate, so that the income comes to the beneficiaries less the tax. If the tax so suffered by any beneficiary in a year of assessment exceeds his liability to tax for that year, a claim may be made for repayment of the excess tax suffered.

Minor beneficiaries

Claims for repayment of tax may be made by the trustees on a minor's behalf, but the conditions of the claim depend on the nature of the minor's interest.

If the minor's interest is *vested*, the trustee can claim year by year in respect of the full allowances due to the minor, and this claim for repayment can be made within six years of the end of the fiscal year to which the claim relates. If the trustee neglects to do this, the minor, on coming of age, may claim, but only in respect of the six fiscal years prior to that in which he makes the claim. The minor will be entitled to the gross income arising from his share of the trust, which will have borne basic rate tax only. If the trust is a discretionary or accumulation trust, claims can be made for the repayments due to the minor in respect of payments to him for his education or benefit. This type of trust is taxed at the basic rate plus 16 per cent additional rate tax, so the payments made on behalf of the minor are grossed at 100/55 for the purposes of arriving at his taxable income.

DEATH OF LIFE TENANT

Upon the death of a life tenant it will be necessary to apportion the income for the year in which the death occurs in order to ascertain what is due to the estate of the deceased life tenant and his successor.

The proportion of income due up to the date of the life tenant's death will form part of his estate, while any balance must be dealt with according to the terms of the trust. That is to say, if another life tenancy follows, the balance will form part of the income, or if the property is given to some person absolutely, it will form part of the capital.

Example 7

Property is held in trust for *A* for life, with remainder to *B* absolutely upon *A*'s death, and *A* dies on 30 June. What apportionments would be necessary, assuming the income actually received by the trustees was as follows, and taking income tax into account at 29 per cent?
a. Interest on £12,000 2½% consols due and received on 5 July.
b. Interest on loan of £1,000 at 6% payable annually each 31 December, received 1 January following the death.
    The following apportionments would be necessary:

	£	£
2½% consols:		
Interest received, *less* Tax at 29%		£53.25
Proportion due to life tenant:		
6 April to 30 June, 86 days	50.32	
Proportion due to remainderman:		
5 days	2.93	
	£53.25	
Interest on loan:		
Interest received, *less* Tax at 29%		£42.60
Proportion due to life tenant:		
1 January to 30 June, 181 days	21.12	
Proportion due to remainderman:		
184 days	21.48	
	£42.60	

Outstanding expenditure will require similar apportionment, e.g. rates, taxes, ground rents, etc.

Example 8

Crispin Day died in 1980. On 1 January 1987 the opening balances in the estate ledger were:

	£	£
Estate account		45,400
£36,000 3% government stock 1990 (interest 1 February and		
1 August) at 75	27,000	
£24,000 3% British Transport guaranteed stock,		
1988–98 (interest 1 January and 1 July)	17,400	

Ground rent upon 'Green Acre' of £36 per annum due half-yearly on 30 June and 31 December	840	
Balance at bank:		
Income	220	
Capital	160	
Trustees' expenses (income)		42
Holly Day's income account		178
	£45,620	£45,620

Under Day's will, the income from the holding of £36,000 3% government stock 1990 was payable to his sister, Anne Ewell, for her life, and subject thereto the income of the estate was payable to the testator's niece, Holly Day, for her life.

All income was received on the due dates.

The other information relevant to the year to 31 December 1987 is:

1987

Feb 15 The balances due on income account as on 1 January 1987 were paid including, the trustees expenses, and the income received on 1 February 1987 was paid to Anne Ewell.

May 31 Anne Ewell died.

July 20 Day's trustees sold £4,065 3% government stock 1990 to meet the tax for which they were accountable by reason of Anne Ewell's death. The stock was quoted *ex div.*, the amount received from the broker being £72 per £100 of stock, net after brokerage.

July 31 Day's trustees paid inheritance tax of £2,927.

Aug 15 Holly Day was paid £256 on account of income, and the personal representatives of Anne Ewell paid the balance due to her estate.

Oct 4 The costs, amounting to £27, in connection with the assessment of the tax were paid.

Dec 31 Trustees' expenses (chargeable to income) amounting to £54 were outstanding on this date.

You are required:

a. to write up the trustees' cash book for the year to 31 December 1987; and
b. to prepare the estate balance sheet as on 31 December 1987 assuming that Holly Day was still alive on that date.

Take into account income tax at 29 per cent. Work in months and to the nearest £. Ignore capital gains tax.

See p. 324 for Crispin Day's trustees' cash book.

Balance Sheet
31 *December* 1987

	£		£
Estate capital account	42,324	*Investments on capital account:*	
		£31,935 3% government stock 1990	23,951
Income account: £		£24,000 3% British Transport	
Amount due to Holly Day 365		guaranteed stock 1988-98	17,400
Outstanding Expenses 54	419	Ground rent upon 'Green Acre'	840
			42,191
		Cash at bank on capital account	133
			42,324
		Cash at bank on income account	419
	£42,743		£42,743

CRISPIN DAY, DECEASED
Cash Book

Receipts (Dr)

Date	Particulars	Income £	Capital £
1987			
Jan 1	Balances b/f	220	160
	3% British Transport stock – half-year's interest (net)	256	
Feb 1	3% government stock – half-year's interest (net)	383	
June 30	Ground rent on 'Green Acre' – half-year to date	18	
July 1	3% British Transport stock – half-year's interest (net)	256	
July 20	Proceeds of sale of £4,065 3% government stock at 72 *ex div.* (after brokerage)		2,927
Aug 1	3% government stock – half-year's interest to date (on £36,000 stock) (net)	383	
Dec 31	Ground rent on 'Green Acre' – half-year to date	18	
		£1,534	£3,087
Jan 1	Balances b/d	401	133

Payments (Cr)

Date	Particulars	Income £	Capital £
1987			
Feb 15	Trustees' expenses	42	
	Holly Day (balance of income account, 31 December 1986)	178	
	Anne Ewell		
July 31	Inheritance tax on death of Anne Ewell	383	
Aug 15	Holly Day – on account of income	256	
Aug 15	Personal representatives of Anne Ewell	256	2,927
Oct 4	Costs – re tax assessment		27
Dec 31	Balances c/d	419	133
		£1,534	£3,087

Note: The payment to Anne Ewell's personal representatives on 15 August is 4 months accrued income on the government stock.

Note: The entries in the estate account may be summarized as follows:

	£	£		£
Inheritance tax on death of Anne Ewell		2,927	Opening balance	45,400
Loss on sale of £4,065 3% government stock at 72	2,927			
Less: Probate value £4,065 at 75	3,049	122		
Costs re assessment of inheritance tax		27		
Balance c/d		42,324		
		£45,400		£45,400
			Balance b/d	42,324

Example 9

Henry, the life tenant of the Agincourt Will Fund, died on 31 December 1986, unmarried. The balance sheet of the Fund as on that date is given below:

	£		£
Capital account	60,000	Investments:	
Income undistributed	240	£30,000 British Gas 3% guaranteed stock 1990–95	18,000
		(Interest 1 May and 1 November)	
		£50,000 British Transport 3% stock 1988–98	42,000
		(Interest 1 April and 1 October)	
		Balance at bank on income account	240
	£60,240		£60,240

Under the terms of the will, on the determination of the life interest, the fund was divisible equally *in specie* between three nephews of the life tenant, David, William and Robert, who have all attained their majority.

£35,000 British Transport 3% stock was sold on 14 January 1987 realizing £29,850, and on 17 January 1987 inheritance tax amounting to £27,000 was paid in respect of the fund passing on the death.

For the purpose of appropriating the investments between the remaindermen a revaluation (on a *cum div.* basis) was made, the figures being:

	£
£30,000 British Gas 3% guaranteed stock	19,500
£15,000 British Transport 3% stock	12,900

In order to keep the respective holdings in convenient amounts it was agreed that the stocks should be divided in this way:

	3% British Gas £	3% British Transport £
David	15,000	–
William	5,000	9,000
Robert	10,000	6,000

Costs amounting to £53 in connection with the assessment of tax and the appropriation scheme were paid on 11 February 1987. On the same date transfers giving effect to the distribution were made out.

You are required to prepare:

a. a statement showing how the investments of the fund have been dealt with;
b. the trust capital account, and
c. the personal accounts of the four beneficiaries.

Take income tax at 29 per cent. Work in months and to the nearest £. Ignore capital gains tax.

a.
AGINCOURT WILL FUND
Statement showing Disposal of Investments

Investment	Nominal value	Income accrued due to life tenant	Value	Valuation 11 Feb 1987	Profit on revaluation
	£	£	£	£	£
British Gas 3% guaranteed stock	30,000	107 (2 months)	18,000	19,500	1,500
British Transport 3% stock (transferred in specie)	15,000	80 (3 months)	12,600	12,900	300
				Proceeds of sale	Profit on sale
British Transport 3% stock (sold)	35,000		29,400	29,850	450
		£187	£60,000	£62,250	£2,250

Distribution in Specie

	British Gas 3% guaranteed stock 1990–95		British Transport 3% stock 1988–98		Total
	Nominal Value	Valuation 11th Feb 1987	Nominal Value	Valuation 11th Feb 1987	Valuation 11th Feb 1987
	£	£	£	£	£
David	15,000	9,750	—	—	9,750
William	5,000	3,250	9,000	7,740	10,990
Robert	10,000	6,500	6,000	5,160	11,660
	£30,000	£19,500	£15,000	£12,900	£32,400

b.
Trust Capital Account

1987		£	1986		£
Jan 17	Inheritance tax	27,000	Dec 31	Balance b/f	60,000
			1987		
Feb 11	Costs	56	Feb 11	Profit on revaluation and	
	Estate of Henry:			realization	2,250
	Income accrued to date of death	184			
	Balance, divided equally:				
	£				
	David 11,670				
	William 11,670				
	Robert 11,670	35,010			
		£62,250			£62,250

Beneficiaries accounts

1987 Feb 11		Henry's exors	David	William	Robert		1987		Henry's exors	David	William	Robert
		£	£	£	£		Jan 1	Undistributed income	240	£	£	£
	Investments per schedule	427	9,750	10,990	11,660		Feb 11	Accrued income to date of death	187			
	Cash		1,920	680	10			Share of trust capital fund		11,670	11,670	11,670
		£427	£11,670	£11,670	£11,670				£427	£11,670	£11,670	£11,670

Notes:

a. The deceased life tenant's estate is *not* entitled to any apportionment of the proceeds of any investments sold *cum div.* in order to wind up the estate, but it *is* entitled to such an apportionment in regard to investments distributed *in specie.*

b. The cash position is as follows:

	£
Opening balance	240
Proceeds of sale of British Transport stock	29,850
	30,090

	£	
Less: Inheritance tax	27,000	
Costs	53	27,053
		3,037

	£	
Less Payments to beneficiaries:		
Henry's executors	427	
David	1,920	
William	680	
Robert	10	£3,034

Exercise 19

1. During a tenancy for life commencing 31 December 1984 default was made in the payment of the half-year's interest due 1 July 1986 on a mortgage of £2,000 at 5 per cent per annum. The property was realised by the Trustees on 30th June 1987, the net proceeds amounting to £1,800.

    How should the £1,800 be apportioned as between capital and income?

2. Prepare from the following data the executor's accounts at 31 December, *X*, the testator, having died on the 30 June previously:

	£
£10,000 6% Central loan, at 85	8,500
Household furniture	1,500
Cash at bank	4,470
Testator's share in partnership	9,000

There was a liability to capital gains tax agreed at £190.

The interest on the Central loan was received on 1 November for the half-year. The household furniture was sold and realized £1,700. The partnership share was settled on 30 September with 6 per cent per annum interest to date. On 1 October the executors purchased £12,000 4½% Blank loan at 100, interest payable half-yearly on 31 March and 30 September. The following amounts were paid:

	£
Inheritance tax (on account)	2,000
Funeral expenses and debts due at death	300
Testamentary expenses	150
Executorship expenses	50
Capital gains tax	190

Income tax to be taken into account at 29 per cent, and apportionments to be made in months. Provision should be made for payment of the balance of inheritance tax of £334 but interest thereon is to be ignored.

3. *A* died on 1 February, leaving the residue of his estate to *B* for life, with remainder to *C*. The will did not exclude any rule of equitable apportionment. Part of the residue consisted of shares of a hazardous nature, valued for probate at £1,000 and producing a net annual income of £45. The shares were sold on the first anniversary of the death for £1,200. How should the amount due to the life tenant for the first year following the death be computed? On what authority would the apportionment be made? Income tax may be ignored.

4. Explain the rule in *Allhusen* v. *Whittell*. Assuming the following figures: how would the payment of debts, legacies, etc., be apportioned?

what would be the income of the life tenant for the first year?

	£
Capital at date of death	10,209
First year's income	1,571
	£11,780
Funeral, debts, testamentary expenses, etc.	£4,729

5. Part of the residue of the estate of *X*, who died on 1 April, consisted of a loan of £5,000 on mortgage at 6 per cent per annum interest payable each 31 December and 30 June. The interest due in June following the death was not paid, and upon sale on 30 September the security realized only £4,000. How should this sum be apportioned, and under what rule? Apportionments may be made in months.

6. Matthew died on 30 June 1985. His estate, after legacies, CTT and debts had been paid, was left to his three sons, Mark, Luke and John, equally. Wide investment powers were given to his trustees.

The sons were under 18 years of age at Matthew's death, but Mark became 18 on 31 March 1987.

On 31 March 1987 the capital assets were:

	£
14,000 Romans Plc ord shares at cost	16,700
21,000 Corinthians Plc ord shares at cost	29,600
9,000 Ephesians Plc ord shares at a 30 June 1985, valuation	11,000
3,000 Philippians Plc ord shares at a 30 June 1985 valuation	3,700
Bank balance	2,100
	£63,100

Accumulated income had been invested on 1 July 1986 as follows:

1,400 Romans Plc ord shares at cost £1,302
3,000 Corinthians Plc ord shares at cost £3,810

The investment income received was:

	Capital	Accumulation
	£	£
Year to 30 June 1986	4,110	Nil
Nine months to 31 March 1987	3,060	600

The following maintenance payments had been made:

	Mark	Luke	John
	£	£	£
31 December 1985	70	70	170
30 June 1986	300	500	600
31 December 1986	270	220	470

Mark's entitlement was satisfied by:

Capital: 2,000 Corinthians Plc ords, 3,000 Ephesians Plc ords, the entire holding in Romans Plc and cash for the balance.

Income: the entire holding of Romans Plc plus the balance in cash.

On 31 March 1987 the valuations were:

Romans Plc ords, 95–97; Corinthians Plc ords 156; Ephesians Plc ords 89–91; Philippians Plc ords 139–141.

Prepare the accumulations account from 30 June 1985 to 31 March 1987 when the distribution was made to Mark: a distributions account for both capital and accumulations in respect of Mark; and the balance sheet on 31 March 1987 after the distribution had been made.

Appendix I
Audit Programme for Trust Accounts

The audit of trust accounts may be effected under the provisions of the Public Trustee Act 1906 or the Trustee Act 1925, or by arrangement between the beneficiaries and trustees. The following specimen audit programme will be found suitable in the majority of cases, although slight modifications may be found necessary in practice.

1. Examine the authenticated copy of the will and of any codicils thereto, noting carefully all provisions with regard to:
    a. property specifically mentioned;
    b. general, specific and demonstrative legacies, and the disposal of the residue;
    c. investments authorized;
    d. directions to carry on the business;
    e. payment of annuities;
    f. creation of trusts, statutory or otherwise, for minors or other beneficiaries;
    g. allocation of property for payment of debts.
2. Examine the official tax account and corrective account to ascertain that all assets and liabilities have been brought into account, and to check the amount of inheritance tax paid. Examine the private books etc. of the deceased and compare with the official account.
3. Vouch the opening journal entries with the official account, noting that all necessary apportionments have been made. Similarly vouch the corrective accounts.
4. Vouch the debit side of the cash book and verify all receipts by examining brokers' sold notes, auctioneers' accounts, counterfoils of dividend and interest warrants, etc.
5. Vouch the credit side of the cash book, and verify all payments by examining brokers' bought notes, Inland Revenue receipts for taxes paid, etc.
6. See that all adjustments regarding taxation have been made, and verify payments or amounts reclaimed.
7. Check the bank account by comparing and reconciling the bank entries in the cash book with those in the bank statement, and obtain a certificate of the balance from the bankers.
8. See that all apportionments required by the Apportionment Act 1870 or by the rules of equity have been made correctly.
9. Examine the rent records and check with tenants' leases and agreements. Obtain certificates from local agents of arrears, and verify allowances to tenants and enquire into all outstandings.

10. See that all income that should have been received has been received and enquire into all outstandings. Also see that no income has been brought into account unless received during the period covered by the audit, but that full provision has been made for accrued expenditure.

11. Examine the trustees' minute book for authority for all transactions such as purchase and sale of investments, etc. Examine all correspondence relating to such transactions.

12. Examine the audited accounts of any business carried on by the trustees.

13. See that all investments are registered in the names of all trustees and obtain certificates from them that they hold such investments on behalf of the estate, free of all incumbrances. See that all investments are authorized by the terms of the will, the Trustee Act 1925, Trustee Investments Act 1961, or other statutes, and that profits and losses on the realization of investments are properly recorded.

14. See that any special trusts created are kept distinct in the accounts and that all receipts and payments in respect of them are properly accounted for, and that accumulated income is invested in authorized securities.

15. Vouch the distribution of the estate with the terms of the will.

16. Ascertain whether any *devastavit* has been committed in respect of capital and report on any irregularities or deficiencies in the accounts.

17. Verify the existence of all investments, properties, etc., by inspection of the certificates, title deeds, etc.

18. Prepare an appropriately worded audit report.

Appendix II

Recommendations on Accounting Principles

The Council of the Institute of Chartered Accountants in England and Wales makes the following recommendations to members regarding the accounts of deceased persons' estates and the more general types of trusts (excluding special trusts such as pension funds and unit trusts). Whilst it is recognized that, subject to the observance of any relevant legal considerations, the form in which accounts are prepared is a matter within the discretion of the trustees, it is hoped that these recommendations as to what is regarded as the best practice will be helpful to members who either act as trustees themselves or whose advice or assistance is sought by trustees. The recommendations which follow were made in the era of estate duty and before the introduction of inheritance tax. It is considered useful to reproduce them here since in principle the views expressed remain quite valid. References throughout to estate duty should now be construed as references to inheritance tax.

INTRODUCTION

1. The main object of trust accounts is to demonstrate that the trust funds, including the income thereof, have been applied in accordance with the provisions of the trust instrument. They should also convey to beneficiaries and other interested parties, as well as to the trustees, information about the transactions and the current state of affairs of the trust. Trust accounts may also be useful for taxation and other purposes.

2. Special considerations, which are not necessarily dealt with in the following paragraphs, obtain in the case of trusts under the Settled Land Act 1925 and those for which prescribed forms of account exist (e.g. certain charities).

3. Trust accounts differ from ordinary commercial accounts in a number of ways because of different underlying circumstances. For instance there are many trusts where income is separately accounted for, thus lessening the need for production of annual accounts, and, in the case of established trust, where changes of investments are infrequent and the income is mandated to a single life tenant, the interval between accounting dates may be several years and the accounts might deal only with capital transactions. Accounts dealing with all or selected aspects of the trust will be required in the following circumstances:
    a. where there is a distribution or other significant change in the trust fund or in the rights in it;

b. in the case of the estate of a deceased person which is settled for any period, when the initial administration of the estate has been completed, i.e. when the final estate duty figures have been settled, testamentary expenses paid, and the investments assembled into a fairly permanent portfolio;

c. at selected invervals, to show changes in capital accounts, even when there are no other matters to be dealt with.

If accounts are prepared less frequently than annually, particular care will be necessary to ensure that the underlying records are kept up to date and that the investments come under regular review by the trustees.

4. The following taxes have been repealed, or were operative for one year only:
    — special charge, imposed by the Finance Act 1968, by reference to investment income for the year to 5 April 1968;
    — special contribution, imposed by the Finance Act 1948, by reference to investment income for the year to 5 April 1948;
    — legacy and succession duties, repealed by the Finance Act 1949, as respects deaths occurring on or after 30 July 1949.

    In as much as these taxes were chargeable to capital and, where separate funds are involved, perhaps disproportionately to those funds, their incidence may still be relevant in trust accounts. In paragraph 57 guidance is offered as to the treatment of special charge: the same general principles would have applied to special contribution and legacy and succession duties, but these are not dealt with in detail.

5. In addition to being accountable for money and other assets actually coming into their hands, trustees are responsible for the administration of the trust. The extent of their responsibility and the way it has been discharged will, therefore, not be apparent unless the periodical accounts deal with both these aspects. This will involve the recording of all the assets and liabilities of the trust, including, for example, interests in expectancy and foreign estate. The balance sheet will then show the position of the trust as a whole and not merely those assets which have come into the hands of the trustees.

6. There is a fundamental distinction in trust accounts between income and capital. Often there are interests in income and interests in capital which conflict and the drawing of this distinction is essential to show the relative positions of those concerned.

7. Various special aspects of the administration of trusts make it necessary to consider how to deal with·
    a. the three ranges of investments ('narrower', 'wider' and 'special') if the Trustee Investments Act 1961 is applied;
    b. investments acquired by the trustees from a testator or settlor which, but for special powers to postpone sale or to retain, would be unauthorized;
    c. assets which have not yet come into the trustees' hands;
    d. accumulations of income, and investments made therefrom;
    e. special legal considerations such as statutory and equitable apportionments, deeds of family arrangement, court orders;
    f. the linking of taxes (e.g. estate duty, capital gains tax) with the particular funds out of which they are payable.

8. Some trustees, and many beneficiaries, may know little about accounting. Trust accounts should, therefore, be as simple and clear as is consistent with the showing

of sufficient detail for a proper understanding of the transactions. These requirements can be fulfilled by using schedules and subsidiary accounts for many matters of detail, cross-referencing them to the main accounts. It is desirable that trustees should sign the accounts and that beneficiaries should formally signify agreement with their personal accounts: clarity and simplicity of presentation, by making the accounts more easily understood, will help adoption of this procedure.

9. The accounts and their underlying records may have to be examined because of a dispute (e.g. between trustees and beneficiaries) or, in the case of discretionary settlement, to calculate estate duty on the death of a beneficiary. Under the Finance Act 1975 there is no capital transfer tax liability on the death of a discretionary object. In addition to emphasizing the need for clarity and adequate detail, these possibilities indicate that accounts, vouchers and records generally should be kept for a longer period than if they were commercial documents.

10. Trust accounts are the responsibility of the trustees. An accountant preparing accounts for trustees should submit with them a report reciting any instructions given to him and stating the principles adopted in presentation and any special factors, problems or outstanding matters. These recommendations do not deal with the form of either such reports or audit reports. However, the accountant should make it clear whether or not he has audited the accounts.

11. It will usually facilitate a clear understanding of the accounts if a short history is attached showing the incidents which led up to the position displayed by the accounts, the names of the trustees and a brief explanation of the devolution of the funds. If the trust instrument(s) is complex, such explanation may be restricted to present interests in income and such indication of succeeding interests as is feasible within the compass of a short note.

12. For quoted investments, a stockbroker's valuation of the portfolio may accompany the accounts and this valuation, together with the accounts, should ideally give sufficient information to enable the capital gains tax implications of investment policy to be considered.

13. The recommendations below may not apply fully throughout the entire field of trust accounts but it is considered that the fundamental principles should not differ in substance from those now recommended. It must, however, be emphasized that trusts are so varied in their nature that there should be flexibility in the manner of presenting accounts and that a standard form is neither practicable nor desirable.

14. The following paragraphs contain references to statutory and equitable apportionments, and to the operation of the Trustee Investments Act 1961. Nowadays, many wills and settlements specifically exclude the former, and, by incorporating their own wide investment powers, override those in the Act.

15. **Recommendations.** It is therefore recommended that the following principles should normally be applied in connection with the records and the preparation of accounts of trusts.

GENERAL PRINCIPLES

16. Trustees should maintain records from which, in the light of the trust instrument(s)

and legal considerations, periodical statements of account can be prepared. The records and/or the trust accounts should preserve all the information that may be required at future dates (possibly long deferred) for any review of the trustees' transactions and for capital gains tax purposes. Although traditionally it has been recommended that this should be achieved by keeping books on complete double-entry principles, less formal methods are now acceptable provided that those principles govern the preparation of the trust accounts. Similar considerations apply to the presentation of the accounts.

17. There should be prepared and kept with the trust documents a short history of the trust and a summary of the relevant provisions of the will or other trust instrument(s). However, the original terms should be consulted where necessary. Other information which might be suitably recorded and kept readily available and up to date would include the trustees' names and addresses, and the names and addresses of present and future beneficiaries, their dates of birth (especially where the attainment of a specified age is relevant to the will or settlement), the dates of their marriages (where this is likewise relevant), and their relationship to the testator or settlor. It may be appropriate to set out some or all of the above information in a statement attached to the accounts.

18. The date to which accounts are made up should be decided according to the circumstances and will not necessarily be the anniversary of the creation of the trust. Having regard to the taxation liabilities of the trust and of the beneficiaries, it may frequently be convenient for accounting periods to correspond with fiscal years; but in some cases it may be necessary for accounts to be made up to the anniversary of the trust's creation if the rules of law relating to equitable apportionments are applicable or if there are other special circumstances. The nature of the trust assets, the dates on which income is receivable, the due dates of annuities, are all factors that may affect the selection of the most convenient accounting date.

19. Income and capital transactions should be segregated clearly. This may be assisted by the use of separate columns in accounting records.

20. Periodical accounts should normally consist of:
    a. balance sheet of the whole of the trust estate;
    b. capital account, summarizing capital transactions either from the commencement of the trust or since the last account;
    c. income account, where appropriate;
    d. schedules and subsidiary accounts explaining in greater detail the major items appearing in the balance sheet, capital account and income account, showing separately the figures for any special funds

21. The balance sheet, capital account and income account should be presented as simply as possible, all details being relegated to the schedules and subsidiary accounts.

BALANCE SHEET

22. The various items in the balance sheet should be grouped under appropriate headings, so that significant totals are readily apparent. Presentation becomes even more important when the Trustee Investments Act 1961 has been applied

and the capital account and the assets represented by it have been divided into narrower-, wider-, and special-range parts.

23. Where there are differing interests in the same trust the accounts will consist of two or more self-balancing sections, and can be made more understandable if the balance sheet layout is designed with this in mind. For instance, if there are few liabilities, it will probably be better to deduct them from the assets than to show them on the liabilities side. In this way the liabilities would be confined to the various funds and beneficiaries' current account balances, and the net assets by which they are represented would appear by sections immediately opposite them. This form of presentation is not always possible, but whenever it is, it should be adopted.

Distinction between capital and income

24. Capital items should be clearly segregated from income balances, either by appropriate grouping, or possibly by the use of separate columns.

Comparative figures

25. Comparative figures should be included if they serve a useful purpose. Normally, however, the supporting schedules will be more informative than any comparison of total figures with those on the previous accounting date.

Capital account

26. Generally the capital account in the balance sheet will show the balance of the capital funds held, so far as they have been ascertained. If the Trustee Investments Act 1961 has been applied, the division of the fund into two or three parts should be shown, but in that case it is important to show the total of the capital account and not merely the amounts of its parts. Where distributions of capital have been made to beneficiaries it is permissible, and sometimes necessary (e.g. where advancement has taken place), to show the original capital available for distribution and the amount of the distributions to date.

27. Where the valuation of a significant part of the fund has not been agreed for probate or stamp duty purposes, the capital account should be amplified by way of note to that effect. This would also apply where the value of the assets is known to differ materially from their balance sheet amount.

Liabilities

28. Where appropriate, liabilities on capital account (e.g. estate duty, capital gains tax, unpaid legacies) should be distinguished from those on income account, which themselves should be analysed so as to segregate balances due to beneficiaries from other liabilities.

29. Accruing liabilities on capital account are normally provided for but in special or difficult circumstances may alternatively be recorded by way or note. An example would be where the Trustee Investments Act 1961 has been applied and it is not known from which part of the fund a liability will be paid. (For treatment of accruals on income account see paragraph 67.)

30. It is normally preferable to deal by way of note with:
    a. known liabilities whose amounts cannot be determined with substantial accuracy;
    b. contingent liabilities including:
        i. guarantees given by a deceased;
        ii. potential capital gains tax on an unrealized but recorded appreciation of the trust's investments;
        iii. estate duty on an *inter vivos* settlement should the settlor die within seven years of the endowment;
        iv. estate duty in a discretionary settlement in the event of the death of a beneficiary;
        v. estate duty on the death of a life tenant (subject to the exemption under the 'surviving spouse' rule).

    Where it is desirable to indicate the financial effect to the beneficiaries, an amount should be set aside to meet the possible liability covered by the note, or should be dealt with in the covering report.

Tax on capital gains

31. In normal cases it will be possible to quantify any outstanding liability in respect of tax on capital gains. In these cases it should be treated as a creditor and charged against the surplus which has been added to capital.

32. Where allowable losses have been established, the cumulative total available to be carried forward should be noted.

33. If payment of capital gains tax is postponed under the provisions of the Finance Act 1965, Schedule 10, paragraph 4, provision should be made for the whole of the tax, and a note added explaining the period over which the instalments are payable.[1]

34. If it known that there will be a future deemed disposal for capital gains tax purposes under the Finance Act 1965, section 25 (e.g. 15-year period) this should be stated in a note.[1]

Assets

38. In normal circumstances investments will appear in the balance sheet under a few broad classifications with the detail appearing in schedules attached. Where, however, there are few investments, no changes having taken place during the year, it would be permissible to detail them in the balance sheet. The total market value of the quoted investments should always appear on the face of the balance sheet as well as in the schedules.

39. Where the trustees have applied the Trustee Investments Act 1961 they should have earmarked specific investments to each part of the fund. It is most important that this allocation should be strictly maintained at all times and that the total of the investments of each part of the fund should appear, either in the balance sheet or in the investment schedules.

---

1. As a result of the Finance Act 1972 the provisions of Points (33) and (34) will no longer apply. Paragraphs 35 to 37 have been officially deleted.

40. Where the trustees of a deceased person's estate have power to postpone the sale of unauthorized investments, such holdings may need to be distinguished in the accounts so that points of equitable apportionment or investment policy can be understood.

41. The circumstances in which an asset is acquired by a trust will determine the value at which it is brought into the trust books. If it devolves on the trustees as part of a deceased person's estate, the probate value (normally the market value at the date of death) will be adopted. If it is a gift from a living settlor, the market value at the date of the gift will likewise become the book value. If the asset is purchased at arm's length by the trustees, cost will be the basis adopted.

42. On the eventual disposal of an asset, its cost or its market value at the date of acquisition, as appropriate, will generally become relevant for the purpose of computing capital gains tax. It will be convenient if the cost or market value appearing in the accounts is made to agree with that which will govern the capital gains tax position on disposal. Where small realizations of investments (e.g. sales of fractional shares and rights to new shares) have taken place and where the proceeds are less than 5 per cent of the value of the investments, the proceeds would be deducted from the cost or market value. It is not suggested, however, that assets acquired before 6 April 1965 should be restated at their market value at that date, unless there is some circumstance or occurrence such as a part-disposal which renders it obligatory to adopt that value for capital gains tax purposes subsequently.

43. The other significant departures from the general principle set out in paragraphs 41 and 42 would be:
    a. where, because of a provision in the trust instrument, the accounts would be difficult to understand or inappropriate if capital gains tax base values were adopted;
    b. where investments are held in unit or investment trusts and those trusts' net capital gains are apportioned among the investors. In those cases the amounts so apportioned are to be treated for capital gains tax purposes as representing additions to the cost of the holdings concerned. A memorandum should be kept of these amounts but it would normally be preferable to ignore them for book-keeping purposes unless they became significant, when they would probably be dealt with in accounts by way of note.

44. The assets of a trust may become subject to estate duty or capital gains tax, or both, while remaining within the ownership of the trustees, e.g. on the cesser of a life interest. On the happening of such an event, the current values agreed for duty or tax purposes should be adopted in the accounts. In this way not only will the duty or tax borne be shown to bear a proper relationship to the assets involved, but the base for subsequent capital gains tax liabilities will normally be established in the books.

45. There may be a revaluation of trust assets for reasons unconnected with taxation, e.g. in order to effect a division of the trust funds for the purpose of applying the Trustee Investments Act 1961 or of carrying out some provision of the trust instrument. If such a revaluation is adopted in the accounts, consideration should be given to the impact of capital gains tax should the assets be disposed of at their new book amounts. If a material liability to tax would result, at least the position should be disclosed in a note on the accounts. It may, however, be preferable to

create a provision for the potential capital gains tax liability out of the surplus on revaluation. In the event of a partial distribution of capital to one or more beneficiaries, the potential capital gains tax liability must be taken into account in order to preserve the interests of all beneficiaries. In such circumstances a provision should be set up and, if any of the investments are realized to make the partial distribution, the tax arising should be set against the provision.

46. Stockbrokers' valuations may be attached to trust accounts, and if they are made at the balance sheet date, they may be used as a substitute for the investment schedules. It must, however, be remembered that in many cases they will not agree with the balance sheet total for investments because the book amount will not be included as part of the information.

47. Where statutory apportionments arise, any income apportioned to capital should be credited to trust capital account and not used to write down the investments concerned (see paragraph 66). To do otherwise would be meaningless unless accrued income were similarly dealt with on all investment transactions.

48. The composition of cash and bank balances as between capital, income and special funds should be shown. If the grouping adopted for the balance sheet as between capital, income and special funds makes it necessary, the bank balance(s) will have to be divided so that the appropriate amounts appear under their proper headings in the balance sheet, but the aggregate bank balance should also be shown.

49. A note should be made in respect of any known assets of which the amounts cannot be determined with substantial accuracy, for example, reversions and claims for damages.

Special funds

50. Where special funds arise by reason of the existence of separate trusts or settled funds within the main administration, the capital and liabilities of such special funds should be stated under separate headings and the corresponding assets should also be stated separately. The treatment of special charge on different funds will depend on the circumstances of the life tenants or annuitants (see paragraph 57). Where it is desired to show a special relationship between the funds (e.g. they are particular fractions of residue) it will be necessary to show the original capital of each fund inset, with the charge and related professional fees as deductions.

CAPITAL ACCOUNT

51. The opening entries for any form of trust record will be derived from the cost or acquisition values of the assets concerned (see paragraph 41).

52. For deceased persons' estates, the opening entries should show the assets and liabilities at the figures applicable for estate duty purposes, a balance being struck to show the net estate subdivided, if necessary, to show:
     a. property on which duty either has been paid or is currently payable;
     b. property not currently assessable to duty; and
     c. property exempt from duty.

53. The capital account for any period should show, suitably classified and in adequate detail, the extent to which the trust capital account has been affected by matters such as:
    a. surpluses or deficits on realizations;
    b. taxation of capital gains;
    c. adjustments of book figures to capital gains tax base values;
    d. estate duty;
    e. special charge imposed by the Finance Act 1968;
    f. administration expenses;
    g. changes for estate duty purposes as shown in corrective affidavits;
    h. legacies, or appropriations to special funds; and
    i. statutory or equitable apportionments.

54. Separate figures should be presented for each part of a trust which has been split in accordance with the provisions of the Trustee Investments Act 1961; this may be achieved by presenting one account with several columns.

Estate duty

55. Where appropriate, the capital account should show the total on which estate duty is payable and the amount paid; also, the information relating to estate duty should include matters such as the lower rate of duty applicable to agricultural property and a reference to any property which is aggregable for duty purposes though not forming part of the estate for which the trustees are accountable. Any other material matters affecting the estate duty should also be stated in the capital account. If the detail is considerable, it should be relegated to a supporting schedule.

56. In some cases the agreement of valuations for estate duty purposes may be a protracted matter extended over several years; for example, where the estate includes interests in land, unquoted shares, or business goodwill. Where this occurs, the fact of the estate duty being provisional should be stated with an indication, where appropriate and practicable, whether the outstanding amount involved may be material.

Special charge

57. Where special charge is paid out of a trust it is charged to capital in the same way as estate duty. Where particular funds are directed by a will to be free from duty the special charge may prove to be a charge against the residuary estate but normally it will be a charge upon the funds whose income gives rise to the tax paid. Where more than one person is interested in the income of one undivided fund then the various payments of the special charge will be charged to the capital of that fund and future shares of income will be adjusted. Professional charges for dealing with special charge will be dealt with in the same way as the tax itself.

Comparative figures

58. Comparative figures for the preceding period will not normally serve a useful purpose in the capital account.

Special funds

59. Special funds, dealt with separately in the balance sheet, should have their separate capital accounts (see also paragraph 50).

INCOME ACCOUNT

60. The purpose of an income account is to inform those interested as to the amount, sources and division of income and, occasionally, to assist in the understanding of the taxation position. The main emphasis, according to circumstances, should be one or more of:
    a. the stewardship of the trustees, when much detail will be shown;
    b. the pattern of income, when the grouping of the figures will be used to produce significant totals, for instance, the income from fixed interest and other types of investment or, possibly, the significant diversification of investments. This will help the appraisal of future requirements and budgeting;
    c. division of income, as in cases where apportionments are made or there are several funds each with a different life tenant;
    d. assistance to beneficiaries and trustees in adjusting or understanding their taxation, where, for example, relief is available against surtax for estate duty on accrued income (section 19, Finance Act 1956) or there are assessments on property income.

61. The form of the accounts must be that which is most apt to the trust, comprehensible to trustees and beneficiaries (who may not be business-trained) and useful in managing the trust. Items should be grouped in appropriate classifications; for example, interest on government securities, dividends, interest on mortgages, rents, business profits, credit from realized capital on equitable apportionments. All items involving considerable detail, such as investment income, should be included in total only, with supporting schedules showing the details. If appropriate, comparative figures should be given.

Income

62. The trustees are normally required to account for income when it is receivable, so that the account will not generally include accruing income. Items in the hands of agents, such as rents collected but not handed over to the trustees, should be regarded for accounting purposes as having been received. Consideration should be given to the effect of any distortion caused by the exclusion of accrued items, for example, where a company alters its dividend-paying time-table and, as a result, the accounts include more or less than a normal year's income. Where material distortion occurs, a note on the accounts or a reference in the accompanying report will be necessary in most cases. Income received in advance of due date should be carried foward in the balance sheet.

63. Where a trade is carried on by trustees, the usual accounting principles applicable to a trading concern should be followed so far as relates to the trading profit and a note on the accounts will be necessary to indicate that this basis has been applied. The trading activity will sometimes have an accounting year which does not coincide with the trust accounting year and the results should then be incorporated

in the trust accounts on the basis of the trading year. Again an explanatory note on the accounts will be necessary.

64. Where there are relatively few changes on capital account, an income account, not accompanied by a balance sheet, may be acceptable. There will also be cases where no formal account is needed, for example where all income is mandated to one life tenant or where the disposal of income is so straightforward that a copy of the Inland Revenue form R59 or R59A (Trust Estate: Statement of Income for the year ending 5 April) is an acceptable substitute.

65. Income may be received:
    a. gross but liable to income tax by direct assessment;
    b. net after deduction of tax;
    c. net under special arrangement, e.g. building society interest;
    d. exempt from tax, e.g. National Savings Certificates interest.
    It should be made clear whether the income is shown gross or net and any charge for tax should be related to the income being taxed. The form of presentation will depend largely on the circumstances of the trust, in particular the types and number of sources of income and the period(s) covered by the accounts.

Statutory apportionments

66. In accounting for deceased persons' estates, investments are normally shown cum dividend. Where, in such a case, all or part of a dividend after death is apportioned to capital, it should not be deducted from the book amount of the investment but should be added to the balance of the estate capital account. Thus the investment will continue to be accounted for at probate (and capital gains tax) value. Where the investment is shown ex dividend then the dividend apportioned to capital will usually be credited to the account for those dividends which are separately shown in the Inland Revenue affidavit. Ultimately any balance on this account will be written off to estate capital account.

Expenditure

67. The income account should include all amounts payable in respect of the accounting period including, where material to a proper view of the distributable income, amounts accrued up to the accounting date but not then due for payment. Annuities payable are not normally accounted for on an accruals basis although there will be cases where an income account would give an incorrect view of the amount of the surplus income if no accrual were made.

68. Items of expenditure and other deductions from income should be grouped in appropriate classifications, for example, administration expenses, interest on overdraft, income tax, interest on estate duty and other taxes, annuities, transfers to capital as a result of apportionments.

Tax on income

69. The charge for income tax will exclude tax on short-term gains under Case VII of Schedule D,[1] as that will be a charge against capital. As indicated in paragraph

1. Schedule D, Case VII, was abolished by the Finance Act 1971.

65, the treatment of the charge for tax on income will depend upon the form of presentation of the accounts. Where tax has still to be assessed on income shown in the accounts, due provision should be made. Any adjustment to the tax of earlier years should be shown separately.

70. There may be cases where the presentation alone cannot make clear how the tax is related to the income shown in the accounts, for instance where:
    a. tax is assessed under Schedules B or D and the charge does not represent standard rate on the income for a particular accounting year;
    b. the rule *In re Pettit* applies (i.e. certain annuities paid free of tax);
    c. trust income is assessed to tax directly on the life tenant.
    In all such cases an appropriate explanatory note should be made in the accounts.

Balance of income

71. The income account should show the balance available after debiting all items chargeable against income. It should show the manner in which the net balance has been applied by the trustees, for example amounts divided amongst the beneficiaries and transfers to accumulations accounts, indicating the bases of division in cases such as those where adjustment is required for interest on advances of capital to beneficiaries.

SCHEDULES AND SUBSIDIARY ACCOUNTS

72. Wherever possible, detail should be relegated to schedules and subsidiary accounts, leaving only the significant totals in the main accounts.

73. Appropriate cross-references should be given in both the main and the subsidiary documents.

Investments

74. The investment schedule should be so prepared as to enable totals in the main accounts to be identified readily. The grouping of the items in the schedule should therefore correspond with the grouping adopted in the balance sheet and it may be necessary to present more than one schedule. Where the trustees have applied the Trustee Invesments Act 1961, the schedule(s) should show clearly to which part of the fund each investment has been allocated.

75. Special funds dealt with separately in the balance sheet or income account should in any case have their separate investment schedules.

76. The following information will normally be relevant in the investment schedule(s) although it may not all be necessary in every case:
    a. description, nominal amounts and book amounts of investments; also in the case of quoted investments, the values at 6 April 1965 where relevant for capital gains tax purposes and, unless a broker's valuation is attached, the market values. In the case of investments outside the Scheduled Territories, the extent to which the premium on investment currency[1] has been taken into account in arriving at the valuation should be stated. In the case of unquoted

1. Abolished with removal of exchange control regulations in 1979.

investments, a valuation will not normally be available. It may, however, be helpful for the schedule to include the date of the latest valuation and the value placed on them;

b. in the case of mortgages, details of the amount, security, rate of interest, and due dates thereof, with particulars of any arrears of interest;

c. the gross or net amount of interest and dividends (see paragraph 65);

d. acquisitions, disposals and revaluations of investments during the period and resultant surpluses or deficits;

e. statutory apportionments of dividends between capital and income, shown item by item (equitable apportionments do not usually fall to be dealt with item by item and should therefore be explained in the capital and income accounts by narration or, if appropriate, by reference to a separate schedule);

f. in the case of real estate and leasehold estate, the probate value, cost or other book amount, as applicable, with such details as tenure, property expenses suitably analysed, rents receivable and particulars of any arrears;

g. in the case of life assurance policies, the aggregate premiums paid to date (plus, in the case of an existing policy acquired, the value at the date of acquisition), brief details of the sums assured and maturity dates of the policies and, if relevant, their surrender values.

Accounts with beneficiaries

77. Accounts with beneficiaries should generally be presented. This is particularly important where the details are complicated, for example where there are periodical payments on account of income, accumulations accounts, maintenance accounts, or special difficulties. It is desirable that beneficiaries should be able to verify easily any amounts shown in the accounts as having been paid to them.

Capital cash summary account

78. A capital cash summary account, containing in summarized form all significant information regarding the receipts and payments on capital account during the period covered by the accounts, may sometimes be helpful in larger estates. The information shown by such a summary account is not normally apparent in the capital account, which includes transactions other than receipts and payments. The summary account therefore provides a link between the capital cash shown in the balance sheet and that shown in the previous balance sheet.

Other schedules

79. Examples of other matters, for which separate schedules should be prepared where the detail involved makes it desirable, are the following:

a. debtors;

b. creditors;

c. taxation, where the tax position of the trust is complex;

d. executorship, administration or management expenses on both income and capital accounts;

e. pecuniary and specific legacies, showing those paid or satisfied;

f. estate duty, where the detail is considerable, showing specifically any amounts charged to individual beneficiaries.

Appendix III

Rates of Inheritance Tax from 18 March 1986

Commencing 18 March 1986 Death rates

Cumulative chargeable transfers (gross)	Rate on gross	Tax on band	Cumulative tax	Cumulative chargeable transfers (net)	Rate on net fraction
£	%	£	£	£	
0 – 71,000	0	Nil	Nil	0 – 71,000	Nil
71,000 – 95,000	30	7,200	7,200	71,000 – 87,800	¾
95,000 – 129,000	35	11,900	19,100	87,800 – 109,900	7/33
129,000 – 164,000	40	14,000	33,100	109,900 – 130,900	⅔
164,000 – 206,000	45	18,900	52,000	130,900 – 154,000	9/31
206,000 – 257,000	50	25,500	77,500	154,000 – 179,500	1
257,000 – 317,000	55	33,000	110,500	179,500 – 206,500	1⅔
Over 317,000	60	—	—	Over 206,500	1½

Lower rates

Cumulative chargeable transfers (gross)	Rate on gross	Tax on band	Cumulative tax	Cumulative chargeable transfers (net)	Rate on net fraction
£	%	£	£	£	
0 – 71,000	0	Nil	Nil	0 – 71,000	Nil
71,000 – 95,000	15	3,600	3,600	71,000 – 91,400	3/17
95,000 – 129,000	17½	5,950	9,550	91,400 – 119,450	7/33
129,000 – 164,000	20	7,000	16,550	119,450 – 147,450	¼
164,000 – 206,000	22½	9,450	26,000	147,450 – 180,000	9/31
206,000 – 257,000	25	12,750	38,750	180,000 – 218,250	⅓
257,000 – 317,000	27½	16,500	55,250	218,250 – 261,750	11/29
Over 317,000	30	—	—	Over 261,750	3/7

Appendix IV
Rates of CTT from 26 March 1980

5 APRIL 1985 – 17 MARCH 1986

Lifetime

Cumulative chargeable transfers (gross)	Rate on gross	Tax on band	Cumulative tax	Cumulative chargeable transfers (net)	Rate on net fraction
£	%	£	£	£	
0 – 67,000	0	Nil	Nil	0 – 67,000	Nil
67,000 – 89,000	15	3,300	3,300	67,000 – 85,700	³/₁₇
89,000 – 122.000	17½	5,775	9,075	85,700 – 112,925	⁷/₃₃
122,000 – 155,000	20	6,600	15,675	112.925 – 139.325	¼
155,000 – 194,000	22½	8,775	24,450	139,325 – 169,550	⁹/₃₁
194,000 – 243,000	25	12,250	36,700	169,550 – 206,300	⅓
243,000 – 299,000	27½	15,400	52,100	206,300 – 246,900	¹¹/₂₉
299,000 +	30	—	—	246,900 +	³/₇

Death

Cumulative chargeable transfers (gross)	Rate on gross	Tax on band	Cumulative tax	Cumulative chargeable transfers (net)	Rate on net fraction
£	%	£	£	£	
0 – 67,000	0	Nil	Nil	0 – 67,000	Nil
67,000 – 89,000	30	6,600	6,600	67,000 – 82,400	³/₇
89,000 – 122,000	35	11,550	18,150	82,400 – 103,850	⁷/₁₃
122,000 – 155,000	40	13,200	31,350	103,850 – 123,650	⅔
155,000 – 194,000	45	17,550	48,900	123,650 – 145,100	⁹/₁₁
194,000 – 243,000	50	24,500	73,400	145,100 – 169,600	1
243,000 – 299,000	55	30,800	104,200	169,600 – 194,800	1²/₉
299,000 +	60	—	—	194,800 +	1½

13 MARCH 1984 – 5 APRIL 1985

Lifetime

Cumulative chargeable transfers (gross)	Rate on gross	Tax on band	Cumulative tax	Cumulative chargeable transfers (net)	Rate on net fraction
£	%	£	£	£	
0 – 64,000	0	Nil	Nil	0 – 64,000	Nil
64,000 – 85,000	15	3,150	3,150	64,000 – 81,850	3/17
85,000 – 116.000	17½	5,425	8,575	81,850 – 107,425	7/33
116,000 – 148,000	20	6,400	14,975	107.425 – 133.025	¼
148,000 – 185,000	22½	8,325	23,300	133,025 – 161,700	9/31
185,000 – 232,000	25	11,750	35,050	161,700 – 196,950	1/3
232,000 – 285,000	27½	14,575	49,625	196,950 – 235,375	11/29
285,000 +	30	—	—	235,375 +	3/7

Death

Cumulative chargeable transfers (gross)	Rate on gross	Tax on band	Cumulative tax	Cumulative chargeable transfers (net)	Rate on net fraction
£	%	£	£	£	
0 – 64,000	0	Nil	Nil	0 – 64,000	Nil
64,000 – 85,000	30	6,300	6,300	64,000 – 78,700	3/7
85,000 – 116,000	35	10,850	17,150	78,700 – 98,850	7/13
116,000 – 148,000	40	12,800	29,950	98,850 – 118,050	2/3
148,000 – 185,000	45	16,650	46,600	118,050 – 138,400	9/11
185,000 – 232,000	50	23,500	70,100	138,400 – 161,900	1
232,000 – 285,000	55	29,150	99,250	161,900 – 185,750	1 2/3
285,000 +	60	—	—	185,750 +	1½

15 MARCH 1983 – 12 MARCH 1984

Lifetime

Cumulative chargeable transfers (gross)	Rate on gross	Tax on band	Cumulative tax	Cumulative chargeable transfers (net)	Rate on net fraction
£	%	£	£	£	
0 – 60,000	0	Nil	Nil	0 – 60,000	Nil
60,000 – 80,000	15	3,000	3,000	60,000 – 77,000	3/17
80,000 – 110,000	17½	5,250	8,250	77,000 – 101,750	7/33
110,000 – 140,000	20	6,000	14,250	101,750 – 125,750	¼
140,000 – 175,000	22½	7,875	22,125	125,750 – 152,875	9/31
175,000 – 220,000	25	11,250	33,375	152,875 – 186,625	1/3
220,000 – 270,000	30	15,000	48,375	186,625 – 221,625	3/7
270,000 – 700,000	35	150,500	198,875	221,625 – 501,125	7/13
700,000 – 1,325,000	40	250,000	448,875	501,125 – 876,125	2/3
1,325,000 – 2,650,000	45	596,250	1,045,125	876,125 – 1,604,875	9/11
2,650,000 +	50	—	—	1,604,875 +	1

Death

Cumulative chargeable transfers (gross)	Rate on gross	Tax on band	Cumulative tax	Cumulative chargeable transfers (net)	Rate on net fraction
£	%	£	£	£	
0 – 60,000	0	Nil	Nil	0 – 60,000	Nil
60,000 – 80,000	30	6,000	6,000	60,000 – 74,000	3/7
80,000 – 110,000	35	10,500	16,500	74,000 – 93,500	7/13
110,000 – 140,000	40	12,000	28,500	93,500 – 111,500	2/3
140,000 – 175,000	45	15,750	44,250	111,500 – 130,750	9/11
175,000 – 220,000	50	22,500	66,750	130,750 – 153,250	1
220,000 – 270,000	55	27,500	94,250	153,250 – 175,750	1 2/9
270,000 – 700,000	60	258,000	352,250	175,750 – 347,750	1 1/2
700,000 – 1,325,000	65	406,250	758,500	347,750 – 566,500	1 6/7
1,325,000 – 2,650,000	70	927,500	1,686,000	566,500 – 964,000	2 1/3
2,650,000 +	75	—	—	964,000 +	3

9 MARCH 1982 – 14 MARCH 1983

Lifetime

Cumulative chargeable transfers (gross)	Rate on gross	Tax on band	Cumulative tax	Cumulative chargeable transfers (net)	Rate on net fraction
£	%	£	£	£	
0 – 55,000	0	Nil	Nil	0 – 55,000	Nil
55,000 – 75,000	15	3,000	3,000	55,000 – 72,000	3/17
75,000 – 100,000	17½	4,375	7,375	72,000 – 92,625	7/33
100,000 – 130,000	20	6,000	13,375	92,625 – 116,625	1/4
130,000 – 165,000	22½	7,875	21,250	116,625 – 143,750	9/31
165,000 – 200,000	25	8,750	30,000	143,750 – 170,000	1/3
200,000 – 250,000	30	15,000	45,000	170,000 – 205,000	3/7
250,000 – 650,000	35	140,000	185,000	205,000 – 456,000	7/13
650,000 – 1,250,000	40	240,000	425,000	465,000 – 825,000	2/3
1,250,000 – 2,500,000	45	562,500	987,500	825,000 – 1,512,500	9/11
2,500,000 +	50	—	—	1,512,500 +	1

Death

Cumulative chargeable transfers (gross)	Rate on gross	Tax on band	Cumulative tax	Cumulative chargeable transfers (net)	Rate on net fraction
£	%	£	£	£	
0 – 55,000	0	Nil	Nil	0 – 55,000	Nil
55,000 – 75,000	30	6,000	6,000	55,000 – 69,000	3/7
75,000 – 100,000	35	8,750	14,750	69,000 – 85,250	7/13
100,000 – 130,000	40	12,000	26,750	85,250 – 103,250	2/3
130,000 – 165,000	45	15,750	42,500	103,250 – 122,500	9/11
165,000 – 200,000	50	17,500	60,000	122,500 – 140,000	1
200,000 – 250,000	55	27,500	87,500	140,000 – 162,500	1 2/9
250,000 – 650,000	60	240,000	327,500	162,500 – 322,500	1 1/2
650,000 – 1,250,000	65	390,000	717,500	322,500 – 532,500	1 6/7
1,250,000 – 2,500,000	70	875,000	1,592,500	532,500 – 907,500	2 1/3
2,500,000 +	75	—	—	907,500 +	3

10 MARCH 1981 – 8 MARCH 1982

Lifetime

Cumulative chargeable transfers (gross)	Rate on gross	Tax on band	Cumulative tax	Cumulative chargeable transfers (net)	Rate on net fraction
£	%	£	£	£	
0 – 50,000	0	Nil	Nil	0 – 50,000	Nil
50,000 – 60,000	15	1,500	1,500	50,000 – 58,500	3/17
60,000 – 70,000	17½	1,750	3,250	58,500 – 66,750	7/33
70,000 – 90,000	20	4,000	7,250	66,750 – 82,750	1/4
90,000 – 110,000	22½	4,500	11,750	82,750 – 98,250	9/31
110,000 – 130,000	25	5,000	16,750	98,250 – 113,250	1/3
130,000 – 160,000	30	9,000	25,750	113,250 – 134,250	3/7
160,000 – 510,000	35	122,500	148,250	134,250 – 361,750	7/13
510,000 – 1,010,000	40	200,000	348,250	361,750 – 661,750	2/3
1,010,000 – 2,010,000	45	450,000	798,250	661,750 – 1,211,750	9/11
2,010,000 +	50	—	—	1,211,750 +	1

Death

Cumulative chargeable transfers (gross)	Rate on gross	Tax on band	Cumulative tax	Cumulative chargeable transfers (net)	Rate on net fraction
£	%	£	£	£	
0 – 50,000	0	Nil	Nil	0 – 50,000	Nil
50,000 – 60,000	30	3,000	3,000	50,000 – 57,000	3/7
60,000 – 70,000	35	3,500	6,500	57,000 – 63,500	7/13
70,000 – 90,000	40	8,000	14,500	63,500 – 75,500	2/3
90,000 – 110,000	45	9,000	23,500	75,500 – 86,500	9/11
110,000 – 130,000	50	10,000	33,500	86,500 – 96,500	1
130,000 – 160,000	55	16,500	50,000	96,500 – 110,000	1 2/9
160,000 – 510,000	60	210,000	260,000	110,000 – 250,000	1 1/2
510,000 – 1,010,000	65	325,000	585,000	250,000 – 425,000	1 6/7
1,010,000 – 2,010,000	70	700,000	1,285,000	425,000 – 725,000	2 1/3
2,010,000 +	75	—	—	725,000 +	3

26 MARCH 1980 – 9 MARCH 1981

Lifetime

Cumulative chargeable transfers (gross)	Rate on gross	Tax on band	Cumulative tax	Cumulative chargeable transfers (net)	Rate on net fraction
£	%	£	£	£	
0 – 50,000	0	Nil	Nil	0 – 50,000	Nil
50,000 – 60,000	15	1,500	1,500	50,000 – 58,500	3/17
60,000 – 70,000	17½	1,750	3,250	58,500 – 66,750	7/33
70,000 – 90,000	20	4,000	7,250	66,750 – 82,750	1/4
90,000 – 110,000	22½	4,500	11,750	82,750 – 98,250	9/31
110,000 – 130,000	27½	5,500	17,250	98,250 – 112,750	11/29
130,000 – 160,000	35	10,500	27,750	112,750 – 132,250	7/13
160,000 – 210,000	42½	21,250	49,000	132,250 – 161,000	17/23
210,000 – 260,000	50	25,000	74,000	161,000 – 186,000	1
260,000 – 310,000	55	27,500	101,500	186,000 – 208,500	1 2/9
310,000 – 510,000	60	120,000	221,500	208,500 – 288,500	1 1/2
510,000 – 1,010,000	65	325,000	546,500	288,500 – 463,500	1 6/7
1,010,000 – 2,010,000	70	700,000	1,246,500	463,500 – 763,500	2 1/3
2,010,000 +	75	—	—	763,500 +	3

Death

Cumulative chargeable transfers (gross)	Rate on gross	Tax on band	Cumulative tax	Cumulative chargeable transfers (net)	Rate on net fraction
£	%	£	£	£	
0 – 50,000	0	Nil	Nil	0 – 50,000	Nil
50,000 – 60,000	30	3,000	3,000	50,000 – 57,000	$\frac{3}{7}$
60,000 – 70,000	35	3,500	6,500	57,000 – 63,500	$\frac{7}{13}$
70,000 – 90,000	40	8,000	14,500	63,500 – 75,500	$\frac{2}{3}$
90,000 – 110,000	45	9,000	23,500	75,500 – 86,500	$\frac{9}{11}$
110,000 – 130,000	50	10,000	33,500	86,500 – 96,500	1
130,000 – 160,000	55	16,500	50,000	96,500 – 110,000	$1\frac{2}{9}$
160,000 – 510,000	60	210,000	260,000	110,000 – 250,000	$1\frac{1}{2}$
510,000 – 1,010,000	65	325,000	585,000	250,000 – 425,000	$1\frac{6}{7}$
1,010,000 – 2,010,000	70	700,000	1,285,000	425,000 – 725,000	$2\frac{1}{3}$
2,010,000 +	75	—	—	725,000 +	3

Appendix V

Answers to Selected Exercises

Solutions to the Exercises which are contained at the end of each chapter are given below in connection with all questions involving the compilation of accounts or portions thereof, or of statements which would eventually find a place in the accounts of personal representatives or trustees.

EXERCISE 3

1. Personal chattels to widow absolutely.
   Pecuniary legacy of £85,000 plus one half of residue to widow absolutely.
   Remaining half of residue to father absolutely.
2. The widow will be entitled to a legacy of £40,000 plus chattels together with a life interest in one half of the residue (£20,000).
   The other half of the residue will be divided as to:

Each son	£5,000	
Granddaughter	£5,000	absolutely or on statutory trusts
Each grandson	£2,500	

   This kind of situation compels the sale of the matrimonial home unless the widow enters into some kind of arrangement with the rest of the beneficiaries.
   The half of the residue in which the widow has a life interest will be divided on the widow's death in accordance with the circumstances prevailing at the time.
3. Personal chattels to husband absolutely.
   Pecuniary legacy of £85,000 plus half of residue to husband absolutely.
   As to the remaining half share of residue, one half (of this half) to each brother absolutely.
   Note that step relations are not recognized and cannot benefit under intestate succession.

EXERCISE 7

14. Widow: £15,000 net and life interest in £8,875. Children: immediate distribution (excluding B): C £3,937 (£5,937 *less* £2,000), D £4,938 (£5,938 *less* £1,000); ultimate distribution: B £916 (£9,916 *less* £9,000), C £3,980 (£9,917 *less* £2,000 and £3,937), D £3,979 (£9,917 *less* £1,000 and £4,938).
15. Specific legacy of £1,000 on deposit at Barclay's Bank is adeemed. Legacy to D lapses, unless he was a descendent of X and leaves issue which survive X. Legacy to G is demonstrative, and he will receive £1,000 from sale of consols. Legacy to E becomes a general legacy. General legacies, £4,000, cash available, £3,400, abatement, $\frac{3400}{4000}$ A, B, C and E, £850 each.
16. Widow: legacy £2,000, personal chattels £1,800, statutory legacy £13,000 (£15,000 *less* £2,000), life interest in £5,475. Son A: legacy £1,000, share of residue: immediate distribution £2,488 (£3,488 *less* £1,000), ultimate distribution (on death of widow) £2,737. Son B, share of residue: immediate distribution: £2,987 (£3,487 *less* £500), ultimate distribution, £2,738.

EXERCISE 8

6. Capital transfer tax: £1,250.
    Distribution: wife £35,000, son £33,750.
8. Capital transfer tax: £9,250.
    Distribution: wife £50,000, daughter £40,750, charity £50,000.
10. Net estate: £100,000 (£120,000 *less* £20,000 loss on sale of investments). Capital transfer tax liability before quick succession relief: £23,750. Quick succession relief: £4,750. Final capital transfer tax liability: £19,000.
14. Widow: £40,000 net plus life interest in £30,000 (half of £60,000).
    Immediate distribution:
    B: £1,000 (£10,000 less advance of £9,000)
    C: £8,000 (£10,000 less advance of £2,000)
    D: £9,000 (£10,000 less advance of £1,000)
    Ultimate distribution (ignoring capital transfer tax):
    B: £10,000
    C: £10,000
    D: £10,000
15. Specific legacy of £1,000 on deposit at Barclays Bank is adeemed. Legacy to *D* lapses, unless he was a descendant of *X* or leaves issue who survive *X*.
    Legacy to *G* is a demonstrative legacy and he will receive £1,000 from the sale of Consols.
    Legacy to *E* becomes a General Legacy.
    General legacies now total £4,000 (i.e. £1,000 to each of *A, B, C* and *E*) so each abates by $\frac{3,400}{4,000}$ giving *A, B, C* and *E* £850 each.
16. Widow: Legacy (under will)   £ 2,000
    Statutory legacy   £38,000 (£40,000 less £2,000)
    Personal chattels   £ 4,800
    Life interest in   £23,475
    Son *A:* Legacy (under will) £ 1,000
    Son *A:* Share of residue   £10,737 (½ × £23,475 (less £1,000))
    Ultimately, on death
    of widow   £11,737
    Son *B:* Share of residue   £11,237 (£11,737 less advance of £500) immediately
    Ultimately, on death
    of widow   £11,737

EXERCISE 9

6. a. E Plc dividend treated as pre-death income, not estate income (*Potel* v. *IRC*).
       F Plc dividend treated as estate income (*IRC* v. *Henderson's Executors*).
       Revised estate income: £1,100 + (497 × 100/71) = £1,800.
    b. 1986/87 £710 × 100/71; 1987/88 £4,260 × 100/71.
    c. 1986/87 95/644 × £7,220 = £1,065 × 100/71 = £1,500.00.
       1987/88 365/644 × £7,220 = £4,092 × 100/71 = £5,763.38.
       1988/89 184/644 × £7,220 = £2,063 × 100/71 = £2,905.63.
    d. The level spread in (c) coupled with basic rate changes; administration expenses not allowable for tax purposes will reduce the payments to the life tenant.
7. Statement of trust income 1986/87: Schedule D, Case I (6,000 + 1,940 − 1,520) £6,420; Schedule A (1,130 − 430) £700; life tenancy 8% × 40,000 = 3,200 × ½ = £1,600; loan stock 10% × 2,000 = £200; BS1 284 × 100/71 = £400; sub-total £9,320; *less* loan stock for IHT £100, and executors annual sum £500; sub-total £8,720. Tax at 29% = £2,529; net £6,191. Gross £8,720 *less* tax £2,529, *less* administrative expenses £90, *less* mortgage interest £900. Final total £5,201 available for *U*. RI8SE gross £7,325, tax £2,124, net £5,201. *Notes:* (1) On death there is a discontinuance and commencement of the trade. (2) Stock should be at cost on death. (3) Life tenancy income is received after death and is estate income (*Wood* v. *Owen*). (4) Loan stock interest is not apportioned. (5) Remuneration of executor is an annual sum and is allowable for tax purposes. (6) As there is no spouse to occupy the home, mortgage interest is not available for relief. A mortgage from a relation is outside MIRAS.
8. b. Schedule D, Case IV on £3,200.

c. £3,200 at 29% = £928. Claims under section 426(5), ICTA 1970: income not liable in UK £3,400, income liable in UK (net) £1,420; total £4,820. 1,420/4,820 × 928 = £273. £928 *less* £273 = £655.

d. 1,420/4,820 × 3,200 = £942 × 100/71 = 1,326. 3400/4,820 × 3,200 = £2,257. Total £3,583.

EXERCISE 10

7. a. Capital transfer tax payable if paid by Mr Jones: £352.94.
   b. Capital transfer tax payable if paid by Peter: £300.00.

EXERCISE 12

1. Additional capital transfer tax payable by transferee: £900.00.
4. a. Capital transfer tax payable £10,450. Distribution of estate: widow £100,000; son £89,550.
   b. Capital transfer tax payable £29,350. Distribution of estate: widow £100,000; son £70,650.
6. Capital transfer tax payable: £36,545.45. Distribution of estate: exempt share to widow £38,455; legacy to son £75,000.
8. Capital transfer tax payable: £44,769. Distribution of estate:

	£
Tax free legacies to nieces (2 × £15,000)	30,000
Legacy to nephew, net of capital transfer tax	16,698
Exempt share of residue to widow	65,088
Balance of residue to son, net of capital transfer tax	43,445
Inland Revenue — capital transfer tax	44,769
	£200,000

EXERCISE 13

4. The capital transfer tax payable on the death of Mr Graves amounts to £44,850 of which £25,415 is payable by the trustees.
7. The first ten-year anniversary charge is £2,900.00.
8. The exit charge payable by the beneficiary is £144.43.

EXERCISE 17

1. Cash balances: capital Dr £21,244, income Dr £249. Apportionments: debenture interest, capital £250, income £50; deposit interest, capital £12, income £3; mortgage interest, capital £80, income £40; dividend, capital £834, income £166, mortgage interest, income £40.
2. Cash balances: capital Dr £492.12, income Dr £266.32. Apportionments: government stock 5 Oct, capital (87 days) £15.11, income (5 days) £0.86; 5 Jan received £15.97; debentures, capital (152 days) £87.98, income (32 days) £18.52; rent 1 Nov, capital (60 days) £48.91, income (32 days) £26.09; 1 Feb received £75.00; war loan, capital (121 days) £46.28, income (62 days) £23.72; B Plc, capital (334 days) £643.84 (i.e. £1,143.84 *less* £500), income (31 days) £106.16.
3. Estate account totals: £55.758 (debits: capital transfer tax £6,960, testamentary expenses £200, legacies £200, balance £48,398; credits: balance £53,143, profit on shares £2,615 (i.e. £9,721 *plus* £300 *less* £7,406)).
   Income account totals: £750 (debits: interest on capital transfer tax £19, testamentary expenses £30, accrued expenses £40, life tenant's accounts £661; credits: interest on Universal loan £600, rents £150).

Life tenant's account totals: £661 (debits: cash £200, balance £461; credit: income account £661).

Balance sheet totals: £48,859 (liabilities: estate account £48,398, life tenant's account £461, assets: 6% Universal loan £23,325, furniture £600, freehold property £24,000, cash—income £501 *less* creditor £40, capital £473).

Accrued rent ignored until received.

EXERCISE 18

1. Cash book (credit side) total £9,000: widow £2,000; Charles £1,000; executor £1,000; brother £500; son (residue) £4,500. Specific legacy to aunt lapsed through ademption.
2. Abatement of pecuniary legacies 16,542; 27,570, i.e. six-tenths. Net legacies payable: widow £6,000; sons (each) £3,000, sister £600; gardener £36; charities £906.
3. Residue £27,000 *plus* advance £3,000. Division: *A* £10,000 (land £9,000, cash £1,000); *B* £10,000 (shares £1,000, furniture and chattels £2,000, cash £7,000; *C* £7,000 (cash £7,000).
4. Estate capital account: credit balance b/f £40,000; debits: loss on revaluation — shares in Commas Plc £3,500, shares in Full Stops Plc £500, law costs £120; balance to be shared £35,880: *A* 11,960, *B* £11,960, *C* £11,960.
   Personal account *A*: credits — share of estate £11,960, cash (from *A*) £2,940; debits — furniture £100, shares in Full Stops Plc £5,500, shares in Commas Plc £9,300.
   Personal account *B*: credits — share of estate £11,960; debits — house £2,300, shares in Commas Plc £9,300, cash £360.
5. Cash balances: capital Cr £31,714, income Dr £20.
   Receipts: £11,300 capital.
   Apportionments: income £511.20 and £2,215.20 = £2,726.40.
   Payments: capital £3,000, £40,400, £1,600, widow £40,000 and £14; income £20, £28, maintenance £100, widow £2,520.
   Estate capital account: balance Cr £12,120 (debits: CTT £1,600, widow £8,686 and £14, widow £40,000, chattels £3,700; credits: £65,000, house profit £1,000, revaluation profit £120.
   Division of estate residue: capital balance £64,520 *less* widow £40,000, chattels £3,700 and life interest £8,700; balance remaining £12,120, held equally for Roderick and Roberta.
   Income: received £2,726.40 *less* paid (20 + 28 + 2,400) £2,448 = £278.40, divided half (£139.20) for widow and one quarter each (£69.60) for children, *less* £50 maintenance per child, £19.60 each.
   Balance sheet: capital fund £12,120 (represented by £43,400 Wickham 12% stock at 101 = £43,834 *less* bank overdraft £31,714 = £12,120); income fund £39.20 (represented by bank balance £39.20).

EXERCISE 19

1. Apportionment under *Re Atkinson*: capital debt £2,000; arrears of interest due to income (18 months) £150, i.e. capital £1,674.42 (2,000/2,150 × £1,800); income £125.58 (150/2,150 × £1,800).
2. Estate account totals (first part): £23,470 (debits: funeral expenses and debts £300, capital gains tax £190, balance (net principal value) £22,980; credits: Central loan £8,500, household furniture £1,500, cash £4,470, partnership £9,000).
   Estate account totals (second part): £23,251 (debits: inheritance tax £2,000, testamentary expenses £150, provision for inheritance tax £334, balance £20,767; credits: balance £22,980, profit on household furniture £200, Central loan capital portion of interest £71).
   Cash book balances: capital Dr £601, income Dr £227.
   Apportionments: Central loan, capital (2 months) £71, income (4 months) £142; partnership, income (3 months) £135.
   Income account totals: £277 (debits: executorship expenses £50, balance £227; credits: Central loan £142, partnership £135, interest on inheritance tax ignored).
   Balance sheet totals: £20,994 (liabilities: estate account £20,767, income account £227;

assets: Central loan £8,500, Bank loan £12,000, cash at bank — capital £601 *less* inheritance tax provision £334, income £227).

3. Apportionment under *Howe* v. *Dartmouth (Re Fawcett)*: life tenant 4 per cent on £1,200 (net proceeds), £45, i.e. £45 from net income and £3 from proceeds of sale.

4. a. Available income producing fund: £6,110.67, i.e. £10,209 *less* £4,098.33 (10,209/11,780 × £4,729).

   Apportionment of debts etc. in ratio 10,209: 1,571: capital £4,098.33, income £630.67.

   b. Income of first year: £940.33, i.e. £1,571 *less* £630.67.

5. Apportionment under *Re Atkinson*: capital debt £5,075, i.e. mortgage *plus* 3 months' interest; arrears of interest due to income (6 months) £150, i.e. capital £3,885.17 (5,075/5,225 × £4,000), income £114.83 (150/5,225 × £4,000).

6. Accumulation accounts: income £4,110, divided as to Mark, Luke and John £1,370 each *less* maintenance Mark £370, Luke £570, John £770. Balance as at 30/6/85 Mark £1,000, Luke £800, John £600. Income £3,060, divided as to £1,020 each. Accumulations income: £600, divided in the ratio 10:8:6, Mark £250, Luke £200, John £150. Deduct maintenance paid Mark, £270, Luke £220, John £470. Revaluation profits: Romans £42; Corinthians £870, total £912, divided in the ratio 10:8:6, Mark £380, Luke £304, John £228. Final balances: Mark £2,380, Luke £2,104, John £1,528.

   Capital account: b/f credit £63,100 *less* revaluation losses of £2,500 (i.e. loss on Romans £3,260, profit on Corinthians £3,160, loss on Ephesians £2,900, profit on Philippians £500). Mark's share ⅓ of £60,600 = £20,200, final balance £40,400.

   Distribution account: income credit £2,380, debit Romans £1,344, balance paid in cash £1,036. Capital share credit: £20,200. Debits: Corinthians £3,120, Ephesians £2,700. Romans £13,440, balance paid in cash £940.

   Balance sheet: capital fund £40,400 (represented by 19,000 Corinthians at 156 = £29,640, 6,000 Ephesians at 90 = £5,400, 3,000 Philippians at 140 = £4,200, bank balance £1,160, total £40,400).

   Accumulation accounts: Luke £2,104, John £1,528, total £3,632 (represented by 3,000 Corinthians at 156 = £4,680 *less* bank overdraft £1,048, total £3,632).

Glossary

Abatement A *pro rata* reduction among creditors (or legatees) when the funds available are insufficient to satisfy the creditors (or the legatees).

Accumulation The continual increase of capital by the re-investment of income.

Ad colligenda bona defuncti A grant of administration for the preservation of property made in order to protect the assets during a delay in the application for a grant.

Ademption The sale or other disposition by the testator, during his lifetime, of the subject-matter of a specific legacy.

Ad litem A grant of administration for the purpose of an action, in order that the estate may be represented in the action.

Administration The process of dealing with the estate of a deceased person, i.e., collecting the assets, paying the debts and taxes and distributing the balance of the estate amongst the persons entitled.

Administrator A person appointed by the court to administer the estate of an intestate, or of a testator when an executor has not been appointed or the named executor will not or cannot act.

Advancement A payment or a distribution to a beneficiary of a part of his share of capital before the time fixed for his attainment of an absolute interest in possession.

Affidavit A sworn statement supported by oath administered by a Commissioner for Oaths.

Aggregation The adding together of all property (with certain exceptions) which passes, or is deemed to pass, on the death of a person, in order to determine the rate of inheritance tax.

Ambulatory (of a will) The quality of revocability at any time before death.

Ancillary probate A subsidiary grant of probate given in respect of a grant of probate obtained abroad, giving powers of administration of the foreign executor over movable property in the United Kingdom.

Animus revocandi The full and free intention to revoke a will.

Animus testandi The full and free intention to make a will.

Annuity An annual sum payable for a given number of years or until the death of the annuitant.

Appropriation The application of property, e.g. for or towards the satisfaction of a legacy or annuity.

Attestation clause A statement made at the end of the will above the signatures of the witnesses, which declares that the will has been duly signed in the presence of the witnesses, who attest the will and sign it in the presence of the testator and of each other.

Authorized securities Those securities in which trustees are permitted to invest trust moneys by the Trustee Act 1925, or by other statute, and any other securities which are expressly authorized by the will which created the trust.

Bequest Gift by will of pure personalty, i.e. legacy.

Bona vacantia Ownerless property which passes to the Crown or the Duchy of Cornwall or of Lancaster.

Breach of trust Any act done, in relation to a trust, by a trustee which he is not entitled to do, either by the terms of the trust, or by the rules of equity or by statute, or the omission to do any act that should have been done in relation to the trust.

Caveat A notice in writing to the Registrar warning him not to issue a grant of probate without giving notice to the person lodging the *caveat* (the *caveator*) or his solicitor.

Cessate grant A supplementary grant of administration made after a grant limited in duration has expired by the effluxion of the time for which it was granted.

Cesser of interest The determination of an interest, which thereupon passes to another.

Chattels Personal property, things; chattels personal are movable things and chattels real are leasehold interests in land.

Chose in action Property consisting of a right to sue in the courts to enforce a claim.

Chose in possession Property consisting of rights over things actually in possession.

Citation A notice issued by an executor applying for probate in solemn form calling upon every person who could possibly benefit from the invalidation of the will, to appear and show cause, if any, why probate should not be granted.

Codicil An instrument executed by a testator subsequent to a will but attached to or referring to the will with the object of adding to, cancelling or altering, the provisions of the will.

Commorientes Persons who die together — at the same time.

Constructive trust A trust inferred by law, and not by reference to the presumed intention of any party, in order to preserve the equities between those persons interested in the property forming the subject of the trust.

Contingent legacy A legacy which transfers no interest at all unless a specified but uncertain event happens.

Contingent will A will which is to come into operation only if a specified but uncertain event happens.

Cum div A quotation in respect of stocks or shares, indicating that the price includes all dividends or interest accrued to date.

Cum testamento annexo A grant of administration, with the will attached, which is made where the testator does not nominate an executor in his will, or when the executor nominated will not or cannot obtain a grant of probate.

Cumulative legacy A legacy which is additional to one previously given to the same legatee.

Cy-près Name given to the doctrine relating to charities whereby effect is given as nearly as may be to an intention of a donor or testator which cannot be carried out literally.

De bonis non administratis A grant of administration over the property not yet administered.

Demonstrative legacy A pecuniary legacy payable out of a specific fund.

Dependent relative revocation The ineffective revocation of a will under a misapprehension as to the effect of the revocation or destruction.

Devastavit A breach of trust involving loss to the estate.

Devise A gift by will of real or leasehold property.

Devisee The person entitled to a devise.

Devolution The passing of property by process of law.

Domicile The country in which a person resides with the intention of making it his permanent home.

Donatio mortis causa A gift of pure personalty made by a person who is expecting to die, on the understanding that if the death does not occur, the gift is to be void.

Double probate Where some of several executors to a will do not prove, they may obtain a grant of probate later, such grant being termed a double probate.

Durante absentia A grant of administration made during the absence abroad of the legal personal representative, the grant operating until the personal representative returns within the jurisdiction of the High Court.

Durante dementia   A grant of administration made during the temporary insanity of the sole legal personal representative.

Durante minore aetate   A grant of administration during the minority of the sole legal personal representative.

Equitable apportionment   A rule of equity deemed to carry out the unexpressed intention of the testator in order to give effect to and protect the respective rights of the life tenant and the remainderman.

Estate   A term meaning the property of the deceased person to which he is beneficially entitled.

Excepted estates   Certain small uncomplicated estates in respect of which no formal Inland Revenue account need be submitted for inheritance tax purposes.

Ex div   A quotation in respect of stocks or shares, indicating that the price does not include any dividend or interest accrued to date.

Executed trust   A trust in which the settlor has given detailed provisions of the trusts created by the instrument.

Executor   A person appointed by a will to administer the estate of a deceased person, i.e., to collect the assets, pay the debts and taxes, and distribute what remains according to the terms of the will.

Executor according to the tenor   A person nominated by implication in a will to act as executor, e.g., where some person is requested to perform acts which are normally performed by an executor.

Executor de son tort   A person who interferes with the property of a deceased person by performing duties which are normally those of a personal representative.

Executor's assent   Any act, express or implied, on the part of an executor which shows his intention to part with his interest in the legacy or devise in favour of the legatee or devisee.

Executor's oath   An affidavit sworn by an executor, declaring among other things, that he believes the will to be the true last will of the deceased and that he will carry out all the duties of administration.

Executor trust   A trust in which the settlor has not given detailed provisions of the trusts but has left it to the trustees or beneficiaries or the court to interpret his broad instructions into detail.

General legacy   A legacy which cannot be specifically identified by the personal representative, e.g., a gift of £100 or a picture (where the testator does not refer to any particular picture).

Gift inter vivos   An unconditional gift of property made before death.

Grant save and except   A grant of probate entitling the executor to administer that part of an estate not reserved for a second executor to administer.

Grant caeterorum   A grant of administration or probate giving powers of administration over the rest of the estate not covered by other grants.

Holograph will   A will entirely in the handwriting of the testator.

Hotchpot   The bringing into account by a child of an intestate, where the child has had an advance in the parent's lifetime, of the sum so advanced before the reckoning of the child's share in the residuary estate.

Implied trust   A trust implied from the presumed, but unexpressed, intention of a party.

Inland revenue account   A declaration of the assets of the estate of a deceased person which must be submitted to the Capital Taxes Office of the Inland Revenue.

In loco parentis   In the position of a parent.

Interest in expectancy   *See* Reversionary Interest.

Intestate   A person who has died without making a valid will.

Issue   All lineal descendants of a person.

Joint tenancy   Concurrent interest in property where the same interest is held under the same instrument by two or more persons in the same right, with the right of survivorship incidental. Joint tenants have one estate in the whole, not in shares. *See* Tenancy in common.

Lapse   The failure of a legacy or devise owing to the death of the legatee or devisee before the testator, except where the deceased legatee or devisee was a descendant of the testator and left issue of his own which survived the testator.

Latent ambiguity   Hidden double meaning.

Legacy   A gift of pure personal property by will.

Legal personal representative   The executor or administrator of the estate of a deceased person in whom is vested the administration and distribution of the estate.

Legatee   The person to whom a legacy is given.

Letters of administration   The authority given by the court to enable a person to administer the estate of a deceased person where there is no will or no executor capable of acting.

London Gazette   The official newspaper in which various notices on executorships, bankrupties, liquidations etc., are required to be inserted. The statutory advertisement for claims against the estate of a deceased person must be inserted therein.

Maintenance   The application by the trustees, for the benefit of the beneficiary, of the whole or part of the income from property held in trust.

Marshalling the assets   Arranging the assets in the proper order of application where the estate is solvent but insufficient to meet all legacies and devises.

Minor   A person who has attained the age of 18 years.

Nuncupative will   A will made orally before witnesses.

Partial intestate   A person who has died without wholly disposing of his property by his will.

Patent ambiguity   Obvious, or unhidden, double meaning.

Pendente lite   A grant of administration made while an action is pending regarding the validity of a will.

Per capita   By heads, i.e., according to the number of beneficiaries.

Perpetuity   A limitation which must vest after the utmost period allowed by law.

Personal chattels   All household furniture and personal effects, except goods used for business purposes, money, bank balances or securities for money.

Personal representative   *See* Legal personal representative.

Personalty   All movable property, e.g., furniture, trade stocks, etc., money, private business and share in partnership and securities and leasehold interests; all property except real property.

Per stirpes   By families, i.e., by representation of a dead claimant by his issue taking his share.

Portion   A gift made by a father or person *in loco parentis* to one of his children, or to a person to whom he has placed himself *in loco parentis*, with the intention of discharging the moral obligation to provide for the child.

Power of appointment   An authority given to some person (called the donee of the power) to nominate the person who shall take certain specified property belonging to the person creating the power (called the donor of the power).

Preference   The right of a personal representative (except a creditor-administrator) to pay any one creditor of a particular class before another of the same class.

Probate   The legal recognition of the validity of a will.

Realty   All interests in land other than leasehold interests.

Remainderman   The person who takes the capital of an estate on the death of the life tenant.

Residuary devisee   The person who takes the remainder of the real property after the payment of all debts and legacies charged on such property, and after the satisfaction of all gifts of such property.

Residuary legatee   The person who takes the remainder of the personal property after the payment of all debts and legacies payable thereout.

Resulting trust   Trust of which the beneficial interest results or returns to the creator of the trust.

Retainer   The right of an executor to retain a debt due to himself in preference to other creditors of equal degree.

Reversionary interest   Any right to the ownership of property at a future date.

Satisfaction   The gift of a thing in extinguishment of a prior claim.

Settlement   An arrangement by which property is held on trust, generally for several beneficiaries in succession, some of them unborn at the time of making the settlement.

Specific legacy   A gift of a thing identified by the testator in his will, e.g. 'my horse Shergar'.

Statutory trusts   The trusts upon which, under Section 47, Administration of Estates Act 1925, the residuary estate of an intestate is held for the benefit of the class of relatives entitled thereto, until they attain an absolutely vested interest.

Substitutional legacy   A gift of personalty made in lieu of a previous gift, where the testator indicated that it was not his intention that the legatee should take both gifts.

Successor   The person entitled to the beneficial interest passing under a devise of freehold or leasehold property.

Sui juris   Of full legal capacity.

Tenancy in common   Concurrent interests in property where the tenants have several distinct, though undivided, interests in respective parts of the property. (*See* Joint tenancy.)

Testamentary expenses   The expenses incurred in obtaining probate or letters of administration, paying inheritance tax and debts, and realizing the assets.

Testator   A person who makes a will.

Trust   A trust is an arrangement by which property is handed over to one or more persons called trustees, or validly declared by the owner to be held by himself as trustee, to be applied for the benefit of some other person, or persons, called beneficiaries, of whom any trustee may be one.

Trust corporation   The Public Trustee or any corporation either appointed by the court in any particular case to be a trustee or entitled to act as a custodian trustee under the Public Trustee Rules 1912.

Trustee   The person who holds property on behalf of another person and to whom is committed the administration of a trust.

Trustee securities   Those securities in which trustees are permitted to invest trust moneys by virtue of the provisions of the Trustee Act 1925 (as amended by the Trustee Investments Act 1961).

Vested legacy   A legacy which transfers an immediate title to the legatee, even though the payment is deferred to some future date.

Warning   A notice entered by an executor at the Principal Probate Registry and served upon a *caveator*, calling upon him to enter an appearance within six days to show cause why probate should not be granted.

Will   Any valid declaration of a man's intentions as to the property which he can dispose of after his death, which he requires to be performed after his death.

Index

Abatement 80–1
Accounts 224–52
  annuity funds 286
  Apportionment Act 257–66
  audits
    under Judicial Trustee Act 250
    under Public Trustee Act 249–50
    under Trustee Act 250
  books employed 245–9
  business interests 255–7
  capital 336, 339–41
  cash book 245–6, 253–4
  corrective 172–3, 247
  documentary evidence 248–9
  duties of personal representatives 251
  estate 247, 254, 286
  examination techniques 280
  final 266–7
  ICA recommendations 332–44
  income 247, 341–3
  investments 257, 265, 286
  ledger 246–7, 254
  mortgages 254–5
  official 247, 249
  see also Apportionments; Distribution *and* Trust accounts
Accumulation and maintenance settlement 212–3, 219
Accumulations 57
Active service death 128, 185
Actual military service 4, 5
Ademption 81–2
Administration
  acts before probate 21, 30
  expenses 113, 170
  see also Grant of probate; Letters of administration
Administrators 1
  death of 35
  trustee or 63
  see also Personal representatives
Advancement 82–3
  from trust fund 87–8
Age
  of executor 22–4
  of testator 4–5
  see also Minors
Aggregation 101–2, 149–50
Agricultural property relief 140–2, 155, 186, 230–2
  companies 142
  ownership period 141–2
Alteration
  of dispositions 154–5, 242
  of will 11
Ambiguity, in appointment 22
Ambulatory wills 9
Animus revocandi 9, 10

Annuitant 2
Annuities 2, 89–90
  in distribution accounts 285–9
  income tax and 100, 109–11
Appointment
  devolution in default of 2
  executor, of
    conditional 24
    express 21–2
    implied 21, 22
    latent or patent ambiguity 22
  power of 2
  trustees, of 64–6
Apportionment 257–66
  disbursements, of 318
  equitable 302–17
  expenditure and receipts 266
  interim and final dividends 258–65
  purchase and sale of investments 265
  statutory 165–7, 342
  see also Trust accounts
Appropriation 42
Assent 91–2
Assets
  choses in action 40–1
  collection of 38–42
  contracts and torts 39–40
  in balance sheet 337–9
  intangible 1
  money 38–9, 80
  order of application 49–53
  tangible 1
  tracing 91
  wasting 303–6
  see also Distribution of assets
Attestation 6, 28
Audits 249–50
  for trust accounts 330–1

Balance sheet 335–9
Bankruptcy 49
Bare trustee 239
Beneficiaries *see* Donee; Legatee
Bereavement allowance 103
Bills of exchange 40–1
Bona vacantia 17, 33
Business, continuation of 41–2, 100
Business accounts 255–7
Business books 248
Business property relief 155, 185–6, 230–2
  minimum ownership period 138–9
  rate of relief 139–40
  relevant property 137–8
  value 139

Capacity
  of executor 22–3